LEADING OUT

LEADING OUT

WOMEN CLIMBERS REACHING FOR THE TOP

▲ ▲ ▲

EDITED BY RACHEL DA SILVA

PREFACE BY ARLENE BLUM

SEAL PRESS

Design by Clare Conrad.
Cover photos: Top: Climbers on Deming-Easton Glacier on Mt. Baker, WA. Photo: Sheri Simmons. Middle: Catherine Freer. Photo: Kathy Phibbs collection. Bottom: Woodswomen leadership course, 1989. Photo: Kathy Phibbs collection.

Interior art by Joan and Carla Firey:
Title page and pages 1 and 107, oil paintings by Joan Firey.
Page 233 and essay title pages, watercolor by Carla Firey.

Library of Congress Cataloging-in-Publication Data

Leading out : women climbers reaching for the top / edited by Rachel
   da Silva.
    p. cm.
    ISBN 1-878067-20-6
    1. Woman mountaineers—Biography.   2. Mountaineering—History.
  I. Da Silva, Rachel, 1951–   .
  GV199.9.L4   1992
  796.5'22'0922—dc20   92-16763
  [B]   CIP

Printed in the United States of America.
First printing, October 1992
10 9 8 7 6 5 4 3 2 1

Foreign Distribution:
In Canada: Raincoast Book Distribution, Vancouver, B.C.
In the U.K. and Europe: Airlift Book Company, London

Grateful acknowledgement is made for the use of the following previously published material: "Explorations" by Dorothy Pilley. Originally appeared in *Climbing Days*. Copyright © 1989 Hogarth Press. Reprinted by permission of the publisher. Copyright by Devin-Adain, Publishers, Inc., Old Greenwich, Connecticut, 06870. Permission granted to reprint "Manless Climbing" from *Give Me the Hills* by Miriam Underhill, © 1971 Chatham Press. "On the Heights" from *Climbing Blind* by Colette Richard, translated by Norman Dale, Translation © 1966 Hodder and Stoughton Ltd., London and E. P. Dutton & Co., Inc. Used by permission of the publisher, Dutton, an imprint of New American Library, a division of Penguin Books USA Inc. "First Professional Season" by Gwen Moffat. Originally appeared in *Space Below My Feet*. Copyright © 1961 Hodder and Stoughton Ltd. Reprinted by permission of the author. "Phyllis Munday: Grand Dame of the Coast Range" by Cyndi Smith. Excerpted with permission from *Off the Beaten Track: Women Adventurers and Mountaineers in Western Canada* (Coyote Books, Jasper, 1989). Reprinted by permission of the author and publisher. "Miss Dish Speaks Out" by Kathy Phibbs. Originally appeared in Women Climbers Northwest newsletter. Reprinted by permission of the author. "Passport to Insanity" by Louise Shepherd. Originally appeared in *Wild* magazine. Reprinted by permission of the author. "Risky Business" by Alison Osius. Originally appeared in *Rock & Ice* magazine. Reprinted by permission of the author. "Everest: My Journey to the Top" by Bachendri Pal. Originally published by the Director of the National Book Trust, India, © 1988. Reprinted by permission of the author. Portions of "Queen of All She Surveys" by Maureen O'Neill originally appeared in different form in *Backbone* and in *Woodswoman News*. Reprinted by permission of the author. "St. Exupery" by Sue Harrington. Originally appeared in *Climbing* magazine. Reprinted by permission of the author.

EDITOR'S ACKNOWLEDGEMENTS

A friend asked me recently how I got the idea to do this book—did I just decide it needed to be done and that I was the person to do it? The answer to the first part of the question is an obvious yes but the second part is more ambiguous. I make no claim to being any more than an intermediate climber and I have never considered myself a writer per se. But as I became more intrigued by the culture of climbing my sense of adventure and need for challenge propelled me in this direction. I was not necessarily "the person to do it," but I was a person excited about doing it, and I knew enough about women's publishing to trust that this was enough.

From the beginning, Faith Conlon and Barbara Wilson of Seal Press shared an infectious excitement about the project. Without Faith's early involvement and her exhortation that I get a computer, this book would still be in the file folders and I would be lost in the eternity of a hunt-and-peck hell. In her role as back-up editor and strategist, Holly Morris was instrumental in broadening this collection and turning it from a group of exciting essays into a wide-ranging, inclusive anthology and her care and enthusiasm always made the work more fun.

Many people gave generously of their skills and resources: Sara Eaton, Maureen O'Neill, Kristen Laine, Mark Smith, Mikel Vause, Sallie Greenwood, Sandra Schwarz, Virginia Baker, Ed Ninman, Evilio Echeverria, Alison Osius, Suze Woolf, David Mazel, Sue Giller, Arlene Blum and Bill Pilling. Cathy Johnson contributed her extraordinarily careful and patient copyediting skills, and Clare Conrad came up with the great cover design early on, making the book beautifully *real*. Rayne Engle dove into a morass of jumbled voices and surfaced with precious Women Climbers Northwest herstory.

Women who inspired me to start, and then to finish, this book include Kathy Phibbs, Debra Barnabee, Sheri Simmons, Elizabeth Rothman, Nancy Czech, Wendy Roberts, Denise Mitten, Nancy Dienes, Ginger Esty, Ruth Nielsen, Adair Dammann, Danielle Cameron, and my mother, Marjorie Nelson Steinbrueck. A memorable high point was one long evening spent with my mom thinking up book titles. Her gems, like "Dr. Rangelove and Her Partners in Climb," "FootSoar" and "The Ascent of Women" cry out for books to go with them and had us in hysterics until way past bedtime. And finally, Terri Moore built our home, and kept its fires burning through all these distracted months. I owe her labors of love.

To all the contributors who put up with my months of silence and then mad last-minute requests, thank you for your faith in this project, your thoughtful and always-prompt responses, and your occasional irate letters that got me going again. This is your book. Lead out!

This book is dedicated to
Hope Barnes, Nancy Czech and Kathy Phibbs
whose spirits always greet us
in the mountains.

Contents

THE ROPE BETWEEN US
Beyond the Climb

PREFACE

This book would have been of great value to me in the 1960s when I began to climb. I was an overweight out-of-shape teenager from Chicago who had never been good at sports when my chemistry lab partner at Reed College in Portland, Oregon, asked me if I wanted to climb Mt. Hood.

After a long evening of studying, we drove up to Timberline Lodge at the base of the mountain, and began climbing at 2:00 a.m. My lab partner later told me that when we started walking uphill, I began gasping so loudly that he doubted I would make it out of the parking lot. I kept gasping, but moved slowly and steadily upward until the early morning sun rose and turned the glacier into a place of dazzling beauty. I stopped gasping. When I reached the top of Mt. Hood, I felt a peace and happiness I had never known before. I was at home.

In the years that followed I climbed with growing enthusiasm, getting strong and fit and making many close friends in the process. As I did more challenging routes, I began to dream of high altitude expeditions in exotic locations. However, when I applied to join an expedition to Alaska in 1965, I was told that women did not have the physical strength or emotional stability to climb high mountains.

Knowing little of the long history of women's climbing, I was somewhat discouraged by statements that women were not suitable for expeditionary mountaineering. Nevertheless, I persevered and did succeed in making some good climbs in the 1960s. But it would have been much easier if I had known more about the experiences of other women climbers.

In 1970, I received an announcement about a climb of Denali where women would only be permitted to go as far as base camp to help with the cooking. This prompted me to try to organize a women's team to Denali. We would be the first all-women's expedition on the mountain and the responsibility and reward would be ours. Our 1970 expedition was a great success, with all six members reaching the top.

The climb of Denali inspired me to begin investigating the written history of women's mountain adventures. The recorded accounts begin in 1808 with the ascent of Mont Blanc, the highest peak in the European Alps, by Maria Paradis. Mont Blanc had received its first ascent only twenty-two years before Maria decided to try to climb it. Then, in 1838, forty-four-year-old Henriette d'Angeville began a three-decade long climbing career with a memorable ascent of Mont Blanc, made notorious both for Henriette's flamboyant attire and the prodigious quantities of rich meats, fruits and spirits her party carried to the summit. "She goes as well as we do, and fears nothing," commented one of her guides. On the summit she was hoisted onto her guides' shoulders as they exclaimed, "Now, Mademoiselle, you shall go higher than Mont Blanc!"

To pursue their sport, early women climbers had to overcome the constraints of awkward clothing as well as restrictive social and physical expectations of the day. Many women climbers would wear climbing pants or bloomers hidden beneath their skirts. Upon reaching the difficult part of the ascent, a climber would hitch up her skirt with an elaborate system of rings and ties, or daringly take off the skirt and hide it under a rock, to be retrieved after the climb. In her 1859 book, *A Lady's Tour Round Monte Rose*, Mrs. Cole suggests, "Small rings should be sewn inside the seams of the dress and a cord passed through them, the ends of which should be knotted together in such a way that the whole dress may be drawn up at a moment's notice to the required height."

In 1883 Elizabeth Le Blond reported that her mountain experience served to loosen "the shackles of conventionality." A genteel young Victorian lady, she had never even dressed herself without the help of a lady's maid and "was none too sure on which foot should go which boot." She was sent to the Alps for her health in the summer of 1881 when she was nineteen and immediately fell in love with the mountains. Returning in the winter to England and the constraints of Victorian society, she fell ill again. The next summer she went back to the Alps and stayed for the winter, making several first winter ascents.

Her mountaineering career included many outstanding forty-plus hour ascents and a manless and guideless climb of Piz Palu in the Alps in 1900. Elizabeth wrote fourteen books on a variety of mountaineering subjects and became the first president of the

Ladies' Alpine Club in 1907.

Over the next six decades women's participation in climbing rose and fell with the political and social tides. Then, in the 1970s, women began tackling the world's most challenging mountains in record numbers. History was made on May 16, 1975, when a team of Japanese women ascended Mt. Everest. Junko Tabei, an English translator and self-styled "housewife" from a suburb of Tokyo, became the first woman to climb to the highest point on earth. The expedition is little known outside Japan, where it received mixed reviews. While Junko's accomplishment was generally applauded, some of the Japanese press criticized her for leaving her husband and two children for her "selfish hobby." "Scaling Mount Everest was easy compared to overcoming discrimination in Japan," Junko responded.

Meanwhile, in Poland, China and India, women climbers had been making ascents of the world's highest and most difficult peaks. In these socialist and communist countries, political ideology emphasizing the equality of men and women encouraged women to climb to the highest places. After becoming the second woman to climb Mt. Everest in 1975, the Tibetan climber Phantog asserted, "Chinese women have a strong will; difficulties can't stop us. We climbed the highest peak in the world. We really hold up half the sky."

In 1978, I led a team of thirteen women in making the first American ascent of Annapurna I (26,500 feet) in Nepal. We were both the first women and the first Americans to ascend the tenth highest mountain in the world. Countless volunteers and supporters from all over the world contributed to our climb and shared in our victory.

The experience of leading that historic expedition and writing about it in *Annapurna: A Woman's Place* changed my life. Prior to the expedition I was a biophysical chemist and mountain climber. Now I am a writer and leadership trainer. *Annapurna: A Woman's Place* is not only an account of our ascent of Annapurna I and a testament to our success, it is also a part of a continuing written legacy—begun by the many women climbers and explorers who came before us and carried on by contemporary climbers.

Common to many of the hundreds of accounts of women climbers I have read is their honesty and their willingness to share personal emotion. For it is the psychological, rather than the physical, journey up the mountain that is of value to the reader. When we see pictures of down-clad figures laboring up an icy Himalayan peak or rock climbers in Lycra scaling steep crags, we often wonder why people climb. And when the climbers are women—supposed to be the life-giving rather than life-risking sex—we are even more intrigued. Why would a woman choose to challenge gravity, rock and ice to climb a mountain? What led her to these steep and dangerous places? How does she integrate this sport into her personal and professional life?

Leading Out, a varied and vivid collection of intensely personal essays answers those questions and thoughtfully relates the multi-faceted experience of women and mountain adventure. The topics range from climbing with young children to climbing as one grows older to climbing blind. There are equally enthralling accounts from the most serious technical climbers as well as light-hearted holiday makers. We learn about the accomplishments of women climbers from North and South America, Europe and Asia, from the 1800s to the present.

While these essays eloquently set forth the breadth and depth of women's experience of climbing, they also provide women with needed heroes and role models, and provide men with inspiring examples of women's capabilities. The physical strength, courage and organizational ability needed to bear children and raise a family are similar to those required to orchestrate an expedition to a remote Himalayan peak. All these accomplishments should be recognized and celebrated. Knowledge of the extraordinary deeds of these women can help each of us to climb our own metaphorical mountains and to live our lives with strength and confidence.

Arlene Blum
Berkeley, California
May 1992

INTRODUCTION

In spite of all the dramatic metaphors about skyscraper canyons, New York's Upper West Side doesn't feel anything like Yosemite. As a kid I played in the parks: balancing on my tiptoes from cannon ball to cannon ball at Grant's Tomb, scrambling over the sharp-edged boulders shoring up the lighthouse under the George Washington Bridge. Sometimes I gazed into the blazing, polluted sunset across the wide Hudson River at the New Jersey Palisades—that impossibly vertical rock wall that seemed to stretch for miles along the river, daring me to cross—and dreamed of what lay beyond.

It wasn't until many years later, after our family had moved to Seattle, that I discovered the mountains through cross country skiing, and fell in love with both the sport and where it could take me in fall, winter and spring. But I had never quite figured out what to do with summer, that virtually useless season when it's too hot to do anything strenuous below 4,000 feet. In 1985 my partner introduced me to rock climbing, coaxing me up a terrifying 5.4 route at Index, a rock climbing area in the Cascade foothills. I was immediately hooked. I took a basic mountaineering skills course that summer, and joined Women Climbers Northwest. Now I knew what summers were for.

Through WCN meetings I learned about climbers and climbing. Helen Thayer held us spellbound with stories of the challenges she was preparing to tackle on her upcoming solo ski to the magnetic North Pole—polar bears, ice mountains, the ice pack breaking up under foot. Carla Firey gave us her own Northwest history lesson—a slide show of climbing trips with her legendary parents, Joan and Joe. Jill Lawrence, a top British climber, came to town with a travelogue of women's rock climbing around the world. WCN's monthly potlucks often included educationals on mountaineering safety, and the newsletter was a good place to find out about how to help clean up a backcountry campsite or when the next climbing meet was. I felt like I was a part of a much larger community, sort of an international sisterhood that stretched back into history and all around the world. I knew that if our group existed, there must be many other women like us and I wanted to know more about them.

I started to explore women's climbing history through its literature. I recently had been given a copy of Luree Miller's wonderful book, *On Top of the World: Five Women Explorers in Tibet* and read about Alexandra David-Neel's middle-age journey of self-discovery. In Elizabeth Fagg Olds' *Women of the Four Winds* I learned about Annie Smith Peck's courage, patience and drive as she travelled and climbed in South America. And Nea Morin's mountaineering autobiography, *A Woman's Reach,* inspired me with her history of women's climbing, from early "manless" ascents to Himalayan expeditions in the fifties. I was completely captivated by the passion of these women. I found books by other climbing foremothers such as Mrs. Aubrey LeBlond, Fanny Bullock Workman, Dorothy Pilley, Miriam O'Brien Underhill and Gwen Moffat in libraries and used book stores. Although most of these mountaineers and explorers did have some independent source of financial support that allowed them to pursue their passion, not all had it so easy. Gwen Moffat set an inspiring example by combining her sport and her understanding of human nature into a means of making a living as a mountain guide and writer.

The end of World War II signalled a return to peacetime pursuits, and climbing was one of these. Claude Kogan, with Raymond Lambert, wrote a riveting account of their pioneering 1954 attempts on two Nepalese peaks in *White Fury.* Monica Jackson and Elizabeth Stark, members of a British women's team that explored and climbed in Nepal, described their 1955 expedition in detail in *Tents in the Clouds.* Although women were discovering mountaineering in ever greater numbers during this period, climbing literature about the sixties and seventies tapers off to a trickle. In fact, Arlene Blum's watershed *Annapurna: A Woman's Place,* published two years after her 1978 expedition, heralded the re-emergence of women's voices in climbing and adventure writing.

The early eighties were a boom period in women's climbing. All-women expeditions from Japan, Poland, Canada, Italy, Chile and elsewhere showed up regularly in the various alpine club journals. The International Women's Rock Climbing Meet took place in Britain in 1982 with representatives from Europe and the U.S. attending. Women's climbing groups were springing up near various climbing centers, and magazines and books began sporting pictures of women climbing. In fact, Michael Loughman's excellent manual, *Learning to Rock Climb,* became something of a touchstone for many novice climbers. With its dozens of well-photographed examples of good technique enthusiastically demonstrated by climber Amy Loughman, and an excellent pep talk to women climbers right up front, this book made a substantial contribution to the development of women's climbing in the eighties.

In August 1987, *Climbing* magazine came out with a special Women's Issue. Focusing on the diverse array of talent and energy among women in the sport, this issue was a breath of fresh air in the locker room of popular climbing literature. But beyond this, the half-dozen climbing magazines available nationally still collectively offered less than a dozen articles a year by or about women, and the track record for books on climbing was even worse. Many women climbers and expedition leaders were being virtually ignored by the climbing media; this was statistically corroborated by the National Sporting Goods Association 1990 census which counted 1.8 million women rock and mountain climbers in the U.S., nearly forty percent of all climbers! With this many women actively involved in the sport, it was hard to believe that publishers and editors were gender-blind in making their selections. It was not until 1990 that books specifically about or by women climbers began to appear, such as *Rock and Roses* and *Women Climbing: Two Hundred Years of Achievement.*

The need for a comprehensive collection of women's writing on climbing seemed obvious. Our community, which was undoubtedly more diverse than the one hundred or so members of Women Climbers Northwest, needed a forum to speak about our experiences and about aspects of our sport that might never find their way into print any other way. I envisioned a collection of writing by climbers from all over the world, a grand *pot pourri* of history, autobiography, humor, philosophy, fantasy and technical writing covering the full range of women's experience of the sport. I talked to Seal Press, a feminist publisher with a record of support for new writing by women, to see if they would be interested in such a project and they responded enthusiastically. I drafted a call for submissions and sent it out to the climbing magazines and to over one hundred of the more than two hundred fifty women listed in the *1989*

International Directory of Women Climbers. I wrote first to women from outside the U.S. and then to American climbers who seemed most likely to write about their experiences—climbers, especially young, active ones, tend to be notorious do-ers, not writers-about-their-doings. Excited and hopeful, I waited for the responses to pour in.

I discovered two things immediately: climbers don't keep the same address for very long (they're out *doing*) and, this project wasn't going to be simple. I went back to the Directory and sent out another mailing. I joined Stonewall Climbers, a gay and lesbian climbing organization and put a notice in their newsletter. I cajoled friends, trying to make essays I wanted, like "Race and Class in Mountaineering" and "The History of Northwest Women's Climbing" sound fun and easy to write. I even took on a couple projects myself as deadlines approached. I went back to the library and rediscovered some early writers. There was a great deal of material there as exciting today as it was when it was written. It was hard to choose, but I wanted to present a range of climbing experience and show how much these women not only enjoyed their sport but gave to it as well.

Little by little a marvelous collection of stories materialized. Dorothy Pilley and Miriam O'Brien Underhill began climbing guideless and guiding others in the twenties and thirties, and their joyful and often hilarious stories remind us of the multitude of foremothers who broke trail for us in many ways. Other pioneers like Gwen Moffat, Phyllis Munday and Colette Richard show us how far a strong love of the mountains—and the friendships made there—can take us.

I received responses from Norwegian, British, Indian, Canadian, Argentinian, Chilean, Mexican, Venezuelan, Brazilian, Ecuadoran, Australian and New Zealand climbers. I was thrilled, as each new piece came in, at the thoughtful and unique approaches they offered and the range of subjects they covered. Bachendri Pal, the first Indian woman on top of Mt. Everest, sent her long autobiography and I was hard-pressed to edit out any of its fascinating detail. Janet Roddan, Jeanne Panek and Louise Shepherd each write about intense, tough climbs in wonderfully rich but very different styles. Louise Heinemann's story of her solo trek over a high pass in Baltistan shines with finely crafted images of the people, culture and landscape of that war-torn region of Pakistan.

Several of the pieces in this collection focus on a particular expedition, yet each writer approaches the dynamics and issues affecting her group differently. Denise Mitten and Deb Piranian climbed in Nepal and China, respectively, with large, all-women groups. Both expeditions had to deal with incredibly demanding conditions and a wide range of experience levels among group members. These writers explore perceptions of success and failure, illuminating the process of their resolution. Sue Harrington and Ann E. Kruse address the challenges of two- and three-person climbing teams, where the entire effort depends on every member being up for the task. They write beautifully about facing these storms—without and within.

The exceptional growth of women's participation in climbing in the 1980s is well reflected in this collection. Laura Waterman writes with humor and insight about the first women's winter traverse of The Presidential Range in New Hampshire. This period of ferment wasn't limited to North America or Europe. The story of the formation of the Latin American Women Climbers' Union and three profiles of some of its most active members are presented here. Women Climbers Northwest, the oldest group of its kind in the U.S., was formed during this time, too. Kathy Phibbs, a friend and great climber, and a founder of WCN, had hinted that she would write an essay about the history of women's mountaineering in the Pacific Northwest. Kathy died in a climbing accident before she had the chance to start on it, but that piece, which I refused to go to press without, appears here as a result of several women's enthusiastic and detailed efforts.

How do girls and women learn to climb? If you're lucky enough to be a child today, you might learn in a special class for moms and kids! Diane Bedell takes us through one such class she teaches in Minnesota. If you were like Susan Rogers and had a friend who was as eager as you, you might have spent the best parts of your childhood bouldering. Kristen Laine got a later start, but found other women who encouraged and taught her. Her essay on her development as a woman and a climber is a deeply thoughtful analysis of what many women go through in pursuit of their dreams. And what's it like to be a mom with an infant and still keep climbing? Nancy Kerrebrock assures us that chalk and baby powder are not mutually exclusive.

But learning to climb is not the same as learning to crawl. While the latter is best done on a purely instinctual level, the former demands a consciousness about things that most people and even many climbers never think about. Susan Edwards hypothesizes in her essay on movement that the enjoyment we get out of climbing and our own kinesthetic awareness are interdependent. And then she proves it.

Some of us never think about climbing's risks except when we buckle on our helmets. Others stop climbing for a while or forever when the mountains claim a loved one. Maureen O'Neill writes eloquently about the risks we accept, the fears we fight, and the special bond we share when we climb with women. For some, climbing can be a powerful healing medicine. Lorna Millard's story of recovery from an attack inspires our trust and passion.

Lorraine Bonney writes about a labor of love she was a part of, the Everest Environmental Expedition, or E-3. Movingly and often humorously, she tells us about the efforts of a few dedicated people who cared enough to travel halfway around the world to take a stand against garbage and waste. In another corner of the world, one not usually associated with climbing, Alison Osius takes us buildering with her family. The sometimes conflicting roles of daughter, guide and tourist weave in and out of her funny, wry tale. And finally Miss Dish, that climbing mentor par excellence and arbiter of fine manners in the mountains, has lots to say about climbing etiquette and the future of the sport.

For at least two decades now climbing has been pulled and sculpted by new forces in several different directions—sport climbing, soloing, super-light ascents. At the same time, the women's and environmental movements have had a profound effect on climbers' attitude toward the mountains and the mountaineering experience. This collection both reflects the past and shines a light on the route before us. I hope you find these stories as challenging, exciting and joyful as I have.

Rachel da Silva
Seattle, Washington
June 1992

FOLLOWING HER LEAD

FOREMOTHERS

MANLESS CLIMBING

Miriam O'Brien Underhill

▲ ▲ ▲

The following excerpt from Miriam O'Brien Underhill's autobiography Give Me The Hills *takes place in 1929. Miriam joined the Appalachian Mountain Club in 1920, and spent several seasons hiking, rock climbing and doing modest alpine ascents in New Hampshire and the Alps. By 1926 she was eager to accept the challenges of the Italian Dolomites and the Aiguilles of Chamonix, and climbed with some of the most outstanding guides of the day: Antonio and Angelo Dimai of Cortina, and Alfred Couttet in the Alps. Within a few years she was leading difficult rock climbs. This excerpt, from the chapter "Manless Climbing," beautifully describes the process of learning to lead and then taking on the challenge of one of the top climbs of the day.*

THE GRÉPON

Very early I realized that the person who invariably climbs behind a good leader, guide or amateur, may never really learn mountaineering at all and in any case enjoys only a part of all the varied delights and rewards of climbing. He has, of course, the glorious mountain scenery, the exhilaration of physical acrobatics, the pleasure that comes from the exercise of skill, and these acrobatics often require skill to a considerable degree. But he is, after all, only following.

The one who goes up first on the rope has even more fun, as he solves the immediate problems of technique, tactics and strategy as they occur. And if he is, as he usually is, also the leader, the one who carries the responsibility for the expedition, he tastes the supreme joys. For mountaineering is a sport which has a considerable intellectual component. It takes judgment to supply the ideas, to make wise and proper decisions on the route, the weather, the possibility of danger from stonefall, avalanche, concealed crevasse, etc., and above all, to know what one's own capabilities permit. This exercise of proper judgment is of more consequence than in most sports, for mountaineering (like lion-hunting or white-water canoeing!) is a game with a real and sometimes drastic penalty for failure. You don't have merely to pretend that it is important to play the game well.

I saw no reason why women, *ipso facto,* should be incapable of leading a good climb. They had, as a matter of fact, already done so, on some few scattered occasions. But why not make it a regular thing, on the usual climbs of the day? Henry de Segogne went to some pains to explain to me why a woman could never lead a climb. There is a lot more to leading, said Henry, then first meets the eye, a lot that must be learned, and that is best learned by watching competent leaders attentively and coming to understand their decisions. Women, however, never bother to do this. Since they know that they will never be allowed to lead anyway, they just come walking along behind, looking at the scenery. Therefore, even if they were given an opportunity to lead, they would be completely unprepared. I didn't find this argument too convincing, but I did realize that if women were really to lead, that is, to take the entire responsibility for the climb, there couldn't be any man at all in the party. For back in the 1920s women were perhaps a bit more sheltered than they are today. And in any emergency, particularly in an outdoor sport like mountaineering, what man wouldn't spring to the front and take over? I decided to try some climbs not only guideless but manless.

The first step along this path was to learn to lead the rope, with a competent man behind. Early in 1927 in the Dolomites I had done a little leading where the going was pretty easy, although it did worry dear old Antonio almost intolerably. With Angelo I could lead all I liked, just so long as we were out of sight of his father, but the places I went with Angelo were almost invariably too difficult for me to go up without the security of a rope from above. For it does make a difference! You need a much greater margin of safety when you are leading; with a rope from above that would hold you if things got too tough for your ability, you can launch out on pitches much nearer your limit.[1] Later in the summer of 1927 I laid plans to lead the Grépon at Chamonix and my guide Alfred Couttet agreed to come along as second man. I took this decision late in the season and the weather was never favourable for the attempt. The next year, however, I did lead the Grépon, taking with me the porter Georges Cachat.

The Grépon now, in these days of improved technique and equipment and thereby higher standards of difficulty, does not count for so much as it used to. Even in those days many longer and much harder climbs had been done. But it was at that time among the most renowned of the Chamonix Aiguilles, having for many past years enjoyed the reputation of being one of the finest rock-climbs in the Alps, and it was still a climb that not all the licensed Chamonix guides could lead. On September 8, 1928, Georges Cachat and I traversed the Grépon with me in the lead. Everything went well. Although not attempting to hurry, we were on the summit a little after ten and back at the Montenvers at one-fifteen—good average time for a competent party. That was on a Saturday. Early Sunday morning, asleep in my bed at the Hotel des Alpes in Chamonix, I was awakened by a congratulatory cablegram from my mother back home in Dedham, Massachusetts. Black Magic! I could think of no other way she could have learned about this. It developed however that Black Magic had been helped out by the machinations of the Associated Press.

But I still wanted to do the Grépon really manless.

The next season, having found out that leading was simpler than it had looked from a distance, I turned to real manless climbing. In spite of Dean Peabody's later observation that it must have been hard to find a woman who was "strong physically and weak mentally," I had many women friends who were excellent climbers and I was able to persuade some of them to go with me.

---

[1] Either a rope from above, or with your rope running through a nearby piton in the modern manner, which amounts fundamentally to the same thing. The essential point is that there should be some arrangement that will prevent your being killed if you fall off.

My first manless climb was an ascent of the Aiguille du Peigne with Winifred Marples on August 14, 1929. The Peigne, shorter and easier than the Grépon, still presents the same type of climbing up its bold, precipitous walls of good, firm Chamonix granite. We spent the night before our climb at the little chalet of Plan de l'Aiguille, just under the Peigne. That evening we walked out a little to look over the route we should have to take the next morning, while it was still dark, up across the grassy alplands and rocky moraines, towards the peak. That's something you never worry about when you go with a guide, but before each manless climb I always scouted the start of the route. It would be entirely possible, and embarrassing, I think, to get lost leaving the hut.

The ascent of the Peigne went off well, and three days later, August 17, Alice Damesme and I made the first manless traverse of the Grépon. Starting from the Montenvers at 2:35 a.m., in three hours we had reached the Rognon des Nantillons, a rocky promontory emerging from the lower end of the Glacier des Nantillons. This was the standard breakfast spot and where we joined several other caravans bound for the various peaks above. Naturally, on an occasion like this, everyone chats a bit about their various projects and when, under questioning, it developed that Alice and I planned to do the Grépon it caused some commotion.

"Vous deux seules?" was the incredulous exclamation.

They were too courteous to laugh at us outright, but we did intercept quite a lot of sideways glances and barely-concealed smiles. Alice and I pretended not to notice. Breakfast over, the other parties all held back and allowed us to lead off up the glacier and over the bergschrund to the rocks below the Charmoz-Grépon Col, that depression between the Charmoz to the north and the Grépon to the south. The present-day route varies in some minor points, but we followed of course the route of 1929. The weather was none too good, with a lot of clouds and mist. Still, the only party actually coming down was Bradford Washburn's movie crew, who had decided that there would be no sun for pictures that day.

The bergschrund really did give us quite a lot of trouble but we couldn't waste much time on it with that large and rapidly-growing audience below. Finally we crossed under a big boulder and then squirmed up a steep narrow crack between the boulder and the ice, clawing away with our axes for holds on the outside of the ice wall.

Above the bergschrund we started up easy, half-familiar rocks but soon we felt sure we were going much too far to the left. There was mist all around us and we could see very little. The routes to the Charmoz and the Grépon diverged about here and we might well be on our way to the Charmoz. We wouldn't have asked directions of any of those men for the world! We were playing a game and we must abide by the rules: no help from men! With a few rapid, surreptitious whispers we took our decision: we would go right ahead with feigned assurance, and if we later found ourselves on the Charmoz we would traverse both peaks and pretend that was what we had meant to do all along. (I believe we might have done it, too!) But later we found a way to edge over to the right and get near the proper couloir. It was not the usual route. As we approached the col, still on the north bank of the couloir, the rocks were steep, icy and loose. When the porter Alfred Burnet, who was already at the col, first saw us through the mist, he excitedly shouted that he would throw us down a rope. We declined, with thanks, this superfluous rescue.

As we got still nearer the col along came Armand Charlet with Guido Alberto Rivetti of Biella, Italy, whom we met there for the first time. They had come over the Charmoz, bound for the Grépon, and we took it for granted, since they had reached the col first, that they would go right along up the Grépon ahead of us. We were a little disappointed since we had hoped to be the first to climb the Mummery Crack. Perhaps Armand realized this, and it reinforced his decision.

"We will have lunch here, Monsieur," said he, casually, as he sat down.

Guido Rivetti looked astounded, as well he might. It was no time for lunch, and hardly a suitable place for it, either. And such a suggestion to come from that speed demon Armand! But he caught on at once: something was about to happen here that Armand wanted to watch.

The summit ridge of the Grépon, as almost every mountain climber knows, resembles a crenelated wall, approximately horizontal, with five or six great spires or pinnacles. The traverse of the Grépon consists in reaching this ridge at its north end and climbing over and around the pinnacles to the south, where one descends to the Col des Nantillons. On the west side the sheer granite wall drops in one sweep 1,500 feet to the upper reaches of the Glacier des Nantillons; on the east, nearly 5,000 feet to the Mer de Glace. To attain the ridge in the first place, from the Charmoz-Grépon Col, it is necessary to tackle one of the most famous climbing problems of the day, the Mummery Crack. It does not lead directly from the col, but starts somewhat off to the side, above the precipice to the west. This narrow crack is climbed by a caterpillar motion. You jam in the right hand and the right foot, and raise them alternately, first supporting your weight on your foot and working your hand higher, then holding everything on your jammed fist and again wedging the foot a little above. The left hand feels over the outside of the slab clinging, as Mummery says of another of his climbs, "to slight discolorations in the rock." There is not much for the left foot to do. All this takes place pretty far up in the air. Not only is the crack itself sixty feet high, but there is nothing below its base to break the view for another thousand feet. The second man, assuring the rope from a little notch just above the col at the side, would not be of much use if you once started bounding down the cliffs below the crack. Climbers have fallen out of the Mummery Crack but no leader has ever fallen from near the top of it and lived! The ascent of this crack is easier if you stay well outside and insert your hand and foot just a short distance. But the exposure is so great that there is an unconscious urge to jam yourself inside the crack as far as possible. This leads to tense and rigid muscles and is the shortest route to getting stuck and having a serious struggle. The key to an easy ascent of the Mummery Crack is complete relaxation.

Alice and I changed our boots for light climbing shoes. There was no question of who should lead: I had already had that pleasure; it was Alice's turn. When I was firmly installed at the little notch above the col where the second man does what he can to belay the rope for the leader, Alice started off in a matter-of-fact way although there was around us an atmosphere of some tenseness and excitement. Nowadays climbers, starting from the col, reach the midpoint of the crack by a traverse on small holds and a couple of pitons, but then it was the custom, at least for the leader, to climb the whole crack from the bottom. To reach the base of the crack it was necessary to descend forty to fifty feet from the notch. The rocks in the couloir here were icy and loose, and Alice dislodged quite a sizeable one. Considering that several parties were already congregated at the col, we were surprised to hear a vehement outcry from two more still in the couloir below, as they heard this rock bounding down towards them. They successfully took shelter.

"Are you up the Mummery Crack?" shouted Maurice Damesme, Alice's husband, who was traversing the Charmoz that day with Winifred Marples and Rene Picard, and who could not see us for the mist.

"Almost," cheerfully replied Alice, who had not yet reached its base.

At the bottom of the crack Alice left her rucksack and started up. The take-off is a difficult pitch, not vertical but overhanging for about the first eight to ten feet, so that Alice was leaning backwards as she tried to pull herself up the smooth rock. She did not get it instantaneously, but soon she did, and was climbing upward smoothy and confidently. It was, as might have been expected, the performance of a real expert.

"Dites donc!" shouted the boys down below in the couloir. "Is it safe to come out now?"

Alice stopped short just where she was and called down to them the most ardent apologies.

"Toutes mes excuses. . . ."

This indeed testified to a poise and sangfroid quite out of the ordinary!

The boys poked their heads out from behind their rock and I was immensely amused to watch the expressions on their faces when they saw where Alice was, and that there was no one above her. In reply to her apologies they stumblingly assured her that it was indeed a pleasure and an honour to have rocks knocked on you by a lady who . . . Still, they couldn't quite believe it.

About this time it occurred to me that even though the day was cloudy I should like to have a picture; my camera, however, was some six feet away. Alice offered to wait until I got it. Never mind, Armand was bringing it to me. As I accepted the camera from him I realized that this was our first deviation from the manless principle!

Midway up the crack an outward-sloping shelf affords a welcome rest. From there on, although the crack is somewhat wider and the angle eases off a little from the vertical, still this second thirty feet continues to be laborious and fatiguing, particularly for the climber who has climbed the entire sixty feet. When Alice reached the top, the watching crowd broke into enthusiastic and well-deserved cheers.

Then in my turn I went down the couloir to the base of the crack, and for the first time realized that our two rucksacks should have been pulled up from the notch on the side, and not all the way from the bottom. It was no easy job for Alice to haul these things up sixty feet with our nailed boots and other heavy gear inside.

When I had led the Mummery Crack the preceding year it had seemed to me surprisingly easy and I was astonished this time to find it had once again become much more laborious. There is indubitably a stimulation to going up first, it seems to me; the excitement and elation bring on a real increase in strength and skill.

The usual custom for a guided party then was to have the tourist swing across on the rope to the middle platform, but today Armand refused to allow Guido Rivetti to do this.

"Today, Monsieur," he suggested, "I don't think that today, since two ladies have climbed the crack from the bottom, it would be appropriate for a man to take an easier route. Would it not be better if you started where they did?"

"But naturally. Of course," Guido Rivetti replied, shaking with laughter as he made his way down the couloir to the take-off. Some climbers could easily have been inconvenienced by this, but since Guido Rivetti was one of Italy's foremost alpinists and had made many difficult climbs guideless, he was more entertained than discommoded.

From the top of the crack Alice and I called to Maurice to reassure him and started on, with me ahead for the moment, up through the Trou du Canon and out onto the Mer de Glace face. After a little traverse there is a short chimney with an overhanging block closing in the top, a tricky pitch, although of course not long. I remembered how uneasy Georges had been the year before when I had gone up here. A few snowflakes had drifted down as I was climbing the Mummery Crack and now we were caught in a brief but severe blizzard of snow, with a high wind and extreme cold. We stopped in a sheltered place to put on our sweaters and mittens. We should really have changed to our nailed boots again too, but for the moment it seemed just too cold to do so, and we kept on as we were.

Then came the other famous pitches on the Grépon, the Boite aux Lettres, that narrow crack where you wriggle through sideways with the crack going on down indefinitely below you, the Rateau de Chèvre, and the Grand Gendarme. To get off this Grande Gendarme to the notch on the farther side, a descent of fifty sheer unclimbable feet, you rope off—but not in the usual way, straight down as the rope hangs, which would land you not at the notch at all but somewhere out on the Mer de Glace face. Instead, laying the mid-point of the rope over a little projection, you then slide down the sharp vertical edge of the summit block *à cheval* holding one strand of the rope out on the left wall and one on the right. The start is sensational, backing off into space with a drop below of more than a thousand feet. I have seen big, strong men (but, to be honest, men inexperienced in climbing) hesitate before getting up their courage to do this even though they were held firmly on a second rope by a guide above. Alice and I were not held on any second rope. Being too lazy to carry two ropes, we were climbing on my 150-foot alpine line. When we needed it for roping down, as here, we took it off our waists.

The actual summit of the Grépon is a large flat rock. The Rivetti-Charlet party had passed us on the traverse but here we four met again and had lunch together, watched (since the snowflurry had stopped) through the telescope in Chamonix by my mother and Christiane, Alice's little girl. (Christiane today will not permit her children to do any mountain climbing with Grandma and Grandpa, but will allow a little skiing!) It was a gay lunch, enlivened by an impassioned oration, no less, by Guido Rivetti on the humiliation suffered by a man, and a man who had considered himself a good climber, at being escorted over the Grépon by a guide on a day such as this.

To leave the summit of the Grépon you rope off on the Mer de Glace side, where the drop to the glacier below is a vertical mile. Armand had already placed his *corde de rappel,* which he invited us to use. Just casting to the winds all our scruples about taking aid from men, we accepted. As Alice was roping down and I was belaying her, I saw Armand's hand shoot out a time or two to grasp her rope. He thought in time and did not touch it, but his desire to do so was almost irresistible. From the Col des Nantillons we went down the glacier in the usual way to the Rognon, where we met Maurice, Winifred and Réné.

"The Grépon has disappeared," said Etienne Bruhl, sadly, that evening in Chamonix. "Of course," he admitted, "there are still some rocks standing there, but as a climb it no longer exists. Now that it has been done by two women alone, no self-respecting man can undertake it. A pity, too, because it used to be a very good climb."

A. F. Mummery, that superlative climber who made the first ascent of the Grépon in 1881, wrote: "It has been frequently noticed that all mountains appear doomed to pass through the three stages: an inaccessible peak—the most difficult ascent in the Alps—an easy day for a lady." He went on to say: "I must confess that the Grépon has not yet reached this final stage, and the heading . . . must be regarded as prophetic rather than as a statement of actual fact."

EXPLORATIONS

Dorothy Pilley

▲ ▲ ▲

Dorothy Pilley first climbed in Wales and the English Lake District in her teens, and immediately fell in love with rock climbing. She was already active in the Fell and Rock Climbing Club when she became a charter member of Britain's Pinnacle Club, formed in 1921 to promote women's rock climbing and expeditions. She was co-editor of the Pinnacle Club's Journal up until 1948 and its fifth president. Introduced to alpine climbing in 1920, she went on to become one of the most active and best known climbers of the period.

Her autobiography, Climbing Days, *published in 1935, from which the following excerpt is taken, describes in rich detail the mountains, culture and especially the people she came to love. The chapter "Explorations" covers some of her earliest and most exciting rock climbing explorations in Wales. I.A.R. is I.A. Richards, her climbing partner and future husband.*

New climbs, by my second year, had become somewhat an obsession. This was largely the fault of I.A.R. who would at any time give up a perfect day, when any number of standard climbs, as yet unvisited by us, would have "gone," to poke about round neglected corners of the crags in search of something new. In fact our association opened with a new climb, the Spiral Variant on Glyder Fach, as our third expedition. With Philip S. Minor I had been strolling up and down the road outside Ogwen Cottage, wondering what we should attempt together, when I.A.R., in a green corduroy suit and a blue "onion-seller"s' tam-o'-shanter turned up to suggest the Oblique Gully. At the time this was a fearsome-seeming cleft to me, with great overhanging walls concealing pitches of I knew not what difficulty. I had never been on the Glyder Fach climbs before, with their peculiar balance and finger-tip grips, so different from the comforting horizontal-bar handholds of Tryfan. When we came out of the narrow exit chimney I felt that my mountain education had taken another step forward. A June day had turned cold as December, dark grey clouds wrapped the mountain and finely divided water was blowing in gusts every way. P.S. Minor wisely decided that the Chasm Route was no place for a man of his scale. Once, according to him, in the Manchester Special Constabulary the Sergeant ordered all those with size No. 6 boots to take one pace forward, and so on up to size No. 11, P. S. Minor had not yet had occasion to move. "Size 12?" tried the Sergent. In vain. "Size 13!" No result. Then the Sergeant came to look at the boots himself and gave the problem up.

The chasm is a curious place where the main mass of the Buttress near its top is split with an extraordinary deep cleft. It seems as you slide down it, or force yourself up, to give just enough room for the tip of your nose if you press the back of your head hard against the opposing wall. About the darkest point in the heart of the mountain the cleft turns at right angles and it is possible to get very firmly fixed here in what is known appropriately as "the vertical vice." Even when the rest of you is through, your boots are apt to stay obstinately behind, and double-jointed legs are useful. We two wriggled our way down and out and went to join Minor who had walked round. I have rarely known a colder half-hour than our sandwich pause at the foot of the cliff. The wind lashed with whips of rain at the crags and made it very hard for me to see what I.A.R. was talking about when he tried to point out to me the lines of the main climbs above and sketched his idea of a new one.

Next day, as is the way with Welsh weather, all was changed. The cliffs were positively steaming in the sunshine as we roped up. Even I.A.R.'s usually melancholy black spaniel, Sancho Panza, was full of *joie de vivre*. In fact he became a positive nuisance to us through his eagerness to join in the climb. The Glyder Fach cliff was no place for him, however. Most new climbs in Wales involve a large amount of "gardening." This means cleaning away from the route anything which is not permanent—grass, earth, loose stones, wherever they may embarrass the climber. Panza, whining and bobbing about far down below at the foot of the climb, was always in the direct line of fire of anything we had to throw down. Whenever we disinterred some particularly large stone out of the recesses of a crack, and threw it sideways away from him, off he would charge to chase it, usually following it in a series of somersaults down the scree.

The most persistent and successful pioneers of this epoch in Wales, E.W. Steeple and Guy Barlow—the inventors of the Grooved Arête Route on Tryfan—used to carry what they called a "pioneer pick" for gardening purposes. White gashes, where mats of turf had been cut away, would appear mysteriously on the cliffs and the discerning would recognize their handiwork and speculate as to what they were "up to." Later, on some new climb of their creation, one could detect, in the character of the climbing, the special marks of their excellent taste in pitches, for many climbers have a distinctive style which is recognizably their own.

I.A.R.'s speciality in those days was high steps. Being loose in the limbs he seemed to like using footholds near his chin. Analytic and scientific by disposition he would sit at the top of a pitch and give me the most extraordinarily detailed instructions as to the precise movements which would bring me up with the least stress and strain. He was in fact of the cautious-controlled type *in excelsis,* tentative in his movements and always seemed able to come back without difficulty from any position, however experimental—a sign of conscious, deliberate planning of the balance. Perhaps through being not particularly strong, he seemed to me to be more reflectively aware of how his holds were supporting him than any other leader I had ever followed. I felt, as I reached the top of the first "new climb" I had ever been on, like Christopher Columbus sighting a new world.

I have heard those who are not interested in new routes maintain that a taste for pioneering is governed, chiefly, by a desire for fame. If so, the fame is slight, ephemeral and worthless enough. But certainly the impulse to find new climbs is obscure. It is a part of that general passion for the unseen and the unvisited which is behind so much travel and exploration. A passion not less strong because it is not easy to justify rationally. After all, most deserts are deserts because they are not worth much in themselves. Central Asia is underpopulated for very good reasons. But to come up some steep and, at a distance, impossible-looking wall of rock into a grassy corner of the cliff that you know has never been visited before by a human being, to sit there speculating upon whether you can force a way onwards up the wall above, to try half a dozen lines before you hit on the secret of the escape, is to go through a range of elemental feelings—not less enjoyable because it is so surprising that one should be able to enjoy them within sight of motor-cars on a main road.

The quest for new routes can become a mania, of course, leading one, since the possible lines on attractive cliffs are limited, to unfruitful haunts on disintegrating, or vegetation smothered, or overhanging or waterlogged masses of rock that the sagacious have long ago decided are not worth investigation. One such near Gorphwysfa, too small and too broken up to yield anything really interesting, occupied us all one wet Easter. It became known to us as Lethargica, either because it was suitable to wet and lazy weather or because we were too sluggish to think of anything better or because we happened to be suffering at the time from a mild attack of an influenza that was being written up in the newspapers as a cousin of *encephalitis lethargica*. Wrapped up to the limit of our resources and repelling the preferred local remedy for the disease (a stocking full of hot bacon and potatoes to be wound tightly round the throat), we tramped out daily in the rain to go through the series of hopeful surmises and final disappointments that are the normal fate of the hunter of new climbs.

But at times there was better game on foot. There were four days one Whitsuntide, sandwiched between two night-journeys from and back to London, which will always be for me an epitome of all that Welsh climbing has to offer of its best. The car from Bangor Station rushed up between the stone walls in the early morning through an air filled with hawthorn scent over the moist freshness of the young uncrumpling fern. The great barrier of the Glyders ahead was in sunshine as we swept up the last winding mile, but Tryfan was still shadowy above the lake as we breakfasted at the slate table that stands like an altar in Ogwan Cottage Garden above the water. We used to pass the tea-pot and the porridge out of the window and carry them across on sunny and windless mornings. C.F. Holland and I.A.R. were waiting for me. Holland had been a white-faced invalid fresh from hospital when I last saw him, with one arm in a plaster cast from shoulder to elbow. A piece of shell had taken away much of the bone between and the surgeons were building up a bridge out of slivers bent from the sound sections. His prospects of climbing again seemed poor and I remember feeling sad for him as he told us of his days on the Central Buttress of Scafell with Herford before the War. Short, tough, virile, and, as far as I could see, not knowing what fear meant, he was not the man, however, to let a mere smashed-up arm interfere for long with his wishes. He had been in the mountains all through the spring and news had come from time to time of most improper ventures for a plaster-cast to attempt on the crags. When we met, I found that he had recently developed one of his characteristic enthusiasms—for the Devil's Kitchen of all places.

The Devil's Kitchen is one of the most notorious climbs in North Wales and deserves its ill-fame. It is the great cleft up in the decaying limestone wall above Llyn Idwal, a dark, dank, noisome ravine with slimy, rotting cliffs echoing at all seasons with the splash of its waterfall, an ill-omened place associated with fatal accidents and daunting escapes from disaster. To this grim spot Holland had suddenly taken a liking, after tiring of daily scents of the Black Cleft—a somewhat similar affair on a smaller scale over in the Llanberis Pass. When we arrived we found he had been making a series of solitary ascents and descents of the climb. Nothing would satisfy him but that we should begin by coming with him to be convinced that it was not nearly so difficult or dangerous as people supposed. It was quite a sound climb, he insisted, and if it were in the Lake District people would be going up it every day! Cleverly he asked me whether I wouldn't rather like to be the only woman to have been up the thing.

On the wave of his unquenchable ardour we set off, stopping at Idwal shore for a swim. At the door of the Kitchen one goes into shadow and the huge, bulging, 400-foot walls seemed to hang over one threateningly. Daylight comes down through the scimitar-shaped gap above and you make a watery way over a large jammed boulder and up by a semi-detached pinnacle from which the inner recesses and the climb itself are revealed. It is easy climbing so far, and sometimes a tourist who has penetrated to this point believes himself to have "been up the Kitchen" and tells you so with emphasis. But the real climb up to the plateau above is quite another matter. Perhaps these pitches up the South Wall would not be really difficult elsewhere. But the water falling noisily down, the gloom, the splashed ooze everywhere, the peculiar texture of the rocks, rather like slippery and brittle toffee, combine to make the scene far from cheerful to a would-be climber. Holland's spirits, however, rose as we approached. He had lately become a devotee of "rubbers" (gym-shoes), even on wet ground, where most climbers—bar the latest "tigers"—find that they slip as treacherously as on ice. The rubber shoe had just come in and divided the climbing world as sharply as later the question of oxygen or no oxygen for Everest was to do. "Dangerous and dishonest, and quite out of the true tradition of the sport," said one party. To which the other replied, "What about the nails in your boots, the rope and your carefully chosen ice-axe? Equally they make climbs much easier." The same dispute arises with every technical innovation which in any way changes the standard of difficulty. I am not sure that the Devil's Kitchen was much easier in rubbers, but Holland insisted that we should only enjoy the climb if we joined him in this footgear. So, with for my part a feeling that it would be good to get the thing over, we took off our boots, left them to be fetched later, and got ready.

The first pitch was a winding discontinuous sort of crack in the steep wall with a number of wobbly holds and a few small spikes that seemed so likely to crack away in the hand that one hardly liked to pull on them. It leads to a little sloping shelf, the size of a small door-mat, and another rather similar crack goes on upwards to a fairly roomy sort of bulge or bracket. Roomy here means that you can stand on it and turn if you want to. From this bracket a line of small bosses leads sideways over one or two flanges, where semi-secure black rocks stick out, to a point just above the lip of the waterfall, whence you can step on to solid level ground and climb over it. Holland, with the ease of a bird hopping from twig to twig, flipped up the first crack in a moment. Remarking that it was hardly worth while stopping, he went on up the second, and began to shout down praises of the holds and especially of the belay he had on his airy perch. I was glad to hear of this, for as soon as I was launched up the crack the holds all seemed to me of the sort that really will not bear inspecting, much less using! Spray from the waterfall was splashing all round, its racket made communication with the others difficult, and I was very glad to reach the half-way ledge, and still happier to join Holland, rather breathlessly, on his bracket. His belay proved to be surprisingly reassuring and I held his rope while he went off along the traverse. One or two of the blocks he passed seemed to be not far off giving way and I made a mental note of them before turning to bring I.A.R. up out of the pit towards me. He too seemed glad enough to be up nearer the sunlight and further from the nerve-racking din of the cascade. We changed ropes round the belay and calling to Holland that I was coming, I made my way as warily as I could across the giddy gangway of the traverse. I was almost on terra-firma, when with a snap like a mouse-trap one of the chief holds of the passage, a jutting block that I had finished stepping on for more than a minute, broke away, seemingly of its own accord, and toppled down into the chasm. It was a startling confirmation of one's suspicions about the whole place, and I.A.R. came across even more gingerly than I had. On the whole, I suppose I was glad to have done it, but I have never felt anxious to do it again. This was in 1918 after a long spell of, I think, deserved neglect. From time to time the climb comes into a brief vogue among the "tigers" of the moment. It is being much climbed just now. Perhaps if frequented enough it will become sounder. But that is not enough for me; they will have to divert the waterfall before I fancy going up it again.

Collecting the boots, we dashed off to the Western Gully of Glyder Fach, a climb of a different class, far more difficult but infinitely safer. It is a strenuous as well as a delicate affair, and after my night journey I was tired enough before we got up it. My arms felt as weak as lambs' tails as I waggled them over the rocks looking for non-existent holds. The main long scoop-pitch is climbed by jamming the knees; you screw them into a corner and they stick. I have never been able to see exactly why, and I watched Holland's progress upwards as though he were a magician.

Our great dream was a climb above the Idwal Slabs, since known as the Holly-Tree Wall. It had been I.A.R.'s pet project for years, ever since he had been second to Mrs. Daniell in her climb. Hope—the name looked forward to the projected completion of the climb by a continuation up the steeper cliffs above—is an extraordinarily elegant route. It goes up for 400 feet over solid, smooth, perfectly clean and sound slabs. A line of holds—pockets and wrinkles in the surface of the unbroken rock—just large enough and near enough together for comfort, leads from one ledge to another by stretches of about eighty feet. Where they are needed, neat little belaying-pins appear as though set there on purpose. The slabs are steep enough to give you, if you have not been climbing for a while, a sense of height exposure as you tiptoe up them. They are just half an hour from Ogwen, tucked away in a sheltered corner of Cwm Idwal. How many an evening have I spent upon them, working out with I.A.R. new variations across them, crawling down in rainstorms (recommendable, as wet clothes cling to the surface of the slabs and assist descent), or going up to look into new notions about continuations upwards. Always our eyes came back to the same point. Right in the middle of the upper wall, flanked on all sides by smooth, apparently holdless faces of rock, was a holly tree. But, as we had often proved, reaching it would be no easy matter, nor, to an eye looking from above, would an escape upwards from the recess in which it grew be easy. Our explorations had led to this result, that a party in form would be needed and a perfect day for the attempt. If it was successful, we should have on the cliff nearest to Ogwen a continuous climb of 700 feet in length, counting Hope, as our reward. A climb on the soundest, most interesting kind of rock and with fine possibilities of natural continuations still higher. This was the project, it was familiar enough to us all—in fact all through the winter I had been receiving drawings of the cliffs from I.A.R. with new suggestions for attempts.

I.A.R had to take a rest day, and Holland's idea of a "day off" for me before the big effort, was to take me up the Bochlwyd Buttress and the Hawk's Nest Climb on Glyder Fach. As I lay in bed that night, wondering if my stiffness would ever let me get up again, I went over in my my mind all our many previous attempts. They had been at times very discouraging, but we had never been there in really good weather and feeling strong. Perhaps this time the fates would be the last!

The perfection of the weather was arresting as we walked up past the shores of Llyn Idwal the next morning. Hot though the morning was, one of us was carrying an ice-axe—of which more anon. By the boathouse was Cochram, the painter at work upon a large water-colour, with an enthusiastic amateur at his elbow explaining each stroke of his brush. He told us a wonderful story of a brother painter who was up there one windy day doing the enormous charcoal sketch of the Devil's Kitchen that now adorns Ogwen Cottage Coffee-Room. Whether the devil did not approve of his art, or for whatever other reason, there came suddenly a most astonishing roar of wind in the Kitchen and the Llyn waters rose in water-spouts and came charging across towards him. Off they went, sketch and sketcher together, clear up into the sky, right over the wire fence and souse into the pool among the peat-hags below the path on the other side. After this artist finished his sketch of the Kitchen inside Ogwen Cottage—which is supposed by some to account for the results.

We were soon up Hope and gathered, in carefully controlled excitement, at the foot of the problem. We became very business-like. I was stationed up to the right, round a corner by a belay, while I.A.R., with Holland to give him a shoulder and an axe, if he needed them, went to the attack. They chose a corner well to the right of the now usual start. (The corner that later became the start of Other Kingdom or, as it has recently been called, the Piton Climb.) Unfortunately for me this took them out of sight and I could only judge progress from the voices and the movement of the rope. Presently a kind of crisis seemed to develop. I was told to flick the rope up, if I could, over the crest of the flange of rock that was hiding them from me. To my joy it went at once where we wanted, and a moment later a call to me to come round showed that a first success had been gained. There was I.A.R. comfortably standing on a ledge that had several times resisted our former attempts to reach it. Now it was Holland's turn; and, when his legs had finished waving in the air and he had declared the place quite impossible without assistance from the rope, it was mine. I looked at the pitch aghast. So far as I could see, there were no holds anywhere. I looked up at Holland, grinning down diabolically to me with rope over his shoulder ready to lift a mountain if necessary. "Do you suppose you can pull me up bodily?" I asked, feeling like a piece of macaroni.

As everyone knows, pulling a person up bodily is not at all like giving them some help. Holland's cheerful "Come along!" was encouraging and as best I could I addressed myself to the pitch. There was a kind of sloping scoop for an elbow but it was covered with compressed slime, and there were some wrinkles like those on a walnut on the other side of the corner but I couldn't find any way of keeping my feet on them. "Pull!" I said, "pull!" and the rope grew tighter and tighter: "Pull!" and I could hear Holland breathing deeper and deeper. But nothing further happened. I didn't soar aloft at all. I merely hung there with my toes just off the ledge I had started from and my head jammed in a recess under the ledge Holland was standing on. He declared that he was "endeavouring to pull up half the mountain as well" and that the turf ledge he was standing on was starting to come away! Plainly this would never do. And besides, a start to a climb that invited the assistance of an axe seemed unsatisfactory. So the two above renewed their explorations. Soon I was watching enthralled a series of climbing manoeuvres that led them across and down to the left to a belay at the head of what is now the First Pitch. And then it was my turn again. Somehow I struggled up it, I seem to recall largely by finger-nail holds in a thin mud that came away as I scratched.

After this initial pitch every movement of the climb was a delight. Small recessed holds led across and up a clean steep rounded slab of rock, pockmarked as though some biting acid had been splashed upon it. How firmly those rough hollows took the toes of one's rubbers! In a very few minutes I.A.R. was writhing among the prickles of the holly-tree. It was a very robust growth, leaving little or no room to squeeze oneself past between its trunk and the walls of the deep little cleft it grows in. Deep enough for us all three to gather there, though I was left perched amid the worst of the prickles wishing I had on the leather coat I sometimes wear in winter.

It is impossible to be happier than we were in this strange lofty little eyrie. The wall is so steep that the lower reaches of the slabs, though tilted themselves at a fair angle, flatten out beneath. You look out to the dark opposite wall of Y Garn and the firm line of the Devil's Kitchen cliffs on one side, and on the other, across the opening of the Ogwen Valley with its glimpse of raft-like Anglesey, the summit slopes of the Carnedds look infinitely remote and high in a dim haze of sunshine. Ordinarily all this, and especially the far-awayness of the Carnedd summits, is more than half a pain. Its beauty is full of aches and queer qualms very like hunger. Hunger for what, though? But now, in our Holly-Tree Niche, I found I could face up to all those half-intolerable quickenings from the scene. One need not either smother the yearnings or submit to the ache. There were ways of changing them into something quite different, and in this discovery one seemed to grasp, fleetingly, both the reason for our ecstasy of the moment and, ultimately, the best reason why we climb. In this illumination a new person was really looking out on the world.

Down below we could see Cochram still at work by the lakeside, a tiny active figure, with his amateur now sitting on a boulder beside him. The bluff rocks were warm to the hand, a light breeze tempered the sunshine, we were alone in a world of our own, in a place that had hitherto only existed, so we felt, in our imaginations. If one could land suddenly in Robinson Crusoe's island itself (not Juan Fernandez or any other island that a ship has ever sailed to) one would know, I fancy, something of the same exultation.

Now began a determined struggle with the narrow crack above the tree. As Holland later wrote: "We inspected the fierce-looking crack that now confronted us and which is invisible from below. First one tried to climb it, then the other. We stood on the tree in turn and sweated in vain attempts to ascend; in turn we fell exhausted into the safe but painful embrace of the tree. It was no use; the victory was with the enemy; we could do no more." Why it beat us I do not quite know, since a few days later, I.A.R. hit on a method which took him up it easily. But this time first I.A.R. and then Holland wrestled arduously and pertinaciously with it, but in vain. Down went our spirits like a barometer before a thunder storm. Had we triumphed so far to be beaten in the end, and was this prickly recess to be the delusive end, the grave of our over-mounted hopes? In a grim disconsolate mood Holland went down to traverse out to the left, without much expectation in any of us that any possible route lay that way. Soon he was far out on the bare, almost vertical wall at about our level. He felt, as he said afterwards, "like a sparrow on the housetops, though without a sparrow's advantages as to the methods at his disposal of removing himself therefrom." But to us he looked like a little eagle with his aquiline nose and intent fierce air as he stood poised on a narrow ledge scanning the rocks above him. Twice he levered himself up and twice his boot-nail slipped from an almost imperceptible toe-scrape and he "dangled on handholds that were none too satisfying." Then quickly his hands went up to what were evidently mere finger-tip holds, up went one boot—it seemed to nothing—and, with a swift springy movement, he was rising. A moment later his knee was on the crest of the wall and he was over the difficulty.

Soon we were beside him, back in a rapture again. To have just the holds you need on a first ascent of such a wall, no more and no less, gives every step the flavour of a victory. At the hard step there is almost one hold too few, or rather the holds are small enough and distant enough to make you really enjoy the large round handholds and the comfortable bay in the crags at which you arrive by these means. In the bay we sat down to relish the moment. Everyone who has enjoyed a first ascent will understand our sublime content.

Reverie can still follow the remainder of the climb step by step. I like to recall most the turn and turn about mood in which Holland and I.A.R. divided the pitches above. They worked out very evenly, giving two more minor climaxes. At the top, on one of the wider quartz-floored terraces that make this part of the Glyder Fawr such a regal lounging ground, we sat down to review again what had happened. We were all feeling a little surprised at our good fortune. It struck us all, however, that another start to the climb, if we could find one, would be preferable. Suddenly the happy notion came— Why not go down the climb at once, and look at the possibilities again from above? Also, why not take the opportunity to clean away one or two bulges of turf that had proved awkward? We regretted this last after-thought a little later. The turf as we threw it down disgorged showers of moist earth that spread out over the reaches below and filled the holds with a sprinkling of greasy mud, horribly troublesome to feel in rubbers. We were cursing ourselves heartily by the time we reached the holly-tree to find the stretch below only manageable with a rope doubled round its trunk—so desperately slippery had the holds become through our gardening. The alternative line for the first pitch (now the standard route) proved to need much cleaning. However, in the end we disinterred a sufficiency of holds and got down it, only to begin at once to go up it again. We had to test its adequacy as the open pitch of the climb. By this time, we were beginning to feel a little like a complicated human pendulum doomed to swing up and down on our climb forever.

A year or so later more cleaning revealed another finger-hold just where it was most needed on this first pitch. Recently again this has disappeared, to the regret of many and the joy of some. This pitch is now approximately of the same difficulty as on the first ascent. So climbs change.

With this route—since Hope gives some 400 feet and the Holly-Tree Wall about 230—a very long climb is available on Glyder Fawr. Above, by way of Abraham's Chimney and a stretch known as "the lava slab," it is possible to continue over perfect rock, interesting throughout, right on to the main upper cliff of the mountain; and with the Central Arête for a finish, you have something like 1,400 feet of good climbing.

Our fourth day took us up the Great Ridge of Criegiau Gleision—aerial climbing on rock that made one uneasy by its appearance of fragility. And so to finish off with a struggle up the Gribin Angular Chimney and a slide down the Monolith Crack before the night journey back to London. How the contrast shook one! To go back to gloves and high-heeled shoes, pavements and taxi cabs. Walking with an umbrella in Piccadilly, one felt as though with a little more strain one would become a case of divided personality. This time yesterday! One lay munching a dry sandwich on a rocky ledge, plucking at a patch of lichen and listening to the distant roar of the white Ogwen Falls. It wavered, faded, and grew again louder and louder as the breeze caught it. What had such moments to do with to-day, and what reckoning could compare the personality now moving through the noisy street on her way to meet people who knew her in one guide only, with that other personality that came to life only among such a different order of existence and was known only to such other minds and assessed by them for such other qualities. The strangeness of the dual life made, in those days, a cleft, a division in my mind that I struggled in vain to build some bridge across. Kind, firm friends would say, "All good things come to an end," or "You can't expect all life to be a holiday." But to me, and to climbers before and after me, this was no question of holidays. It went down into the very form and fabric of myself.

Oh these spring days!
A nameless little mountain
In the morning haze.

Matsuo Basho (1644–94)
Translated by H.G. Henderson

FIRST PROFESSIONAL SEASON

Gwen Moffat

▲ ▲ ▲

*Gwen Moffat was the first woman guide appointed by the British
Mountaineering Council, and climbed professionally for twenty years
in North Wales, the English Lake District, the Highlands, the Isle of
Skye, the Swiss and French Alps and the Dolomites. This excerpt,
from the chapter "First Professional Season" in her autobiography*
Space Below My Feet, *published in 1961, describes her first summer
of guiding. It is 1954, and her daughter, Sheena, is five. Johnnie is
Johnnie Lees, an excellent climber and mountain rescue expert, the
object of Gwen's affections, and future husband.*

I left Fort William in April and spent the Easter holidays with
Sheena in Sussex. I was very relieved to hear her talk about her new
school with obvious enjoyment. Life became less complicated. All I
had to do now was make enough money to pay school fees three
times a year. These seemed exorbitant, but I had the comforting
thought that if anything happened to me—such as temporary illness
or unemployment—she was happy and safe. By the time I was on
the road north again, heading for Langdale, I was feeling, if not exactly confident, at least a little aggressive towards the Enemy watching for that first slip.

I hitched north. I couldn't afford to go by train because my salary included expenses and I must keep these to a minimum. By nightfall that first evening I had reached Windermere. The last bus had left for Ambleside so I walked down to the shore and found a patch of grass where I could lie and listen to the ripples a few feet away. It was a clear, starlit night with no wind. After a while I became aware of something moving in the bushes.

I stared at the dark tangle of brambles until my eyes ached, wondering when this nasty man (who had, obviously been very close when I undressed) would leap out on me. But the rustling continued and no one came. Reluctantly, I crawled out of the bag and crept across the grass to the bushes. In the light of my torch I found a hedgehog grubbing for worms.

I lay on my back and stared at the stars and remembered another night, years ago, when I came to an old straw stack in the Cornish cliffs, and thought a tramp had staked his claim before me, for the straw rustled without visible agency, and closer inspection showed that it *moved*. It was full of rats. I had been too tired to move on, so I pulled the drawstring of my sleeping bag over my head and hoped that they wouldn't eat their way through the down. They left me alone, but ate a neat hole in my rucksack and left nothing of my food but crumbs.

Langdale was basking in spring sunshine when I arrived the following morning. The first course was not due to start for another week and my object in coming early was to familiarize myself with the easier climbs in the district. I pitched my tent in a field full of new lambs and celandines and went out to look for a climbing partner.

I met a girl called Maureen, six feet tall and correspondingly strong. The first day was lovely: dry, with chance sunlight and cloud shadows racing across the fells. We went to Scout Crag because I wanted to assess its qualities as a nursery cliff, and did a few routes, before moving up to Pavey Ark.

We scrambled up Jack's Rake to the foot of Rake End Chimney and sat there, idly contemplating the climb. I had put on my spectacles in order to see the cliff better, and out of the tail of my eye caught a movement on the wall of the gully below. There was a sheep on a tiny ledge about forty feet above the bed of the gully.

My heart sank. It is quite impossible for me to abandon any animal in difficulties. If I find a wounded bird I must take it home or kill it. If a sheep is stranded on a cliff it must be rescued. And here we were, just the two of us, with one rope. It meant going down to the hotel and rousing Sid Cross to action or doing it ourselves. The disadvantage of the latter course was that two ropes were necessary to be safe (and always I wanted to be *safe*) one for the sheep and one for the rescuer. We stared at the sheep gloomily, willing it to do something: to jump up the rocky rake by which it had plainly descended, or to jump off and take the decision out of our hands.

The sheep lay down, stood up, tottered, and lay down again. It was obvious it had been there a long time. Its little ledge was bare of grass.

We would do our climb, we said, and descend again. Perhaps by then—disregarding the length of time the ewe had been marooned—something would have happened.

We did the climb, hurriedly and preoccupied. Back on Jack's Rake we stared at her again. She was still there.

We decided that Maureen should tie on to the middle of the rope, belay at the top of the gully wall, and haul us both up: the sheep and me.

Rather foolishly I started climbing up the gully before she was in position and found myself perched, delicately, on a steep slab with a tiny excrescence for one foot, nothing for the other, and my hands resting lightly on the rock above. I yelled for the rope and Maureen retorted that I would just have to wait. I waited, trembling, until the two ends came down, and I could tie on.

It was something like forty feet to the ledge, which was roughly triangular in shape. The easiest line—and easy only in comparison, for I was on a tight rope all the time; it was too hard to *climb*—went up to one side of the ledge, with the result, of course, that by the time I'd pulled myself level with the lip, the sheep, instead of moving to the back of the haven, was six feet away at the other end, stamping her feet and threatening to jump off if I moved another inch.

I clung to the ledge, motionless and silent, while Maureen—out of sight some distance above—asked petulantly what was keeping me. I couldn't shout for fear of startling the sheep so I told her in a gentle, reassuring monotone. I told her that if I could persuade the ewe into the back of the haven, I could leap on her. I also told her that the ledge sloped outward and was filthy with mud and sheep droppings; that the ewe looked very big, and that when I yelled she was to hold me as tight as possible, but to leave the other rope free so that I could secure the sheep.

I stopped talking to Maureen and addressed myself to the sheep. She flared her nostrils at me and twitched her ears. After five minutes of my steady monologue she retreated calmly into the back of the haven. I mantelshelved onto the ledge and threw myself on top of her.

I was quite determined to get her on her back. She was equally determined to stay upright. We fought like a couple of jungle beasts, and in the middle of it I was horrified to realize that we were sliding towards the edge. I had yelled to Maureen as I pounced, but things happened so quickly—and nylon is so elastic—that my rope was not yet tight. It didn't tighten until we were literally on the brink. When the pull came on my waist, I was dragged back from the edge, lost my footing, and fell. The sheep fell on top of me; I had my arms round her waist, my fingers deep in the wool, when I saw the spare rope disappearing up the wall. As I yelled for this to come back, the sheep got one hoof free, stood up, and planted it in my mouth.

This was the last straw. With a convulsive heave I turned over and got on top of her. We lay there, panting, glaring at each other.

I managed to work a sling round her head and under her front legs. There was a knot in the end of the spare rope and I clipped her on with a carabiner and stood up, retaining a tight hold on the rope. I shouted to Maureen that I was going to try to drive the ewe up the rocky rake at the side of the ledge and both ropes were to be kept very tight. I let the sheep stand up, showed her the rake, gave her a word of encouragement, and threw her at it.

She *did* try; she got up a few feet and then, despite the tight rope, came rolling back into my arms.

I kept her pinned on her back, and knelt beside her, studying the rock. Above the haven, and directly below Maureen, was an overhang. It wasn't a very big one, and I suggested that she should try to pull us both up at the same time.

When we were ready she started to pull. She was very strong. The sheep and I rose gently up the rock, my feet scrabbling for holds while the sheep pretended to be dead and went completely limp. But still we rose, myself clutching the rope with one hand, pushing the sheep above my head with the other. When Maureen paused for a second the sheep sat on my head. After we'd risen about ten feet I emerged from the wool (which smelled abominably) and screamed to Maureen to relax. The sheep was in an inverted diving position with its front legs vertically above its head, and the sling just caught round its front hoofs.

Maureen took her orders literally. She relaxed, and the sheep came back into my arms. We went down to the ledge again where I fastened another sling round the other end (I had tried to do this before, but the sheep had been too fat, then).

Up we went again, as far as the overhang where the sheep stuck, and started to make horrible noises. Maureen hauled me to the top and I peered down the overhang. The ewe was twirling now, and as her head came out from the rock, we heaved together. She came up like a fish, and, directly she felt the grass, she was on her feet. We threw ourselves on her (for we weren't off the cliff yet) and lay there in a tangle of limbs and wool until we had recovered sufficiently to lead her off the cliff.

It was not until several sheep rescues later that I learned the advisability of taking sheep down to the farm after they have been rescued, so that they can be confined in a small space and fed slowly, otherwise they will kill themselves after their long period of starvation.

We finished the day with an ascent of Cook's Tour, then trotted down to the Old Dungeon Ghyll, full of our rescue, to spend the night like the Ancient Mariner, pinning people in corners of the bar and telling them all about it. No one believed us, although they admitted we had been very close to sheep because of the smell.

At the end of the week I met my first course. They were four young men all of whom had had previous experience of rock climbing. I tried to appear cool and businesslike, but now that I was confronted with the situation after weeks of brooding over it, there was an element of hysteria in my welcome. Despite the fact that I had to pass or fail them at the end of a fortnight, I was the one on trial.

On that first morning I took them up Middlefell Buttress: five of us, all on one rope. It was slow, cold and boring. They climbed faster than I did, surrounded with an almost visible aura of masculine resentment. So I took them to Gwynne's Chimney on Pavey Ark, and as they struggled and sweated in that smooth cleft, with sparks flying from their nails, and me waiting at the top with a taut rope and a turn round my wrist, I knew that I had won. The atmosphere—when we were all together again—was clean and relaxed. They could look me in the eye and say, "Have we got any more like that? I thought it was going to be easy when you went up it . . ."

And I could laugh and say, "You'll be leading it by the end of the week."

I was no longer a woman with a reputation, but an instructor with a technique superior to theirs, and now we could settle down to work.

I took them to Bowfell Buttress—not five on a rope this time, but in two parties. The great difficulty of these courses was that there was only one leader: myself. When Johnnie ran Mountain Rescue courses, with pupils who were more experienced generally than mine, he never had more than two novices to one instructor. I might, after the first week of an Intermediate course, weed out another leader, perhaps two, who could take the strong seconds up a Difficult, even a Very Difficult, but I was always very wary of letting people lead, and the parties kept close, on parallel climbs, with myself tense and watchful and almost unaware of my own climb, all eyes for the other two leaders.

During the first few days, however, I was extremely cautious, with the result that the students received only half the rock climbing I thought they should have. When we went to Bowfell Buttress I sent two people on a walk to the summit by way of Brown Ghyll and Crinkle Crags while I took the other two straight to the cliff and climbed. We met on the top and the two who had climbed reversed the walk while I led the others up the Buttress.

By the second day of the course I had recovered my sense of proportion and was astonished when I remembered my fears of the last few weeks. Certainly the work was extremely exacting but it was, on the whole, fun. I forgot the Enemy watching for a slip and reveled in the easier classics in Langdale. The two basic moods on a climb were, first, delight while I was actually climbing perhaps tempered a little by the necessity to tell a dreaming second to watch me and not the view, and then the sense of confidence and responsibility as my seconds followed when I approved their style and neat movements; and realized with amused surprise that they had watched me carefully. Usually I had no doubt that they were better than the day before.

It was capricious weather. The day might be spent in the hotel doing theory with the rain curtains drifting down the dale, and the night—clutching the tent poles as the gales came roaring down on me, shaking and snatching at the canvas, while the guy ropes strained and slackened, and the stream rose, and finally I slept from sheer exhaustion. One night mine was the only tent left standing. Even the proper mountain tents were blown away and one of the caravans behind the farm was tossed over like a doll's house.

In contrast there were hot still days on Gimmer when, at lunch time, we sunbathed at the foot of the cliff; or (the same place) in mist when Oliverson's seemed as exposed as a climb on Scafell, and another day so hot that we were too lazy to tramp all the way to Pavey Ark, but turned aside and, in shirt sleeves and sneakers, ran up and down all the little routes on Tarn Crag.

Despite the pleasure I was taking in climbing, I had been looking forward to the end of this course, for I was to go to Skye for six weeks, and Johnnie was in Kinloss. But he was posted suddenly to Topcliffe in Yorkshire, and we had only one day together in Langdale before I left for Scotland. I wasn't very miserable. My days were so full now that I had no time for anything else but climbing; after I had cooked my supper at night and written up the day's report, I was ready for bed. It was very different from being warden at the youth hostel where I had far too much time in which to wait for Johnnie and wonder why he didn't come.

My courses on Skye were not to start for three weeks; until then I was fully booked with private clients. I traveled north with the best of my students from the Langdale course. He was waiting to do his National Service, and had engaged me for a further week.

We broke our journey at Fort William and I took him up Tower Ridge in two and a half hours. There was no snow left except in the last gully before the summit plateau. The rock was bare and nail-scratched and very easy. I told him about our great climb here back in the winter and pointed out the gap where Johnnie had worked for so long in the moonlight trying to find a way up the other side. Even I found it unbelievable that here, where we scrambled gaily out of the gap, I had wondered if we would survive the night if we had to bivouac, and—where I had crept, terrified, along the unstable snow of the Eastern Traverse—now we walked casually, carrying coils.

From Fort William we headed west, along the Road to the Isles, crossed to Skye by steamer, and came at last, in the dusk, to Glen Brittle and the Black Cuillin.

The incongruous bulk of the old wooden youth hostel loomed ahead and, with a wary eye on the sky and remembering those gale-swept nights in the tent in Langdale, I was deeply thankful that, for the next six weeks, I should not be camping. The peaks were very clear, but one felt no uneasiness about the weather if one slept under a roof, with a good fire to dry clothes and cook food.

Despite the abnormal clarity of that evening the weather didn't break completely. There were showers during that first week but we climbed almost every day. We did nothing eventful and had no excitement and my client disappointed me by saying that he thought Scottish climbing dull and the walks to the foot of the cliffs far too long. My next client was very different. He was a dentist from Shropshire, a windfall in that he had come north to climb with Jim Cameron, the Coniston guide, but Jim, on his way to Skye, had fallen in Clachaig Gully and was now in a Fort William hospital. He had recommended me to the dentist.

Mr. Bellamy took over so closely from my other client that they overlapped and one day I had them together on Sron na Ciche. I was elated with the trade and began to think that now, with school fees paid, a debt to my mother honored, and money still rolling in, I could go to the Alps in August. I wrote jubilantly to Johnnie making plans for Chamonix.

My second day with Mr. Bellamy was a complete fiasco. I had become quite confident in myself as a guide, and I lost my client in Coire Lagan.

I knew that the Black Cuillin were magnetic in places so I never carried a compass; it was quite useless. I thought I knew Coire Lagan, too, and this day we had intended to do Collie's Route on Sgurr Alasdair. We walked into mist at about a thousand feet and continued, following the track up into the corrie. We negotiated the *roches moutonnées* below the lip of the upper corrie, and then started to traverse screes diagonally upward to the foot of Alasdair.

Mr. Bellamy was a happy little man, enjoying everything: views, company, climbs, walks—even that long walk up shifting scree to the foot of Collie's. He had great faith in his guide, too, so that when, to my astonishment, we came out on a ridge at the top of the scree (when we should have been at the foot of a cliff, hundreds of feet below any ridge) and I, after a discreet mental calculation, identified it as a point on the southwest ridge of Sgur Sgumain, he accepted it and turned meekly to start the long, diagonal descent to Collie's.

We came to a cairn at the foot of a cliff. Below we could hear the sound of a fair-sized stream. That, I told him, was the burn running into Coire Lagan. He looked at me with admiration. We roped up.

Suddenly the mist shifted and began to disperse. I looked down the slope and saw the stream and the lochan. Everything seemed the wrong way round. The stream was running *out of* the lake, not into it.

We were on the Lagan Buttress of Sgurr Deargl. Collie's and Alasdair were opposite, on the other side of the corrie. Since the moment I identified Bealach Coire Lagan as the southwest ridge of Sgumain I had been a hundred and eighty degrees out in my calculations.

The only emotion Mr. Belamy showed was concern that I should feel so humiliated. Determined that he should climb, I took him up Sgumain. We went slowly, watching the mist clear from the main ridge, with Sgurr Dearg appearing occasionally above the cloud bands and looking twenty thousand feet high.

He didn't seem disappointed with his day; he was the kind of man who can be happy in the mountains under any circumstances, but I had the sneaking feeling that I was not giving him his money's worth. However, I quieted my conscience on the last day when, with a heat wave starting, we climbed on Sron na Ciche in shorts and shirt sleeves, and the rock was like sandpaper. We reached the Cioch by way of the Cioch West and finished the day with Archer Thomson's route on the Upper Buttress. I had never been on this climb before; we both thought it was a delightful little route. It is only a Difficult and the holds are enormous—but when you look down, you seem to be suspended in space above the plunging depths of the Cioch Gully. We came racing down the screes of the Alasdair stone shoot where the dust rose in clouds behind us and the sun beat relentlessly as in a desert, and we cooled off by the limpid water of the lochan.

The heat wave continued. My engagement ended and Mr. Belamy drove me south to Glen Coe where I was due to climb with

Monica Jackson. And how we climbed! Not hard stuff, nothing more than Very Difficult, but we took full advantage of that glorious weather, out early in the morning and coming home in the dusk.

I hitchhiked back to Skye through miles of flaming rhododendrons, and then caught the bus from Armadale to Broadford where every wood and field was drenched with bluebells—and I met a man at Broadford who had known Collie, Mallory, Irvine and Odell and talked about the old days with a nostalgia that had me almost in tears.

There was a lot of mail waiting for me at the youth hostel, among it a letter from Johnnie saying he was in a hospital in Yorkshire with a broken back. He had gone to his parents' home on leave and decided to test—or stretch—an old hemp rope by abseiling on it out of a bedroom window. He put the rope round a bed and leaned out of the window horizontally with his feet on the ledge. The last thing he remembered was seeing the bed move towards him across the floor. Then he was lying on his back in the rockery. He said he would probably be fit for the Alps.

Dazed and appalled, I took the letter to a German doctor who was staying at the hostel and he assured me that a squashed vertabra was not too bad, that Johnnie wouldn't be a permanent cripple. I felt a little better and wrote fourteen pages to him before I went to bed, swearing mildly in my relief that it hadn't been worse, feeling all the time the horror of that moment when the bed started to move across the floor.

There was never any monotony in our lives.

The heat wave passed but the weather stayed dry for the first course. This was a Beginners' and we were to make a film for the Mountaineering Association. The cameraman was Norman Keep, the M.A. treasurer. I had four beginners, two of whom, a restaurant undermanager called Paul and an Italian countess, Dorothea Gravina, were already competent on rock. The other two, George and Mary, had no experience. I approached this course with some trepidation. I had heard guides say they wouldn't take Beginners' courses on Skye for higher wages than I was getting—and others said they wouldn't take Beginners' courses under any circumstances. The Cuillin are not suitable for parties of novices with one leader. The climbs are long and difficult to escape from in an emergency: too long to have more than two novices behind you. And if I climbed with two only, I was committed to sending the others for a walk, and "walks" on the Cuillin are scrambles of a high standard.

The first day I played safe and taught ropework on the boulders in Coire Lagan. With the hope that something had been learned, I took two of them on the long and easy Amphitheatre Arête in the afternoon, leaving the others, under the leadership of Norman, to traverse the skyline of Coire Lagan. Two people fell off that day and one retreated from Sgurr Thearlaich with an attack of nerves. People falling off was a secondary consideration, since they were roped and with me, but nerves on the ridge was worrying. I decided to keep the party together in the future.

The following day the course went into Coire na Banachdich where a fine sweep of rock ran up to the main ridge. We split into two parties, with Paul and Dorothea leading through on a route parallel to mine, following a line which I picked out as we climbed—a very moderate route, well within their limit. I had George and Mary on my rope, and Norman filmed us from an easy gully.

Roped, we went well. It was when we took the rope off that we had trouble. We were coming down the ridge of Sgurr Dearg, a blunt edge, not particularly exposed, and broad enough to walk along without using our hands. I had the most competent people in front and bringing up the rear. I was in the middle with Mary in front of me and George directly behind. Suddenly aware that the footsteps behind had stopped, I turned and saw George, very white, standing motionless on the crest. He was quite unable to move—how long had he been looking at the drop and calculating how far he would fall when he slipped? He stared at me miserably.

The whole caravan had stopped. Quietly I told him to come on, but he couldn't move. I uncoiled the rope and gave him an end. He muttered something about its being no use.

I said confidently, "If you come off, I shall jump over the other side."

He said nothing, but when I moved on, carrying coils, he followed, and we had no more bad moments that day.

Such situations, although saved, were very shattering to the one who had the responsibility, and by the last morning I was getting ready to breathe a hefty sigh of relief that the course was over. But Norman wanted to film me climbing, and abseiling off, the Inaccessible Pinnacle. To reach it I gave them one last ridge walk in the same climbing order as on Sgurr Dearg. I was ignoring the first three, giving all my attention to George who was coming down a steep section of the knife-edge to the level part where I was standing. Below the cliffs dropped away on either side. Unlike Sgurr Dearg, this *was* exposed. Paul and Dorothea had continued past the level section and were about a hundred feet ahead. By a coincedence I looked away from George for a moment, and saw Dorothea leaping back towards me with her arms outstretched and a terrified look on her face. I shouted to the last men to stay where they were—and then I don't remember moving, but it must have been fast because I heard the rocks falling as I scattered the rotten crest off the ridge. When I reached Dorothea, Mary was scrambling back onto the ridge where she sat down, trembling a little and speechless, her face completely drained of color.

Fortunately she kept up a running commentary on all her movements and, being a parson's daughter, "Oh dear," in sepulchral tones, meant she was at the end of her tether. Dorothea, hearing this, coupled with the sound of a slip, had turned to see Mary clinging to her last handhold. She had raced back, wedged a shoulder and foot under the girl, and levered her back onto the ridge.

I stood there, breathing hard and staring at them. We all looked about a hundred years old. Then I went back for Norman and George.

The day ended with Dorothea and me performing for the film on the Pinnacle. The course ended with my asking Norman—as an officer of the Mountaineering Association—to recommend that, after this season, no more Beginners' courses should be held on Skye.

Looking back on that first course, it seems full of harrowing incidents. Perhaps I should have picked easier sections of the ridge for walks, but where on the Black Cuillin is there a day's walk which is perfectly safe?

Whether I was more cautious with the next course or that they were, in general, less clumsy, is a debatable point, but the second week was less trying; the only casualty being myself, spraining an ankle scree-running, and gashing a foot abseiling—barefooted—into the sea.

It was a bad summer. For weeks on end the Skye courses climbed through rain and gales: wet to the skin, numb with cold, and miserable. The lines above the hostel stove were festooned with steaming clothes and one night I found a sock in the soup. Then I returned to the Lake District, back to camping, and it was more difficult to dry clothes, my sleeping bag was a sodden mass of feathers, and the field flooded and a cow put her horn through the tent. Tired and nervy, I crawled to the Old Dungeon Ghyll hotel for succor and Sid Cross and his wife welcomed me with open arms. When Johnnie arrived three days later, I was replete with Cumbrian hospitality, climbing well again, and straining at the leash at the thought of the Alps.

PHYLLIS MUNDAY: GRAND DAME OF THE COAST MOUNTAINS

Cyndi Smith

▲ ▲ ▲

WHEN PHYLLIS MUNDAY first started climbing, around 1910, women wore bloomers. "We'd start off from home with a skirt on—you were never seen with bloomers or a pair of pants—it just wasn't done in those days." They would take the streetcar from home, and as they started hiking up the trail, they'd cache their skirts under a log. This meant, of course, that they always had to return the same way, or they couldn't go home on the streetcar!

Over a period of nearly thirty-five years, Phyllis and her husband, Don, explored the mountainous regions of Alberta and British Columbia, coming to know the Coast Mountains like no one else has before or since and claiming many first ascents in the process. While doing research for *Off the Beaten Track,* a book about women explorers and mountaineers in Canada, I came to realize that "Phyl," as she was known to all, had few equals among mountaineers, men or women.

Phyllis was born in Sri Lanka on September 24, 1894, but grew up in Canada. Her father, a tennis champion for many years in both Sri Lanka and in Vancouver, British Columbia, felt that, with proper help and guidance, his daughter could be a tennis star, but Phyllis had other ideas. Her eyes were forever turning toward the hills around Vancouver. She wanted to climb mountains, for "there was something about getting away often, in the wilds, as we used to call it, that appealed to me more than anything else, and I wanted to go up to the mountains."

Her first real climb was of the Lions (1,646 meters), near Vancouver, with the British Columbia Mountaineering Club (BCMC) when she was about sixteen years old. After the climb her father asked, "You've climbed one mountain, why do you want to climb more?" Phyl infuriated him by pointing out that "he'd played more than one game of tennis!"

Near the end of the First World War, Phyl was employed as a clerical worker in the orderly room of the Military Annex of the New Westminster General Hospital. She also served with its Voluntary Aid Detachment. (Phyl was involved with the St. John's Ambulance first aid all of her life.) It was here, in 1918, that she met Don Munday, a twenty-eight year-old soldier and mountaineer who was recovering from a war injury.

Phyl and Don were married on February 4, 1920. Phyl's mother hosted a gala wedding for them and was exasperated when they bypassed the reception to rush home to exchange wedding clothes for knickers and boots. Two hours later they were off to their beloved mountains.

Their only daughter, Edith, was born on March 26, 1921. A few weeks later they took her up to their cabin on Grouse Mountain. Edith was only eleven weeks old when she accompanied them up Crown Mountain (1,503 meters). On the first of July the same year they traversed the Seymore Valley and continued down the Stawamus Valley into Squamish with Edith along. On this trip the Mundays stayed in a cabin owned by the Britannia Mining Company. A monstrous baking pan was perfect for bathing the baby, but when three geologists from the mine came along, they were stunned to see a baby in a bread pan on the oven door!

The Mundays raised their daughter to be thoroughly comfortable and unafraid in the outdoors. Edith remembered being a happy child, but in retrospect wondered if she didn't take "second place to a mountain."

In 1924, Phyl and Don attended the Alpine Club of Canada's (ACC) annual camp at Robson Pass. They had just returned from an ascent of nearby Mumm Peak (2,962 meters) when the autocratic club president, A. O. Wheeler, announced that they would have "permission" to climb Mount Robson (3,954 meters), the highest peak in the Canadian Rockies. This was despite the prevailing impression that no woman would be allowed to attempt the "big climb," at that time regarded as beyond the physical endurance and mountaineering skill of women. The group included the Mundays, Fred Lambart, A. W. Drinnan, Annette Buck, J. F. Porter, Austrian climbing guide Conrad Kain and his assistant, Joe Saladana. Phyl wanted no favored treatment: "Having seen my lady companion's pack lightened, unbeknown to her, of the supplies she was going to carry, led me to guard mine closely."

High camp was located at timberline on the southwest face, above Kinney Lake. There were three tents, a stove, cooking utensils and bedding. Although it rained during the night, the weather was good when Conrad woke the group well before daylight.

Conrad called us at 2:30 a.m.; at 3:30 we were on our way to test the perils of the climb for ourselves. At about 8,000 feet we gained the ridge behind the little black peak of the west face, in time to see the ice-front of the southwest face discharge a mass of ice down cliffs where exceptionally big avalanches are sometimes hurled 5,000 feet into the valley of the Little Fork. Nearly a thousand feet higher the same glacier has broken through the ridge to fling ice down bare cliffs for 6,000 feet almost to the trail along Lake Kinney.

What concerned us more intimately was that we had to cross the cliffs for nearly 100 yards directly under the glistening and shattered wall which, 100 feet in height, hung far out over the way we must go.

From this and the greater wall somewhere above, tremendous avalanches had fallen just after the previous party passed—some assurance that less remained to threaten us. A few stray blocks came down with crashing reports as they shattered on the rocks, but we passed safely.

More good rock climbing followed for about 2,000 feet, the shining white peak in sight most of the time, and seemingly close at hand. So far we had performed so that Conrad had not roped us, but now we had to work across the cliffs 200 yards under the upper ice-wall, and then actually climb its 150-foot face. The wall extends for more than a quarter of a mile, sloping diagonally upwards—close to Lake Kinney we had passed remains of an avalanche fallen 8,000 feet from this wall.

The ice-cliff, amazingly overhanging, fantastically sculptured, grunted uneasily. Conrad coached both rope parties carefully; we gathered up the slack of the ropes, and worked out along a protruding shelf. Perhaps a fairly steady head and foot are needed for one to trot rapidly along a ledge with 8,000 feet of thin air immediately below; nevertheless it is fairly certain that no one in the party actually saw just then the void below or the ice menace above.

In one place the ice sloped back slightly, and here Conrad decided to force a passage, and plied his ice axe vigorously, working out diagonally far beyond the base of the ice wall—surely the dizziest place imaginable, but obviously the only way. Cutting small handholds, he stood on one foot and chopped the final step to surmount the crest of the ice, over which he disappeared. I had anchored him with the rope around my ice-axe thrust in a hole in the ice. Now it was my turn to follow—without a professional guide I had scaled as difficult ice-walls before, but never with such an excess of nothingness under my heels, or so much impending above.

Just above this point they were held up on the glacier when Saldana fell through a snow bridge. He was quickly extricated, but he had lost his ice axe, which took an hour to recover. This delay proved costly later. On the main ridge, the ice terraces reminded Phyl of "breakers on a rough sea."

The slope above is unlike anything elsewhere in the Rockies—an absolute chaos of ice blocks on a slope of not less than forty-five degrees; domed with snow, and bristling with gleaming icicles, they were a never to be forgotten sight, fairylike perhaps, but sinister, hostile, menacing. Even in the bright sunlight, we shivered if we stopped. When a cloud crossed the sun the cold was intense.

Around, between, under the ice blocks we climbed, the rotted snow often subsiding beneath us, necessitating the use of the rope to get the rest of the party across the holes. Sometimes we crawled on hands and knees across doubtful places, or even lay down and wriggled. Utmost care was required to avoid giving some of the shattered masses just the jar which might set them going, probably to disrupt the whole slope.

It was late in the afternoon before Conrad negotiated the last, short face section, disappeared from view, then pulled the rope in quickly. Phyl climbed onto the summit and was greeted by Conrad, who extended his hand and said, "There, Lady! You are the first woman on top of Mount Robson," and almost pumped her arm off in congratulations. For her it was the achievement of a four-year ambition.

Darkness overtook them on the descent. They sought shelter

that night in some rocks and finally reached their high camp at five o'clock the next morning where the other climbers welcomed them with soup, toast and tea. Two hours later they left for the long tramp back to base camp at Robson Pass. Theirs was only the third ascent of the magnificent peak.

In the early spring of 1925, Phyllis and Don Munday joined a friend, Tom Ingram, on an early-season attempt of Mount Arrowsmith (1,817 meters), near Port Alberni on Vancouver Island. While stopped for lunch and casually scanning the horizon with binoculars, Phyllis spotted a high peak in the Coast Mountains across the Strait of Georgia. It was shining like a beacon through a break in the clouds that hugged the mountains. She pointed it out to Don, who immediately took a compass bearing before the clouds obscured it once again. To them, it was the "far off finger of destiny beckoning."

The mountain lay due north on a line passing near the head of Bute Inlet. Phyl and Don guessed the mountain was about 250 kilometers away, in a virtually unknown and unmapped area. It seemed to dwarf the surrounding peaks. Could it be a monarch, never before discovered? Don wrote that "I do not recall that Phyl or I suggested in words to each other that there lay our future goal . . . we took that for granted from the moment we first spotted it." They christened it Mystery Mountain. Their search for the mountain and attempts to ascend it are unequaled in mountaineering circles.

In September 1925 the Mundays set out to reconnoitre Mystery Mountain, accompanied by Tom Ingram and Athol Agur. They traveled on a Union Steamship Company boat to Orford Bay in Bute Inlet. A trapper took them another forty kilometers in his motorboat to the head of the inlet. After toiling straight up from sea level, they gained the summit of Mount Rodney (2,391 meters). On the skyline one peak towered over all the others: Mystery Mountain. Who would believe their estimate of its height as more than four thousand meters? At 3,954 meters, Mount Robson was still believed highest in the province. "At least Phyl and I knew we must return again," wrote Don, "not as assailants, but in a spirit closer to veneration."

The only plausible access route seemed to be via the Homathko Valley. This was a fifty kilometer long trench, with steep flanks 2,400 meters high, and the head seemed blocked by a large glacier.

The scene was anything but encouraging.

But during May 1936, they made two trips to Homathko. The first trip was a reconnaissance to see if the route was feasible. On the second one, they spent a week freighting five weeks' worth of supplies as far up the Homathko River as they could, using a four-meter rowboat with a "kicker" (outboard motor), and a canoe. On May 31 the whole party set out together: Phyl, Don, Tom, Athol, Johnnie Johnson and Don's brother Bert. Edith was left at a logging camp on Bute Inlet in the care of a friend of the Mundays and her daughter. Phyl missed Edith terribly on these extended trips—she would glue Edith's picture in the front of her diary and wait for her letters.

As they headed into Homathko Valley, Don wrote that it "lost itself in a cavernous gloom as unwelcoming as the dark lair of some unknown beast." The valley floor was awash from heavy rain and flooding glacial streams; they crossed and recrossed creeks, usually on narrow, sagging tree trunks. Willows, alder, brush, silt, rotting trees and devil's club, "the most diabolical plant in North America," threatened to bar their passage every step of the way. After thirteen days they had traveled barely fifty kilometers from tidewater and were a meagre one hundred meters above it. Don estimated that they had averaged more than 160 kilometers per person relaying their supplies in three trips.

For another week they battled their way up to Waddington Glacier, attempting to get as close as possible to their goal. After climbing a peak to scout the area, Phyl became snow-blind. Although the affliction was painful, it was fortunately temporary. Tea poultices placed over her eyes eased the burning sensation somewhat, but for days Phyl was led by hand as they moved camp. Still, she continued to carry her share of the loads.

With a scant four days' food rations left, they decided on June 23 to make a final push for the mountain. They left camp at nine o'clock in the evening, aided by generous moonlight and an acetylene lamp. At 5:15 a.m., in the glorious sunrise, they crested "Mystery Pass" and had their first full view of Mystery Mountain. They spent the next twelve hours working their way closer to the mountain, but alas, time had run out. They returned to tidewater.

"Alpine starts" or late-night arrivals were not unusual for the Mundays. Occasionally, when pressed for time, they made twenty- or thirty-hour scouting trips from base camp. As they began to tire, they sometimes had visions. Once Phyl went to sit down, thinking she was on a heather slope, but she was actually on a glacier. Leading the party at such times was a sought-after position, as the extra responsibility made it easier for the leader to stay awake. About such times, Don commented that "my wife and I bring to this kind of night travel a glad confidence in each other that one not knowing us well might brand foolhardiness."

Hoping for an easier route to Mystery Mountain, the Mundays tried an approach from Knight Inlet in July 1927. Knight Inlet was fed by the mighty Kliniklini River and the outflow of the Franklin Glacier. The struggle along the valley was much less trying than that along the Homathko the year before. They made three unsuccessful attempts on their Mystery Mountain, the final time being chased down from a subsidiary summit by a severe storm. Subsequently they were stormed in for a week. When the weather lifted, the new blanket of snow made the mountain too treacherous to climb. They returned to Vancouver, disappointed but not defeated.

Always the Mundays outran the map-makers. When weather made it impossible to try for the main tower of Mystery Mountain, their objective, they would explore the surrounding area. Phyl's philosophy was that "there isn't any one mountain worth throwing your life away on. So if it (the condition of Mystery Mountain) wasn't good, we'd go off and do something else . . . but every time— it doesn't matter whether it's storm or sunshine—it's always worth it." In 1927 J. T. Underhill's survey party established the height of Mystery Mountain as 4,016 meters, and within months the Canadian Permanent Committee on Geographic Names had officially named it Mount Waddington. The Mundays had the pleasure of naming most of the features in the Waddington area.

It seems amazing that the Coast Mountains—formidable and savage—had remained unexplored for so long compared to the other wilds in Canada. But there were no roads or railways in the area, nor aircraft landing sites, so the range remained unknown. The wet, stormy climate, all-but-impenetrable forests and raging rivers keep the mountains isolated even today.

Don and Phyl returned to Waddington again in 1928, accompanied by Don's brother Bert. They climbed intermittently because of poor weather, making only two first ascents, of Mount Whitetip and Mount Myrtle. On July 8 they arose at 1:15 a.m. for yet another attempt on Waddington. After hours of struggling along the northwest ridge, they topped what appeared to be the final peak—only to discover the soaring main tower across a gap to the east. It was adorned with huge feathers of ice, like "ostrich plumes," formed by rain and snow freezing in the high winds off the Pacific. It was "a nightmare molded in rock" and seemed impossible to climb. Don wrote in his diary that it was "thrilling to see a so uncompromising face" on Waddington. Soaking wet, and with darkness approaching, they were forced to turn back. More than five years would pass before they could attempt Waddington again.

Phyl was a very strong woman, frequently carrying a thirty-kilogram pack, and she never took the lightest load. She was an excellent rower, and to her often fell the laborious and risky river and inlet crossings. Don and Phyl were fairly equal in climbing ability. They took turns leading, but in rock-climbing situations where there was a touchy left handhold, Phyl would lead because of Don's war-wounded left arm. They climbed on many different kinds of rock and "always seemed to find a route somewhere or other where we didn't seem to need a piton." Phyl was one of only three women to receive the Alpine Club of Canada's Silver Rope award, in recognition of leadership capabilities.

Although Phyl was considered an equal on the mountain, the traditional woman's chores of sewing, cooking and taking care of camp still fell to her. She spent the winters experimenting with drying different foods, but little was lightweight. The menu was usually very simple. Bannock was a staple. Phyl would make it in a baking tin, put it on the fire, and then set up the reflector so that it would brown and cook on top. That way she didn't have to flip it, and she could attend to other chores while it was cooking. In camp Phyl would cook food for the next day's climb: boiled pudding, beans, rice, pilot bread. Chocolate, nuts and raisins served as "iron rations" when they were climbing.

Rainy days in camp were spent fixing gear, waterproofing boots with dubbin, washing, baking and so on. Phyl and Don made most of their own gear—one, because very little was available commercially and two, because it saved them money, their only income coming from Don's pension, his freelance writing and Phyl's secretarial wages.

Climbing in the notoriously poor weather of the Coast Mountains, the Mundays were often caught in rain and snowstorms. In such instances they would retreat as quickly as possible and bivouac if necessary. On one trip, they had 150 hours of rain out of 152 consecutive hours! These conditions undoubtedly aggravated Phyl's arthritis. Most nights she had to wrap her knees in cold towel compresses and cover them with light rubber sheets in an attempt to keep the swelling down. She made light of this process, calling it "a bit of a nuisance."

In 1930, with the use of skis, the Mundays prepared to attempt the mountain that had been recently named for them. Mount Munday was on the long southeast ridge of the Waddington massif. They skied to Mystery Pass and up the slope as far as they could. A cold wind precluded much time on the summit (3,505 meters), and they were soon enjoying the ski run back down the glacier. Overtaken by darkness, they continued trekking through the night, keenly atuned to the "disturbingly brilliant" stars and Milky Way.

The Mundays ventured yearly into the Waddington area from 1931 to 1935, filling in more blanks on their maps and making a few first ascents, but never attempting Waddington again. During eleven trips in twelve years, Phyl and Don spent a total of fifteen months exploring the area. They attempted to climb Mount Waddington sixteen times, coming as close as fifty feet from the summit, but never actually reaching it.

Then, in 1936, while exploring the Kliniklini Glacier, Phyl and Don heard that Fritz Wiessner and Bill House had accomplished the long-coveted first ascent of Waddington on July 21, using pitons and extra rope. The Mundays took it well. "We seemed to manage and do all the climbing we needed without carrying all those things," says Phyl. "I suppose we could have done much more in the (way of) rock work if we had had more pitons. We had only two, but we never used them." House later admitted that he wouldn't want to repeat the climb.

For the next three seasons, 1937 to 1939, Don and Phyl, accompanied by Edith, Henry Hall and Hall's friend Hermann Ulrichs, explored the Bella Coola area, some six hundred kilometers north of Vancouver. They made the first ascent of Mount Stupendous (2,728 meters) and attempted Mount Saugstad three times without success. Edith was sixteen years old, and this was the first time she had accompanied Phyl and Don for any serious climbing. They were very impressed with how well she handled the hard days on the mountains.

Progress was slow in this untracked wilderness. The great depths of the valleys—rising some 2,500 meters or more from sea level—and their consistently steep sides made ascents difficult. The valley bottoms were often choked with tangles of alders.

One year the whole family assisted in fighting a small forest fire near Bella Coola. Women couldn't be included on the payroll, so Phyl and Edith listed only their initials. They received the small sum of eight dollars for their hard work!

After a hiatus during the war years, the Mundays were back on the Homathko in 1946. Their explorations gave them the first ascent of Reliance Mountain (3,134 meters). Although Reliance Mountain was their final first ascent, the Mundays continued to climb in the Coast Mountains and in the Rockies. They also continued to enjoy skiing. When the conditions were excellent, it "made the marrow in my bones bubble," according to Phyl.

Don and Phyl shared their last Alpine Club camp in the Freshfield group in 1949, where they climbed Mount Freshfield (3,336 meters). Phyl was fifty-five and Don fifty-nine. In November that year Don fell ill; six months later, on June 12, 1950, he died at Vancouver Military Hospital.

After Don died, Phyll continued to do the easier climbs into her sixties and to attend the annual ACC camps (she attended more than thirty in all), where she frequently attended to the many cuts and bruises in the "blister tent." She served as hostess for eight summers during the 1960s at the ACC Clubhouse in Banff. She continued to get inquiries about the Waddington area from people who were planning trips, and her correspondence was full of requests for opinions and photographs—more than she could fulfill. She was truly the Grand Dame of the Coast Mountains.

Phyl loved photography. She started with an ordinary Kodak Brownie, but soon graduated to a good bellows camera and finally to an Exakta, which was her favorite. "It's so exciting when you're focusing on something very small—the centre of a flower or even the veins and petals." Her color and black-and-white photographs of mountain scenery won her acclaim in mountaineering circles.

On all their outings, the Mundays were meticulous in their observations and recordings and kept detailed records of their climbs.

They both photographed panoramas, and from these and his compass readings, Don made photo-topographical maps.

Phyl collected and pressed flowers, and she made an insect collection for the Provincial Museum of British Columbia (now the Royal British Columbia Museum) in Victoria. Phyl never considered herself a botanist, just a lover of those "brave little things growing all on their own." She always felt that their collecting and mapping made her and Don see and observe a lot of things that they might have otherwise missed.

Phyl's kinship with the outdoors was very special, and she frequently berated the general public because "they just go up there and they see the mountains away off in the distance, and come down like it was the last moment they had to live. . . . They just don't *see* anything . . . people today don't seem to respect nature." She loved nature in all its forms, from the wonderful cloud effects to the most minute spider or ant. "Nothing appealed to me like it (nature)," Phyl said, "and for a long time I didn't go to church because the mountains were my great cathedral."

Phyl always found it difficult to find words to describe her love of climbing: "There just aren't any words, but on a mountain you are so very close to nature. Mother Nature can be severe with the careless, but I always feel a friendship with mountains, almost as if they were human."

Phyl really enjoyed snow and ice climbing, because conditions change all the time, whereas "rock is rock." The thrill of exploration and discovery was the main factor for Phyl: "I'm not a rock monkey as such, not at all like the rock climbers today. I wouldn't want to hang on a string for hours and hours feeling around for something. I'd want to get going and get on the mountain. I'd rather have an easier mountain and get on top."

Phyl had only scorn for some of the modern climbers and mountaineers who rush in, bag peaks and rush home again. "They don't give you the feeling that they have any reverence for it all, love for it all, adoration for it. It's just accomplishment and nothing else." Phyl and Don were not only mountaineers, but also true pioneers and explorers.

Besides the British Columbia Mountaineering Club and the Alpine Club of Canada (she joined the latter in 1920), Phyl was also a member of the Ladies' Alpine Club, the American Alpine Club, the Carlisle Mountaineering Club of England, the Appalachian Mountain Club and the Varsity Outdoors Club of Vancouver. She and Don were elected to the Appalachian Mountain Club for "outstanding feats of climbing and exploration in the coast range of British Columbia, and for vision and efforts which have opened up a spectacular new region to mountaineers." Phyl is the only mountaineer to be the recipient of honorary membership in three international mountaineering clubs: the Ladies' Alpine Club (1936), the Alpine Club of Canada (1938) and the American Alpine Club (1967). She was the only woman so honored by the American club. In 1970 she received the ACC's badge for outstanding service, and the following year she was named honorary president. She had trained ACC members in ice and snow climbing, and in mountain first aid. Phyl was also the editor of the *Canadian Alpine Journal* from 1953 until 1969.

Her crowning honor came in 1973, when she was named a member of the Order of Canada. She was also conferred with the title and degree of Honorary Doctor of Laws from the University of Victoria.

Phyl never considered whether she was a role model for other women climbers: "I don't know what women really thought of me. . . . If a person enjoys it (mountaineering) and you are strong enough, and well enough to do it, and you can hold your own with a party . . . then there is no reason in the world why a woman can't do it." She felt that the reason a lot of women are discouraged in mountaineering is because the group sometimes travels off too quickly to start with, and they can't keep up. Her secret was to travel at a steady pace, one which she could hold to all day. As she grew older gracefully, it was obvious from Phyl's tremendous vigor that she had paced herself properly, when others had burnt themselves out. "She gave to everybody a sense that you don't go beyond your limits, your capabilities, that you had to think of the team, the others, of the party," remembered one Vancouver climber.

Phyl climbed some one hundred peaks, nearly a third of which were first ascents. Many others were first ascents for women.

A young climber once asked Phyl why she and Don went into the Mount Waddington area so many times and didn't even reach the summit of the main tower of Waddington. She replied:

We didn't go into the Waddington country just to climb one mountain and run out and leave it. We went in . . . to find out all we possibly could about glaciers and mountains and animals and nature and everything about that particular area—completely unknown before we went into it—so that we could bring out the information for the interest of other people as well as ourselves.

"What a life we've had," said Phyl, when I spoke with her in 1988 in Nanaimo, British Columbia. "Nothing can take away our mountain memories." Phyl Munday died on April 11, 1990.

The Biggest Party of the Year (47) Sliding on The
Paradise Glacier - Sept. 1st 1919.

*The Mountaineers sliding on Paradise Glacier, Mt. Rainier, Washington, September 1, 1919.
Photo: Special Collections Division, University of Washington Libraries*

Top: Members of the 1924 Alpine Club of
Canada camp who climbed Mt. Robson.
Front row (l-r): Joe Saladana (assistant
guide), Don Munday, Phyl Munday, Albert
MacCarthy, Annette Buck, Harry Pollard.
Back row: Malcolm Geddes, Thomas
Moffat, Fred Lambart, A. E. Drinnan,
James Porter.
Photo: Whyte Museum of the Canadian
Rockies, Banff, Alberta, Canada

Right: Anna Howard Price, first woman to
climb Mt. Shuksan and member of several
other first ascent parties in the first and
second decades of this century.
Photo: Whatcom Museum, Bellingham,
Washington

Opposite page: Looking at Mt. Adams,
circa 1910.
Mountaineers Collection, Special
Collections Division, University of
Washington

Jake Shidell
Summit Guide

Alma D. Wagen
"Lady" Guide

Top: Mountaineers outing to Washington's Olympic Range, July 1907, Mt. Noyes. Photo: Melvin A. Krows. Special Collections Division, University of Washington Libraries

Left: Alma Wagen, the first woman mountain guide employed by the U. S. government and Jake Shidell, summit guide at Mt. Rainier. Alma worked in the early 1920s in Mt. Rainier National Park, guiding clients like John D. Rockefeller, Jr. up the mountain.
Photo: Mountaineers collection; Special Collections Division, University of Washington Libraries

Opposite page: Janet Roddan on Polar Circus, Alberta, Canada.
Photo: Barb Clemes

Top: Kathy Phibbs climbing
at Joshua Tree.
Photo: Kathy Phibbs
collection

Left: Jeanne Panek climbing
at Smith Rocks, Oregon.
Photo: Jeanne Panek
collection

Louise Shepherd cutting loose on Pilot Error, grade 20, Mt. Arapiles, Australia,
1985.
Photo: Louise Shepherd collection

Nyrie Dodd climbing Three Dimensional in the Grampions, Australia.
Photo: Louise Shepherd

ON THE HEIGHTS

Colette Richard

▲ ▲ ▲

In Maurice Herzog's Foreword to Colette Richard's autobiography,
Climbing Blind, *published in 1967, he writes that the book "tells of a*
girl who one day resolved to become a mountaineer and a cave-
explorer. She let nothing stand in her way. She explored the princi-
pal caves in the Pyrenees. She climbed in the most beautiful, but not
the least dangerous, region of the Alps, the Massif de Chamonix. She
'did' the Mont Tondu, the Col du Geant, the Infranchissible (11,000
feet) and the Mont Blanc du Tacul (over 13,000 feet)—difficult climbs
even for experienced mountaineers. But Colette Richard came late to
mountaineering; and she had another handicap—she is blind."
Climbing Blind *is written with a joy and sense of continual dis-*
covery nearly unmatched in climbing literature. As its author says,
"To those who know the mountains I would say that it is not sight
alone that matters, and that I hope to show them other things. Those
who do not know them I hope to teach to love them. The secret wish
of mountaineers is to cause others to share the joys they discover in the
heights."

I was born at Versailles in a humble dwelling very near the palace.
When I was two my eyesight failed almost completely, leaving me
with only a faint perception of light, able to distinguish between

sunshine and darkness like a normal person with their eyes tightly closed.

My parents taught me a love of Nature, and as a little girl I played with other children either in the Great Park of Versailles, which was like my private domain, or on the land adjoining it, where my father had a vegetable garden near the pond known as the Pièce d'Eau des Suisses.

At school I became passionately interested in geology and geography; I dreamed of volcanoes and mountains. My holidays were spent in a village in the Gatinais, where my younger brother and I played together in an old quarry. It was there, amid the fields and woods, that my longing for adventure was born. My love of mountains grew with the years, with the books that were read to me and those that I read to myself in braille. But I have always had an intense longing for space and great expeditions.

We are all to some extent imprisoned by life, and the thing we most ardently desire is always slow in coming, so that often we feel that it will never come at all. But with patience and courage, if we want them enough and love them enough, all things come in the end, however long the time may be.

In 1953 I visited my first mountain—a small one certainly, but still a mountain. Providence sometimes arranges things to suit us. I went as a tourist for reasons of health, because I was badly in need of a change from city life, and on the fourth of August that year I first set foot on the Mer de Glace. My dream of becoming a real climber never afterwards left me. In all of us there is a sleeping star which, consciously or unconsciously, we seek to grasp.

My love of mountains was such that it absorbed all my thoughts, even to the point of wearying me, but it stimulated me as well. My friends, seeing the fascination they had for me, found it hard to understand why. Why go to the mountains, they wondered, when one cannot see them?

It is a large question and a strange one, but one which I find it easy to answer. We do not need to see mountains in order to love them, any more than we need to see, or even hear, a person who is dear to us. Their presence is enough. For me it is enough that mountains exist.

People describe landscapes to me. I picture them, and I note the reactions of my companions, their delight, their exclamations of wonderment when a new prospect is disclosed at a turn in the path. The landscape I imagine may not be the real one; it may be more or less beautiful than reality; but what does that matter? For me it is real and it possesses its own truth.

I believe strongly in the truth of my inward feeling, and it is the idea I have of things which gives so much *value* to my mountains. Snow, rocks and glaciers, no doubt I idealise all these a little; but if I endow the things and people I love with so many qualities, I recognise their faults as well.

I do not go to the mountains for the same reasons as other climbers, and that is all that can be said. We approach them in a different way. And so people are often surprised by my evocation of the mountains, and my love of them. But sight is only one of our senses. There are all the things one perceives by other means, things one knows by intuition, things one can hear and touch and smell and taste. In the foothills there are waterfalls, flowers, cattle bells and raspberries.

What one experiences at higher altitudes is to my mind more precious and rare because it is difficult of access: the wind in the peaks, the footsteps of the rope-party in the snow, the steady crunch of the ice-axe sinking into it, the falling stones which whistle as they fall, avalanches, the sounds coming from the glacier's depths... And there is also, which is wonderful to me, the reflection of brilliant sunshine on untrodden snow, the warmth, the quiver, the extraordinary light that is to be found nowhere else.

There is the keen, cold air that stings the cheeks, the delicate, almost imperceptible scent of snow which has in it something of pine, of grass and of flowers. There is the use we who are sightless must make of our hands, the feeling of rock and snow.

There is the wonderful comradeship of the climbing-party, the friendship and mutual trust; the atmosphere of the mountain huts where one shelters; the nights of waiting and the mornings of setting out; the plans, the prospects, the difficulties to be overcome on an awkward climb. There are the debates about the weather, which one prays will be perfect, because that is the first requisite if the climb is to be a success.

All these simple matters, which in another book might sound merely commonplace, so much padding, here assume a special significance. The guide who escorts a blind climber up a mountain is undertaking a great responsibility.

There is the poetry of darkness in the mountains, when the party sets out before the sun has risen. There are all the things I have forgotten to mention, which may be termed the local colour of the mountain peaks.

Why do I climb mountains? Quite simply because the mountains and I had to meet. I go for my pleasure and to conquer myself. I know of nothing more deadly than inaction, whether physical or mental. One needs to try one's strength and one's willpower, to triumph over one's destiny, to remake oneself, to put one's muscles to use.

I do not climb mountains in order to break records of height or altitude. Those things do not interest me. I do it because I love the beauty and simplicity of a way of living which brings confidence, which confirms resolution and calls for courage.

Is it difficult to climb when one cannot see? Is it not more dangerous than for a person possessing sight?

A mountain is a great lady who must not be treated lightly. She is not easily mastered by anyone, still less by a person without eyes. She is in the first place a friend; for friendship is the best of what we give and take from one another. To conquer her calls for great patience and perseverance; one must learn to know her.

In practice one needs to be in good condition, capable of walking for very long stretches, with the least possible fatigue and expenditure of effort, over every kind of surface, rocky for preference. The ideal ground for persons without sight is that of the mule-tracks at an altitude of between 6,000 and 8,000 feet. I shall come back to this. And it goes without saying that a blind person must always be well escorted, accompanied by experienced guides and team-mates.

Unquestionably climbing is more difficult for a blind person—I mean, climbing in the *high mountains*. It is also more dangerous and entails a greater expense of energy, besides inducing a state of constant nervous tension in every member of the team. One ends by acquiring a certain technique, tricks and devices which one perfects with every climb.

Does blindness produce vertigo? Are the blind more susceptible to heights than normal climbers?

No, I do not think that, lacking sight, one can suffer from vertigo in the ordinary sense of the word—that is to say, see the world spinning round one, so that one is tempted to fling oneself into the void. In this respect the blind have an obvious advantage, although it is one that we would prefer to do without.

My friend Monsieur Arthur Richard of Morzine, who is the only blind Frenchman to have reached the summit of Mont Blanc (21st July, 1959) once said to me, referring to a newspaper article which talked about the extreme perceptiveness of the blind, "Those of us who claim to be conscious of the change of altitude after climbing thirty or forty feet are certainly remarkably sensitive—to the point of making themselves ridiculous. The change is only perceptible in thousands of feet. You know it by a sense of space, a sort of headiness . . . the smell of the air."

The remark is a very interesting one. What Monsieur Richard, a great observer and born mountaineer, calls with so much truth and precision "the smell of the air" is what I would term, more fancifully, "the scent of snow." Although physical vertigo does not exist for us, we may still experience a very strange feeling, a sort of "moral vertigo" if I may so express it. This can be terrible. Certainly it is in part imaginary, and it is something against which one has to fight with all one's strength. Above all one has to keep one's head, behave even more calmly than usual and do nothing capricious (I can see my climbing companions smile as they read those words!), which is not always an easy matter.

Our master once said to us at school, "We see much more with our minds than with our eyes," and the words are perfectly applicable here. One perceives, with all one's senses alert. The mind registers impressions. One has to concentrate without becoming overstrained. Everything varies according to the inner mood, and it is very important to be good-humoured.

The blind are conscious of space. Obviously they cannot measure depth, especially when it is a matter of thousands of feet. But the sense of space has a great effect on them, and it is not always an unpleasant one. It may, on the contrary, be wonderfully exciting. Everything depends at such moments on the general mood of one's team-mates, the coolness and deliberation of those who guide and direct the climb.

I shall return to this matter in talking of my own climbs; but I can say at once that if one is overtaken by that kind of panic at some very unpropitious moment, practice and experience do much to relieve it. I was far more frightened on my first climbs than during the later ones.

As in life, the important thing is to gain utmost confidence in oneself, and above all to trust the rope which links one to one's comrades. It is also important that they should clearly describe the movements to be made, and the scene in general; but they alone are the judges of this.

I have learnt that for a blind person who attempts mountaineering the two most essential virtues are obedience and trust. I cannot pretend to possess them entirely, a whole lifetime would not be enough for me to acquire them. And what I have said about mountineering applies equally to exploring the subterranean world. This is not really surprising for the two worlds are one—the mountain and what is hidden in its heart.

Le Mont Tondu

On the sixteenth August, 1960, we climbed to the Tré-La-Tête shelter, a height of about 6,000 feet.

The track was an easy one. I went with Monsieur Piraly and the Abbé Meynet. Meynet was a good friend and a good mountaineer, and we jokingly called him the apprentice-guide.

Let me say at once that it was not because there was any thought of death or the last sacrament in our minds that we had brought a priest with us. On the contrary, we were all in high spirits, and Meynet had come simply for the pleasure of doing so. In these days a great many priests take up mountaineering, following the example of Pope Pius XI, who wrote admirably on the subject and has left us the beautiful form of benediction for ropes and ice-axes.

We reached the shelter at about five on a beautiful summer evening, and I was wildly happy. We had talked all the way telling tales of guides and accidents, of which there is never any lack, and joking and laughing and thoroughly enjoying ourselves. There had been no hurry, and Piraly had stopped here and there to gather mushrooms. The undergrowth smelt of damp earth, humus and moss. A party of about a dozen climbers had passed us, also making for the shelter, which meant that we should have plenty of company. Towards the end of the climb the track narrowed and we had to go in single file, taking care where we put our feet. The air was growing cooler, and we could hear in the distance the tinkling of cow-bells. When we reached the shelter Piraly stood on the verandah telling us the names of the peaks to be seen on the horizon. He knew them all, and each one had its history. Meynet and I greatly admired his erudition, although, of course, it was part of a guide's job, and one of the most delightful, it must be said.

We went inside. I was enormously hungry. We dumped all our equipment in a corner, rucksacks, anoraks, jerseys, ropes and ice-axes. It is what every climber does when he comes stamping into a shelter, but to me it was wonderful.

We were greeted by other guides who told us of the expeditions they and their parties were planning for the morrow. They were men from Gervais and the Contamines, and I liked their sing-song accents. One party was going on to the Bérangère, another to the Miages and others to l'Infranchissable or, like ourselves, to the Mont Tondu, the Shorn Mountain.

The great question was the weather, but everyone was sure it would be fine. We had to turn in early, because the alarm-clock was set for three in the morning.

It was a long time before I fell asleep . . . There have been many tragedies in the Massif of Tré-La-Tête—that of the Skier, of the youthful party from the Contamines and of the Dutchmen. Everyone knew about them, but all hoped that this time the Great Lady would be kind. Well, I had Piraly and Meynet to look after me, and there could be no better escort. Still, this was my first real climb in the high mountains. A real glacier, and a big one, was no laughing matter. But it was what I had been dreaming of all my life. I was twenty-five years old—why should I not succeed?

When the alarm went off I seemed scarcely to have slept at all. I carefully dusted my feet and ankles with talcum powder—they had a hard day's work ahead of them!—and laced my heavy boots.

Piraly and Meynet took nothing but black coffee, saying that one climbs better on an empty stomach. It may be so, but all the same I ate three slices of bread-and-butter and drank two glasses of strong tea.

In the general-room of the shelter people were talking doubtfully about the weather. It was not cold enough, they said, and the sky threatened rain, which meant snow at the higher altitudes. But

Piraly was not worried.

"We're going, my children. It'll be fine. The clouds will lift at ten."

We set off at four o'clock, to be plunged into the silence and poetry of darkness on the mountains. There was a soft, moist breeze.

Meynet felt cold. He was seriously afraid of bad weather and he had not brought an anorak. We teased him, and then Piraly went back to the shelter to get him one. I was reminded of the scolding I had been given for setting out for the mountains without a raincoat. I was tempted to laugh, but I thought it tactful not to say anything. All was well with Meynet once he had the anorak on. Piraly was full of optimism, and his experience as chief of rescue-parties for that district made him a reliable judge of the weather. I trusted him to guide my footsteps and felt sure I should not regret doing so.

We were going up the Tré-La-Tête glacier, but first we followed its left-hand lateral moraine. Piraly remarked in passing: "This is where the three Dutchmen were killed last year. One slipped and the other two lost their grip. They were found on the glacier two hundred feet below."

We proceeded in Indian file, taking extreme care. I bumped now and then against the rocky wall on my left, which sometimes overhung us and from which water constantly dripped. The face was scored by the progress of the glacier in reaching its present was scored by the progress of the glacier in reaching its present level. Nearly all the European glaciers have moved downwards since the beginning of this century, and Tré-La-Tête was no exception. The fact is striking when one considers the deep gorge at its mouth, and I recalled a sentence I had read: "A glacier is a river of ice which tends to sharpen the contours and reliefs of its bed, instead of smoothing them as flowing water does."

Gradually we worked our way down the moraine until we reached the glacier. It was dirty here, littered with stones and debris. We moved along it, always keeping to the left side, for nearly a mile. Piraly told us about the formation of the *moulins,* circular holes caused by melt-water bubbling up to the surface. The water swirls round in these wells with an impressive, roaring sound, and can be heard at great depths. The glacier at this point was about a thousand feet deep.

We now roped ourselves, and for the next few hours our fortunes would be linked for better or for worse. Holding our ice-axes in our right hands and the rope with our left we advanced steadily and slowly, making precise, careful movements.

"The first time one is roped for a climb one has a drink to celebrate," said Piraly. I said nothing, having been roped before.

We veered presently to the right to avoid the dangerous zone of seracs, huge, over-hanging ice-masses liable to fall at any time. The day had now dawned, shyly and hesitantly, and a light wind was blowing. It was pleasant to hear our feet crunch on the untrodden snow. I had a feeling that mine were treading a path they had been always destined to tread. I was in my natural element, and a feeling of wild joy possessed me—the joy of surpassing oneself, of freedom, of profound peace. Names rang in my ears—Tré-La-Tête, la Grande Muraille, la Bérangère, la Lex-Blanche (so sadly celebrated). Yesterday Odette, Yvonne and Rolande had said to me, "Will you think of us when you're up there?"

The very bad snow conditions of that year of 1960 were not making things easy for us; there was two feet of fresh snow. We were slowly gaining height, but it would require great staying-power to reach the Tondu.

Piraly was first on the rope and I was in the middle; this was real climbing. Now and then we had to jump a crevasse, or go round the ones which were too wide for me, which took longer but was less hazardous.

"Here's another narrow one," said Piraly. "Put your foot there, on the edge—a bit further, beside mine." He held my left hand while I used my ice-axe to measure the width of the crevasse. "Right-jump!"

The glacier was exactly as I had imagined it to be. I did not feel at all strange. I felt that I was coming to love the mountains more and more, but that I should need great courage.

Here and there Piraly tested the depth of the snow with the handle of his ice-axe to make sure that it did not conceal a hidden crevasse. We proceeded for the most part in silence, but at intervals Meynet talked about the difficulties he had encountered on a previous climb, and this became the main topic of the day.

On the far right of the glacier we followed a moraine path of small loose rock fragments. For me this part of the climb was very difficult and dangerous. I did not know where to put my feet. The stones constantly shifted under my weight, and I had great trouble in keeping my balance. I made constant use of my hands, feeling the stones to make sure of their firmness before setting foot on them. I was nearly always either on all fours or crouching. Those wretched stones caused us to lose a lot of time. Although we were roped I had to solve my own problems, for the guide's function was to lead the way and shift stones that were obviously unsafe. Meynet, behind me, gave me what guidance he could in placing my feet; he was very patient.

We had not yet devised methods to enable us to get along faster. Piraly was not used to leading the blind, still less in the mountains, and this was only too clear. I did not yet know him very well, and I was afraid of making too many suggestions. It would all sort itself out in time. I was convinced that I should return to the mountains. I knew it. But it would never be easy for me . . .

Truly, happiness is not achieved by doing things easily. Later climbs were to seem to me at times more difficult than anything I had read about; but there were other times when they seemed simpler.

I tried to follow my natural instincts. There was a kind of tenseness about our rope-party of which we were all conscious in varying degrees. For Piraly it was a matter of pride to get me up Mont Tondu, and also he wanted to please me, and anyway it was his job. He may have had his doubts about it, but he was very anxious to succeed. As for Abbé Meynet, he was simply there to help, and he did his best to be useful. In a way he was at the opposite extreme from Piraly—happy to be making this climb for the second time.

For myself, I was going to the Tondu to carry to its peak the tiny flame in my heart.

We continued to gain height, and the loose, rough surface went on and on. It seemed to me interminable and it was exhausting. I was not happy, because I could not help realising how easy it would be to break a limb on the unstable path. I tried to avoid letting the rope drag on the ground in case it got frayed—it was a good perlon rope—and I took particular care to avoid getting my feet caught in it.

"Would you like a drink?" asked Piraly.

"Yes, I would, rather. The air's very dry."

"We're getting on," he said. "We've lost a bit of time on the moraine, but we'll get there. We aren't doing too badly, all things considered."

Was he laughing at me or trying to cheer me up? He was certainly trying to encourage me. The people of Savoy seldom pay compliments. I remembered how he had said, "You have a talent for rocks," at the climbing-school.

Over to our left we could hear the rattle of stones as they plunged down on to the glacier. Otherwise there was complete silence.

We were now at a height of about 8000 feet and there was snow in the chinks between the stones. I had to be doubly careful because the coating made them very slippery. If my feet were not thoroughly educated after this exercise, they never would be!

But nobody felt like laughing. Piraly talked in an encouraging tone, indicating the best path. I don't know how I managed not to scrape all the skin off my hands on those sharp edges of rock; it was almost miraculous.

"Well, that's over," said Piraly.

At last we were all together again.

We went gently, very gently, up the long slope of fresh-fallen alpine snow, no sound but the scrape of the ice-axes on the rock beneath. All my life I had dreamed of holding an ice-axe in my hand, but now there was no time for dreaming, because the mountain allowed me no respite. The slope grew steeper and finally very steep. At every step one had to make an effort to plant one's foot securely in the snow.

I tried to find a method. The best was to feel the way with my hands, so I resumed my painful progress, bent double. We were all breathing deeply, matching our movements to the rhythm of our breath. Piraly helped me by making good big footprints in which I put my feet.

The snow was beginning to burn my fingers. It was time to put on the gloves Rolande had given me before I set out. We were now on a long rope, at some distance from each other. It was very hard going, the stretch of soft snow seemed endless. If the surface had been harder I could have put on crampons. Weariness was beginning to overcome me. I sat down in the snow, but Meynet called me to order.

"You can stand still and rest for a minute on an ascent, but you must never sit down. If you do your legs get stiff and you find it harder than ever."

It was a little past eight in the morning when we reached the Col des Chasseurs, at a height of nearly 10,000 feet. This was the only spot on that particular climb where we could allow ourselves to stop for a short time and have something to eat.

The day was fine but very cold. I had no appetite at all. All I wanted was to rest and drink great gulps of iced tea out of the leather flask. To keep going I forced myself to swallow some bread and ham.

My spirits revived. We passed through other steep, endless snowfields and I went on all fours, finding this the most effective and least tiring method. I wanted to live the present moment as intensely as possible. My companions were plunged in their own thoughts—to get to the summit . . . I wanted to experience for a few moments the sense of tremendous solitude in the presence of the mountains, to feel quite alone, remote from everything, a thousand miles from civilisation . . . But it did not happen. That spiritual state was denied me, and I was rather sad.

Things turn out strangely. Sometimes in the valleys of men, when one is surrounded by people, one feels horribly alone; but here on the seventeenth of August, 1960, at a height of 10,000 feet, I could not feel alone. Why was it? Down below, at the chalet, they must be thinking of our party—that is the great human fellowship. Yet scarcely anyone knew that this morning we were on the Tondu. So . . . ?

We had to make a short traverse to the left—just when I thought our troubles were over. Piraly went ahead to secure us. I did not like our being widely separated, because as a rule we were closely roped, but here it was necessary. Meynet was some yards behind me. We went very cautiously, wholly concentrated on the business of putting hands and feet in the right places, while Piraly watched us.

"Take it easy. It's slippery."

"Listen, Piraly," said Meynet. "If Colette loses her grip what do I do? It must be a two-hundred-foot drop."

"At least!"

Meynet was really marvelous. My position was certainly a strange one, my feet in two small toe-holds, my fingers clutching icy rock, my face turned up to the sun, which had just appeared. I did not move; I held my breath so as to hear better. I had a feeling that I was trembling and that my fingers were slipping. I was frightened. The blood was pounding in my veins. I felt—or better still, I heard—the void on my left.

(As all blind people know, it is our ears that enable us to perceive a wall, or a break in a wall at a street-crossing, because they sense the thickness of the air in relation to a fairly close solid object.)

Yet in my heart I was glad to be feeling this fear, this anguish of terror, because to do so is to be vulnerable. All climbers know it from time to time, and one needs to know it at least once in one's life, because all other fears seem trifling in comparison.

"Everything all right?" asked Piraly.

"Yes, but I wouldn't want it to go on too long."

"Well, hang on. I'm going to take a photograph. A formidable slope with a crevasse at the bottom—you'll look splendid!"

This was pure Piraly and it produced a burst of laughter from us both. Those seconds seemed very long, but I forgot to be afraid, I was laughing so much.

"Now move, Colette!"

The sharp order restored my calm, but I still did not move a finger. The rope grew taut—I had to move at all costs. Sentences ran through my mind like sparks blown from God knew where— "Courage is to be afraid and be the only one that knows it . . . If you were never afraid what would be the use of courage?"

I mastered myself and moved on until I had come up with Piraly. Then we repeated the process. It was a long, slow business. My companions were fortunate since they could see our objective, the summit, and reckon how far we had to go. I could not, and that made it much harder. The summit meant little to me until I was on it.

A small outcrop of rock bothered me. "What shall I do?" I asked Meynet.

"You must sort it out for yourself. I'm hanging on by my eyelids, and I'm not a bit keen on falling."

"Really, Colette," said Piraly, "what a way to climb! I thought I'd taught you not to hang on with your knees."

It was tough going for my companions as well as for me. I was like a baby which wants the walk to be over, and I surprised myself by asking: "How much longer is this going on?"

The silence had become heavy and solemn. The sun warmed me. We took several photographs. We had been seven hours on the ascent (two and a half hours longer than the normal time) but the snow conditions were very bad and I was lacking in experience.

We reached the terminal ridge, which was long and snowy. A friendly rope-party passed us in the opposite direction, greeting us with shouts of encouragement. Now that victory was so close I ventured to sit down and rest, and Piraly said that for a person who could not see, any climb must be considered twice the effort, so I had really done it twice over.

At last we were at the summit, 3,196 meters, by French reckoning. It was an unforgettable moment, an immediate reward for all our efforts. I felt compensated for all the troubles in my life, a life so well worth living.

I embraced my guide. Within myself I tried to evoke the great silence which is an act of immense thanksgiving. I thought of my parents, my family, the friends who would never see this spot, and indeed were far from supposing that on this morning, at eleven o'clock, I was treading the snow at a height of 10,000 feet.

We were surrounded by high mountains which Piraly named for us. The Italian frontier was not far off and we thought of Mont Rose, about 15,000 feet. Where we stood was like the end of the world. I longed to see all the peaks, but perhaps if I did I should love them less. Things are very well as they are.

The sky was clouding over.

"Quick, Meynet," said Piraly, "You take the lead. Colette, you keep beside me. Dig your heels well in."

"I'm slipping."

"Go carefully."

The slight alarm I felt climbing down the steep slope of the ridge was instantly dispelled on the Tondu glacier, which I glissaded down—it was glorious! The sheer intoxication of sliding! Those were unforgettable minutes which will brighten all my life. A blind girl on the Tondu glacier! And Meynet produced a splendid phrase: "The mountains are wonderful on the way down!"

We laughed like mad creatures, happy and proud of our hard-won victory. Only God can measure the worth of our effort.

In moments of great fatigue during the ascent by the other route that morning, I had now and then found myself counting my footsteps—"One for mummy—and for auntie—one for so-and-so . . ."—like a child being made to eat its soup.

"All the same, it was a difficult climb," said Piraly.

"Yes, and now it's over."

"If we were to do it again you'd find it much easier—there wouldn't be the fear of the unknown."

"I'm sure you're right—but perhaps it would be less wonderful."

"Watch out, we're in the avalanche area. I can see there's been a new fall—it must have happened after that party we passed half an hour ago went by."

In the pocket of my anorak I was clutching a small pebble which will always be precious to me, for I picked it up on the summit of Mont Tondu and it is the souvenir of a great adventure.

A Brief History of Women
Climbing in the Coast
and Cascade Ranges

Rachel da Silva, Jill Lawrenz & Wendy Roberts

▲ ▲ ▲

SEVERAL HOURS FROM the major cities of the Northwestern United States and Southwestern Canada—Seattle, Portland and Vancouver, British Columbia—lie thousand-foot granite crags for rock climbing, some of the highest and most heavily glaciated volcanos in North America, and thousands of peaks that provide challenging backcountry opportunities. In his encyclopedic *Cascade-Olympic Natural History*,[1] Daniel Matthews points out that "local relief, measured as the total ups and downs on a fifty-mile line crossing [the North Cascades] exceeds that of any comparable breadth of U.S. Rockies or Sierras, and approaches that of the Alps." Fred Beckey, the region's pre-eminent mountain historian, says about them: "Washington's Cascades have the most glaciers, densest and most magnificent forests, and least disturbed wilderness in our contiguous western states. They are the southern limit of a typical Northwest Coast alpine topography which extends to Prince William Sound in Alaska. . . ."[2] Included by geography if not by name is British Columbia's Coast Range, that continuation of the Cascade

---

[1] *Cascade-Olympic Natural History*, (Portland, Oregon: Raven Editions, Portland Audubon Society, 1988)

[2] *Cascade Alpine Guide: Columbia River to Stevens Pass* (Seattle: The Mountaineers, 1973)

Range north of the Fraser River. "Our region," though crossing state and national boundaries, is united by a culture of mountaineering as well as by geography.

Dr. Christine Mackert, a two-time past President of The Mazamas, speculates that people who came to this region were pioneers in spirit and took advantage of the wealth of nearby mountains as a way to express this enthusiasm for the new, unexplored territory in which they found themselves. Many of these settlers were immigrants from Scandinavian countries such as Norway and Sweden, whose long, rugged shorelines and backbones of snow-capped mountains they found reflected in the Cascade region. Immigrants to Canada, often from the north of England or Wales, brought with them a love of hill and mountain walking shared by both sexes. That these pioneers looked to the sea and the mountains for their livelihood and recreation is no surprise. Others, emigrating from large Eastern and Midwestern cities to escape the urban blight of the day, or the limitations of their lot in life, fell in love with the clean, rugged country and the opportunities it offered.

Hundreds of people discovered mountaineering on trips organized by one of our region's several early climbing organizations, The Mazamas, The Mountaineers, and the British Columbia Mountaineering Club. Virtually all the early climbs up into the second decade of this century, in the days of the horse-drawn wagon and pack trains, were multi-day affairs, but compared to outings in the more remote Interior Ranges and Rockies in Canada, for example, many peaks in our region were accessible to amateur mountaineers on weekends or week-long holidays. One hundred ninety-three people, thirty-eight of them women, reached the summit of Mt. Hood during The Mazamas' inaugural climb on July 19, 1894. The Mountaineers, founded in Seattle in 1906, organized large outings into the Cascades or Olympics every year from 1907 through 1964 when the U.S. Wilderness Act was passed, limiting the size of camping groups. The British Columbia Mountaineering Club (BCMC) was founded in 1907 to offer an alternative to what for many people were the inaccessibly remote and lengthy Alpine Club of Canada summer climbing camps in the Canadian Rockies. The BCMC organized climbs closer to home, in the Coast Range and elsewhere nearby, and thus enabled more working class men and women to discover mountaineering. Thus, geography, accessibility, and a pioneering spirit of adventure contributed to the region becoming a cradle of mountaineering activity.

With help from the likes of Fay Fuller, a charter member of The Mazamas, and other early feminists, women were accepted and valued within these climbing groups from the beginning, and were expected to participate in all but the most physically demanding aspects of mountaineering. Just as women were central to the building and development of culture in our region, their participation in leisure pursuits like hiking and climbing was essential to the development of the family spirit of these climbing organizations. Women found they could enjoy the beauty and challenge of the outdoors without having to leave the comforts of home for very long, as their homesteading foremothers or the "lady explorers" of the day had done. Photos from early outings show Mountaineers and Mazamas members cavorting in fancy dress costumes at "tea parties" held at base camp before the climb.[3] Men and women in nearly equal number play-acted with abandon, developing a familial closeness that helped perpetuate the organizations and the friendships forged there. Indeed, many of the strongest climbing teams in the first few decades of this century were husband and wife teams: Don and Phyl Munday, Eric and Emmie Brooks, Ida and Everett Darr, to name just a few.

These outings also allowed both sexes to extend the limits of their everyday roles. Women could carry backpacks, men could cook, and strangers could live in closer proximity to each other than they would in town. To the public at large, mountaineering was still a fairly odd and suspect activity. Having the support of their "family" of fellow-climbers behind them, girls and women were more easily able to validate and pursue their love for the outdoors.

The fitness craze of the late 1800s and the advent of the bicycle as a popular sport in the 1890s contributed to a wider acceptance of women's participation in sports and in particular, mountaineering. As Canadian climber Ethne Gibson pointed out, the advent of the bicycle in the 1890s offered women a tremendous new freedom. Up until then, women, having to ride sidesaddle, required help in mounting or dismounting their horses. And it was an ungainly and

---

[3] The Mountaineers photo collection, housed at the University of Washington Special Collections, Northwest Section, Suzzallo Library.

uncomfortable means of transportation. The bicycle allowed for easy, quick mobility, and it was cheap: it didn't require feeding.

As a result of the labor-saving innovations of the industrial revolution at the beginning of the twentieth century, middle class women were beginning to carve out more leisure time for themselves. Many early women climbers often were the daughters of business owners or the wives of professionals and sometimes had their own careers or worked alongside their husbands. They weren't quite the vagabond rock-jocks of the late twentieth century, but definitely stood on their own two feet, literally and sometimes financially as well. Later on, some women even came to earn their living from the mountains: guiding, running pack outfits and teaching mountaineering skills.

Many women fought hard for the right to be treated as men's equals, and often had to be crafty about it. Phyllis Munday had to guard her pack lest some "well-meaning" associate help her out by lightening it when she wasn't looking.[4] Fay Fuller refused help over the hardest parts of her climb of Mt. Rainier because she felt she deserved to reach the summit only if she did it unaided, just like the men. By going out into the "wilds" and purposefully sharing the work of campcraft and mountaineering, these women were sending down the roots of a new order of things, proving that women had the same rights and needs to participate in "physical culture" as men did.

They may have been inspired by the writings of the few but widely publicized women explorers of the day, like Annie Smith Peck, who wrote of her life and climbs in South America, or Fanny Bullock Workman and her husband, whose exhaustive travels on bicycle in Africa and on foot in Asia opened the eyes of armchair travelers everywhere. Women were also getting information about campcraft and outdoor life from magazine articles and self-help books like *Woodcraft for Women* (New York: Outing Publishing Company, 1916.) The author, Mrs. Kathrene Gedney Pinkerton, having lived in the Canadian woods, gave sage advice on the gamut of concerns that faced the novice camper. From clothing (it was important, she pointed out, to slowly lengthen the time each day that

---

[4] See Cyndi Smith's essay "Phyllis Munday: Grand Dame of the Coast Range," p. 40

one would go without the support of a corset until one didn't require it at all) to "going alone" in the woods (learn all the trails around camp, and carry two compasses so that if you get panicked you won't be tempted to believe that it's the compass that's wrong!) to what she calls the Spirit of the Open:

> A love of the out of doors, although dormant, lies within most women. That it is so infrequently exhibited is due, to a large extent, to the means that are taken to awaken its spirit. No woman of any force will enjoy the role of passive observer for any length of time.... The open is a place of doing, of exertion, of physical triumph. A woman, to really know and understand it, must learn at least one out of doors activity sufficiently well to enjoy it. That interest will carry her beyond the petty things.... It will give to her a strong body, controlled nerves, and a poise and calmness of mind. It will open to her an enchanted playground in which she will find another plane of comradeship with the men of her family....

How could any young woman reader withstand Kathrene's exhortation! No wonder The Mazamas and The Mountaineers climbing clubs had no trouble signing up scores of climbers, often more than thirty percent women, for their outings.

The period after the First World War offered women new opportunities they hadn't found open to them before. They developed a new confidence in themselves as workers in industry during the War; in Seattle many had participated in the General Strike of 1919 and had had their eyes opened to the world; and they had worked for and won the vote.

This was also a period of increased access to the mountains. Instead of having to take a train, a pack train and then often make a lengthy approach on foot to base camp, climbers began using the automobile with greater frequency. Climbing holidays further afield—to the Selkirks and the Rockies—became easier. While tents and down sleeping bags had always been available if you could find them and afford them, Army-surplus gear after World War II put camping essentials within reach of many more people. This period corresponded to a dramatic rise in the number of new members of organizations like The Mountaineers—membership quadrupled between 1937 and 1947.

Many women who started climbing because of their husbands'

interest found that it offered a way for them to spend time with their husbands as equals—an experience most women of the day never knew. Sometimes this gave their relationships a special strength; other times it gave the women an independence that made "normal" married life intolerable. Women trip leaders within The Mazamas or The Mountaineers discovered the joys and challenges of being out front. Some of them saw the value of being role models for other women and took pride in demonstrating that women were every bit as good as men.

But what about the women who found they didn't fit in with the region's climbing groups as they were structured, or who discovered climbing on their own or with other women? Although women's climbing groups, such as England's Pinnacle Club, founded in 1921, had flourished in Europe for decades, there was no similar movement in this area until the late 1970s. Individual women were pushing the standards in rock and alpine climbing, but it was extemely rare to see women out together "alone" on the trails. Here and there small groups of friends came together to share childcare and climb or hike together, but the idea of forming a group akin to the Pinnacle Club didn't gain a toehold in the Northwest until the 1980s. Women Climbers Northwest formed then, and colleges and climbing organizations offered all-women's outings and courses with greater frequency and involved more participants than ever before.

The full story of women's mountaineering experience in this region is yet to be told. Some women, already "stars," don't make their way into these pages simply because of space limitations. They are here, nonetheless, encouraging us, leading us on. This brief overview highlights some of the major achievements, turning points and role models that may begin to define our history.

I
"I Expect to Have My Example Followed . . ."
Before the Vote

August 26, 1867, Miss Frances S. Case and Miss Mary Robinson were the first women to climb to the summit of Mt. Hood (11,245 feet). Case and Robinson, described as "two single girls from Salem," climbed the south side route with a group of several men. They left camp at timberline at 7 a.m. and reached the top about six hours later. They spent an hour admiring the view, left several mementos of their visit and were back in camp at 5:05 p.m., excited about their adventure.

John M. Garrison, who was in the party, reported to *The Oregonian:* "This achievement is something for them to boast of, as they are undoubtedly the first white females who ever stood on the summit of Mt. Hood. The late ascent, by ladies, of Mt. Adams, dwindles into insignificance compared with it, and henceforth Miss Case and Miss Robinson are entitled to the first distinction as female adventurers."

▲ ▲ ▲

"Hurrah! I have been to the top of Mount Tacoma and am safely back. Five of us spent all night in the crater. Am perfectly satisfied, but Oh! It was hard work," Fay Fuller wrote to a friend in Tacoma from Paradise Camp, at the foot of Mt. Rainier (14,410 feet), August 12, 1890.

In 1890 Fay Fuller was twenty years old, social editor of her father's newspaper, the *Every Sunday,* and a school teacher in Yelm, Washington, twenty-five miles south of Tacoma. One of Fuller's students was Christine Van Trump, whose father Philemon Van Trump was one of the first men to climb Mt. Rainier (also called Tahoma, the more generic of several Indian names). Van Trump came to his daughter's school to talk to the students about Mt. Rainier, and Fay was greatly impressed by his climbing stories.

In the summer of 1890 the Van Trumps invited Fay to accompany them to Mt. Rainier. Three years before, she had climbed to about 8,500 feet and had been frustrated in her ambition to go further. Although she was not sure she would be allowed to climb to the summit this summer either, she came prepared to do so. She wore a thick, blue flannel bloomer suit, heavy calfskin boys' shoes, loose blouse with innumerable pockets in the lining, and a small straw hat to protect her from the sun.

"The costume . . . will amuse present-day climbers. I had it made at the time when bloomers were unknown and it was considered quite immodest. How anyone could have scrambled over the rocks thus attired is now inconceivable," said Fay in an interview years later.

The Van Trump party left Yelm on horseback on Monday August 4, 1890 and arrived at Paradise on August 8. Fay found several people at Paradise who were planning an ascent and when she expressed her hope of reaching the summit, she was invited to join them.

"Before starting I donned heavy flannels, woolen hose, warm mittens and goggles, blackened my face with charcoal to modify the sun's glare, drove long caulks and brads into my shoes, rolled two single blankets containing provisions for three days and strapped them to my shoulder under the arm to the waist, the easiest way by far to carry a pack, shouldered one of Uncle Sam's canteens, grasped my alpenstock and was resolved to climb until exhausted."

The party arrived at Camp Muir where they spent the night.

"At 4:30 we rose and shouldered our blankets ready for the hard day's work. Not waiting to eat breakfast, we nibbled some of the melted chocolate, now frozen solid, and began the ascent. . . . We climbed and climbed until we stood at the foot of the Great Gibraltar. This is one of the most dangerous and difficult points of the journey. Standing on some of the high narrow backbones of the ridges we could look down on either side to a long glacier where one wrong step or several loose rocks giving way would land one in the unknown world."

According to Len Longmire, a member of the party, Fay Fuller refused assistance from the men at difficult spots and stated that if she could not achieve the goal without their help she would not deserve to reach it.

After seven hours of difficult climbing, they reached the top of Gibraltar cliff. "We then knew the most dangerous part was over, but were prepared to be disappointed yet, for the crevasses looked broken and numerous, and breathing was getting more difficult. . . . I could sometimes only travel fifteen feet for loss of breath, being obliged to stop and rest, but only a moment or two is needed to recover, when your lungs are ready again, you think, to climb a long distance, but not so; quickly exhausted, soon refreshed, is the rule, and it is not possible to do otherwise. . . . We moved slowly on, the rim of the crater in sight. . . . At last we stood on the rim of the big crater, where the wind was blowing so strongly we could hardly keep our footing, and oh, it was bitter cold. . . . The middle peak was some ways off, and for fear anything should happen we hastened on to the great high knob and at 4:30 p.m. August 10, 1890, we stood on the tip top of Mount Tacoma. It was a heavenly moment; nothing was said—words cannot describe scenery and beauty, how could they speak for the soul! Such sensations can be known to only those who reach the heights. The scene below was a wonderful panorama.... The glaciers of the Nisqually, Cowlitz, Carbon and White rivers were seen, and the valleys and prairies beyond."

Violent wind soon drove them to the shelter of the large volcanic crater, where they steamed themselves warm before taking shelter for the night in an ice cave on the eastern side. After rubbing their feet with whisky, the climbers settled down to a comfortless night in their light blankets. Fuller says she was the only one to sleep, but even she had wakeful spells during which she watched the meteors overhead and listened to "God's music," avalanches and the wind.

"In the crater we left our names in a sardine can, a brandy flask, and a tin cup. The hairpins which tried to serve as a button-hook, but miserably failed, were found by the Hitchcock party (who made the summit the next day) and they laughingly remarked that it proved to them that a woman had been to the summit."

That a woman had climbed what was considered the highest mountain in the country on an equal footing with men was big news and a strike for women's rights. "I expect to have my example followed by a good many women," said Fay. She became a charter member of The Mazamas, the Portland-based climbing club, when they formed in 1894 and climbed Mt. Rainier with a Mazamas group of fifty-eight in 1897. She continued to blaze trails for women, covering the waterfront, the courts and the markets of Tacoma as a journalist, a decidedly unladylike job. She later became port collector, reputedly the first woman to hold such a position in the United States.

▲ ▲ ▲

Mt. Baker, a 10,778-foot volcano fifteen miles south of the Canadian border, was in Nooksack tribal territory when it was first climbed in 1868. It was known by its Lummi Indian name Kulshan, meaning broken or damaged, because of its irregular, jumbled appearance. In August 1891, a party under the leadership of J. O. Boen of La Conner made the third ascent of the mountain, the first from the east side. Sue Nevin, the leader's sister-in-law, was a member of the party. She is described as a "brave Iowa girl, a vivacious young woman just out of her teens."

Leaving La Conner August 10, the party made its way up the Baker River to Baker Lake, then up Boulder Creek and "an unbroken mesh of briery jungle for a whole day and a half" to the snowline, where they rested for a day. From snowline the party followed the northern part of Boulder Glacier to the east breach of the volcano's crater. They picked their way through crevasse fields and then scrambled over rock to within one hundred feet of the summit. Here they ran into a huge crevasse some twenty-five to thirty feet across and fifty to seventy-five feet deep, where they stopped. After some delay and discussion, Robert Woods, resolving to make one more effort, left the party and found the end of the crevasse where he let himself down. After an hour's persistent work with his ice axe he succeeded in getting up the other side of the crevasse.

Woods brought the rest of the party up, and they reached the summit at 4:30 p.m. August 24, 1891. They placed their names and addresses in a bottle, and tied it to a stick shoved in the snow. Details of the descent are not known, but the party probably raced the fading daylight back to camp.

▲ ▲ ▲

Not all women took to mountain climbing avidly after trying it. Another early climber in the North Cascades, Mrs. John Geoyther (her first name is lost to us) wrote this story of an outing to the hills in 1898, starting from the town of Whatcom, Washington (now Bellingham, near the Canadian-U.S. border). It is obvious from her account that her party encountered some very serious scrambling on the way to the summits of the Twin Sisters (6,932 feet).

"We left sometime early in August—just don't remember the day of the month—never thought then that we were making *history.* Wanted to go camping so tried for the Twin Sisters. The four of us women wore full-length skirts and long puffed sleeves instead of the nifty outing garments and climbing togs of the present day.

"We went by way of Park at the head of Lake Whatcom. Reached the summit the third day. There were no trails. It was awful work. Climbed both peaks. Would never do it again.

"Miss Johnson stumbled over a tent rope where we were camped on our way back and broke her leg. Tony was sent out for help and brought back four men. It took a whole week to get her out on a stretcher and she was in the hospital for over a year."

▲ ▲ ▲

In the summer of 1907, The Mountaineers organization of Seattle had its first annual outing to the heart of the Olympic Peninsula, Mt Olympus. Mountaineers wishing to go on the outing were instructed to "have shoes well nailed with cone-headed Hungarian or hobnails and these should be in the ball of the foot and extend back nearly to the heel," and furthermore, "all women of the party who expect to go on side trips or climb any of the peaks, must be prepared to wear bloomers or better still knickerbockers, as on all these trips no skirts will be allowed."

The Mountaineers hiked three days from Port Angeles, Washington, on the Olympic Peninsula to the head of the Elwha River near the base of Mt. Olympus (7,965 feet) and established a camp there. Mary Banks, a member of the party, wrote that the real part of the trip was the "views to be had from the mountains, rather than the mere attainment of summits." On July 30, she was one of the first women to climb Mt. Noyes (6,100 feet) southeast of Mt. Olympus along with Alida J. Bigelow, Winona Bailey, Grace Howard, Anna Howard, and Lulie Nettleton. Mary Banks's record of their hilarious descent follows:

> On the return from Noyes, when the first steep snow slope was reached it proved too great a temptation for the leader to resist. He called for everyone to follow, but to under no circumstances let go of their alpine stocks. He suddenly disappeared down the steep incline, little suspecting that for many of the climbers this was the first time they had seen someone coast down a slope let alone coast down a slope themselves. When the leader reached the bottom of the snow slope he stopped and looked behind him.
>
> I have coasted down many a mountainside with far larger parties, hailing from Boston to Los Angeles, but never have I dreamed of the variety of ways it might be done until I saw those thirty-nine coming down. Not only were they coming down thirty-nine different ways but some seemed to be coming down all thirty-nine ways at once—head first, feet first, sideways, some a whirling tangle of arms, legs, and alpine stocks, snow flying. Others clutched vainly at the air in futile effort to retard their lightning progress.

Dangerous? Possibly, but so funny that when I had somewhat recovered from laughing I was really alarmed lest the grave professor
would collapse from merriment, and it was with difficulty that those
below overcame their laughter in time to stop the flying progress of
others ere they reached the rocks.

The next day everyone was belatedly taught the many appropriate
uses of the "alpine stock." This one outing put many women on
Olympic summits: Mary made the first female ascent of Mt. Queets
(6,480 feet) on August 1, the first female ascent of Mt. Barnes (5,993
feet) was made by Lulie Nettleton and Alida J. Bigelow on August 4,
and the next day Ida Kracht climbed Mt. Christie (6,179 feet.)

A week later, on August 13, Anna Hubert became the first
woman to climb Mt. Olympus's Middle Peak (7,930 feet) and West
Peak (7,965 feet). Several women made the first female ascent of
Mt. Seattle (6,246 feet). Dr. Cora Smith Eaton was the first woman
to climb the East Peak of Mt. Olympus (7,780 feet). She also made
the first female ascent of Cougar Peak of Mt. Seattle.

▲ ▲ ▲

The goal of The Mountaineers' annual outing of 1910 was
DaKobed, the Great Parent, or Glacier Peak (10,541 feet), in the
North Cascades. An expedition-style climb, fifty-seven people were
in the climbing party, nearly half of them women. The Mountaineers took four days hiking forty-four miles in to Buck Creek Pass
from the train depot near Nason, Washington. "The long tramp in
hardened muscles," Lulie Nettleton reported. From Buck Creek
Pass members took try-out trips to practice with the alpenstock and
gain confidence for the final climb. They climbed Sunset Hill and
Liberty Cap (6,800 feet). Southeast of camp they climbed unnamed
peaks from 6,000 to 7,800 feet. "Thus, when, on August 3, the party
left camp for the great ascent, not one of the fifty-seven was physically fit for a very strenuous trip," reported Nettleton. The Mountaineers blazed a trail through very rough country from the Suiattle
River to timberline.

The men, doctors, lawyers, professors, and men of the most sed-
entary occupations in town, made splendid woodsmen, and forming
in a long line looked quite formidable with alpenstocks bristling,
hand axes gleaming and heavy packs on their backs. The horses followed, loaded with supplies, and then the line of twenty-five

women, wearing packs containing their sleeping bags, brought up the rear.

They were to be up at 3:30 a.m., so they went to bed early. Nettleton wrote, "Had not hideous dreams of seeing the line of people starting off while you could not get your boots on intruded themselves, the night would have been pleasant. When the morning whistle sounded we crawled out of our bags and made hasty preparations for the day. Shivering with cold and excitement, [we] tried to manipulate shoe strings which, in the dark, seemed possessed of evil spirits."

After breakfast at 4:30 a.m., the party fell into line in their assigned places and were off as the gray light of dawn touched the peaks around them. The weather conditions seemed favorable, the party in fine spirits. They followed a ridge above camp, first on grassy slopes, then pumice, and from there to the snow. The ascent then followed snow slopes for 2,500 feet, crossing the Cool Glacier to an arête between the Chocolate and Cool glaciers. They reached the summit at 11 a.m., after six-and-a-half hours of climbing.

"Thus was accomplished the first club ascent of Glacier Peak, and for the first time women stood upon its summit," exclaimed Nettleton. In all, twenty-four women participated in the ascent.

▲ ▲ ▲

Anna Howard Price, who had been on The Mountaineers outing to Mt. Olympus in 1907, became the first woman to climb Mt. Shuksan (9,127 feet), Mt Baker's closest neighbor. Years later she wrote about her trip. Her story has been somewhat abbreviated here, but she made many detailed observations of the splendid wilderness through which she traveled.

In 1908 I went to the summit of Mt. Baker with The Mountaineers. There were many of us on that climb who wanted to make the ascent of Mt. Shuksan also but it could not be done at that time. Four years later, however, my husband and I prepared ourselves for an outing to Shuksan. My ambition was to be the first woman to climb this wonderfully picturesque mountain.

We took up the trail at Concrete on the Skagit River and followed the course of Baker River and up Swift Creek nearly to its source where it is merely a tiny rivulet, taking the forest rangers' trail most of the way. . . .

Mr. Price engaged a packer to bring our bedding and supplies along as far as this, leaving us at an old cabin built here at one time by some prospector.... The next morning, we prepared our packs of "grub" and blankets, cutting the weight to the last ounce, but taking on our backs all that would be needed to carry to some point the first day where we could make temporary camp.

We picked our way slowly up the divide between Swift and Shuksan creeks, passing from one ridge to another, until we came to a place where there is a plateau strewn with great boulders as if some demon had hurled them down upon the place from the awful cliffs of Shuksan above and beyond.

We were now in comparatively open country and here on this plateau we came to the beautiful mountain lake discovered by Mr. Asahel Curtis and my husband in 1906 and which has since been named Lake Ann, after [this] writer who has the distinction of being the only woman, at least the only white woman, who has ever seen it to date.

The lake is deep. The azure of a clear sky was reflected and the waters were blue—oh, so blue!—that indescribable blue you see sometimes in the pot-holes on the glaciers. It was at this place we came face to face with Shuksan, the glorious! Great spots of black rock divided with tracts of white snow, such a marvelous view of astonishing contrasts!

We gazed long at the Hanging Glacier on the face of Shuksan, just opposite us, and higher up at an almost perfect duplicate of it, each having two sources which join and in that joining push outward over a great cliff hundreds of feet high, dropping immense bergs occasionally into the chasm below. This is the real beginning of Shuksan Creek.

To go on, we would have to drop down an almost perpendicular hillside, it looked like, slippery with its thatching of heather, but with here and there an outcropping of rocks and a few friendly trees, but Shuksan was our goal and we had not yet reached the base of it, where climbing would count for anything. So a thousand feet down we dropped to the bottom of the canyon, where, meek and humble in the presence of the stupendous walls of rock and ice, we stopped to have our lunch.

Then on, and up a long talus slope and on and up till we were passing into the spray of the waterfall. We crossed the foaming torrent on the rocks and began again the sturdy climb of Shuksan. But it was good climbing. Along here we found a trail blazed with locks of white [mountain goat] wool.

At this place the rocks rise by successions of shelves from two to eight feet and where one shelf runs out you simply climb like Mr. Goat to the next one higher up. . . . It was now getting late in the afternoon and we were pretty well up to the region of perpetual snow where we had planned on making temporary camp. . . . Mr. Price soon located the old wind-break he had helped to erect six years before when he and Mr. Curtis made what they believed to be the first ascent of Shuksan. There were a few rusty tin cans lying round. We both got busy and gathered a good pile of dead wood for our all-night camp fire.

That night it was cold and our bleach-wood did not give off very much heat. In the gray dawn of the early morning we ate our breakfast then left our blankets and supplies and all extra weight behind and started hopefully for the summit.

The heights were wonderfully beautiful when the sun came up and poured its rays through great banks of clouds off in the direction of the Cascades, but the summit of old Shuksan could not be seen. Slopes were good, the snow was crisp and firm beneath our feet and after long, hard climbing we reached the shoulder of the mountain and the last, long snowfield on the top came into view.

The snow ahead looked very level compared with the work we had just been doing, but it was a long distance, perhaps about two miles across to the base of the highest pinnacle of bare rock, but upward steady toil. The nearer we approached this jagged pile of rocks the less I liked the looks of it.

These steep, black, rocky projections, and there are several of them, rising about the snowfields, are literally broken into blocks and fragments and set up on edge forming dangerous walls and chimneys. I've climbed Baker, Rainier, and the Olympics and a few other high peaks but this particular part of Shuksan threatened altogether too much risk, considering the number of persons and the limited equipment. It would not have been so dangerous perhaps had there been a larger party.

I had come to climb to the very tip of this peak but when it came to picking out footholds in uncertain niches in the steep wall of rocks where it didn't look feasible to get back down, once you did get up, I confess it set me to thinking: There was but one life to live, and it would take three days to reach help in case of accident, which might mean the death of both of us. Then there were the fifteen-month-old twins I had left at home—Billy and Betty—who couldn't get along very well without a mother, so, silently and sadly, but perhaps thankfully, we turned about.

There is nothing more to be said.

But some day I would like to try it again.

▲ ▲ ▲

Ann Dillinger and Anna Louise Strong were contemporaries, climbing and organizing outings for The Mazamas climbing club during the pre-World War I years, but no record exists as to their having climbed together. It is likely that they at least knew each other, since both of them claim to have done the first winter ascent of Mt. Hood! It was Dillinger who, in 1914, probably came up with the idea of doing a winter ascent and, after several attempts, was in the party that finally succeeded, on March 7, 1915. Strong was on the third winter ascent, later that year.

Strong left ample record of the reasons she took up mountaineering in her autobiography *I Change Worlds*. A Seattle activist, she used the mountains as an escape from the deep desperation she felt as she struggled against the growing militarism of the pre-war period. She was also very active in the area of child welfare and organized trips for young people to Mt. Rainier.

On the other hand, we have little information about Ann Dillinger except what can be found in the Mazamas Journal. She must have started climbing at least by 1912, because starting in 1913 she organized numerous trips for the group. In July 1914 she was lauded in the Journal for "superintending two large excursions to Mt. Hood. . . . On the first, one hundred seventeen and on the second twenty-seven persons reached the summit and returned without accident, and helped materially to increase our membership. More success to Ann! Long may she climb!" The following year, as leader of a 120-person climb of Mt. Hood via the Cooper Spur route, Ann saved the life of an ill climber she was attending to at the rear of the line. A massive avalanche, triggered by the rest of the party climbing above them, buried Ann and the climber up to their necks, and they were saved from being swept down the mountain only by Ann's quick thinking and alpenstock anchors. Ann climbed Mt. Hood twenty-four times, several times accompanied by her aunt, Mrs. C. E. Dillinger, and was very active in The Mazamas up through 1916. However, after her marriage in 1919 record of her activities evaporates and her subsequent life remains a mystery.

▲ ▲ ▲

The Mazamas also had their early rock climbers. In the summer of 1915, shortly after the first complete ascent of Rooster Rock in the Columbia Gorge area was made—without ropes—in April, Margaret Griffin (Raymond), Mary Hart and four others climbed the rock. On this ascent, which Margaret describes in the Mazamas Journal, they were roped and used "life belts," but while "none of the climbers were forced to resort to their actual use . . . they were invaluable, nevertheless, as a source of encouragement." Margaret Griffin remained very active in The Mazamas until she died at the age of 103 in 1989.

II
"IT'S A GREAT LIFE, IF YOU WANT TO DO IT!"
Between and After the Wars

Jane MacGowan's parents were married in 1910 atop Bell Jack Peak, north of Mt. Rainier. It should have come as no surprise to them, then, that their daughter would take up climbing. Jane remembers that she had always wanted to be good at some sport, but tennis and other more traditional women's sports didn't excite her. When she discovered mountaineering, however, she was thrilled. She joined The Mountaineers in 1929, and by 1931 she was spending every summer weekend in the Cascades. She was serious about her new sport. "We were peak-baggers for pins!" she laughs, remembering The Mountaineers' policy of giving out commemorative pins to members for climbing entire groups of peaks. Jane still has all her pins.

As a teacher, Jane's summers were free, so she joined the Alpine Club of Canada and went on the club's extended outings. It was on one of these trips, to the Selkirk Range in British Columbia, that she met her future husband, George. He was an excellent climber, having done first ascents with Jack Hossock, Wolf Bauer and others. Jane, Jack's wife, Mary, and climber Katherine Hood from Tacoma often rounded out these parties. In 1940 this group, plus several others, made the fourth and probably first "guideless" (not employing paid guides) climbing expedition into Canada's Bugaboo Mountains. Jane recalls that they had to deal with several severe hailstorms, chopped down trees to get across the resulting swollen rivers and finally ran out of food. "The worst part, for me, was always getting across the bergschrund, crossing from glacier to rock. Once I was on the rock I was fine. I really enjoyed rock climbing the most." This shows in her climbing itinerary: both before and after World War II, the family climbed in the Canadian Rockies, returning several times to the gorgeous Lake O'Hara area, the Wind Rivers, and Mt. Garibaldi. Both her children climb, and her son has some first ascents to his credit.

▲ ▲ ▲

"My most exciting climb? Well, that would have to be St. Peter's Dome . . . or maybe Martin Peak." Ida Zacher Darr was reminiscing. Her daughter, Lori, helped out by supplying dates from Ida's journal entries, kept up in some detail from 1934 onward. "St. Peter's—do you know that one? Yes, like Rooster Rock, only steeper. It was practically all piton work, though. The rock was pretty rotten then. Nowadays people hardly ever climb it. Too dangerous. I don't know what we were doing up there!" But she was up there, with five men, in June 1940. "Was it pretty daring to climb in those days? Well, I'd say you had to really want to go climbing. There weren't too many women who did it then. But it's a great life, if you want to do it!"

Ida Zacher got her start climbing with The Mazamas, climbing Mt. Hood in 1934 and Three Fingered Jack in central Oregon the following year. She participated in parties that established several new routes on Mt. Hood in the late 1930s, including one inside Crater Bowl. Ida and her husband, Everett Darr, are credited with twenty-four first ascents in Washington and Oregon, and Ida has one solo first: Martin Peak (8,511 feet), in July of 1936. That same summer she and her husband spent two weeks in the North Cascades, climbing and exploring. They attempted to be the first up Bonanza Peak (9,511 feet) and got to within three hundred feet of the summit via the Holden Lake face. Their route development was credited with the successful climb of this face the following year. That was just the first of many climbing trips in the North Cascades. The following summer the Darrs, along with several friends including Joe Leuthold, climbed Bonanza by the Northwest Buttress, and in July and August of 1940 the couple did at least seven first ascents or new routes in this area, including Tupshin Peak, Devore Peak,

Mt. Buckner and Mt. Goode, all rugged North Cascades summits between 8,320 and 9,200 feet.

▲ ▲ ▲

"All this nonsense about what women are 'allowed' to do—we never thought about that! My father never said we couldn't use tools, or that sort of thing! We lived in the country, had an orchard, and if you wanted to do something, you just did it! It didn't matter if you were a girl or boy." Ethne Gibson, the widow of one of Canada's foremost mountaineers, Rex Gibson, states her strong opinions in a lovely British accent. She started climbing in 1936, when she was twenty-four. Did she do any first ascents with her husband? "No, he had already done them all!" she laughs. But she climbed with him throughout the 1930s and 1940s, attending many of the Alpine Club of Canada camps in the Selkirks and Rockies. They climbed in the Bugaboos—her favorite climb was there—and in Wales and the Cumberland district of Britain, from which her parents had emigrated. Now living in B.C.'s lower mainland, she still takes an active interest in the Vancouver Section of the ACC.

▲ ▲ ▲

In the summer of 1931, Milana Jank, an experienced skier and climber from Munich, Germany, visited Mt. Baker Lodge and made quite an impact. On her first climb of the season on June 29, she became the first woman to climb Baker via the Park Glacier and Cockscomb Ridge and the first woman to ski the peak.

Milana had become a "Mountain Sports Instructor" at Mt. Baker Lodge. She set out to repeat the June 29 climb of Mt. Baker solo. She left Mt. Baker Lodge at 2 a.m. on July 13. By eleven o'clock she was near the summit. People watched her through a telescope from Table Mountain and reports of her progress were sent back to the lodge. It was quite a show. But Milana didn't reach the summit of Mt. Baker this time. She was unable to get across a crevasse on the upper Park Glacier at the foot of the ice wall, and in the hot July sun avalanches of ice and snow were continually falling around her. Nine days later, on July 22, Milana tried again. This time she followed the tracks of a mountain lion through the maze of crevasses and over Rainbow Glacier and reached the top. Two days later, Milana, now Assistant Guide at Mt. Baker Lodge, made her first ascent of nearby Mt. Shuksan, guiding Dorothy Ruff of Sacramento, California, up the mountain. They climbed a variation of the Fisher Chimneys route, which Jank later described as more dangerous than the normal route. This was the first all-women ascent of Mt. Shuksan. It seems a testimony to her skills that Jank was permitted to guide a client alone without ever having been up the mountain before.

In 1926 the British climber Dorothy Pilley, along with I. A. Richards and Benton Thomson, made the summit of Mt. Shuksan over a new, direct route up the White Salmon Glacier and the north face. The following year, Esther Buswell, Winnie Spieseke and Harriet Taylor accompanied the developers of the Fisher Chimneys route, Clarence Fisher, Dr. Emmons Spearin and two others, on the first complete ascent of the route.

▲ ▲ ▲

Emmie Milledge Brooks was already a weekend mountaineer when she met her husband, Eric, while teaching school near Vancouver, British Columbia. She introduced him to the idea of mountain climbing, and they went on to explore many of the peaks and more inaccessible regions of the Cascades and the Coast Range.

Emmie and her women climbing partners were exploring the peaks of the lower Mainland long before it was common for women to climb "on our own, no men around to help us out and show us the way." She recalls how she and her friends had to wear their skirts to the trailhead, reached in those days by streetcar, where they hid them in the brush and retrieved them before going home. An excellent rock climber and proficient mountaineer, Emmie Brooks led the first all-women ascent of Mount Garibaldi in 1932.

Other climbers associated with the Coast Range during this period are Kate McQueen, who joined the Alpine Club of Canada in 1914 and participated in some of its earliest camps, Polly Prescott, who climbed with the Mundays and others, and the Mundays themselves, one of our region's best-known climbing teams.

▲ ▲ ▲

In the 1940s and 1950s, when Margaret Oberteuffer, Agnes Dickert and Lorita Leuthold were exploring the region's mountains, one could be in the "backcountry" like Cascade Pass in the North Cascades or the Sisters area in Oregon and not see a soul except those in your own party. The spirit of adventure and sense of being pioneers was strong in all of them.

"My mother tried hard to raise me as a nice lady, but I was always a tomboy!" Margaret Oberteuffer laughs, remembering. She learned hiking and camping skills through her participation in Camp Fire Girls, and as the oldest child in her family found herself easily drawn to guiding and leading others. In 1947 Margaret and her husband, Bill, joined The Mazamas. They climbed all the major peaks in the Oregon and Washington Cascades, and took climbing trips to the California Sierras and the Tetons. "We didn't do the scariest or most difficult routes, but we enjoyed the mixture of rock and snow climbs. We liked the comradeship in that kind of experience and wanted to share it with others." The Oberteuffers were among the first handful of parties to complete the Ptarmigan traverse in the North Cascades around 1956, and later led a Mazamas climb of their new route. The also guided many other outings for the club.

▲ ▲ ▲

The secretary of the Mountaineers Climbing Committee and a member of the Board of Trustees for five years, Agnes Dickert loved climbing. Agnes and her husband, Phil, were married in 1931 and joined The Mountaineers the same year. As Margaret had done with the Portland group, Agnes became very involved in developing the Mountaineers climbing school, working on the first climbing manual, teaching mountaineering skills courses and "leading a climb or two." She lead a climb of Gunn Peak and remembers leading another with Gloria Huntington. In July 1938, she, Lloyd Anderson and Lyman Boyer made the first ascent of Blue Peak, later known as Gunsight (8,198 feet).

She didn't always climb with her husband. "The Climbing Committee would schedule the trips, and I'd go!" But she and Phil did do a great deal of climbing together in the Selkirks, Tetons and Cascades. They often took trips with Jack and Mary Hossock, another ardent climbing team, and spent several weeks with them in the Canadian Rockies, climbing Castor, Pollox, Uto and other peaks in the area. Agnes was the first woman to climb Big Four (6,135 feet) in the Washington Cascades.

▲ ▲ ▲

Now seventy-three years old, Lorita Leuthold started climbing while in college, and over the next several years she climbed Mt. St. Helens (then 9,677 feet) and Mt. Hood several times. She was astonished to learn that these "modest adventures" usually merited several column inches in *The Oregonian,* so unusual was climbing in those days.

In 1946 Lorita married Joe Leuthold, a pioneering climber who already had many first ascents to his credit. Among these were several new routes on Mt. Hood, Bonanza Peak, Tupshin Peak and St. Peter's Dome in the Columbia Gorge. Climbing with Joe privately, and assisting on over fifty climbs he guided with The Mazamas, Lorita became an avid and skilled mountaineer herself. She climbed in the Canadian Rockies, the Tetons, California and the Oregon and Washington Cascades. Among the most memorable was a climb of Mt. Victoria (3,464 meters) with Joe, via Abbot Pass. The weather was great and they had spectacular views of the gorgeous country. Another was a near-epic late-season ascent of Mt. Rainier, a Mazama outing that they lead together. "We were supposed to go up the Ingraham Glacier, the standard route, but there had been an earthquake that year and the glacier was so broken up we had to go all the way around to the Emmons before we found a safe way through all those crevasses! It was a twenty-three-hour trip from Camp Muir and back!"

What did she like best about climbing? "I made very special lifetime friends with the people we climbed with. Even though most of us don't climb any more, we're still very close." Her daughter, Toni, has been climbing since she was five, and mother and daughter have climbed and skied together in Glacier Park, the Cascades and Colorado.

▲ ▲ ▲

Joan and Joe Firey met through the Sierra Club Rock Climbing Section in the San Francisco Bay area. Both were already climbers when they married in 1950. Starting in the early fifties they made many trips north, to the Washington and Oregon Cascades, the Coast Range of British Columbia and further inland to the Selkirks and the Adamant Range, where they put up new routes. Joan's initial first ascent was in the southern Selkirks, the Badshots, on Mt. Templeman in 1953.

In 1955 Joe was hired by the University of Washington, and the Fireys moved to Seattle with their young daughters, Carla and Nina. Joan worked as a physical therapist and over the next twenty-five years developed her artistic talent as well, producing watercolors and silk-screen prints based on her mountain experiences.

The Fireys are truly a legend in the region's mountaineering history. Every summer but one, between 1961 and 1975, the Fireys added new first ascents to their long list of climbs. In the Washington Cascades, they climbed three of the jagged spires west of Mt. Terror in 1961, and four major rock peaks on Ragged Ridge in 1966 with John and Irene Meulemans; one year later they did the Jagged Ridge traverse between Mt. Shuksan and Cloudcap Peak. They returned several times to the Austera Peak area in the North Cascades, exploring and putting up new routes with the Meulemans and later with their daughter Carla, Dave Knudson, and Frank deSaussure. Along with Carla, Dave Knudson and Peter Renz, they did a traverse of the North Cascades' Picket Range in 1970, doing the first ascent of Ghost Peak (7,840 feet) and the east ridge of Mt. Terror (8,151 feet).

In 1963 Joan and Joe made their first trip into the Monarch Ice Cap area. They did four first ascents this year, and seven others during their many climbing trips in the area, including Mongol Peak, Aurora Tower and Arjuna Peaks. In 1965, on an extended three-week trip to the Neacola Peaks with George and Frances Whitmore, they struggled to get in five days of climbing, thanks to uncooperative weather. In spite of the weather, they managed several first ascents.

In 1968 they climbed Mt. Waddington, getting in and out of that remote area without the benefit of helecopters. Joe Firey recalls that it took five days just to get out to the road. He was glad for the advent of helicopters on later trips. "The use of choppers is a lot less damaging to the environment than all the camps along the trail and trash that comes with that." Joan loved the mixed climbing of the Coast Range. A few years later, on one of several trips they made into the area, Joan and Piro Kramar, a frequent climbing partner, climbed Asperity, only the second climb of this peak and the first female ascent.

Joan was also an avid ski mountaineer. In the company of other active skiers like Nancy and Tom Miller, Irene and John Meulemans, Joyce and Cal Magnussen, Margaret and Frank Fickiesen, and Carla Firey and her husband Jim McCarthy, they explored the West year round. On these ski trips the climbing was almost incidental, although they did carry crampons. The point was to be in these remote areas of incredible natural beauty with friends and family.

In 1978 Joan joined Arlene Blum's American Women's Himalayan Expedition to Annapurna. Margarite Hargrave, a skiing and climbing partner of Joan's in the 1970s, recalls that Joan was very supportive of the idea of women's climbing, and although she turned fifty that year she was determined to go. A chronic lung condition flared up during the climb and kept her from the summit.

After her separation from Joe in the late 1970s, Joan focused more on her art and on developing and defining herself, as woman, artist and climber. She continued to climb and ski with special friends and do first ascents. "She was very opinionated about who she climbed with," remembers Margarite fondly. Joan's outward affect reflected her strong will and determination to achieve what she set out to do. Joan died in 1980.

▲ ▲ ▲

Vera Dafoe started hiking in the fifties as a way to get out of the house with the kids. Several families would go on an outing together, and they alternated childcare chores. She remembers that "someone told me I could climb Mt. Hood, so I got in shape and did it!" Soon she was hooked and began climbing and assisting the leaders on many climbs. After her first husband's death, Vera married avid climber Carmie Dafoe in 1968. "He was a real overachiever," Vera smiles. They climbed a lot all over the western United States, Canada and Europe. "Carmie pushed me toward leading, and by 1971 I was leading Mazamas outings independent of him. I began to see the importance of women being active role models; I believed that it was very important to show that women could climb, and lead, and play a full role in mountaineering. It was as valuable for men to see this as women."

Vera has been leading Mazamas outings for twenty-two years and has witnessed the development of many women climbers. She is somewhat frustrated that during the seventies and eighties, a period of women's increased participation in sports, the actual proportion of women who develop into lead climbers hasn't changed. Out of eighty-plus leaders in The Mazamas, only ten to twelve are women, even today.

Frustrated but not mystified, Vera has some explanations. "In the Basic climbing school, when a male novice seems to pick up things quickly, teachers will tend to say, 'Gee, you're pretty good. You should consider leading!' But when a woman does well, they're more likely to give her a 'you're pretty good for a woman' type of message and never even mention the idea of leading. I've also noticed that in climbing, men often have this very strong drive that they operate from. Driven to adventure. Women aren't usually coming from the same place. Their motives involve being with other people on a climb, getting exercise and being up high, maybe for the views or the excitement."

Vera has forced herself to accept the full responsibilities of leadership. That did not come naturally. She tells a story about a climb she was on with two men. They were traversing a steep, icy snow slope in the Tatoosh Range, south of Mt. Rainier. They had a rope but weren't using it, and she was getting concerned. She finally asked the others whether they thought they should be roped up. No sooner had one of the men dismissed the idea than he slipped and fell several hundred feet, only stopping by a lucky coincidence. Vera has never forgotten this lesson. She trusts her own experienced judgment now, and teaches her students to learn the skills that will make them equally self-sufficient.

Vera never felt that she was a born climber. She "just fell into it." But she kept doing it in part because of this sense of responsibility to women. How does she feel about all-women climbs? In the early seventies The Mazamas sponsored several such outings, but Vera felt they were demeaning—they always had "tea party stuff—costumes and all" and she feels they weren't taken seriously as climbs. Vera doesn't see anything cutesy about women climbing. Does she think women can gain skills and confidence in all-women environments? Possibly, but for her, it's more important to stay in the mainstream and show by example that women are every bit as capable as men. In Vera's case, one hopes the men are as capable as she is.

III

STARTING OUT EQUAL
The Boom Years

By the early 1970s, the number of women who were discovering rock climbing and mountaineering was growing rapidly. From a roster of 4,200 members in 1960, The Mountaineers' membership list had grown to some 7,000 ten years later. It could have been related to the second wave of feminist activism, heralded by authors like Friedan and de Beauvoir, that washed over North America. It had a lot to do with the sport of rock climbing finally reaching a stage of critical mass, with enough participants and a growing culture of its own. Laura Waterman, in her essay, "When Women Were Women in the Northeast"[5] spells out the genesis of women's participation in the sport and how the movement traveled west, with climbers influencing and encouraging other climbers in the Yosemite Valley and further north. During this period of the early 1970s some dozen women were pushing the upper limits of rock climbing at areas from New York to California to British Columbia. Carla Firey, Julie Brugger, Catherine Freer, and Judy Sterner were among them.

Carla had learned to climb with her parents, but decided it would be a good idea to branch out on her own. In 1969 she signed up for one of Bill Sumner's climbing courses at the University of Washington and discovered that she loved pure rock climbing. "I've never been attracted to expedition climbing—all the logistics! And I'm not crazy about snow and ice." But she was attracted to the big walls and solid crack climbing of Yosemite, and from 1974 on she spent every spring in the Valley. She had met Julie Brugger in Sumner's course, and for several years they climbed together in the Cascades and Yosemite. Julie was already leading long, strenuous climbs like Meat Grinder (5.10c) and Lunatic Fringe, another classic 1970s crack climb. By 1976 Carla was leading these and more. When it got too hot to climb in Yosemite, Carla returned to the Northwest. Besides her first ascents with her parents in the early 1970s, she and her husband, Jim McCarthy, did the first free ascent via a new route ("a crummy route called Corkscrew," she warns) on

---

[5] Mikel Vause, Ed. *Rock and Roses: An Anthology of Mountaineering Essays* (LaCrescenta, CA: Mountains N'Air Books, 1990)

Burgundy Spire, "a high-quality route" on Paisano Pinnacle, and several others in the North Cascades.

"By the late seventies there were lots of women leading 5.10," Carla recalls, typically modest. Nevertheless, her 1976 climb of the Steck-Salathe route on Sentinel with Julie Brugger was one of the first all-women ascents of the long free-climbing route. In 1978 she climbed the Chouinard-Beckey route on South Hauser Spire in British Columbia's Bugaboos. She and Jim swung leads: "If I don't participate in leading, I don't really count it. It's the leading that's really exciting."

Carla continued to climb in Yosemite but by 1981 realized that she wanted a change. The climbing bug still stung every spring, but now she and Jim went to the desert, to Utah, to Joshua Tree, to Colorado's steep face climbs. They climbed Castleton Tower in 1981, and many routes in Eldorado Canyon.

Although Carla hasn't climbed as much in the last ten years, she hasn't lost her edge, either. "I really enjoy the gymnastic quality of harder climbs, so these days I don't lead regularly. But when I'm feeling in shape, I can go out and lead climbs of the same difficulty rating as I used to. I just haven't progressed much beyond that." She has been climbing more in British Columbia's Squamish, Smith Rocks in Oregon, and Idaho's City of Rocks. But in 1991 she and Jim returned to Yosemite and Owens River Gorge in California, where she led a 5.11 pitch of a climb she hadn't done before.

Carla has been a member of the Seattle-based Women Climbers Northwest since 1985. She feels that WCN is important for women climbers both socially and as a way to bring more women into climbing through a supportive network of friends and mentors. Her slide shows of family climbing trips are well-loved history lessons at WCN events.

▲ ▲ ▲

Julie Brugger, on the other hand, has never been a member of WCN, preferring to find her climbing partners through friends and on the rock. She remembers first meeting Catherine Freer in 1969 at Castle Rock, a popular climbing area in Washington's Cascades. Catherine was running around, offering advice to stuck or tentative novices. Three years later the two were climbing together seriously in Yosemite. "I remember Catherine was into liebacks, so we did every lieback in the Valley. Then she got into off-widths and tried to talk me into leading all the off-widths!" They were nothing if not driven. "Catherine always thought she should be able to do anything anyone else could do. 'He runs a four-minute mile? I should be able to do that!' She was very hard on herself. But Catherine really loved the mountains. Whether she was scared or not—and she did give a lot of thought to the risks of climbing—she was always a very together climber." In 1982 Catherine was chosen to represent the United States in the first women's rock climbing meet, held in Britain and the following year she climbed Zenyatta Mendata on El Capitan, alternating leads on one of the most difficult aid climbs in Yosemite.

Catherine's climb of Cholatse (21,128 feet) and Lobuje East (20,075 feet) in the Nepal Himalaya in 1984 was perhaps one of her finest mountaineering achievements. She and teammate Todd Bibler climbed Lobuje East, and went on to climb Cholatse's North Face two days later by a new and difficult route. She participated in attempts on K2 and Everest in 1986. Catherine and teammate David Cheesmond died in 1987 while attempting to complete the second ascent of Hummingbird Ridge on Mt. Logan.

What drives Julie to climb? "I don't like the world the way it is and *that* world—she gestures toward the distant, cloudy Cascades— is more like the way it should be." Julie spent many years intensely focused on rock climbing, but her main passion now is mountaineering. She has climbed in Peru, Argentina, Europe and Nepal. She is going to Alaska to climb the North Buttress of Mt. Hunter with her partner Andy de Klerk, and dreams of returning to Nepal.

But a sense of time running out infuses her plans. Since suffering a serious accident five years ago parapenting off a mountain, she is somewhat more cautious, her fears more specific. Nevertheless, she gets out climbing more days than not and finds herself climbing with people ten to fifteen years younger than herself. She laughs about an incident where the mother of a nineteen-year-old climbing partner assumed the thirty-something-year-old Julie was one of his school chums. I asked her what she saw in her climbing future. "It's your mind that stops you before your body," Julie muses. "I know I won't be able to do the hard stuff forever, and yeah, I'll eventually go back to school—but not yet!"

▲ ▲ ▲

Judy Sterner started rock climbing in 1969 in her native California. She took to it avidly, leading within two months of her first day on the rock, and climbing with some of the best climbers of the day: Elaine Matthews, Bev Johnson and Anne Marie Rizzi. She climbed the East Face of Mt. Whitney with Johnson, and the Chouinard-Herbert, one of the longest routes in Yosemite Valley.

Judy learned ice climbing and ski mountaineering when she visited Canada in 1971. She recalls how in the early 1970s ice climbing was the new big thing, and climbers from all over the world flocked to its mecca, Calgary, Alberta. After moving there herself and taking up ski mountaineering in a serious way, she decided to put together a women's expedition to Mt. Logan (6,050 meters), Canada's highest mountain. She hadn't led anything longer than a two-day rock climb in California. But it was 1976; the year before, Junko Tabei had become the first woman to reach the summit of Mt. Everest, women had been pioneering new hard routes in Yosemite and New York's Shawangunks, and the move was on for women to lead major expeditions as well.

Judy started asking her friends—women she'd known and climbed with for years. Many of them, with at least as much experience as she had, turned her down or backed off later. They had been confident enough on the mixed trips, but now they seemed to lack that same self-confidence. It took Judy a full year to put together the team of six. Kathy Calvert and Lorraine Drewes had extensive rock experience. Diana Knaak was both a rock climber and ski mountaineer. Sharon Wood had mountaineering experience, but this was to be her first high-altitude trip. And Kathy Langill was, as Judy put it, "stolen at the last minute from an expedition to the St. Elias Range!"

Their planned route was not a technical one, and it is now the standard route, but the hazards include a very long approach, an excellent chance of awful weather, and the risks associated with high altitude. The expedition was also to be the first ski ascent of the West Summit.

Judy went about organizing the logistics with the same tenacity she employed in finding team mates. In hindsight, they may have been overprepared. By sharing a list of potential donors with another expedition leader, Chick Scott, she raised enough money and "thousands of candy bars." She suspects that they carried too much food, which slowed them down somewhat. After a grueling twenty days of travel on foot and skis, the team got to just below the West Summit before they were forced to turn around to make it back to the heli-camp for their scheduled evacuation. As team member Katherine Calvert wrote in *The Canadian Alpine Journal* (Vol. 61, 1978):

> . . . we felt our own goal had been achieved. We had planned and exe-cuted the first all-women's expedition to Canada's highest mountain and had accomplished it in safety. Yet sadness lingered, as did a rea-son to return, for now we knew we had the ability the mountain de-manded. Before it was only an outlandish idea that the world, in disbe-lief, forced us to realize."

Today, having received her Ph.D. in Social Anthropology, Judy divides her time between doing field work in various countries and life at home in Alberta, Canada.

▲ ▲ ▲

"No, we've never had anything like your women's climbing group up here," Barbara Clemes, from Calgary, Alberta, reports. "There are really only half a dozen women leading 5.11 in Canada that I know of." Barbara ought to know. She, Julie Leino and Jola Sanford all lead 5.12 now and compete in the sport climbing circuits. Tami Knight was the top woman rock climber in Canada for many years, leading 5.10 in the late seventies and early eighties, though Janine Caldbeck and a few others were in that range as well. In the East, Judy Barnes has led 5.12 climbs at Lion's Head in Ontario.

In ice climbing, the number of Canadian women climbers is even smaller. Barbara Clemes, with Ann Campbell from Scotland, did the first women's ascent of Polar Circus in 1987, climbing it again the next year with Janet Roddan, another active mountain and ice climber. Marnie Virtue and Sharon Wood are top ice climbers, but in terms of women leading or climbing with other women, there are very few beyond these.

Barbara is one of only eight women guides certified by the Asso-ciation of Canadian Mountain Guides (ACMG) out of more than one hundred. In 1982, she and Jan St Armand, Elaine Kennedy and

Jane Weller climbed Mt. McKinley (Denali) in Alaska as only the second all-women's expedition to the peak. Janet Roddan teaches rock climbing courses for the Federation of Mountain Clubs (an umbrella group of British Columbia climbing and hiking clubs) and plans to become a certified mountaineering guide in 1992. Nicky Cody, a dedicated rock and mountaineering guide, was tragically killed in October 1991 while teaching at a climbing area in Washington State.

Sharon Wood, an active climber and certified guide, was the first North American woman to climb Mt. Everest. She was one of the eleven members of the Canadian Light Everest Expedition that put two Canadians on the summit via the West Ridge and Hornbein Couloir on May 20, 1986. Her description of the more than two-month-long expedition paints a picture of an incredible effort of teamwork and leadership under some of of the most difficult conditions imaginable on an 8,000-meter peak. Sharon's climbs of Huascarán and Aconcagua are additional feathers in her mountaineering cap.

▲ ▲ ▲

Since the mid-1970s, our region has produced or attracted many top expedition leaders and high-altitude climbers. Kitty Calhoun Grissom received the American Alpine Club's prestigious Miriam and Robert Underhill Award in 1991. Stacy Alison, the first American woman to reach the summit of Mt. Everest, lives and works in Portland, Oregon, and lectures widely on her experiences. She is planning a Himalayan expedition for the near future. And Arlene Blum grew up in Portland, learning mountaineering skills while a student at Reed College. In 1970 she participated in the first all-women ascent of Mt. McKinley and went on to become a dedicated mountaineer and top mountaineering writer. Her 1978 American Women's Himalayan Expedition to Annapurna and the book she wrote about it, *Annapurna: A Woman's Place* (The Sierra Club; San Francisco, CA; 1980) remain centerpieces in the history of women's climbing.

It was this book, in fact, that inspired Jaymi Devans to pursue her dream of climbing. Now thirty-two, she recalls that she did some easy climbs while in her twenties, but the bug really bit when she read about Blum's all-women expedition. In April 1990 Jaymi, a lesbian, joined Stonewall Climbers, a Boston-based gay and lesbian climbing organization. She borrowed a huge pile of back issues of *Climbing* and *Rock and Ice* magazines and set about learning everything she could about her new sport.

Jaymi's first climbing partner was a male fellow-Stonewaller. She learned everything she could from him, and then started looking for other women to climb with. But try as she might, it took her from April until the following January to find someone. She thinks this was due in part to her lack of experience, but more than that, to the fact that there weren't, and still aren't, very many women who lead. "I did over one hundred fifty routes last year, at least one hundred days on the rock," she explains, "and in all that time I saw maybe five or six women climbing together!" She sees lots of women climbing, but mostly with their boyfriends or male climbing partners. Few lead. She feels that "it's very important for women to lead, otherwise it sets up a power dynamic that perpetuates women's dependence. How can you feel like an equal member of your team if you don't lead?"

Jaymi learned "by doing adventure climbing, by going ahead and trying things!" She started leading a couple months after she started to climb, a circumstance she credits with forcing her to become an extremely safety-conscious climber, thinking and re-thinking everything until she's sure she has it right.

Jaymi, Celia Pender and several other women, Stonewall's women's contingent in the West, organized a five-month climbing camp at Yosemite in 1992. Jaymi and her climbing partner did a route on Half Dome in July, and met Celia and other climbers from the East Coast and British Columbia on Snake Dike for a full moon ascent.

Jaymi feels it's very important for women to be able to climb with and learn from other women. She climbs with men and women, gay and straight, but supports Stonewall as a way for people to make connections with other climbers who will be the best mentors for them. She sees herself as a mentor for others, too, down the road. When interviewed, Jaymi had just returned from Yosemite, where she and three other women had climbed Crest Jewel, a ten-pitch 5.10a route, in two teams of two. It's easy to see how Jaymi, Celia and other devoted climbers like them will become the inspiration for a new generation.

▲ ▲ ▲

By the 1980s, women were flocking to sports in greater numbers than ever before. In part because Title IX funding in the U.S. had mandated equal access to sports facilities and programs in public schools, making sports more accessible to girls and women and enlarging the pool of athletic talent. In the field of climbing, women like Lynn Hill and Alison Osius were proving that there were literally no limits to women's climbing ability. These women refused to be categorized as great women climbers; they were simply great climbers.

With foremothers and mentors in relative abundance, women in our region began to discover and pursue climbing in greater numbers. One energetic force in this movement was Kathy Phibbs. An avid rock and alpine climber since her college days in California in the late 1970s, she had made several efforts to form a women's climbing organization, but nothing had really taken hold. Finally, in January 1983, Kathy and several other women, including Gwen Hall, Eve Dearborn and Maureen O'Neill, organized the first meeting of what was to become the Seattle-based Women Climbers Northwest. To their surprise, some two dozen women showed up, enthusiastically endorsing the concept of a women's climbing group.

As a women's climbing organization WCN is unique in the United States in terms of size and duration. Attempts to develop similar climbing networks in other parts of the country have not lasted for more than a few years at a time. In some of these groups, women felt that being serious about climbing meant acting too much like men and that a women's group should be more "laid back" and support other outdoor activities. In others, women were looking for a teaching organization, with authority and strong leadership clearly defined. These qualities are easy to come by in most traditional mixed climbing groups, but rarely describe the functioning of women's organizations.

The success of WCN is also a product of having a core group of women who felt that they wanted to simultaneously push their limits as climbers and continue to climb often, or exclusively, in all-women groups. When Susan Ulery tried to start a chapter of WCN in Portland in 1988, she learned firsthand the value of having that core group of committed climbers. After the initial gathering at which seventy women showed up, rapid attrition set in: some women wanted a formal teaching organization; others didn't want their hard-won climbing skills "tainted" by membership in an all-women organization. As WCN member Kristen Laine recalls, "Some women climbers I knew were very good, but in the ranking view of men, they were never as good as the male climbers they went out with. These women refused to join WCN because they were already afraid they didn't belong, and to be with women would be an admission, saying they didn't belong in the guys' climbing scene. I think some were also afraid they would be labeled as lesbians." Although it took many years for the percentage of lesbians in the group to even reach the percentage of lesbians in the population as a whole, some women experienced this perception of the group as a tool to intimidate potential members.

As Kristen Laine points out, it seems that "men and women define themselves and how they view relationships differently. When two men go out climbing together, it's as if they have a contract, and the contract starts here, goes there and ends here. The rules seem to be clear. I listen to guys setting up trips, and they go down a check list that to me leaves out a lot of things. I think women want to make connections and develop relationships through climbing." WCN members value the honesty that assures that potential climbing partners don't exaggerate their claims to mountaineering greatness. They are more likely to evaluate their skills based on their actual experience than many male climbers.

While WCN is not, officially, a teaching organization, members do pass along their knowledge, and their enthusiasm. Many women who have climbed mostly with men or in mixed groups tell stories about expeditions on which they felt extremely isolated or were ostracized outright. One top Northwest climber got to the last camp before the summit of a major Himalayan peak and opted out of going on to the top with her two male teammates. Being ignored by them another day was more stress than the summit was worth. Similarly, another who went to Peru with a group of male climbers boarded the plane only to find that she literally couldn't start a conversation with any of her team mates. "They didn't want to form a relationship with me because that could sabotage the whole expedition!"

When women go out into the wilderness, they are confronted with issues—such as leadership and responsibility—that many don't get the opportunity to take on in their daily lives. "I've never climbed much with men because I felt I couldn't get my full share of responsibility," Maureen O'Neill explains. "On one climb I did with a guy he always took control at crucial moments. I could have brought it up but I didn't even want to fight that battle with him. I am willing to fight a different kind of battle with women, because I start out on an equal footing with them." Men usually have leaders in outdoor situations, whereas women try to operate on consensus. Reaching consensus can be a frustrating process, but is usually worth the struggle in the sense of unity and self-reliance that results. Rayne Engle notes that often women focus on the process as well as the goal. "They want to make sure the slowest person isn't left completely behind and that she feels a sense of accomplishment as well. "While this is the prevalent attitude in WCN, many people are also climbing at high levels—5.10 isn't that unusual. WCN's philosophy tends to be inclusive rather than narrowly exclusive. Membership requirements are that you are a woman and you learn to climb."

This region is so rich in wilderness opportunities that several organizations run guided outdoor trips exclusively for women. Womantrek and Adventure Associates are the largest of these, but other companies offer llama pack trips, sea kayak excursions and backcountry ski outings. Some, like Woodswomen, based in Minneapolis, also offer leadership training in the Cascades and provide ways for women to gain experience as guides. Guiding or teaching novices in a mountain environment is challenging for instuctor and student alike. But for women to get the most out of their mountain experiences it is often important to give them an opportunity to learn from and with other women.

Even where there are no formal courses taught by women, there can be a supportive mentoring approach that will go a long way towards developing women's skills and confidence. Kathy Phibbs described what she felt was most important about a group like Women Climbers Northwest: "I want to make sure that the knowledge of the people that are here is passed on to people who aren't here, knowledge in terms of skills and history. To me, WCN can be more powerful if the people who have skills pass them along."

Women Climbers Northwest currently has some 125 members and remains the only group of its kind in North America.

Notes on the Sources

Carla Rickerson, head of the Pacific Northwest Collection, Special Collections Division at the University of Washington Libraries was very helpful in suggesting books, scrapbooks and photographic resources during the research on the early years. People who helped by steering us toward early climbers include Malcolm Bates, Phillip Dickert, Jeff Thomas, Jim Olsen, Gary Beyl, Jack Grauer, Linda MacNeil, Dorothy Rich, Paul Wiseman, Bob Lockerby, Celia Pender, Jim Kjelsen, Ken Lans and Nora Layard.

People who kindly agreed to be interviewed or answered technical or historical questions include Dorothy Rich, Nancy South, Edith Pierce, Lori Darr, Debra Barnabee, Helen Hapgood, Tom Hargis, Joe Firey and each of the people who are quoted in the essay. Kristen Laine and Maureen O'Neill contributed invaluable editorial assistance.

A Bibliography of the History of Women's Climbing in the Pacific Northwest and Lower Mainland of British Columbia

Andrews, Mildred T. *Washington Women As Path Breakers* (Dubuque: Kendall/Hunt Publishing Co., 1989)

Beckey, Fred. *Cascade Alpine Guide, Climbing and High Routes, Rainy Pass to Fraser River* (Seattle: The Mountaineers, 1981) *Cascade Alpine Guide, Climbing and High Routes, Stevens Pass to Rainy Pass* (Seattle: The Mountaineers, 1989) *Cascade Alpine Guide, Climbing and High Routes, Columbia River to Stevens Pass* (Seattle: The Mountaineers, 1973)

Bellingham Evening News, The (Bellingham. June 29, July 7, 8, 16, 25, 1931)

Birkett, Bill and Bill Peascod. *Women Climbing: Two Hundred Years of Achievement* (Seattle and London: The Mountaineers and A&C Black, 1989)

Blair, Karen J., Editor. *Women in Pacific Northwest History: An Anthology* (Seattle & London: University of Washington Press, 1988)

Brooks, Don and David Whitelaw. *A Climber's Guide to Washington Rock: Darrington, Index, Leavenworth* (Seattle: The Mountaineers, 1982)

Daily Ledger, The (Tacoma. August 19, 1890)

Daily Oregonian, The (Portland. August 31, 1867)

Easton, Charles F. *"Mt. Baker, Its Trails and Legends."* (Bellingham: unpublished scrapbook, Whatcom Museum of History and Art, compiled 1903–1940)

Figge, John. *Mountaineering on the Nooksack, an Annotated History of the Mount Baker Area* (Seattle: printed by xerographic process, limited handbound series, 1984)

Grauer, Jack. *Mount Hood: A Complete History* (Portland: John F. Grauer, 1975)

Haines, Aubrey L. *Mountain Fever: Historic Conquests of Rainier* (Portland: Oregon Historical Society, 1962)

Hazard, Joseph T. *Snow Sentinels of the Pacific Northwest* (Seattle: Lowman & Hanford Co., 1932)

Leslie, Susan, Ed. *In the Western Mountains: Early Mountaineering in British Columbia* (Sound Heritage Collection, Vol. VIII, No. 4, Victoria, British Columbia: Aural History Program, Provincial Archives of British Columbia, 1980)

McNeil, Fred H. *Wy'east "The Mountain," A Chronicle of Mt. Hood* (Portland: The Metropolitan Press, 1937)

Miles, John C. *Koma Kulshan: The Story of Mt. Baker* (Seattle: The Mountaineers, 1984)

Molenaar, Dee. *The Challenge of Rainier: A Record of the Explorations and Ascents, Triumphs and Tragedies, on the Northwest's Greatest Mountain* (Seattle: The Mountaineers, 1979)

Mountaineers, The. *"The Mountaineer, Volume 1–8"* (Seattle: The Mountaineers, 1907–1915)

Mountaineers, The. *"The Mountaineer, Volume 9–12"* (Seattle: The Mountaineers, 1916–1919)

Olympic Mountain Rescue, *Climber's Guide to the Olympic Mountains* (Seattle: The Mountaineers, 1979)

Pilley, Dorothy. *Climbing Days* (London: Secker & Warburg, 1935)

Robertson, Janet. *The Magnificent Mountain Women: Adventures in the Colorado Rockies* (Lincoln & London: University of Nebraska Press, 1990)

Schlissel, Lillian, Vicki L. Ruiz, and Janice Monk, Eds. *Western Women:*

Their Land, Their Lives (Albuquerque: University of New Mexico Press, 1988)

Schullery, Paul. *Island in the Sky: Pioneering Accounts of Mt. Rainier, 1833–1894* (Seattle: The Mountaineers, 1987)

Smith, Cyndi. *Off the Beaten Track: Women Adventurers and Mountaineers in Western Canada* (Jasper: Coyote Books, 1989)

Strong, Anna Louise. *I Change Worlds* (Seattle: The Seal Press, 1979)

Sunday Ledger, The. (Tacoma. August 17, 1890)

Vause, Mikel, Ed. *Rock and Roses: An Anthology of Mountaineering Essays* (LaCrescenta, CA: Mountain N'Air Books, 1990)

Whitney, Marci. *Notable Women* (Tacoma: Tacoma News Tribune. 1977)

Writers' Program of the Work Projects Administration in the state of Oregon. *Mt. Hood: A Guide* (New York: J. J. Little & Ives Co., 1940)

Meeting the Challenge

Climbs and Expeditions

APRIL FOOLS ON
POLAR CIRCUS

Janet Roddan

▲ ▲ ▲

Polar Circus is a long, alpine climb, 1,500 feet of vertical gain, involving both snow and ice pitches on Cirrus Mountain in the Athabascan Icefields of the Canadian Rockies. Janet Roddan's story relates a female ascent of this route on April Fool's Day, 1988.

The dance with fear fascinates me. Learning to accept fear, to take it in without letting it take over is one of the challenges of climbing ice. Climbing leads me into myself, through my hidden doors, into corners and attics. The doorway through fear always appears ominous, locked shut, insurmountable, impossible. Fear talks to me, whispers my weakness; it speaks of conditions, of my own mortality—it whispers "hubris." Fear sharpens my senses. It dances through my body. It tunes me. It wraps its fingers around my heart and squeezes gently. I learn to welcome fear and the edge it brings me, the whispered warnings, the adrenaline. The tango with fear makes me wise.

Two fireflies glimmer in the darkness. The tiny puffs of light float slowly upward and burn deeper into a maze of ice, snow and rock. Snatches of our conversation drift up. We are on a quest, in search of ice. A note of opera breaks the white silence. We are singing as we approach the climb.

I learn the language; I articulate the right series of moves, body positions, ice axe and crampon placements to dance with a frozen tongue of ice. To talk with the mountain is strong medicine. Ice climbing allows me the privilege of witnessing the world. The couloir leads us into the mountain, up there to wild, silent places that wait, unconcerned with whether we view them or not.

An initial pitch of ice, steep enough to burn our calves, increases the intensity with which we communicate with this frozen world. This pitch is followed by a long, rambling walk, past the Pencil, a once free-standing pillar of ice that now lies broken and crushed in a heap. Then on up to the knoll, where we look out from the dark, claustrophobic couloir to see sun on the peaks. We continue to snake along a snowfield and arrive at last at the base of the route proper, six long pitches of undulating ice...varied, interesting, alpine.

Kafka said, "The words of literature are an ice axe to break the sea frozen inside us." We use our ice axes to shatter our frozen worlds into crystals of ice and fear. One of the strong pulls of ice climbing is the tremendous range of feelings one is forced to endure—tingling, shivering pain...bubbling, shining elation. We hold on, struggling to control the fear that pounds through our veins and capillaries. But just as fear begins to steal into the soul, a good axe placement thunks into the ice. This solid, physical connection to the world causes the fear to recede...first from the arms, then from the mind...then even more gradually fear's fingers release the heart, which eventually slows and quiets. The intensity is replaced with warm, smooth, flowing beats. The rhythm takes hold, and the dance begins again.

The last two pitches of the climb cascade out of the notch like an enormous wedding gown. Today's brides approach slowly, touched by the mystery and majesty of the place. We are filled with our fear and our audacity. We encourage each other; we push each other. Our vows are strong, but it is April, late in the season for ice climbing. The ice is rotten; the climb is falling down. Time melts and falls away along with great chunks of ice as I rail and pound against it. The dance becomes a struggle.

The entire world shrinks to a section of frozen water in front of my face. The ice is dripping wet and soggy. The rhythm has been broken. I force myself to breathe, to generate my own flow, to create my own beat. But nothing feels right. A chasm fifteen feet wide opens up between Barb, my partner, and me. Impossible to return. I fight. I hit hard to get good placements. A big block of ice disengages itself; my tool is embedded in it. Time stops, and in slow motion I swing onto my other ice axe. I "barndoor" open and the block of ice topples over my shoulder. I look down to see the ice explode beside Barb, who suddenly looks tiny and hunched in her small belay stance.

"I don't know about this, Barb," I shout down, hoping she will offer an easy way out. I reason to come down. But she calls back, "It depends on how much you want it." Indeed. How much do I want it? Doubt slides in with spaghetti arms and little shivers that evaporate my courage.

But desire, commitment and an incredible dislike for down climbing drive me. Up. One move at a time. Filled with solemn focus, I proceed. The final veil is gently torn away. The great Goddess reveals her face of frozen water. I witness her dark, foreboding pinnacles, her places of silent, quiet peace, her vistas too vast to contain in a single glance. Tingling, shivering, we arrive at the summit notch at 4 p.m., a happy marriage of fear, sweat, intelligent strength and smiles.

The vast mystery that spreads before us causes us to stop and look and take it in for heartbeats of silence. Endless jagged peaks. The silent contract, the ceremony is almost complete. We rappel down the climb. The ropes pull, snagging a few times just to remind us that it's not over yet. A climb is never over until you are back at the car. And even then, the journey that we are all on keeps going. As we descend, night overtakes us. We turn on our headlamps, tiny pins of light in a blanket of darkness.

The April fools, married with fear and laughter on Polar Circus, return to the car, smiling in the darkness, two tiny fireflies humming and buzzing softly.

EVEREST: MY JOURNEY
TO THE TOP

Bachendri Pal

▲ ▲ ▲

I

My father's name is Kishan Singh Pal. He was born in 1901 in
Bampa, a small mountain village which was part of the border district of Chamoli, in the Garhwal Himalaya. The village spread over
both sides of the river, the gurgling, playful Dhauli Ganga.

My father is short and stocky. Like his father before him and
most others of the area, my father was a small border tradesman.
There were no roads in the region so he used mules, horses and even
goats to carry his goods. He took *atta,* rice, barley, *mishri* (candy-
sugar) from India to Tibet. In Tibet he would either sell or exchange
Indian goods for wool, mineral salts, especially rock-salt, goats and
sheep.

My father, however, was not very successful in business and at
the age of thirty-five decided to move to new pastures. He left
Bampa and made his new home in Nakuri, a small village of about
fifteen houses, perched on the right bank of the Bhagirathi Ganga,
some twelve kilometers south of Uttarkashi.

Kishan Singh married a Nakuri girl, Hansa Dei Negi. Eighteen-
year-old Hansa was half her husband's age but though they were
different in many ways, they got on well. The sturdy, short Kishan
Singh was stern and quick-tempered while Hansa Dei was soft-

skinned, delicate and tall for a Garhwali girl. She spread sunshine around her and was tender-hearted.

My parents raised a happy family. Five children in a row: girl, boy, girl, girl and boy, in that order. I was the third child.

Like all border villagers of the region, we had two homes—one at Nakuri, the other at Harsil. In winter, when Harsil was snow-bound, we lived in Nakuri. For the six summer months we moved up to Harsil, over 2,500 meters in elevation, where there was good grazing for the goats, sheep and the cattle on the higher slopes. Along with the other families which had come from eastern Garhwal, we lived in a small village in the Harsil valley. But the village was washed away in a flash-flood in 1943, making us homeless for the summer months. Ultimately, we decided to stay at Nakuri all year round.

My father stopped his business in raw wool and rearing animals and the family started producing finished goods, weaving carpets and waist-bands worn by the Garhwali women and knitting sweaters. Father also bought a small plot of land some distance away on which he grew food crops for the family. Despite all our hard work there was never enough for the needs of the family.

The first child, a girl, was born in 1945 and named Kamaleshwari. She went to school when she was quite young but had to leave after Class VI. The family could not afford her further education. Kamla had to do her share of work at home and outdoors. She had to fetch firewood and fodder from the forest and carry water for the household. I know what being a girl in Garhwal means. I have done all the back-breaking work myself, but not as much as Kamla Didi did. We, too, learned to weave carpets. My sister was a very good weaver. I was not bad at it either, but I was restless and did not like indoor work.

Next to arrive in the family, six years after Kamaleshwari, was Bachan Singh. My brother was good at his studies but his real love was the mountains and climbing difficult routes. He was also an outstanding sportsman. After his graduation, he was recruited as an Inspector in the Border Security Force (BSF) and prevailed on the BSF authorities to send him to be trained in mountaineering at the Nehru Institute of Mountaineering (NIM) in Uttarkashi. He completed the basic and advance mountaineering courses with top grading.

I was born on May 24, 1954. According to my parents, I was the noisiest of all their children; I cried alot. I kept my parents on their toes. There was never a dull moment in the family after I arrived.

The next child was Upama, three years after me. She studied up to Class IX. I teased my little sister a lot but Upama and I were good friends. Like my elder sister, Upama was a typical hill-village girl, well-behaved, gentle and domesticated. I was the only rebel.

The youngest child of the family, Rajender Singh was born three years after Upama. Raju was strong and a good sportsman. My elder brother was always urging Raju to take part in outdoor pursuits like mountaineering. This made me angry. "Why only Raju? Why can't I also take mountaineering courses?" I would ask. For much as I loved my brothers, I resented the boys getting more attention and opportunities than us girls. I was determined not to take a back seat in the Pal family and to not only do what the boys did, but do it better.

Unlike my sisters who went out only when they had to, I loved going for walks in the forest or the mountains. I would insist on accompanying my father when he went out and threw a tantrum if he refused to take me with him.

One day when I was about four, my father took me to the fields nearly two kilometers away. The next day my parents set off alone. Though I begged to be taken and cried myself hoarse, they did not relent. My brother was asked to keep an eye on me. After some time I fell asleep and my brother went off to play. When I woke up I made straight for the fields where we had gone the previous day. I crossed a number of small water channels and kept going on and on, hoping to find my parents. When my feet could carry me no further, I sat down to wait for them and, after while, I lay down and fell asleep.

There was panic when my parents returned in the evening. I had been missing for some hours and no one knew where to look for me. They feared that I might have gone out and been swept away in one of the rivulets. Poor brother Bachan got a sound thrashing. Following his instinct, my father then took the track of the day before and saw my footprints on the rain-wetted path. He followed the trail and found me fast asleep nearly two kilometers from home. Instead of my parents showing any anger, I showed mine. They only laughed in relief.

When I was young, my elder brother Bachan was my hero. He was strong and confident. When we went on climbs or on walks I could not keep up with him so he avoided taking me with him. One day, he had to go into the hills to cut leaves for the cattle. He left me behind but I followed him quietly.

Bachan was busy lopping branches and did not see me as I approached. He had made a wide swipe with his sickle when he suddenly noticed me. He tried to hold back but it was too late. The point of the sickle nicked my skull.

I started bleeding profusely. I was in pain but I did not cry. In fact, I felt sorry for my brother. He looked worried and scared. He tried to wipe off the blood with leaves. When the bleeding did not stop, he crushed some medicinal plants and pressed them on the wound. The bleeding stopped and brother Bachan washed my face and the other blood-stains in a stream.

Before reaching home, Bachan made me promise that I would not tell anyone about my injury. He also asked me to avoid having a bath for some time.

I kept my word but after a few days my mother noticed how I was avoiding bathing and, catching hold of me, dragged me to the stream. While washing my head she saw the matted hair and when she washed it out the wound started bleeding again. My horrified mother tried her utmost to find out how I had hurt myself, but I was determined not to let my brother down. I kept a stony silence. Finally, my brother confessed. He told Mother how he had hurt me accidentally. Everyone was amazed by my self-control.

I was a great dreamer. I never thought anything was beyond my reach. If a magazine or a newspaper had a picture of the Prime Minister meeting young people, I would declare, "I will meet Indira Gandhi." When a car drove past on the road below our house I would say, "I will own a car when I grow up." But airplanes attracted me the most. Whenever I saw a plane or a helicopter, I said excitedly, "One day I will fly in an airplane." The family was poor and could not even afford the bare essentials. My parents were sad that their child lived in a world of dreams which could never be fulfilled. But the younger members of the family enjoyed my seeming fantasies and egged me on. I did not need much encouragement. I would keep talking about cars, airplanes and the important people I would meet. When my brothers and sisters burst out laughing I would raise my voice, stand up and shout, "Wait, I'll show you."

I joined Dunda-Harsil Junior High School when I was just five years old. As the school's name indicated, it functioned from both Dunda and Harsil. In the winter, Harsil was under a blanket of snow so the school moved to Dunda, five kilometers from my village, Nakuri. Come summer, most of the lower village population, including the school, shifted lock, stock and barrel to Harsil. I enjoyed the long trek every six months. Herding our cattle and cuddling new-born sheep and goat kids, we would pick flowers and berries and play hide-and-seek on the boulder-strewn mountain slopes. When tired, we rode a horse or mule. Being familiar with the camping sites on the way we ran ahead the last two or three kilometers to gather dead wood for cooking. I also loved living in tents, and then there was the excitement of going to school in a new place.

This exposure to nature made me independent and fearless. At the age of ten, I often explored the woods and the hill slopes alone. In spring I would sneak out to watch the flocks of migrating birds which had spent the winter in the plains. I also brought home from my wanderings the popular flower, the 'Brahma-kamal,' and armfuls of the scarlet blossoms of the rhododendron whose petals made a refreshing drink.

I was the most mischievous of my class. One incident I remember clearly concerned a young teacher who had a very fair, smooth complexion. All the girls, including myself, envied her and were curious to know the secret of her beauty. So, one day I slipped out of her class with two trusted friends, and prying open the window, entered her room. We were peering into the many bottles and jars on the dressing table when we heard footsteps outside. We hid hurriedly under the bed. The teacher came in with a long, thin stick which she immediately thrust under the bed. We shrank back to the farthest corner. But then, one of my companions giggled. Punishment followed swiftly. Being the ring leader, I got the maximum number of strokes. The last one got away with half the amount because the stick broke.

There ended my search for beauty. Whenever I think of the incident and the subsequent punishment, I shudder at the thought of beauty aids. I still don't use any makeup.

I wanted to excel in every outdoor activity, particularly in the competitions with boys and would practice diligently before the annual sports contests for races such as the three-legged, sack or those involving threading a needle and balancing a pot of water on the head. Since I did fairly well in my studies, my parents encouraged my interest in games and were very proud when I came home with a prize.

One Sunday morning when the school was in session at Harsil, ten of us, girls and boys, decided to go up the mountain for a picnic. We reached the snowline at 3,500 meters, and were delighted with the feel of crunchy snow under our feet. We climbed higher and higher until one of the girls complained of hunger. Then, finding an exposed outcrop of rock, we settled down for lunch. Assuming we could drink from some hill stream or spring we had brought no water, but at that height (nearly 4,000 meters) everything was under snow. So we quenched our thirst by eating snow.

Our troubles really began on our homeward journey. It was late in the afternoon and the slope was no longer in the sun. The snow had hardened and was very slippery. The climb down was, therefore, not only slow but also dangerous.

To add to our woes, several of the party had headaches and nausea. One boy threw up his lunch. We thought it was due to food poisoning or the contaminated snow we had sucked. There was also a common belief that this strange sickness was caused by the smell of certain flowers and leaves found at these heights. I now know that these symptoms were due to a shortage of oxygen in the thin air which occurs at an altitude of about 3,000 meters.

As darkness descended, we had to halt and make a partial overhead cover with branches. We had no food, no water and spent a cold, miserable night, waiting for daybreak.

When we reached home the following morning, we received little sympathy. Instead, we were rewarded with a beating. But this did not deter me. I had tasted the excitement of climbing the mountains and nothing could now hold me back.

I was nearly thirteen and had passed my Class VIII exam with good marks when my father said that he could no longer afford to send me to school and I should help at home. I had, however, set my heart on higher education, so during the day I did my full share of work and more, and borrowing my friends' school books, I studied on my own late into the night. My keenness and determination impressed everyone and finally my mother and sister Kamla pleaded with Father and I was allowed to join Class IX.

I knew we needed money for my education so I learned to sew and earned five to six rupees a day making *shalwar* and *kameez* suits. My earnings helped me to continue at school. I did well in my studies but even better in sports. I came in first in most disciplines in which I participated and won many cups in field events like the shot-put, discus, javelin and sprinting.

But after I passed the high school examination, my father was firm about my not going to college. It was the same problem: the family didn't have enough money. Then my principal intervened. She wrote saying that I had missed the first division by only three marks and as an "all-rounder," I had a bright future. Once again Father relented and I joined intermediate classes in physics, chemistry and biology, with an eye on doing my pre-medical. Though I passed my intermediate science, I could not cope with the pre-medical examination and switched to Arts. I took Sanskrit in my B.A. chiefy because of my love for the Himalaya. I knew that Kalidasa's *Kumarsambhava* and other Sanskrit literature were rich with references to these mountains, which are called "the measuring rod of the earth" by Kalidasa.

I was allowed to do my B.A. but the family's resistance to my further education continued. It made no difference to my resolve. Nothing and no one was going to deter me.

I won prizes in rifle shooting and first aid in joint competitions for boys and girls. I remember one particular contest in which we were blindfolded and had to dismantle and reassemble a rifle, a sten-gun and a Bren light machine gun against time. I came in first. My class teacher was very happy and taunting the boys, said that girls would now have to defend the country. The boys should wear bangles and sit at home.

After my B.A. I faced no further obstructions to my education, for by then Father wanted me to be the first girl in the village with an M.A. degree. I did my M.A. in Sanskrit from DAV College, Dehradun and then my B.Ed. from Garhwal University, Srinagar.

Higher education had been my first goal. I had, therefore, curbed my strong mountaineering urge. Now that I had an M.A. and B.Ed., I could realign my sights and put my heart and soul into mountaineering.

II

I was keen to join the NIM and become a good mountaineer, despite my mother feeling that it was too risky for girls. But I had not forgotten my father's sacrifices to give me a good education. It was my turn to do something for the family. I applied to a number of colleges for a teaching job but received offers only of temporary low-paid posts, and that, too, at primary level. I was not prone to devalue my hard-earned academic qualifications and declined these.

Instead of sitting home, I applied to the NIM to join their Basic Mountaineering Course but all the vacancies had been filled for the year. I gained admission the following year, however, and learned the techniques of climbing on rock, snow and ice, and experienced the thrill of rappelling, that is, coming down a high vertical rock or ice face in a matter of seconds with the help of a nylon rope. We were also taught camping methods and safe ways of crossing mountain rapids.

Major Prem Chand, NIM's Vice Principal, was the training officer. He was known to be a strict instructor who demanded a very high standard of performance. I thought I had probably done well enough to get the silver ice-axe and a certificate but in fact I had been awarded 'A' grading, and was declared the best student of the course. In his report the Vice Principal even put me down as "Everest material." At that point in time I paid no attention to this.

When I heard that the Indian Mountaineering Foundation (IMF) was planning a mixed expedition to Everest in 1984 and that there was a search for women with talent and experience in mountaineering, I gave it no thought as I could claim neither at this stage. I was, therefore, surprised to receive a letter from the IMF telling me that I had been selected for a screening camp for the Everest expedition. I was asked to confirm that I would attend the camp.

How could they possibly consider me for Everest? I had done so little mountaineering. Everest was indeed a far cry. Being doubtful of my caliber for such an important venture, I didn't reply to the IMF. I thought only of my next training course. In October 1982 I was given a vacancy on an advanced course. During this we learned more advanced climbing skills on rock, snow and ice and climbed Black Peak or Kala Nag (6,387 meters.). We were also given training in planning an expedition.

On this course, too, I got an 'A' grade and was recommended for participation in expeditions. My instructors were very encouraging and said that I had the makings of a good mountaineer. I should take every opportunity to improve my climbing skills. It was about this time that I received a reminder from the IMF about participating in the Everest screening camp. When my instructors learned about my having ignored the IMF's earlier letter and about the reminder, they said, "Don't you realize that you are throwing away a golden opportunity, Bachendri?" At their urging I therefore confirmed my acceptance.

After that I was a transformed person. If the IMF considered me a possible candidate for the Everest team, I could not let them down. I enthusiastically volunteered for all the domestic chores that involved climbing. To toughen myself, I would carry heavier and heavier loads of grass, fodder and firewood home. My choice of the daily routes changed. I would choose steeper and more difficult paths and deliberately went over boulders or climbed steep rock faces to acquire better balance and get over vertigo or fear of heights. All my activities were aimed at making me a really competent climber.

I attended the Gangotri screening camp in the latter half of 1982. My instructors were very pleased with my performance and during this training I climbed Gangotri I (6,672 meters) and Rudugaira (5,819 meters) and gained confidence in my climbing ability. Soon afterward I was informed that I was tipped for the final selection camp in September and October 1983.

I was happy with the manner in which my mountaineering career was shaping up but it did not solve my or my family's economic problems. Then, in February 1983, Brig. Gyan Singh, Director of the National Adventure Foundation (NAF), came to Uttarkashi to run an adventure course for teachers at the NIM and selected seven local, educated women, including me for scholarship.

I confided in this eminent but understanding senior mountaineer and told him that my parents were pressing me to get married to reduce the financial burden on the family. I asked him to find a way for those who were poor to earn a living, using our interest and skill in mountaineering.

Next morning Brig. Gyan Singh asked us to fill in the NAF's application forms to start the "Bhagirathi Seven Sisters Adventure Club." Explaining that this would be a unique organization of girls and women to help other girls find adventure, he promised that the scheme would take care of the monetary worries of trained girls and women. Our morale rose sky high and we got down to training in earnest.

Each of the "Seven Sisters" earned a good report. Brig. Gyan Singh said that our performance was much better than that of the men. By the end of our stay the Brigadier had become like a father to us and, at my suggestion, we began to address him as "Chhote Chacha."

When Chhote Chacha had left Uttarkashi on February 28, 1983, we were in tears. But he promised to return in three months to help us run our own adventure programs. Meanwhile, we were asked to take local children rock climbing. The prospect of running our own program was very exciting. In preparation I used to walk and jog from Nakuri to the rock climbing area in Tekhla, eighteen kilometers each way. This practice greatly helped in toughening me up for the climbing challenges which lay ahead.

The Brigadier arrived as promised on June 1. He brought twenty-five sets of camping and trekking equipment for us to run two adventure courses for girls. With the army's help he also arranged that a tent camp be put up at Tekhla.

The first group from Jamshedpur had thirteen girls. The second party from Meghalaya had fifteen lively Khasi girls from Shillong. The groups were made up to twenty for each course by taking local girls on scholarship. I was made director of the course and Vijaya-Pant deputy director. Jobs like quartermaster and medical assistant were allotted in turn to the other "Seven Sisters." We were paid an honorarium for our work on the courses.

The program was varied. There were three days of rock climbing followed by a day for river crossing, besides camping, learning the use of mountaineering ropes, cooking and safety in the wilderness. A forest ranger accompanied us and told us about the flora and wildlife of the region. Including two short and one long trek, we covered nearly 150 kilometers and climbed up and down a total of 2,500 to 3,000 meters.

Our highest camp during the long trek was at picturesque Dodital at nearly 3,000 meters. Here lush green deodars bordered a beautiful lake full of cold-water fish, including the lovely rainbow trout. We stayed here for three nights. We also went to the top of the ridge to Bakriya-Khal at nearly 4,000 meters. It was the first contact with snow for many of the girls and they were like playful kittens, rolling and sliding on the snowfield and tossing snowballs at one another. Before returning to Dodital they were given some elementary lessons in snow craft, including glissading.

I conducted the first course with Vijaya's help under the supervision of Chhote Chacha. He guided us but left us to work out the details. His most memorable contribution, however, were his talks on a variety of mountain and climbing topics, replete with fascinating anecdotes. Whenever Chhote Chacha shouted, "Girls, here is another story," all of us crowded eagerly round him. When I told him how impressed I was with his method of teaching, he modestly said, "I learnt it from Tenzing."

Using the excuse of catching up with his paper work, Chhote Chacha asked us to handle the second course entirely ourselves. I was rather nervous at first, but with responsibility came confidence and everything went off well. When the children told Chhote Chacha what fun they had on their treks with "Bachendri Didi" I experienced a great sense of satisfaction and achievement.

Towards the middle of July 1983, Brig. Gyan Singh took the well-known mountaineer Chandra Prabha Aitwal (Chandra Didi to me), Vijaya Pant and me to Delhi. By this time Chandra Didi had been elected chairperson and I vice chairperson of the "Bhagirathi Seven Sisters Adventure Club."

In the capital, Chhote Chacha had organized a television interview for us in the popular Ghar-Bahar programme. We were also interviewed by three national dailies. The writeups with our photographs appeared the following morning, and when we were shopping in Janpath, we were stopped by several young people who asked, "Didn't I see you on TV?" or "Are you the ladies whose pictures I saw in the newspaper?" Our small club, the Bhagirathi Seven Sisters Adventure Club, had already started making waves in the capital.

At the end of August 1983 I was invited to the first Himalayan Mountaineering and Tourism Meet in New Delhi. Over two hundred delegates came, including many international figures in the field of mountaineering. Though I was awed by the presence of so many celebrities, I was also greatly inspired. Actually, my encounters with the famous were confined to occasional returns of a smile when I physically bumped into one of them in the crowded convention hall of the Taj Palace hotel.

I could not however keep my eyes off two superstars: the legendary Sherpa Tenzing Norgay, who with Edmund Hillary was the first man to reach the top of Everest, and Japan's petite Junko Tabei, the first woman to have stepped on the highest pinnacle on earth.

I had admired Tenzing since I was a schoolgirl but now that I was so near him I didn't have the courage to introduce myself. Then the NIM doctor's wife, Sherry, asked me to join them for a group photograph and I found myself standing next to Tenzing himself. Though I wanted to talk to the Everest hero I was too tongue-tied and a second later Tenzing was whisked away by some fans.

Almost immediately after the Meet I joined the final selection camp for the "Everest '84" expedition held on Mana mountain, beyond Badrinath. Initially I ran a fever and had to stay back at the Base Camp, I was worried that if I didn't get well and complete the selection camp. I would not be considered for the Everest team. That would be the end of my cherished dream. Fortunately, I recovered quickly and completely and was able to catch up with the lost training schedule quite easily. During this camp the stress was on practice and not the peak. However, I was able to climb up to nearly 7,500 meters on Mana, the highest I'd been until then.

This camp was crucial for entry into the Everest team so everyone strove to do their best. All the others were experienced mountaineers. I was the only novice. However, I felt that I had acquitted myself well in technical climbing, physical effort and in getting acclimatized to heights. Though I could not say where I would stand in the final merit list, I was confident about my prowess as a climber.

When the camp was closed, the participants were required to ferry loads to the roadhead. The majority seemed full of strength and vitality and many rushed down with their loads. I moved carefully and kept a slow and steady pace. Major Prem Chand saw me and remarked, "That is the pace you will have to keep on Everest, Bachendri."

What could he mean? Could I dare hope I had made the grade? Ours was to be India's fourth expedition to Everest. The first two in 1960 and 1962 had been turned back by bad weather within 200 and 130 meters of the summit respectively. In the third, as many as nine climbers had scaled Everest.

Of the 170 or so people from all over the world who had climbed Everest only four had been women. But India's young women had shown their mettle on many mountains. Three had climbed the "Killer" Nanda Devi (7,816 meters) in 1981. Thus the main aim of this expedition was to see at least one, and if possible more, Indian women on the Everest summit.

I was on tenterhooks awaiting the announcement of the Everest team. My family shared my tension and my brother Bachan specially came home to be with me. My chances of inclusion in the team were a subject of daily discussion.

According to the evening ANR news bulletin on October 18, 1983, Col. D.K. Khullar had been selected to lead the Everest expedition and the team would be announced the following morning. I heard the news at Uttarkashi where I had been invited as a guest instructor on a girls' Basic Mountaineering Course.

I hardly slept that night. Getting up well before sunrise, I was at the newspaper vendor's several hours before the boy came with the packets of dailies. My heart in my mouth, I snatched a copy of the paper and opened it with trembling hands. My eyes raced impatiently across the list of the Everest team till finally they rested on the one name I was looking for: Bachendri Pal.

I ran straight to the sweetmeat shop and, after buying some *ladoos,* hopped into the first vehicle which was going towards my village. As I got out of the truck on the road below my village, I looked up and saw Bachan waiting for me on the terrace. He ran down and met me halfway. I had already shouted the good news to him. When we met he hugged me and danced with excitement. By then the entire family and many others had collected. Sweets were distributed. My mother shed tears of joy and my father kept looking at me with pride, stroking my head lovingly.

Six other women had been selected. All were strong climbers and experienced mountaineers. Compared to them, I was a novice. Besides Col. D.K. Khullar and Lieut. Col. Prem Chand, the team included eleven other men.

Brig. Gyan Singh had been confident that Chandra Didi and I would be chosen for the "Everest '84" team and had prepared a pre-Everest self-training program which we started as soon as the selection was announced. Briefly, the training entailed climbing nearly six hundred meters every day with a load of twelve to fifteen kilograms on our backs and jogging eight to ten kilometers.

To match the very hard physical work, we had to eat special protein-rich foods—plenty of milk, greens and of course, sugar. Our daily intake had to consist of 3, 500 to 4 ,000 calories.

People in Nakuri were amused to see me climb up from the bottom of the hill to the top of the ridge with a rucksack full of stones every morning. Someone remarked that I was perhaps trying to restore the height of the eroded hills. My father would join in the fun. "Bachendri has found no job to her liking after her big degrees," he would explain. "She is now preparing herself to be a construction labourer." He would chuckle and repeat this joke to anyone he met. My simple mother, on the other hand, shed worried tears to see her daughter lugging stones to the mountain top.

We reported to the IMF in New Delhi at the beginning of December 1983. For nearly five weeks, the seven female mountaineers were put through a gruelling training program. We spent hours in the gymnasium toughening up our abdominal, dorsal and other climbing muscles. There was also plenty of bending and stretching with rhythmic breathing exercises. Prolonged swimming and jogging helped build up our stamina and improved lung functioning for the maximum use of oxygen under physiological stress.

Then at the height of winter in January 1984, Lieut. Col. Prem Chand, an uncompromising trainer, took us women to Gulmarg and for a month he made us climb up and down steep slopes covered with deep snow.

Brig. Gyan Singh was aware of my desire for economic independence so that I could pursue my love for mountaineering. Immediately after the "Seven Sisters" programs in June 1983, he contacted the Tata Iron and Steel Company (TISCO) in Jamshedpur and persuaded them to employ me for the promotion of adventure. My inclusion in the Everest team helped and I was made Sports Assistant. I was on the company's payroll thereafter and also received a substantial daily allowance for my participation in the Everest expedition.

I could now concentrate on the expedition and on reaching the top.

III

The Everest expedition left Delhi for Kathmandu by plane on March 7. A strong advance party had left much earlier to open the route through the treacherous icefall before we reached the base camp.

After a few days in Kathmandu, we moved to Ziri, four to five hours drive away. Then we had a leisurely eight-day trek to Namche Bazar. Going against the grain of the mountains, we climbed up and down nearly a thousand meters every day, which toughened us up and helped us acclimatize. On the way we met the friendly, cheerful people of the region, paricularly the Sherpas.

Namche Bazar is the most important township in Sherpa-land. Most of our Sherpas came from here and the neighboring villages. It was at Namche Bazar that I had my first view of Everest, popularly called Sagarmatha by the Nepalese.

Gazing at Everest I could see an enormous snow plume, a kind of banner which seemed to fly out of its summit. I was told that this phenomenon was due to the wind blowing at 150 kilometers per hour or more near the peak's upper reaches and driving the powder snow off the mountain. The snow plume could be ten kilometers or more long. Anyone attempting the peak had to face these storms on the southeast ridge, particularly in bad weather. This was to haunt me; yet I was strangely fascinated by Everest and drawn to its tough challenge.

We hill people have always worshipped the mountains. My overpowering emotion at this awe-inspiring spectacle was, therefore, devotional. I folded my hands and bowed my head to Sagarmatha.

After a day here we reached the famous Thyangboche monastery where the incarnate Lama blessed us and prayed for our success and safe return. Thyangboche was not only beautiful but its height, over 4,000 meters, was suitable for acclimatization training. We halted here for two days before moving to our main acclimatization training camp at Pheriche.

When we reached Pheriche on March 26, we got the shocking news of a Sherpa porter having been killed in an avalanche. An enormous snowslide had swept down from Lhola, a depression on the steep ridge to the left of the expedition's route to the Khumbu icefall. Of a ferry party of sixteen Sherpa porters, one had died and four had been injured.

Noticing the gloom the news had cast on members of the expedition, our leader, Col. Khullar, explained that on an expedition of the magnitude of Everest, danger, and sometimes death, had to be taken in one's stride. "We must not be unduly disturbed or deterred by one single mishap," he said.

The deputy leader, Prem Chand, who was leading the advance party, returned to Pheriche on March 26. He briefed us on the nature of our first major hurdle, the Khumbu Icefall. He said that his party had opened the route to Camp I (6,900 meters) just above the lip of the Icefall, and that all major obstacles had been taken care of by bridging, fixed ropes and route-making with flags. But he reminded us that the glacier was a river of ice and the icefall portion was on the move. The erratic shifting of the ice base might undo all the work done, and we might have to reopen the route. My curiosity about these hazards was stronger than my fears but I concealed my feelings from the others.

Before we reached the base camp, we learned of another death. A kitchen attendant had died as a result of acclimatization failure. We were certainly not starting on a promising note.

We halted a night at Gorakhshep, from where I went for a small acclimatization climb to Kala Pathar. From there I had a clear view of Everest, the South Col, Lhotse and the Icefall. It was an awe-inspiring sight. My feeling on viewing Sagarmatha a second time was again devotional. I folded my hands involuntarily and bowed my head.

I had seen the Everest summit twice earlier but from a distance. On reaching the base camp the next day I saw the rest of the Everest massif and its satellites. I stood transfixed, gaping at the much-ruffled solid river of ice enclosed by the towering trio: Everest, Lhotse and Nuptse. We could see that the Khumbu Glacier dove nearly six hundred meters in less than a kilometer, flowing between the near vertical slopes of the western shoulder of Everest to our left and the near shoulder of Nuptse to our right. It was the sharp drop in altitude that caused the Icefall. Its backdrop was the fort-like turreted top of Lhotse, the fourth highest mountain in the world. Facing the strong westerlies, Lhotse could hold no snow near the top. Its rocky crown was therefore grayish black in color.

The Icefall itself was a chaotic cascade of ice blocks and leaning ice towers. We were told that the movement of the glacier caused frequent ice-quakes which triggered the instant toppling of huge ice slabs and other features often balanced precariously at dangerous angles. The thought of a fissure opening up on a harmless surface and developing into a gaping deep crevasse was very frightening. And even more terrifying was the knowledge that throughout our stay, the Icefall would be the daily trudging ground of about a dozen climbers and ferry porters.

Camp I (6,000 meters) was just above the icefall. A couple of hours of climbing steadily nearly five hundred meters over a crevasse-ridden high valley popularly called the Western Cwm (pronounced coom), brought one to Camp II, which was the advance base. Camp III (7,200 meters) was on the exposed Lhotse face and Camp IV at the South Col (7,900 meters) was the last firm base on a windy, cold, inhospitable saddle between Everest and Lhotse. The one-tent summit camp would have to be established at about 8,500 meters on the dangerous southeast ridge leading to the summit.

I was desperately keen to get near the Icefall. The same evening, along with some others, I went up to the point where the Icefall started. This was where the climbers strapped on their crampons to avoid slipping on the ice or hard frozen snow.

The following day most of the newcomers ferried loads to a point halfway up the Icefall. Dr. Minoo Mehta showed us the makeshift bridges with aluminum ladders, logs and ropes, the fixed ropes on ice walls and steep traverses, as well as other evidence of our advance party's engineering handiwork.

The third day was earmarked for a practice climb by ferrying a load up the Icefall to Camp I. Rita Gombu and I, climbing together, had a walkie-talkie and reported our step-by-step progress to the base camp. Col. Khullar was very happy when we announced our arrival, for we were the only two to have reached Camp I.

After we had been told about the topography of the area, I noticed that the Bulgarian expedition had their base camp next to ours. They were climbing by the difficult Western Ridge route and were to return from the summit along our route. We learned later that five Bulgarians reached the summit but paid a very heavy price. Their first summiter, Christo Prodanov, accomplished a solo oxygenless ascent, but perished somewhere quite high up on his descent.

Opening the route and stocking high camps was a slow, exacting operation. Working in small groups and sometimes in pairs, we fixed the route with ropes, and made foot holds and hand holds. Camps II and III were established in good time. Ang Dorjee, Lopsang and Magan Bissa finally reached the South Col and set up Camp IV at 7,900 meters on April 29. This was satisfactory progress.

When I was at the base camp in April, Tenzing visited us with his youngest daughter Deki and made a point of speaking to every expedition member and every Sherpa porter. When it was my turn, I introduced myself saying that I was an absolute beginner and that Everest was my first expedition. Tenzing laughed and told me that Everest was also his first expedition, but explained that he had to go seven times to Everest before he reached its summit. Then, putting his arm round my shoulder he said, "You look a strong mountain girl. You should reach the summit in your first attempt!" These words were to linger with me.

By May 1 the stage was set to launch the ascent plan. Out of twenty loads of oxygen and equipment planned for the South Col, twelve had already reached it. A large ferry carrying the required loads was expected to accompany the first summit party.

Col. Khullar had decided on a major push by three summit teams, grouped for the climb to the Col in two parties which were to start from the base camp on May 5 and 6. The first party, comprised of Prem Chand, Rita, Phu Dorjee, Chandra Prabha and Sirdar Ang Dorjee, reached the South Col on May 7. On May 8 Prem Chand, Rita and Ang Dorjee were to form the first summit team. They would make the attempt to get to the summit and return to the South Col in the evening. The same day, May 8, the second summit team made up of Phu Dorgee, Chandra Prabha and eight Sherpas was to establish the Summit Camp at approximately 8,500 meters. They were to stay the night there and attempt the peak the next morning and return to the South Col by the evening. The third summit team composed of ND Sherpa, Lopsang Tshering, Magan Bissa and I was to reach the South Col on May 8 and attempt the peak on the 9th. The success of this ambitious plan depended on a sufficient number of Sherpas being available to stock the South Col and summit camps.

But this was not to be. Against eight planned, only two Sherpas could go up with Phu Dorjee and Chandra Prabha. Prem Chand, therefore, decided on only one attempt by his party and gave his place to Phu Dorjee for the summit attempt. Chandra Prabha returned with him to the South Col. Phu Dorjee joined Rita and Ang Dorjee to spend the night at the Summit Camp.

The three started from the Summit Camp at 7 a.m. on May 9. After only an hour's climb Ang Dorjee found that his feet were becoming very cold. Fearing frost bite, he decided to turn back. Rita, who was with him, was of two minds. Phu Dorjee, about twenty meters ahead, waited to see if she wanted to go up with him. Unsure of the weather—an eighty-kilometer-per-hour wind blew and there was a thin, cloudy haze—Rita, too, decided to return.

Phu Dorjee's oxygen ran out when he was barely two hundred meters short of his goal. But he possessed extraordinary stamina and determination. Dumping the equipment, he pressed on and was on the summit at 12:30 p.m. This feat gave the expedition the peak and India its first oxygenless solo climb of Everest.

Our party made steady progress from Camp III to South Col on May 8. I was climbing without oxygen because of a shortage of the gas. When I was still more than an hour from the South Col, I found it heavy going and slow, particularly because it was the steepest portion of the climb and a very cold wind had stirred up. Just then, I saw someone coming down along the Geneva Spur. It was ND Sherpa who had come down with an oxygen cylinder for me. I was very touched by this thoughtful gesture. With the oxygen, the climb was quite easy.

Meanwhile, the first Bulgarian pair who had climbed the mountain by the west ridge route were more than twenty-four hours late in completing the traverse by the South Col route. On his return from the summit, Phu Dorjee helped the exhausted summit pair. Later our leader cancelled our summit team's attempt on the 9th to divert ND and Lopsang to the rescue mission. The rest of us therefore returned to Camp II on May 9.

On the Buddha Purnima of May 15–16, 1984, I was at Camp III in a colorful nylon tent camp perched on the ice-encrusted steep slope of Lhotse. There were ten others in the camp. Lopsang Tshering shared my tent. ND Sherpa and eight tough high altitude Sherpa porters were in other tents. I was sleeping soundly when around 12:30 a.m. I was shaken awake by a hard object hitting me on the back of my head and simultaneously by a loud explosion. Then I felt a cold, extremely heavy mass creeping over my body and crushing me. I could hardly breathe.

What had happened? A tall serac on the Lhotse glacier directly above our camp had cracked, crashed down and developed into a massive avalanche. This enormous mass of ice blocks, crushed ice and frozen snow thundering down the near vertical slope at the speed of an express train devastated our camp, which was directly in its path. Practically everyone was hurt. It was a miracle no one was killed.

Lopsang was able to tear his way out of our tent with his knife and immediately began frantically to try and rescue me. Delay would have meant sure death. Heaving and pushing away the large ice slabs, he dug out the hardened snow around me and succeeded in pulling me out of the ice grave.

No tent had been left standing except the kitchen shelter. Lopsang and I clambered there and found ND talking on the walkie-talkie with the leader at Camp II. ND said he had broken some ribs. One Sherpa had fractured his leg and there were quite a few other injuries. Groans of pain and cries for help were audible from all sides. But ND assured the leader at Camp II that all was not lost. The expedition still had a lot of fight in it.

By now most of us had gathered in or near the kitchen tent. From my first aid pouch, I gave everyone painkiller tablets and prepared hot drinks. Being useful helped disperse the cloud of gloom and depression that enveloped me.

The leader promised to send rescue parties without delay. KI, Jai and Bissa, hearing the conversation on their walkie-talkie at Camp I, set off immediately while it was still night. From Camp II a rescue team of four and the Camp II cook moved into action.

Well before dawn we began to dig out our equipment. I was terribly worried about the image of Goddess Durga which I had in my rucksack. Every morning and evening I took it out and drew inspiration and strength from it. So my first act on finding my rucksack was to thrust my hand into the side pocket. To my relief my fingers encountered the ice cold metallic image. I held the holy image tightly and, placing it on my forehead, felt that I had everything I wanted. I had Shakti in my arms. The Shakti which had saved my life a few hours earlier and the Shakti which, I was now sure, would lead me onwards and upwards. The experience of the night had drained all fear out of me.

The rescue teams arrived soon after and by 8 a.m. on May 16 we were nearly all at Camp II. The Sherpa with the fractured leg was brought down on an improvised stretcher. In our leader Khullar's words, "It was a remarkable feat of high altitude rescue work."

The bump at the back of my head had now begun to throb. I felt uncomfortable but kept it to myself, occasionally pressing the bump with my palm. All nine male members had to be sent to the Base Camp because of injuries or shattered nerves. Then Col. Khullar turned to me and asked if I was frightened.

"Yes."

"Would you also like to go down?"

"No," I replied without hesitation.

KI Kumar, Jai Bahuguna, Magan Bissa and Dr. Minoo Mehta were to form the next summit party. I was given the privilege of providing the crucial female element. Lhatoo, Pulzor and all available high altitude Sherpas were to be in the support role. Resources permitting, the support party would make their attempt after the first summit party. There was to be no woman in the second party.

To conserve oxygen for the final ascent, all the male members had to do without oxygen up to the South Col. However, when Bissa's feet became numb after he had climbed halfway, he was advised to switch on his oxygen. I was told to conserve my energy for the next day's final climb by inhaling oxygen at about two liters per minute. My noticeable fitness on reaching the South Col and on the day of the ascent proved that this decision was a wise one.

As soon as I reached the South Col Camp, I began to prepare for the final climb the next day. I collected food, cooking gas and some oxygen cylinders. When Bissa arrived at 1:30 p.m. he found me heating water for tea. KI, Jai and Minoo were still far behind. I was concerned because I had to climb to the summit with them the next day. They were slow because they were carrying heavy loads and climbing without oxygen.

Late in the afternoon I decided to go down to help my teammates and filling a thermos flask with juice and another with hot tea, I stepped out into the icy wind.

I met Minoo just as I was leaving the camp area. KI and Jai were still some way behind. I saw Jai just below the top of the Geneva

Spur. He accepted the drinks gratefully but tried to dissuade me from going further. But I had to meet KI too. After climbing down a little further, I saw KI. He was flabbergasted when he saw me. "Why did you take such a risk, Bachendri?" he shouted. I told him firmly that I was a climber like the others. That was why I was on the expedition. I was physically fit so why should I not help my team mates? KI smiled and drank thirstily but refused to let me carry part of his kit.

A little later Lhatoo and Bissa came down from the South Col Camp to meet us and we returned to such safety and comfort as the South Col, deservedly known as the "most inhospitable place on earth," could offer.

I got up at four o'clock in the morning, melted snow and brewed tea. After a light breakfast of a few biscuits and half a slab of chocolate I left my tent at around 5:30 a.m. Ang Dorjee was standing outside. No one else was about.

Ang Dorjee was going to climb without oxygen. But because of this his feet would get very cold. He thus wanted to avoid long exposure at heights and a night at the Summit Camp. He had therefore to either get to the peak and back to the South Col the same day or abandon the attempt.

He was keen to start immediately and asked if I would like to go with him. Going to the top from the South Col and back in a day would be strenuous and tough and there was the risk of Ang Dorjee turning back if his feet got too cold. I, however, had full confidence in Ang Dorjee as well as in my stamina and climbing capability. Besides, no one else was ready to move at that time.

At 6:20 when Ang Dorjee and I stepped out from the South Col, it was a perfect day. There was a gentle breeze but the cold was intense. I was, however, warm in my well-insulated climbing gear. We climbed unroped. Ang Dorjee set a steady pace but I had no difficulty keeping up with him.

The steep frozen slopes were as hard and brittle as sheets of glass. I had to kick really hard to get the front teeth of my crampons to bite into the frozen surface. I took every step very deliberately on the dangerous stretches.

In less than two hours we reached the Summit Camp. Ang Dorjee looked back and asked if I was tired. I replied, "No," to his surprise and delight. He told me that the earlier summit party had taken four hours to reach the Summit Camp and added that if we could keep our present pace, we would be on the summit by 1 p.m.

Lhatoo was following us and caught up with us when we rested below the South Summit. After drinking some tea we moved on. Lhatoo had brought a nylon rope so Ang Dorjee and I roped up while Lhatoo walked in the middle, holding the rope with one hand, more for balance than security.

Lhatoo noticed that I had been climbing with oxygen at about two and a half liters per minute against the normal four for these heights. After he increased the oxygen flow on my regulator I found even the steeper stretches comparatively easy.

Beyond the South Summit the breeze increased. At that height the eddies of strong winds whipped up the powder snow, reducing visibility to nothing. On many occasions, I had to get into a crouching position with my back to the onslaught of the icy wind saturated with fine particles of bone dry powder snow.

It was terrifying to stand erect on a knife-edge ridge with a sheer drop on either side. I had to dig in deep and secure myself by attaching my waist strap to the ice axe head. There was some tricky climbing between the South Summit and what is popularly known as Hillary's Step. Ang Dorjee and Lhatoo were already over it, but I was still negotiating its vertical face when Ang Dorjee gesticulated towards the top. I was thrilled. The goal was near. With renewed vigor I was on top of the step in seconds. The sun had made the snow soft and climbing was easier here than it had been earlier.

We trudged in the heavy powder snow for some time. Then the gradient started easing off noticeably. A few steps later I saw that after only a couple of meters there was no upward climb. The slope plunged steeply down.

My heart stood still. It dawned on me that success was within reach. And at 1:07 p.m. on May 23, 1984, I stood on top of Everest, the first Indian woman to have done so.

There was hardly enough room for two to stand side by side on top of the Everest cone. Thousands of meters of near vertical drop on all sides made safety our foremost consideration and we first anchored ourselves securely by digging our ice axes into the snow. That done, I sank to my knees, and putting my forehead on the snow kissed Sagarmatha's crown. Without getting up, I took out the image of Durga Ma and my *Hanuman Chalisa* from my rucksack. I wrapped these in a red cloth which I had brought and, after saying a short prayer, buried them in the snow. At this moment of joy my thoughts went to my father and mother.

As I rose, I folded my hands and bowed in respect to Ang Dorjee, my rope-leader, who had encouraged and led me to my goal. I also congratulated him for his second ascent of Everest without oxygen. He embraced me and whispered in my ear, "You climb good— very happy, Didi."

A little later Sonam Pulzor arrived and began taking photographs.

By then Lhatoo had given the news of the "four atop Everest" to our leader. The walkie-talkie was then passed on to me.

Col. Khullar was delighted with our success. After congratulating me he said, "I would also like to congratulate your parents for your unique achievement." He added that the country was proud of me and that I would return to a world which would be quite different from the one I had left behind.

We summiters embraced and thumped one another's backs. Nepalese, Indian and, for my sake, the NAF "Seven Sisters" and TISCO flags were hoisted and photographed. We spent forty-three minutes on the summit. The towering giants Lhotse, Nuptse and Makalu were dwarfed by our mountain. I collected a few samples of stone from a bare patch near the peak.

We started our downhill journey at 1:55 p.m. I knew I would have to be especially careful during the return trip, for more accidents occur while descending than when climbing up. But I was unaware of one fundamental hazard. I took off my snow goggles on the snowless and dark rocky patches assuming that snowblindness was only caused by the glare of the sun's rays reflected from the snow. Besides, the atmosphere was hazy, I reasoned. But snowblindness is due to strong ultraviolet rays at high altitudes and has nothing to do with the snow or the glare.

I paid a heavy price for my ignorance. Both my eyes were affected and I suffered intense pain. On our return to the camp I had to take a sleeping pill, the only one I took during my stay on Everest.

Though Ang Dorjee moved fast, I found I was reasonably sure-footed in downhill climbing, even at the veteran Sherpa's pace. When we were still some distance from the South Col, to my astonishment, I saw Magan Bissa coming up. It was dangerous to be on the exposed southeast ridge in the evening when the temperature dropped sharply, besides the usual dangers of height and environment. Bissa's rucksack was filled with oxygen cylinders and thermos flasks. He congratulated us and gave us some hot drinks and juice.

Then he went up to help Lhatoo and Pulzor and gave them hot drinks. Pulzor had no oxygen mask so Bissa gave him his own. Lhatoo reached the South Col at 6 p.m. while Bissa brought Pulzor to safety on his rope at 7 p.m.

Ang Dorjee and I had arrived at the South Col at 5 p.m. Everyone complimented us for doing the South Col - Summit - South Col trip in only ten hours and forty minutes, including the halt at the top.

As I was entering my tent I overheard Major KI Kumar talking to Col. Khullar on the wireless. "Believe it or not, Sir," he said excitedly, "Bachendri is already back in just three hours. And she looks as fresh as she was when she started climbing up this morning."

IV

The months following my return from Everest were bewildering. But the first week in Delhi was downright nerve-wracking. I had a packed eighteen-hour or longer daily schedule. I was presented to VIPs and there were press conferences, speeches, addresses and interviews.

I received the IMF's coveted gold medal for excellence in mountaineering and numerous honors and accolades which I cannot even remember. The Padma Shri and prestigious Arjuna Award were announced. The functions and fuss were undeniably gratifying to the ego but were extremely exacting on the nerves and body. I would have given anything for twenty-four hours of uninterrupted sleep.

I would not say that I didn't enjoy being the focus of attention and praise but my greatest desire was to be with my parents and sisters and brothers and meet the friends I had in my village, Nakuri.

I set off from Delhi on a sultry June day and arrived at Rishikesh after an eight-hour drive. As the car climbed up the hill road, it began to pour. But despite lashing rain, men, women and children huddled by the wayside villages to welcome their daughter who had, according to them, brought glory to Garhwal, and to Bharat. They had also hastily put up welcome arches. I was running far behind schedule as I halted to receive their greetings and by the time I reached the district border a large crowd had been waiting for several hours to greet me. At 9 p.m. the motorcade reached my village. Despite the rain, the entire village seemed to have come out to welcome me. Beating drums, blowing conches and wind instruments and chanting mantras, talking and shouting they showered me with affection, each one wishing to garland me.

As I pushed my way through the jostling crowd, my eyes searched for two faces. Suddenly I saw them. My father and mother were quietly standing outside a thatch hut. They looked utterly overwhelmed.

I ran to my mother and fell in her arms. We held each other and cried and cried. I looked over my mother's shoulder and saw the blurred figure of my father also crying and looking at me disbelievingly.

On July 1, I presented TISCO's Chairman, Mr. Mody, the TISCO flag which I had hoisted on the summit of Everest. Mr. Mody announced my promotion to Manager of Adventure Programs and said I was to head the Tata Youth Adventure Centre and be solely in charge of all adventure activities in Jamshedpur. In fact, Mr. Mody's encouragement and help for adventure and sports has made it possible for many like myself to pursue their field of interest and excel in it.

It is given to very few to have their dreams come true. I have not only got everything I wanted but have been given far more than I could have wished for. Climbing was in my blood. In the three years before Everest, I had done more climbing than almost anyone I know. In 1986 I climbed Mont Blanc, the highest mountain in Europe, and have also climbed in four alpine countries.

But I also love to be with children. Now I am paid handsomely to teach young people adventure skills—camping, trekking, rock climbing, river crossing, exposing them to the wilderness. I give particular attention to girls in my programs, for I feel that in India we neglect them and discourage them from outdoor pursuits. The love of adventure and living dangerously is as necessary for girls as it is for boys, for it makes for courage, boldness and initiative.

I have met many important people. The two who have inspired me most, however, are Indira Gandhi and Sherpa Tenzing Norgay. When I met Mrs. Gandhi after Everest, she said, "We want hundreds of Bachendris in the country," and urged me to reach out to rural girls.

I met Tenzing the last time in December 1985. He told me that Bachendri no longer belonged to herself. Now everybody had a claim on my attention, my time and on my smiles. He pointed out that climbing Everest and becoming famous had its rewards, but it also had its responsibilities.

Climbing Everest has fulfilled my deepest aspirations and given me everything that I have. I can ask for no more.

PASSPORT TO INSANITY

Louise Shepherd

▲ ▲ ▲

THE STORY BEHIND the first free ascent of Passport to Insanity is one of the great sagas of Australian rock climbing. It is a story of cunning and conspiracy, of epic attempts and retreats, of terror, perseverance, and, for a mere handful, success. Many attempted the climb, but only four people made it to the top, and of those four, only one, a woman from Adelaide, climbed the route completely free.

To understand the fascination this route commands within the climbing community, one must look at some of the wildest country in Victoria's Grampians National Park. The remote southwestern arm of the Grampians, the Victoria Range, is a fifty-kilometer-long, jagged escarpment visible from the Henty Highway. For much of its length it is characterized by high rocky ridges rising out of dense eucalyptus forest. Midway, the ridge abruptly rises to form a prominent blocky monolith, descriptively named the Fortress, accessible only by the negotiation of a treacherously steep, dirt vehicular track, and almost nonexistent foot tracks.

For years, the area was visited only by the most enthusiastic bushwalkers, until in 1971, the notorious Gledhill twins stumbled over it during a rock climbing reconnaissance. They could scarcely believe their eyes. While most of the Fortress is a nondescript massif, the western extremity had split away to create a bold and independent pinnacle over one-hundred meters high, and separated from the parent rock by a giant slot. Buffeted by winds howling up the western slopes over the ranges, leveled by storms and rain, the pinnacle yet retained an enigmatic symmetry. Steep-sided and undercut, it looked impregnable, its summit virginal. It had one weakness as arresting as the pillar itself: a crack which cleanly bisected the lower half of the pinnacle, until, at half-height, it shot straight out through a nine meter ceiling of rock, and then into flake systems leading to the summit.

It was pronounced the best line in Australia. To climb it first would be the biggest coup in years. The Gledhills, more than anyone, were well aware of the implications of its discovery.

"Those were the days," Keith Lockwood was to write later, "of intrigue, secret cliffs and delightfully far-fetched hoaxes."

The Gledhills soon returned with Ian Ross, whom they swore to secrecy and privately hoped would lead them to glory. The crack was fifteen centimeters wide for the first forty meters, the most awkward size for jamming. Ross struggled up a few meters before plummeting on to the alloy tubes he had used for protection. Enthusiasm for the ascent suddenly evaporated, and the party retreated, although bravely vowing to return.

Conspiracy, however, breeds suspicion. Lockwood had his curiousity roused by whispers and conversations chopped off mid-sentence, so he made a solo mid-week excursion to the Fortress. Chancing upon the towering crack-line, his first impulse was to sit down securely and stare, but then he was gripped by a terrifying and compulsive desire to climb the crack and reach the summit.

Lockwood went home but could not rest. He returned at the first opportunity with a partner, Joan Shrameck. Their attempt was aborted even before the rock was in sight. Torrential rain converted the dirt track to a gutter: the car became bogged in the drainage channel, and the trip was spent digging it out.

This heralded a spate of similarly doomed episodes. Nothing, if not persistent, Lockwood next convinced Ed Neve to join him on another attempt. This time, Neve's car had engine failure. The resultant rescue bill stung the impoverished pair even more than the twenty-five kilometer walk-out in rain.

Meanwhile, rumors of the elusive line inevitably reached the ears of entrepreneurial climber Chris Baxter. He and Chris Dewhirst embarked on a furtive foray to the infamous pillar. The climax of the trip was Dewhirst's van hitting a kangaroo and smashing the radiator. Yet another team became lost on the approach march, and spent the whole day fruitlessly scrub-bashing in the wrong direction.

Then, inexplicably, the attempts stopped. Nobody went near the place for years. The Fortress remained aloof, unmolested, intact.

"On a Friday night some years later," wrote Lockwood, "I was showing Joe Friend some photos before driving up to Buffalo. Up came one of the pinnacle and the VW changed direction. No matter that Joe's gear was in another car bound for Buffalo." The two made a courageous attempt despite the prevailing rain. They became lost on the approach, stumbled through dripping scrub and finally arrived at the pinnacle at midday.

Lockwood magnanimously offered the lead to Friend, and then settled into his sleeping bag while Friend headed into the swirling cloud. Passing all previous high points, Friend's progress was punctuated with increasingly hysterical expletives. The crack was interminable. Loose flakes snapped off under body pressure, creating rivulets of sand, chockstones teetered precariously on small points but were slung for protection anyway. During a burst of particularly frantic scrabbling from above, Lockwood was startled to hear a frightened yelp from Friend: "Quick mate, send up my passport— I've just crossed the border to insanity!"

Friend struggled onto a horizontal slot where he belayed up Lockwood. Daylight was dwindling, and an argument ensued about whether to rappel off or bivouac in the slot. The slot was less than one meter high and its floor was littered with fragmented blocks of crumbling sandstone. Lockwood voted to go down. Friend voted to bivy. He even offered to split his chocolate bar with Lockwood. To resolve their differences, Friend produced a coin. "The Hong Kong coin came up heads three times," went Lockwood's account, "which is pretty hard to argue against."

The next morning, Lockwood pushed on to the end of the offwidth, eight meters below the ceiling. From his new stance, it seemed to spear out endlessly above a terrifying void. Their resolve weakened. They were stiff, hungry and freaked out. Retreat was unanimous. They fixed a nut and rappelled off.

A few months later, they made another attempt, but again the roof and bad weather repelled them.

In October 1976 they returned for the third time. Once again, they grunted up the offwidth crack to a horribly cramped belay right under the monster roof. The roof was Lockwood's lead, and it was one of the most demanding leads he had ever done. The crack was almost parallel-sided, therefore hard to aid on nuts, which work best in V-shaped slots. Lockwood spent hours wriggling Hexentrics into the crack, breaking out into a fearful sweat as he weighted each placement. Miraculously, nothing pulled out, and Lockwood arrived at the belay ledge a gibbering wreck, but in one piece.

Fortunately, the last two pitches were not difficult. Once on top, the trauma and fear of the ascent, and each epic attempt and retreat before it, was momentarily forgotten in mutual exultation.

Notwithstanding its checkered history, the route was indelibly written into the annals of Victorian rockclimbing. Certainly no other route had attracted such a gammut of bizarre, ill-fated expeditions. They named it Passport to Insanity.

One weekend at Mt. Arapiles in 1983, Glenn Tempest was expounding on his latest attempt to free the roof-crack of Passport to Insanity. Hand size, he announced, was the crucial factor. Everyone present immediately compared and inspected each other's hand profiles. Malcolm Matheson, who had also been in on the attempt, proudly held his stubby sausage-like fingers aloft and declared he could only get jams up to his knuckles. It was Nyrie Dodd who stimulated most speculation when she displayed her hands, which were thin enough to jam up to the wrist in a number-two-Friend-sized crack. Tempest stated authoritatively, "You'll cruise it," as if Nyrie's ascent was already a *fait accompli*. Thus the seed of Nyrie's obsession to free Passport was sown; an obsession which was to span three years, motivated her to build a special contraption to train on for crack-climbing, and spend a total of six days attempting the roof.

Nyrie was then a twenty-year-old medical student, in her third year at the University of Adelaide. She had begun rock climbing the year before, and, endowed with natural aptitude and bubbling self-confidence, had rocketed up through the grades. She had astonished some of the old guard of the Climbing Club of South Australia by her sheer audacity in trying to lead routes right at her limit, frequently with success. Pixie, keen academic, and hyperactive kid rolled into one, Nyrie sped through life, giggling in high pitch, and infecting all those around her with irrepressible *joie de vivre*.

She plied Tempest with questions about Passport, and he was voluble about the unrelenting horror. The hardware needed to protect the crack was phenomenal: ten tubes, a specially manufactured giant-sized Friend (a mechanical camming device), and a standard rack of Friends, wires and carabiners. Nyrie began to muster the essentials for the onslaught. The big Friend was borrowed from another ex-Passport hopeful. Tubes and extra number-two Friends for the roof (recently-invented Friends protected a climb much better than Lockwood's old-fashioned Hexentrics) were scrounged from other climbers. As for belayers, I was an obvious choice, being ideologically sound. The only snag was that my relative poverty meant that, like Nyrie, I had no transport. Kim Carrigan, however, possessed the necessary vehicle and was also curious to try Australia's "last great problem."

It was a fine February day in 1984 when we arrived at the beginning of the walking track to the Fortress. After a prolonged tussle with the scrub, the cliff suddenly towered above the vegetation and there, perched on the extremity, was the pinnacle with the Passport ceiling in unmistakable profile.

Like Lockwood a decade earlier, we stared open-mouthed at the pillar and the monumental crack-line. I shuddered at the sight of the offwidth, for I had rashly promised to lead it. I was saved from humiliation by the giant Friend. By pushing it ahead of me all the way up the offwidth crack, I practically top-roped the entire pitch. Thank heavens for technology!

By the time I had struggled up the first pitch, it was mid-afternoon. The belay was still in the shade and in such an exposed position that it caught every puff of wind. From my perch the roof looked absolutely preposterous. The lip was actually lower than the back of the roof, which meant that the climber's feet would be higher than her head! I was secretly relieved that it was Nyrie's lead.

Guarding the roof-crack was a strenuous layback and fingertip traverse. Hanging off the traverse, Nyrie's feet barely touched the overhanging wall below, but she managed to plug in a Friend and flop on to it. After a rest, she headed up on the rope for another try. Her hands went into the crack up to her wrists, although her boots only went in half-way, and she could only manage a few moves at a time before resting on the next Friend.

I lowered her down, only to discover that she was too far out in space to reach the belay. Luckily Kim managed to reach her feet and haul her back on to our stance. Kim fared about as well as Nyrie on the roof. Disadvantaged with thicker hands, but advantaged with greater strength, Kim was able to do a few moves free before resting on the rope. But he had no joy stuffing his hands into tight jams and twisting them ferociously to make them stick. We had food and camping gear in the car in case we decided to stay another day, but this was now out of the question.

That year Nyrie took time off from her studies and went on a climbing trip to Europe, but on returning to Australia she had to plunge straight back into another term of medicine. By the summer she had lost some of her European edge, but in spite of that she was still eager to try Passport again so we made plans for another attempt. Nyrie did marginally better than the year before, although she was still a long way from a completely free ascent. She did make an important discovery, however. By removing her boots, she was able to get solid foot-jams up to the ankles.

In 1985 her studies were demanding, and after recovering from severe elbow tendon injuries and a wrongly-diagnosed viral infection, she built a simulated roof-crack on her verandah, on which she trained several days a week, jamming back and forth with a rack of number-two Friends and dangling from her harness.

Nyrie could barely wait to get out on to the rocks again. Steve Monks, a British climber, accepted our invitation to join the expedition to the Fortress.

Back at the pinnacle I was once more on the familiar belay below the roof. Nyrie seconded me, and then carefully taped up both hands and feet to minimize skin abrasion from the roof. Just as she was starting, Steve appeared on rappel at the lip of the roof, armed with his camera. He had found a way to solo up (at grade seventeen!) the back of the pinnacle, up through an unexplored maze of deep chimneys and tottering blocks. He became quite excited when he saw the roof at close quarters. Meanwhile, Nyrie, as on previous attempts, was having trouble moving from the overhanging finger-traverse into the roof-crack. The first few hand-jams were tight, even for her, and it was desperate changing mode from slightly overhung to worse than horizontal! She rested on the rope and removed her boots. Barefoot, she continued across the roof. She looked much stronger than in previous years. Perhaps this time she could do it.

In the late afternoon, Nyrie and I rappelled off, while Steve jumared back to the top of the pinnacle and repositioned his rappel rope over a new route between Passport and the dividing chasm. He spent most of the walk back to the car musing on how many bolts his climb would need, before deciding it could be done British-style, without any.

The following day Nyrie and I prusiked our rope and reached the belay under the roof. On this attempt, she managed for the first time to get established in the roof without any falls. She kept going, slowly getting closer to the lip. There she put in her last number-two Friend, tried to push on, but pumped out and snatched the Friend instead. It was by far her best effort, and Steve and I cheered. Suddenly, success seemed to be within her grasp.

We awoke the next morning to the sound of rain drizzling on the tent fly. The Southern Grampians weather patterns are infamous. In the end, we threw our wet gear into the car for a soggy drive home.

We spent three fine days climbing at Mt. Arapiles before the weather settled in the south and we could return to the Fortress. Nyrie was inspired, and hurried up the track. I nominated myself as photographer this time, leaving Steve to belay Nyrie. They Jumared up the rope which had been fixed previously, while I reclined on top of a large, pointy boulder.

I was just dozing off when I heard an encouraging shout from Steve. Nyrie was at the lip of the roof and had got there without a fall! She hung from hand- and foot-jams for a second, psyching up for the crux. She looked a bit like a mythical nymph, naked but for pink lycra tights and harness. I snatched up my camera—too late! She had pulled over the lip and was cruising up the easy wall above.

On the belay ledge, she stopped, panting but jubilant. After six days of attempts over three years, and months of verandah training, Nyrie had at last overcome one of the largest ceilings in Australia, and certainly the most notorious. It was an outstanding achievement.

Weighted with a rucksack, big-fisted Steve aided and cursed his way across the ceiling. He made it without mishap, and led on through toward the summit. Partway up the last pitch, he found an old crusty bottle sitting on a ledge. Inside was a scrap of paper on which was pencilled a message, left during the Friend/Lockwood ascent, promising a five-hundred dollar reward to the first person who climbed the roof free!

Steve and Nyrie reached the top in the late afternoon. Nyrie bounced around, full of summit joy, while Steve pragmatically rigged the abseil ropes.

We straggled along the walking track towards camp, arguing vigorously about Nyrie's decision to grade the route twenty-eight. She contended that Passport was probably the only route in the world that she could ever climb that others might find as hard as grade twenty-eight. Nevertheless, this was an unprecedented departure from convention, which states that one must grade a route according to how difficult one found it, despite individual advantages. I anticipated the controversy which was sure to erupt from Nyrie's decision.

Postscript: 1991

Five years on, Passport to Insanity awaits a second free ascent. Keiran Loughran, in his recently published Victoria Range guidebook, says of Passport: "Considered by some to be overgraded, though no one has tried to repeat it because it's too hard." (!)

However, the reaction of other male climbers was, predictably, one of entrenched sexism. Chris Baxter proclaimed in *Wild* No. 20, that the route was graded 24–28, depending on the climber's hand size. Nyrie publicly graded her route 28 and made no mention of any lower grade. Never, to my knowledge, has any climber (read "male climber") been questioned, far less in publication, over their grading of a first ascent before a repeat ascent.

The five-hundred dollar reward offered by Joe Friend was retracted by him on the grounds that Nyrie had used chalk, and she probably hadn't free climbed it anyway!

Finally, soon after the controversial grade was published, Kim Carrigan announced his intention to repeat the climb and downgrade it to 26. It seems rather unusual to hear somebody forecast how hard they will find a climb, having experienced only the first few meters of it!

OUT AND ABOUT
IN BALTISTAN

Louise Heinemann

▲ ▲ ▲

Baltistan is a small region in northeastern Pakistan, bordering on China and India. Though historically isolated by the towering Karakoram Range to the north and the Himalaya to the south, tiny Baltistan is now caught in a crossfire as Pakistan and India vie for territory.

"I don't want you to go. You won't go, will you?" insists Shamyla, with considerable intensity for a seven-year-old who knows herself to be generally irresistible.

"I'm afraid I've got to."

"But why? Can't you stay here? Don't go."

There's never been an adequate reason for going off to the mountains. Merely, I like it and am happy there to the point where nothing else compares, but this sounds churlishly ungrateful and selfish to those who aren't equally addicted.

"Come back quick then. How many days will you be?"

I calculate half a day to get there, five or six to cross, by all accounts, and a day back. "Six or seven, I think."

"No, that's too long. Be quicker." I'm flattered by the Princess's command, though I know it's only that she's bored, and her baby sister is too young to be a playmate.

. . .

"Yes, you can do it alone, now that you have the map," reassures Mr. Afridi, lending me the only one he has. It's a photocopy, on a scale such that my entire journey fits into a mere four inches. I head off to the bazaar on my usual pre-trip scavenger hunt round the little box shops for food. Always, one item is inexplicably unobtainable, and this time it's sugar, with all stall holders refusing to admit to possessing any. Shamyla's father, the hotel manager, gives me some and won't accept payment. I unpack and repack my rucksack, wondering what I'm forgetting,

The next day starts with an early breakfast with Shabeer, the cook, who has hard-boiled my bazaar eggs and packed them beautifully into a cardboard picnic box. I haven't the heart to discard this as unnecessary, but am already viewing it as a potential fire lighter. He, too, doesn't understand why I want to go and persists in believing it dangerous. The jeep is loading, and I'm on my way there when I encounter Jaffer, a local man and leader of porters, whom I haven't seen for weeks.

"Asalem Aleikum. Where've you been?"

"Aleikum Asalam. Thalle La."

"Great. What's it like? I'm heading there and you're the only one who's been across so far this season. Did you meet the guys coming the other way?"

I've talked too fast, and he's confused. With very little time, I can only collect that there was much snow, and he thinks I won't make it alone. Out at the jeep, Ashraf, a guide, has forgotten to inform his group of Baltoro-bound trekkers that they're giving me a lift to Shigar, my starting point. The Swiss Germans are as sniffy as the Americans are generous, but I jam myself in regardless and don't explain that it's in payment for my previous day's guiding of them.

"So now, tell about the road," commands Ashraf as the jeep jolts out of town.

There's not much to tell, except that it wouldn't exist at all if there weren't a war going on at the other end of the Baltoro. Naturally, one of the Germans has to contradict, and I decide to keep my information to myself in the future. The same German wants to photograph the view, bridge in foreground. We're in a militarily sensitive area, and the bridge, though old, is plastered with notices forbidding photos. There's also a guard house, complete with guard. I leave this to Ashraf, who grins all the wider for the camera's whirring. The guard ignores us, and I decide I must have underestimated Ashraf's local prestige.

The next photo stop is in a small desert of soft, white river silt. The nonphotographic German complains of diarrhea and "womiting." It must be the food, he declares, as he filters, boils and chlorinates the water. Idly, I speculate that this may be the true cause, but say nothing as I'm still on flagyl to clear my own giardia.

At last, with the arrival of the American-laden jeep, we continue up the barren gray hillside, over the col, and glimpse below the broad river braiding the green of the Shigar oasis. I wish I were continuing forward, to the Baltoro and the high peaks beyond, but not with this mob. I foresee conflicts between the Germans, intent on speed records, and the Californians, wanting to absorb the individual atmosphere of each pebble. I've lost my tolerance for my own kind.

It must be a month since I was last in Shigar, and I notice the barley has grown, the poplar leaves have lost their spring brightness and already there are large green fruit on the apricot trees. We careen through the village, the jeep behaving like a wild animal, knocking corners off mud walls. Children stare, yell and run after us. I'm beyond enchantment or exasperation; being conspicuous has become a fact of my life.

At the police station, Ashraf has to register his group, and though I don't have to be recorded (I'm not going to a restricted area), he wants to show off his acquaintance with the chief of police. The chief is a large, florid man, affecting Western clothes and sunglasses and surrounded by cringing, skinny underlings. Unfortunately, I've met him before. Last year, when I got double-crossed by some of his crooked guide cronies, and used another guide, this chief tried to have my guide's license revoked. Luckily, Mr. Afridi, a stickler for honesty, had more influence.

The chief ignores me till Ashraf has left, and then he turns and accuses me, "You look just like a Balti." Well, I suppose I do, except that no Balti can afford decent footwear or a rucksack. My clothes are not intended as a disguise; they make it easier for local people to accept me. Ironic, really; we're both wearing the clothes of each other's culture. I spend the next two hours keeping my cool, explaining repeatedly that I'm crossing Thalle La, alone. I show them the map, but I don't think they can read the place names, or grasp the concept of river and ridge lines, as they hold it upside down. The Spanish Latok expedition arrives, registers and leaves, their liaison officer suggesting I accompany them instead.

I decide to leave and heave up my rucksack. "But tea . . . ," the underlings insist. It was offered hours ago to prolong my stay. Now it's produced, so I have to drink it and be grateful.

"You will not be able to cross alone," pronounces the fat chief. "There are bears, tigers . . ."

"And an eagle to carry me off," I retort. "If I cannot cross, I shall have to return." I've decided that if I do fail, I'll find a jeep without re-entering his domain.

I'm in a filthy mood, exasperated by the delay, apprehensive, unsure just how big a thing I'm undertaking. I go out and, almost immediately, get lost in a warren of houses. There are no defined streets, just narrow spaces between houses, which are sometimes courtyards, sometimes not. I can't find my way through, although the mud walls are almost low enough to see over. It's like being in a maze, and a crowd collects. Women, children, old men—they can't make out what I am, or what my problem is. A bright girl realizes and steers me through.

Thereafter, I find myself accompanying a group of ragged kids up a hillside. It's dry and dusty, the bare earth sliding under my feet. The pack is heavy, the sun hot and my breath gasping. I'm not too pleased when we reach the summit, and I see the track winding innocently below.

A downhill slither brings me back to the track, which leads, gradually, up a narrow valley. There are fewer fields, houses, trees and more barren hillside beside the river. People are scarce: a man with a donkey, a man with a spade, a man with a load of wood, a couple of laughing women, a man unladen. I stop for a drink and pull out the map, wondering if I can make Baumaphron today. There I must leave this valley for another. It's hard to know how far I've come, only that the day is hot and dry, my pack heavy and the walking hard. I'm sorting myself out to continue when a Westerner comes striding round the corner, slender ski poles clicking along in either hand.

"You've been over Thalle La?"

"Yeah."

"Much snow?"

He indicates a level somewhere on his chest, which approximates to my neck. He and his mates (somewhere behind) have taken only three days, being short of time, and I plod on, apprehensive about the snow, till I calculate that they must have crossed yesterday, midday. If I go over very early when the snow is still firm, I've got a fair chance of avoiding drowning.

Below me, the noisy river is so fast-flowing not a single droplet splashes up on the banks. Even grass has a difficult time growing in this desolate gorge. Earth and stones slither down the slope I'm traversing, making me reluctant to rest for long. A little rain makes me drag out my cagoule, and I sweat worse than ever. I tell myself that I'm getting fitter, though I begin to despair of ever doing anything worthwhile with this fitness, assuming I attain it. After several hours the gorge widens to a valley with a few grassy spots and a huddle of low stone huts. A man asks me to stay, but I'm fixated on Baumaphron, and it's late afternoon already.

At the next settlement, a dog comes after me, silent but hostile. It's the first dog I've seen. Baltis drive their flocks themselves; dogs need feeding, and there's no food to spare. The dog stalks me, growling. I pick up a handful of pebbles, but a kind man hauls the dog off before I have to reveal the inaccuracy of my throw.

Eventually, I think I've arrived. The valley ahead is inviting, but there is a bridge of branches lashed together and a few stone huts where a side valley and stream come in. Uncertain, I dump my rucksack and set off toward the huts. I'm so tired that I don't experience the euphoria and weightlessness that normally come when I leave the sack.

Two shepherds have been watching me from a high vantage point. One skims down to intersect me, muddling amongst the willow scrub.

"Asalam Aleikum."

"Aleikum Asalam. Baumaphron?" It is. Thank goodness, I can relax. I point up the side valley, "Thalle La?" It is. Now it is his turn. He points to me—"Chick?"—and holds up one finger. I nod and grin proudly. "Chick," one, I confirm. As usual, he is puzzled by my singularity, even a little concerned. By now, we're back at my abandoned rucksack. I struggle to my feet with it, wishing he'd offered to carry it. Still, he's got the petrol can. Across the river again, I start looking for a sheltered campsite, inclining toward a border of scrub. The man is first puzzled, then definite that I should come to the huts, so, moving like an automaton somewhat in need of repair, I follow him.

By a semi-subterranean shelter he stops. We've arrived. He mimes a tent, points to some blackened firestones and then asks, "Chocolate?" I drop my rucksack and grudgingly dig out my un-opened packet of toffees to give him some. I'm too tired to care that I've been resisting the temptation to eat these all day; they're sup-posed to be my emergency rations. I find my bag of biscuits and swallow a few, hoping they'll give me more energy. Ali (as he says he is called) reappears, and I give him a handful.

I settle in to the serious business of getting my stove lit, intend-ing to cook dahl. The stove is having a lousy day, too, and keeps going out. Then the rain starts, and I have to stuff my scattered pos-sessions back into the rucksack. Ali is puzzled and mimes a tent again; I try to mime a bivy bag. The rain increases. Ali moves the thorn branches from the hut entrance and mimes going inside, for me and my rucksack. I point to the spluttering stove and use one of my few Balti words, "Shishik," bad. He agrees, and we take the stove, pan and dahl inside too.

The earth floor is a foot or two down. The hut is circular, made of piled stones with a central tree trunk and beams to support the earth roof. I suppose it's about five feet six inches high, but no one has to stoop. Light filters grayly through the doorway, an opposite window hole and a small smoke hole. Carefully, Ali folds and spreads a clean sack on the earth floor. He indicates I should sit there, in the honored guest place. I feel very grateful, very honored.

Above me a couple of sacks hang from the rafters. They contain food and dishes. Three blackened stones mark the fireplace. My stove is still playing silly buggers, so Ali quickly starts a fire, using the thorn branches. After that, it's a bit hazy, for I'm tired and the smoke upsets my lenses, so that I have to take them out. Ali finishes cooking the dahl, but I'm too tired to eat much. I give it to him and Selim, the other shepherd who's reappeared, surprised to find me inside. They milk their sheep and goat flock and make tea with the fresh milk. I've only had dried milk for months, and this tastes great. They lack sugar so I give them half of mine.

The hut is full when a third man comes in. A goat tries to follow him, is repulsed and reappears in the window, only to be driven off again. It gets dark, and I produce a candle, which is set up on a flat stone in the wall. Curled up on my clean sack I doze, and watch Selim, who washes his hands, mixes flour and water, kneads the dough and cooks little round flattened loaves, turning them in the hot ashes. Periodically, I hand round biscuits and toffees; I divide up my onions, garlic, matches and lump of rock salt, and the shepherds accept that there are no cigarettes. When the bread is cooked, I am woken and given a loaf to eat by flickering candle and firelight. It's delicious, but I'm so sleepy I can barely eat. Sad, for Ali is clever and interested. He catches on to the idea of telling me Balti words for objects. I already know stick, fire, pot, and I could've learned so much more if only I'd had the energy to listen and record. Instead, I curl up in my sleeping bag and sleep. One of the animals outside has a bleat like a sick old man's cough, and it coughs all night.

I don't know how early it is, but when Ali wakes me, I don't want to get up. He indicates I should come outside. The stars are still out. Ali has a pitcher of water, cold from the river. He pours it over my hands that I may wash. I am given tea, and, as I refuse anything else, it is time to go. Ali picks up my rucksack, so this time I carry the petrol can as I follow him back, across the bridge to the track up the side valley. He points, "Thalle La." I nod. We look at each other seriously, me wishing I had words to express my gratitude, his old, wrinkled face expressing much concern for this particular female nutcase. "Asalam Aleikum" exchanged, we part. I won't forget him, but already I wonder if I'll recognize him, if I ever see him again.

I start up through the juniper scrub. Hearing movement behind, I turn with hope, but it's only a string of little gray donkeys that belong to the shepherds; corralled every night, they're left free to graze by day. For some distance they follow me, rather too fast. I look back; the confluence, the huts have disappeared already in the steepness of the land, and I can see only the mountains that form the opposite side of the first valley.

I emerge from one scrub thicket to find another conglomerate of shelters. Men are out, some milking the animals. One, in surprisingly good English, calls to me. We chat; he has a large load of firewood for Shigar, has been a Baltoro porter, thinks he recognizes me, picks up my sack and estimates its weight as twenty-five kilograms. I doubt it, but laugh and cease to care if it feels heavy, for perhaps it is. They want me to stay, but I can't.

The next delay is at the last settlement. Again, men come out and call. As usual, they say I can't cross Thalle La alone, and by now I'm beginning to believe it. I actually start bargaining with the goitered headman for a porter. After half an hour, we've got down to a reasonable sum, and I'm thinking how good it'll be not to carry the sack when the subject of snow comes up. I haven't any spare boots. My prospective porter has the usual, useless plastic sandals. He says he can't come, and abruptly I find myself left alone, less resigned than I was before.

The path is steep and muddy. I plough on up, slowly, resentfully, wondering why I consider this to be enjoyable. My goal for the day is the snowline. Above the treeline there is desolate yak pasture; mountains are visible around, but the clouds are heavy and the weather looks bad. I make camp as high as I can, on a spit of earth and boulder immediately below the snowslopes. Though it's only early afternoon, I must've been going five hours or more, and it's cold. The stove has had a change of heart and is behaving itself. I keep it busy, melting snow, boiling water, cooking rice and onions, dehydrated beanfood and always more tea. I'm hard at it all afternoon, in between burrowing into my bivy sack and sleeping bag for the snow showers.

I'm not happy about the route ahead. Sure, I can see roughly where the pass must be, but there's a lot of snow and the Westerner said there was even more on the other side. I can't see any traces of their crossing. My watch blanks out, which is a nuisance, for I'll need its alarm tomorrow. The numbers reappear, but time is somewhat lost. The sky clears for a yellow sunset. The snowslopes are pink.

I sleep well but wake early, if my watch is right. I've changed from local clothes to climbing gear. Momentarily, I feel stronger, more confident, as though my clothes could really transform me. By 5:15 there's nothing to do but leave. On the snow above, I find the footprints. At first, I'm reluctant to use them, thinking their line is unnecessarily circuitous, but soon I'm simply grateful. I suspect I'm not a real mountaineer after all. This trail of prints absolves me from the need to find a route. I don't have to think, decide, evaluate or doubt; I just have to keep putting my feet down.

It gets warmer, and I strip off more and more of my clothing. I no longer go printless, though my tracks are not as deep as those I'm following. I try not to think what I'll do if the weather changes and further snowfall obliterates all tracks. My compass is lost, and I can't orient by sight alone. Whirling snow will confuse me till I may not know which way is down. I push the thought aside and concentrate on climbing the next snowbowl. I count the paces. After twenty, I'm allowed a breather; a minimum of five twenties equals one sit-down. I measure my infinitesimal progress against the rock bands in the snow wall alongside.

The snow will be soft after nine o'clock, if not before. I consider retreating while I can still get down easily. The pass is sure to be higher than it looks. I can't remember how high it is—4,500, 4,800, 4,300—meters, I don't know. If it weren't for the tracks, I wouldn't be here. I am surprised that the terrain seems to have flattened out. Just as there is always a false summit, I'm expecting a false pass. Instead, the ground falls away and ahead is a vista of unfamiliar peaks and ridges. I've crossed the pass and it's only eight o'clock. I'm totally exhilarated.

Suddenly I break through the snow. It's far softer on this side, and I'm thigh deep, crotch deep, head over heels, struggling, rucksack crushing me into the snow. I get tired and angry. Sometimes, I manage a dozen steps safely, holding my breath, tiptoeing, then the thirteenth, fifteenth, seventeenth is the heavy one, and I've capsized again. I wonder if I'll ever get down and out. I know I've got to, but it's exhausting, and I don't seem to progress. I'm thirsty, didn't drink enough on the way up and am paying for it now. My water bottle is stuffed with snow crystals turning to ice and, eventually, I hope, to water.

An hour and a half below the pass, I sprawl onto an isolated mud patch. No other patch is visible, so I'm not safe, but at least I can stop here without sinking. I light the stove, melt snow and drink water laced wlth rehydration salts for an hour. By then, I've reassessed my position. To stay longer is crazy, with the sky clouding over and bad weather drifting about. So I go on. It's colder, but the snow is softer, meaning I sink further, more often. However, the sack is less of a burden, so I must be lower. I'm a bit resentful, having kidded myself that this downhill side would be easy. There seem

to be vast distances of flat rotten snow, with no quick, easy descent.
Once, I'm even rather scared, trying to edge diagonally down a gully
wall. The snow is slithering away around me, and there's a heap of
rocks protruding just where I'll land. Badly, I want to panic, but the
rotten snow won't give me time. I go on, and though I'm not neck
deep at every step, it seems interminable, and I wonder if I'll ever
get down. The joy of it, when I see by the larger grassy patches that I
have done so. Rock and snow give way to mud and grass.

"Well done, Lou," I congratulate myself aloud, for there is no
one else around. I know I've been lucky, that the weather held off,
that the tracks were still there. "Asalem Aleikum," I salute my first,
high-grazing zho[1], I'm so glad to see him. I know I'm safe, know I've
done it. My heart sings, and my tired feet seem to find their own way
across the scree. The zho edges off, and some horses canter away,
but there is no herdsman in sight. Below, the clear water sparkles by
a bright green, flower-starred meadow. By two o'clock, I'm down in
that meadow, laughing up at the sky, not caring how low the cloud
ceiling comes.

I sleep long, but not well, waking to find the end of my bivy bag
being investigated by a large, mottled black-and-white zho. I sit up
and it skedaddles, terrified. Though very big, I think these must be
zho, not yaks, for they seem easily scared, and I've always understood yaks are aggressive creatures. It's a peaceful scene, green
meadows dotted with gray stones, fast-flowing water, peaks around
and above, patches of melting snow, birdsong. Zho are moving
slowly uphill, and I wonder how they know when or where to go,
whether they have any human control or leader and whether they
graze the same slopes all their lives. They go so high on such barren
land, it hardly seems worth the effort.

Early, I swing off downhill, following the river. I have to cross a
deep sidestream. The water is fast and cold, but in the end I'm only
wet, not swept off my feet. With walking, I've dried out before I
reach the first, half-collapsed stone hut. The shepherd seems quite
surprised, and I'm a bit smug, with my "Chick" and "Thalle La"
behind me. Further on are great grass-covered moraine heaps and
beyond them, a spectacular valley opens up. That's the way I'd have

---

[1] A cross between a yak and a cow. The Baltis crossbreed them and have specific names for the
three generations it takes for the zho/zonghi to revert to yak. Yaks are virtually not tameable.

come if I'd kept along the original valley beyond Baumaphron, taking a more northerly, higher pass. I suppose it can't be open yet, but it tantalizes me, and I promise myself that next time, when I have more time, I'll explore it.

I splash noisily through another river. On the further bank, horses gallop freely, fast-moving in the sunshine. This has to be a rich valley to have so many horses and to have them running loose. Usually, they're walled in, prized possessions, fed by hand. The path skirts round a steep hillside, and I realize I'm close to cultivated land. Reluctantly, I abandon my climbing persona and change back to my local clothes. Across the track is a solid wall to stop the zho from getting back into the crops. A way through the wall is knocked out in autumn when the animals are brought down.

Outside the first village, a group of women rush at me, clutching their breasts, stomachs, heads, miming coughing, spluttering, death agonies, clearly wanting medicine. "Doctor, Doghani," I say, indicating the roadhead further on. I've had too much of this recently. I'm getting cynical. If the women are really ill, they need a doctor, not me, and if they're not ill, my supplies of placebos are low. The usual gaggle of people stare and follow while I find my way through the village maze. I wish I could go around the village when I feel like this, but I don't want to trample the crops, and there is no other path.

"Kusomik?" I ask and follow the man who indicates he's also going there. He strides along, dressed in short rubber boots, brown shalwar kameez[2], green pullover and white Gilgiti cap[3]. We cross the river via a bridge, and on a wider track we're joined by a man with two donkeys, almost invisible below their loads of fragrant juniper. I feel slightly like the donkeys, driven to keep a pace when I would have dawdled along alone. The men offer to load my sack onto the donkeys, but as a conqueror of Thalle La, I'm too proud. I'm also too broke, and anyway, it doesn't seem fair to the donkeys. The road improves steadily, and the land around is solidly cultivated. The mountains are only higher glimpses. From Kusomik, Doghani causes confusion as it's also a higher village, so we establish that I

---

[2] A loose, baggy trousers and tunic, worn locally by both sexes.
[3] A round, flat cap with no peak, made of woolen cloth. Worn by men locally and so-called because of its origin further west in Gilgit.

want a jeep going toward Skardu, and I call the roadhead Bara, as do the locals.

The road is crowded, men with burdens, women with children and umbrellas, the donkeys most heavily laden of all. People greet each other, swap destinations and news, walk together a while and gossip. My companion carries a woman's child; a man gives us some of his dried apricots, and the dust rises. Somehow, the atmosphere is medieval, and I find myself thinking of Chaucer's pilgrims (though they rode, not walked) and see for the first time how the situation really arose. The road unrolls into the distance, a white line between the jewel-bright irrigated fields, a ruled line where it has been blasted from the ochre rock walls.

I've established that my companion is Ibrahim, and that he knows me from the Baltoro. Honestly, I don't remember him, but I was with his group only a couple of days. With sixty porters, I distinguished them then only by a bright scarf or flower, or an unusual hat or an old bodywarmer. Ibrahim has changed his clothes since then. Repeatedly, he offers to take the sack, and by late morning Thalle La's conqueror has rather low resistance. We agree on a price, and he adjusts the straps.

At one village, a festival is under way, music and ponies coming in for polo, though I haven't seen a flat patch of grass big enough for clock golf, let alone polo. We walk on, as I'm afraid if I stop I won't start again, and I am supposed to hurry. As always with porters, I'm impressed by Ibrahim's strength, endurance and cheerfulness. At a brief stop for water and biscuits, he grins and says his boots are shishik, he has no socks; somehow Baltis rarely do. The inside of his rigid rubber boots is softened only with a little straw. Of course, the boots don't fit either. He washes the torn blisters, and I rub in antiseptic and stick over plaster and strapping. I thought I was so tough, so smart, but I know I wouldn't be grinning if I had to walk with those blisters, or those boots. Or the rucksack, come to that. Ibrahim strides on, solidly, cheerfully.

This morning's high valley seems a world away. At two o'clock we get to the roadhead and join the guard on the bridge. Contrary to what I was told, the hotel isn't open. I'm unlikely to get a jeep so late in the day. Army convoys veer past, but they won't stop. A crowd of locals collects to discuss me, and after an hour, the local police hear of my existence. They haul me off to the police station at the other end of the bridge.

It's the same, hollow square layout of single story, white-washed, blue-doored buildings as at Shigar. I seem to be spending an inordinate amount of time in police stations; this is my third, and back home I've only been in one ever. However, this is not like Shigar. There are chrysanthemums in the central garden plot and friendly, lounging policemen. Mr. Karim, who seems to be in charge, gives me tea and boiled eggs and promises me a ride in the first civilian jeep. Deciding I'm in safe hands, Ibrahim leaves for the two-hour walk up to his village.

Just before dusk, a jeep arrives, and I'm loaded in. However, a quarter of an hour down the road, the driver realizes darkness is imminent and that he has no lights. We return to the police station, where kind Mr. Karim feeds me and finds me a spare bedstead for the night. The police live in, their homes often being a day's drive away. Despite the time I've spent in this area, I still don't know what these police do, other than register my presence. There is always a cell, complete with bars and padlock, but never a prisoner. Without much language, it's hard to know, but no one rushes in for help or undergoes heavy questioning. The atmosphere is pleasant, sociable. Perhaps my presence alone enforces good behavior, or perhaps I've seen too much television. I think there is little local crime.

I'm woken by the quiet muttering of Mr. Karim's early morning prayers and shown where to wash. I'm given tea and parathas before being reminded, gently, that the jeep is waiting, The driver isn't so relaxed, though his mate smokes, sings and sleeps, snoring. We have more punctures than spare tires, which means many waits for other vehicles to rescue us. Finally, exasperated, I buy my way out and swap to a better-prepared vehicle.

Mid-afternoon, I'm back.

"You're late," says Shamyla.

"I hurried as much as I could," I say, as I brush back my longing for that other high valley. Next time . . .

MOUNTAIN STORMS

Ann E. Kruse

▲ ▲ ▲

STORMS ARE routine on Mt. McKinley. We know its severe and volatile weather is one of the greatest hazards we will face in climbing the mountain. So we aren't surprised to be hit by a storm as we drive from Anchorage to Talkeetna. What surprises us is the storm's ferocity. Heavy rains pelt us, and the wind is so strong it almost blows our van off the road.

On the mountain, the storm does worse damage. High on the West Buttress, tornadoing winds rip a tent from its anchors and send two climbers tumbling down the steep snow toward the Peters Glacier a thousand feet below.

We learn about this incident the next morning at the ranger station as we register to climb the mountain. The ranger has been up all night monitoring radio reports of the rescue effort. Now, over the crackling radio, we hear reports of the difficulty getting a helicopter into the mountain through the low clouds.

We are experienced and equipped to meet whatever hazards and challenges McKinley throws at us. But knowing that two climbers are now struggling for their lives on the very ridge where we plan to be camped in two weeks—well, it humbles us. We now understand that the mountain is in control, not us.

. . .

My climbing partners are my husband, Curt Mobley, and our friend Linda Roubik. Curt and I first met while rock climbing in Maryland fourteen years ago. On our first date, we climbed a 12,000-foot peak in Colorado. We eventually moved to Seattle and got married. On our honeymoon, we joined a group of friends to climb several peaks in the Wind River Range in Wyoming. The day we arrived in Alaska was our tenth wedding anniversary.

It was on the Wyoming trip that Curt and I met Linda. My glowing reports of life as a lawyer convinced her to move to Seattle, start law school and eventually become a lawyer herself. Linda is ten years younger than Curt and I and more athletic than we are, so she routinely leaves us in her dust. To mask the impairments of age, Curt and I claim our slowness is due to our being older and wiser and therefore more cautious.

Our plan to tackle McKinley had been hatched in the sunny warmth of Yosemite Valley a year earlier and we had been planning the trip ever since, getting into condition, buying gear, planning meals. We had squeezed a month away from our work—Linda and I from our law practices and Curt from his work as a research scientist and college professor. After all our planning, we are now in Talkeetna, a small town about two hours north of Anchorage, waiting to be flown by bush pilot to base camp.

Mt. McKinley, at 20,320 feet, is the highest peak in North America. It is part of the Alaska Range, located roughly halfway between Anchorage and Fairbanks.

The Alaska Range forms a natural barrier to the moist air flowing inland from the Bering Sea and the Gulf of Alaska. When this air collides with the cold mountains, the resulting storms drop massive amounts of snow. Over the centuries, this snow has collected and compressed into glaciers, slow-moving rivers of ice, that have carved valleys thousands of feet deep into McKinley's flanks, leaving rocky ridges—called buttresses—between the glaciers.

We plan to travel up the Kahiltna Glacier, gain the ridge of the West Buttress and then follow the ridge to the summit. If successful, we would be on the mountain three weeks, covering sixteen miles on the ground and gaining two and a half vertical miles.

Each year a thousand climbers attempt McKinley. They come from the world over. Three hundred are now on the mountain. Dozens are waiting with us in Talkeetna to fly in and begin their adventure.

Two days after we arrive, the weather lifts slightly, just enough to fly. Our bush pilot deposits us on the Southeast Fork of the Kahiltna Glacier. The injured climbers are finally flown off the mountain as well.

We land at 7,200 feet above sea level. Our food, fuel, clothing, camping gear and climbing gear total 360 pounds. To haul this huge load, we will use not only backpacks, but also sleds strapped to our waists and pulled behind us. We plan to follow a traditional expedition strategy—"work high, sleep low." From each campsite, we will haul a load of food, fuel and gear to a higher elevation, cache our load and then return to spend the night at the lower elevation. The next day, we will strike camp and move everything up to the location of the cache. This climbing strategy will force us to gain elevation slowly, allowing our bodies time to adjust to the stresses of working at high elevations.

After landing, pitching our tent and sorting our gear, our next step is to take advantage of the good weather and move a load three miles up the Kahiltna. We strap on our sleds and skis, and we rope together—Curt in the front, me in the middle and Linda in the rear. For as long as we are on the mountain, whenever we venture beyond the campsite, we will be roped together as protection from another danger on a glacier, a fall into a hidden crevasse.

A good clear track has been worn in the snow by other climbers, making the route easy to follow. But new snow and wind can easily obliterate the track. So every rope length (about 150 feet), Curt plants a wand in the snow. Our wands are made of green bamboo tomato stakes about two feet long, with a luminous orange ribbon taped to one end. With the wands in place, we can easily see our route, even when fog reduces our visibility. As we complete each leg of the journey, we will retrieve the wands and use them to mark the next section.

As we travel up the glacier, we concentrate on putting one foot in front of the other and watching for indentations in the snow that could signal a hidden crevasse. It's hard work. It requires all our energy and attention.

Only when we stop to rest can we let our bodies and minds fully appreciate where we are. The size and majesty of the glacier and its surroundings are awe-inspiring. The Kahiltna Glacier is a mile wide, with rocky peaks jutting straight up from the glacier on each side. In the low clouds, we can see only the very bottoms of the peaks that line the glacier, but we can hear the roar of new snow avalanching off the ridges far above us.

The wind and the avalanches are the only sounds I can hear. I feel the slight breeze against my face and taste the deliciously crisp air with each deep breath. I know I am where I want to be.

After two hours of traveling, we have used the last of our trail wands. It is late in the afternoon, and we're tired, so we dig a pit in the snow, bury our load (to guard against marauding ravens) and mark the spot with wands. Then we head back down to spend our first night on the silent white expanse.

Three days pass before we again see the sun. Working in fog and low clouds, following our wands and the trail, we have moved our camp to 8,000 feet, at the base of a rise called Ski Hill; our cache is part way up Ski Hill at a level section near several existing tent sites.

Existing tent sites are a precious commodity on McKinley. A tent has to be protected from the high winds, either by digging a pit into the snow or by building snow-block walls around the tent. This is exhausting work at the end of the day. Whenever possible, we camp at a tent site a previous party had already constructed. At the spot on Ski Hill where we deposited our cache, several tent sites had been excavated into the slopes. We hope that at least one will be vacant if we decide to camp there.

As the new morning breaks, we are delighted to see the sunshine. Perhaps the bad weather is over. We strike camp, pack our gear, rope up and head up Ski Hill.

As we zigzag up the hill, it starts to get windy and cold. This is not surprising. We are, after all, gaining altitude and rising out of the protection of the Kahiltna basin. But before long the weather starts deteriorating. Clouds move in. Snow starts falling. The winds pick up. Soon a blizzard is howling around us.

We don our wind pants and jackets, tighten our hoods against the blowing snow and bend into the wind. Hauling the sleds over the wet new snow is slow work. The snow falls and drifts over the trail, obliterating it. Even the new tracks made by Curt and his sled disappear in the seventy-five feet between us.

The glacier, the falling snow and the cloudy sky blend into one vast blanket of gray. We are in a whiteout. We can't see the horizon or judge the slope or angle of the snow. In fact, we can't see anything as we climb but an occasional climbing party venturing downward, a tent here and there, and the wands.

The wands are our only guide. Each time Curt comes to a wand, he stops and searches ahead for the next one. When he sights it, he heads in that direction. Finding the wands is not always easy. When the snow is falling lightly, a wand 150 feet away is readily visible. As the snowfall grows more intense, we can barely see each other just seventy-five feet away, much less the wands.

After two hours of this, Curt stops. He cannot see the next wand. He searches every direction that can possibly be "up." Nothing. If we cannot spot the wand, we could be in trouble. Curt would have to head out into the nothingness and stop when Linda reached the last wand. While she stood at our last known on-route location, Curt and I would travel an arc until he came across the wand. We would lose time and energy in this tedious process and risk entering a field of large crevasses that lies just a hundred feet or so to our left. And if the wand has been broken or knocked down, it would be covered by snow and we would not find it. If we cannot find the next wand, we will have to stop where we are and start the hard work of excavating a tent site.

I move up closer to Curt and search for the wand myself. I can see nothing but gray. Standing still, doing no work, I begin to shiver from the cold. I look again, this time farther to the right, directly into the blasting wind. In the distance I can barely make out a faint orange glow that seems to hover above us in the distance, one tiny spot in a 360-degree globe of gray. It's our wand! We head toward it. Once there, we can see that just one rope-length beyond it is our cache. And no more than thirty feet from our cache is a vacant tent site, already excavated and waiting for us.

We have traveled all of one mile in the last three hours. We are tired and cold and hungry. We quickly dig out the foot of snow that has just fallen, pitch our tent and settle in for a long night.

By the next morning, the rear half of our tent is completely buried in snow. I get out and dig, a process we would repeat several times during the next day and a half as the blizzard continued. The blowing snow has covered our sleds, blasted a three-inch coating of snow on the windward side of our skis and filled the opening between the tent and the walls of snow that surround it on three sides.

One might reasonably ask at this point why people climb mountains. The answer undoubtedly differs with every climber. I started hiking in mountains as a child. I enjoyed both the solitude and the joy of discovering something new at each turn of the trail, whether it was a ground squirrel or a waterfall, or a wind-stunted tree or a spectacular sunset. I enjoyed the sights, the smells, the tastes and the sounds so different from those of everyday life in the city. The wilderness was a fairy-tale world. As I grew older I became more curious about what was beyond the trail. I wanted to see what was at the top of a rock cliff or at the end of a glacier. And so I learned to climb. And I am still continually enchanted by the sights, the smells, the tastes and the sounds of the wilderness.

I also enjoy the physical work of climbing. For fifty weeks a year I sit at my desk and work with my brain. People and papers compete for my attention. On McKinley, I can escape to a world where life is reduced to its simplest elements. We haul our gear up the mountain. We melt water, cook, eat and clean up. We sleep. I can focus my attention on one goal only. My body enjoys the exercise. My brain enjoys the rest. And they both enjoy the deep refreshing sleep that follows a day of intense physical labor.

And so I am standing outside the tent at 9,500 feet on Mt. McKinley, shovel in hand, watching the snow fall as fast as I can scoop it up. As I look around me, I know I am just one small speck on this huge mountain. We cannot stop the snow or the wind or the cold, but we can live with it, and we are doing so successfully. In exchange for our cooperation and gratitude, the mountain is letting us see and feel and experience what few people ever have a chance to know. On this climb, my body will feel pain and will suffer injuries but will recover and forget. My soul, however, will experience a deep peace and a soaring exhilaration from which it will never recover. That is why I climb.

The most vivid sensory impression on our climb is that of silence. The only natural sounds are those made by wind and snow, sometimes delicate, sometimes violent; the only artificial sounds, those made by the three of us and any other climbers who are close by. Each sound is measured, identifiable and an item of interest to be mulled over and discussed, like a foreign coin found on a seashore. Inside our cocoon of a tent, in the middle of a blizzard, on a vast glacier, we are isolated from any sounds except nature's and our own. Other people are nearby. Through the falling snow we can see the hazy outlines of three other tents a hundred feet away, and we can see the occupants venture out occasionally to perform the same chores we are—digging snow, collecting snow to melt for water, answering nature's call—but we cannot communicate with them. Our shouts won't carry over the raging wind, and one does not wander around visiting on a glacier because of the danger of falling into a crevasse. We are left to our own devices and entertainment as much as if we had been pioneers on the prairie with no neighbors for hundreds of miles.

Inside the tent we are quite comfortable. We eat fudge and play Scrabble. We melt water, cook meals and read books. In the evening we listen to our two-way radio for half an hour. We had brought the radio primarily for emergency purposes and—luxury of luxuries—weather reports. But we now turn to it for entertainment. We hear a little idle chit-chat. We hear foreign languages and accents. We hear a British party at 18,000 feet on the South Buttress report that they have two days of food left, are doing well in the storm, are optimistic and expect to make the summit. Each word that comes our way is savored. It is our only contact with the world beyond our tent.

We awake late the next day. I look out the door of the tent. For the first time, I can see the other tents clearly. Snow is no longer falling. I stick my head farther out the door. I can now see a clear demarcation between gray and white—some sort of horizon. Could it be the top of Ski Hill?

By the time we finish breakfast, the area is abuzz with activity. For the first time in two days, we can hear numbers of voices. Climbers on their way down are the most anxious to get under way. They have been on the mountain long enough and want to go home. Those descending from above create a trail for those of us who are ascending. Their trail is welcome. It will show us the route, and it will pack down the newly fallen snow. We are in no hurry to get started. Breaking trail in fresh snow is no fun. There are several teams on their way up, and we are happy to let them go first.

. . .

Several days later we reach 14,000 feet. We set up camp in a broad, flat basin directly below the summit. Nestled between ridges on three sides, the basin is sheltered from the worst winds and provides a spectacular view to the south. Because it is flat, well protected and relatively free of crevasses and avalanches, this basin is the resting spot for every team on the way up, every team on the way down and every team just hanging around for various reasons. I count eighty climbers camped there one day. In contrast to our days sitting out the blizzard in isolation, the 14,000-foot camp is an urban experience. There is a lending library (in the tent of a medical research team studying altitude sickness), a solid waste disposal system (a latrine consisting of a wood seat over a pit in the snow, with a spectacular view of neighboring Mt. Hunter), housing problems (we managed to acquire a fine tent site surrounded by snow blocks, with plenty of room for our tent, sleds and all gear; others have even more luxurious accommodations with underground caves for protection in truly bad weather; but the less fortunate have only small tent sites surrounded by miserable little piles of snow), and there are traffic jams and noisy late-night parties. It is ironic that this camp is crowded with people who are there in part to escape from crowds.

The most difficult section of the West Buttress route is the 2,200-foot climb up a steep headwall from this camp at 14,000 feet to the crest of the West Buttress. We plan to spend two days hauling our gear up the headwall. They will be long, grueling days. Once there, we will follow the narrow crest to a camp at 17,000 feet. We will rest a day and then head for the summit.

We fill our packs and head out on the well-worn trail. The trail starts like a sidewalk, then gradually steepens until it is like climbing stairs, and then steepens further until it is like climbing a ladder. At this altitude, just walking on level ground is laborious. Carrying a pack up a steep slope is draining. Early in the day, I can take only one step with each breath I take. Eventually, I have to stop and take four or five deep breaths for every single step.

The inconsistent texture of the snow slows our progress. In places the footing is stable. I place my foot and haul my body up six inches. My calves burn. I rest and catch my breath. I place my other foot and repeat the process hundreds of times, step by slow step. Sometimes the snow collapses when I put my weight on it. The jolt takes my breath away. I cuss. I lean my knees against the steep wall of snow and catch my breath. I have gained only three inches in the last two minutes. I have thousands more inches to go.

My body rebels at the altitude. Nausea. Dizziness. Headaches. Cold hands. Cold feet. The glare of the sun reflecting off the snow makes my eyes water even through my glacier glasses. I feel more miserable with each step, and I know that tomorrow I will have to cover the same terrain with a heavier pack. I push on.

Climbers do not really conquer mountains; climbers conquer themselves. Climbers need not only physical strength and stamina, but also the mental discipline to shut out a certain degree of tedium, frustration, pain and fear that might cause them to stop short of their goals.

But a climber's discipline must be tempered with the wisdom to know when to stop. A climber must assess external hazards—bad weather, crevasses, rock fall, avalanches. A climber must also deal with internal storms—how far do I push to test my limits, without foolishly pushing too far? For each climber there is a point at which the exterior forces overcome the interior mental discipline, where the needs of the body overwhelm the climber's desire to reach the summit. I can feel that point approaching as I drag my body inch by inch up the headwall. I try to forestall it. Just one more hour and we will be on the crest of the ridge. Keep going. One more step. One more step.

"Come up here," Curt yells. He has stopped and is sitting in the snow above me. Although Linda and I take some time to reach him, he is still gasping for air when we arrive at his side. "I can't breathe," he says. "I can't go any further." Resting does not help; his lungs simply cannot get the oxygen they need for the hard work we are doing.

This is an unexpected problem. Even worse, it is a horrible place to decide what to do about it. As we shiver in the cold and try to maintain a stable foothold in the steep snow, we also wrestle with the difficult choices confronting us. Linda and I could continue to the ridge and then return for the contents of Curt's pack. Or we could all return to camp and try again the next day. Or we could let Curt rest longer to see if his condition improves. We have to think not only about our choices today, but also in the days ahead. If Curt were unable to go higher, Linda and I would have to carry heavier loads. I am having a hard enough time with the small load I am carrying now—could I carry a heavier load tomorrow, or the next day, or on summit day? Linda would have no problem, but the difference between her physical abilities and mine would be even more pronounced if just the two of us were to continue. What if we deposited our cache on the ridge and then Curt's condition got worse? Would I be able to leave him down below? What if we left our cache on the ridge and bad weather came in? Would we be able to retrieve it, or would we have to descend and abandon our gear?

The brain does not function well at high altitudes because of the lack of oxygen. At altitude, climbers have to rely upon rote and reflex, not complex decision-making. Even when the brain, after great difficulty, does form a thought, it is difficult to transmit the message to the mouth and then to get the mouth muscles to work well enough to say the words to express the thought. The questions we were wrestling with would have been difficult enough to discuss on a warm day at sea level. But on the side of the mountain at 15,000 feet in the cold and wind, it is virtually impossible. We decide to retreat to our camp at 14,000 feet and consider our options later.

The next day, we do nothing but eat and sleep. The following day, our fourteenth on the mountain, we confront the question again. Curt is feeling no better, and he is convinced he can go no higher. He could keep one of our stoves and sleep in a snow cave if Linda and I want to try for the summit. I am feeling no more confident about my abilities to go higher, and I am worried about leaving Curt alone. Dividing a party is never wise, although this populated camp is a relatively safe place for a lone climber to stay.

Linda is feeling fit, and she is anxious to go on. She is frustrated that Curt's and my physical limitations might cause her to lose the summit she has worked so hard to reach. She considers teaming up with other climbers and discusses the possibility with several.

The weather again enters into the equation. A storm is expected in the next day or so. When it arrives, we will be pinned down wherever we are for several days. It will be bad enough to be stuck at 14,000 feet, but worse still to be stuck high on the West Buttress. We cannot help but remember the climbers who had been blown from that same spot in the storm just two weeks earlier.

We each struggle privately with our own internal storms—to go higher and risk life and limb, or to retreat and risk losing the

chance, perhaps of a lifetime, to reach McKinley's summit?
We decide to retreat.

We had spent nine days traveling from the landing strip up to the camp at 14,000 feet. It takes us only nine hours to travel the same distance going down. We arrive at the landing strip at 10:00 p.m., too late for a plane to fly in. We pitch our tent and crawl into our sleeping bags, fully expecting to wait out a storm for several days. Instead, we awake the next morning to crystal clear skies. We radio for a plane and start packing. Within an hour, we are back in Talkeetna, eating tacos for lunch while watching the storm clouds move in from the southwest.

So it was over. A year of planning. Two weeks of hard work in constant danger. Substantial cash outlay. We did not reach the summit. Was it worth it?

I have been to a place I have never been before and that few people have the opportunity to see firsthand. I have seen sights so dramatic that no artist could possibly capture them in words or on canvas. I have pushed myself to my utter physical limits and then said "no further" while my fingers and toes were all still intact. I have shared this incredible experience with my closest friends. All of our major decisions—the route we selected, the wands we placed, the precautions we took against crevasse falls, the food and clothing we took, when to push on and when to retreat—were made in consultation with an important fourth team member, the mountain itself. We lived with the mountain and bent to its will for two weeks. We were not defeated. We succeeded in this goal, and some other year we may return and learn more about Mt. McKinley, experience a different side of its personality and see a place we have not been before—its summit.

Weeks later we hear from another climbing team that was on the mountain at the same time we were. On the same day we had descended to the landing strip, they had climbed the headwall. They had reached 17,000 feet with no problem. Then the storm came in, and they had to sit out four days of storm before retreating. They did not make the summit.

The two climbers who had been blown off the West Buttress recovered with relatively minor problems. One lost parts of a few fingers to frostbite. Both plan to return to try McKinley again.

A month after we've descended, another storm pummels the mountain. A professional climbing guide is sleeping in his tent on the West Buttress when the wind tears his tent from its anchors and hurls him off the buttress toward the Peters Glacier. As I said, storms are routine on Mt. McKinley.

A LATE NIGHT
ON A HIGH WALL

Jeanne Panek

▲ ▲ ▲

YOSEMITE VALLEY lay under the shadows of the monoliths bordering its rim. The sun reddened, dropping closer and closer to the tips
of distant mountains, sending the shadows farther afield. Below, in
the Valley, a pall of smoke was just beginning to gather, a uniform
haze that rose from the Valley floor with the onset of evening. From
thousands of campsites came the smoke of thousands of camp-
fires—the nightly ritual.

The sun's light had lingered long on us, 1,800 feet above the
north side of the Valley. But the shadows were marching across the
wall toward us—night was nearing, and we still had two pitches to
climb before reaching our bivy ledge. The relaxed and easy manner
of the afternoon slipped away with the sun, the banter, encouragement and laughter between us faded with the light. Strain edged our
voices as we made ready for the next pitch, preparing the haul bag
and exchanging the rack. We were efficient, damn it, why hadn't we
been able to climb the entire eleven pitches in the light? But this was
my first big wall and my second day of aid climbing. No doubt,
therein lay the problem. Who was I to know what was or was not ef-
ficiency? I was the greenhorn and the slow cog in the machine.

With our earlier banter we had been challenging each other not
to succumb to the gravity of the moment. But the strength to keep
doing that was wearing thin. The climb had become marked by an

underlying tension, a push to move as quickly as was safely possible. The tone now was serious, more serious than any climb I had tackled previously.

Being new to big-wall climbing, I brought to it the perspective of an outsider, eager, but also objective and shyly skeptical. I had thought that big walls were the epitome of climbing, the final form of the art. Certainly I was led to this belief by the company I kept, and the stories swapped by that circle of men. Ingrained ideas, nurtured from late nights in a living room, all of us draped over the furniture and dreamy, are not easily banished. But opinion can be changed by the obvious. I was stunned by the differences between this and the climbing I had known. Aid climbing seemed so graceless, almost completely lacking the fluidity and creativity of free climbing. Each aid pitch is an engineering task, as mechanical as free climbing is artistic. Within this framework, and after many pitches, I grew, however, to respect it for itself, for the process. I took glee in the system, in the mechanics, how they all fit together to create progress up the rock. But in my opinion so far, aid climbing lacked the spirit and imagination of free climbing.

Pitch after pitch the ground below became less defined: the trees became dots, and the huge boulders of the talus slope became just a wash of texture between the dots. I was a full ten pitches above my highest climb to date and fifteen pitches above the ground, though I had not spent much time looking down in the last day and a half. I felt no reason to, with spectacular vistas across the Valley, rounded domes of polished slab, distant horns and aretes. And, in fact, the closer and more demanding rock right above me captured most of my attention. Tomorrow I would spend substantial time glancing straight down 2,000 feet contemplating the consequences of a mistake. But tomorrow was a long way off.

Now that I was aware of time as a premium, even Simon's efficient lead seemed painfully slow. I alternately watched him pick his way up an easy ramp, and then, because I needed to distract myself, surveyed the dimming horizon. Even the far rim of the Valley became difficult to discern. Night was closing in. For the first time, I felt the cold penetrating the layers of bunting I had worn continuously for the last two days. I shivered and stomped my feet, while waiting and feeding out rope inches at a time. Simon had reached the 5.9 corner and decided to aid it.

My fingers itched to be on the rock, my arms ached to flex and pull. I hated standing, inactive and waiting, while our fate sealed night around us and pulled the drawstring closed. Simon's headlamp came to life and marked the spot where he was setting up the belay. Finally it was time to move. Unlike the blaze of light that defined Simon, my headlamp was a dim glow, but enough to dismantle the belay, secure my jumars and guide the haul bag next to me as I climbed. I followed the rope and the imprint of the pitch etched in my memory. Unaware of the rock or the features under the rope, I jugged up, focused on Simon and on arriving at the belay. In what felt like an instant I was seated beside him. Simon's face, as tense and impatient as my own, told me that it had taken much longer than an instant—climber's versus belayer's time warp.

"Well, the next pitch is yours if you want it." He looked at me expectantly as if I hadn't already made up my mind to lead off into the dark. Until that moment I hadn't doubted that I would do it; I had accepted it as the luck of the draw. It was my lead, therefore it was my challenge, like any of the challenges we had encountered en route—bad bolts, squeeze chimneys, off-widths. But Simon's implied offer became a temptation—to let just some of this tension slide off my shoulders, to let him guide us out of this situation. As the greenhorn I could legitimately bow to greater experience. I'm not sure what made me shun the offer, whether the challenge baited me or perhaps my own need to refuse the easy excuse that I was new to this. After an obvious pause, almost a thought spoken aloud, I said I'd lead it.

I sorted the rack. I took Simon's headlamp. I swallowed great gulps of water. And I took the map of the route.

As I moved away from Simon, I eased into solitude and soon felt myself surrounded by the night. Tension clung to me like a sweat. It was a given—it flexed when I did, bent with me as I bent. It was inescapable. As the darkness expanded, so my focus narrowed. The rock illuminated by the glow from the headlamp became my entire world, about four feet in diameter. This was no different from the realm that is usually the climber's focus, but the darkness made the delineation undeniable.

My senses were vibrant, tuned only to my small sphere. I felt the warmth of my breath bounce back to me off rock that was verging on cold as my hands pressed against it. It was smooth, solid granite, clean and beautiful, and my fingers and feet sought its edges and undulations. I moved down a ramp, slowly and deliberately. My own personal sense of time had ground to a halt and I moved through a world without reference to any clock. My rack sounded a musical carabiner clink as I unclipped protection, and its weight pulled reassuringly at my shoulder. The acrid gunpowder smell of the granite merged with the sweat-permeated nylon smell of the rack, a heady aroma as I reached to place the piece. I felt no sense of space below me, and gave no thought to the thousands of vertical feet below my heels. Nor did I consider the sweep of the granite face above me, topped with the cornice of rock that characterizes this wall. Those thoughts only came later.

With no distractions but the task at hand, with my focus entirely centered, my mind became a calm voice dictating my actions with an unreal concentration and determination. Never had I felt my thoughts and my movements so closely allied, the physical and the cerebral working in harmony. I was a machine, calculating and methodical, but also fluid and efficient. I reveled in the emergence of this new union from somewhere inside of me, something I had never called to action.

I tugged the topo out of my pocket constantly, trying to match the features in my view with the ones drawn on the map—5.8 double cracks. I thought I found them, but moved further on to make sure, then returned. No doubt, this was where I began to climb up. Music wafted past on a tiny breeze, but it took some time to catch my attention. I must be dreaming, I thought, but there it came again, and I laughed aloud. "I Love the Night Life, Baby" by The Cars was sent our way from the team far across the wall. They had set up their hanging bivy and were clearly very amused to watch our headlamps continue to creep through the night.

I groaned. Our largest Camalot was neatly tucked away in the haul bag, and here was a crack that cried out for it. But I registered only momentary dismay. Calm reason held my emotion at bay—my mind, churning away on its own, had already figured out another solution. This was a stunning crack, straight-sided and smooth, hiding a secondary crack that I could wrap my entire hand around. Its twin, beside it, also rose and disappeared out of view. I ached to climb this free, to drop my hands into the crack and feel the positive contact with the rock. I wished away the darkness, the heavy aid rack and the burden of tension. Instead, I ascended methodically and mechanically in my étriers.

A long bundle of slings hung down in view, a pendulum to somewhere out of my circle of light. I had finished the crack and needed only to move up right some distance over undefined terrain to reach the ledge where we'd bivy. Hope and expectation fractured the calm, emotionless shell and had me squinting up through the darkness, trying to distinguish my goal. The tension eased only momentarily, returning with the disappointment of seeing only what I knew I'd see, vertical rock in the light four feet away from me. Emotion fled, and I moved mechanically up again over a fairly easy face and small ledges.

I finally clambered onto the bivy ledge. The description "big sandy ledges" had conjured images of a spacious landing, inches deep in soft, accommodating sand. The narrow, grit-strewn ledge fell far short of my expectations; I took great gulps of air, and my shoulders sagged. Elation, relief and a final admission of fear swept over me all at once. "Welcome" was all but written on a doormat at my feet. I felt as though I had come home.

Time sped up again, and shortly I heard the rattle of protection being removed from down below. "Don't you love that crack?" I couldn't help but chirp down to Simon. It was unfair of me to intrude; he was still on the climb. Meanwhile I was working the haul bag up, a piston in the machinery of engineered climbing. Bend the knees, pulling the rope down through the pulley, relax and up. Down again, methodical, paced. Then a snag and all my weight wouldn't budge it. No need to panic, it had happened before. I was singing at the task. Down on bent knees—no movement. Stuck. I called down to Simon to work on the haul line. He yelled up that it was no use, he couldn't move it either. I heard the uneasiness in his voice. He just wanted badly to be where I was; the darkness was cloying. He was, after all, wearing my dim headlamp.

His face finally came over the edge, and he hoisted himself up next to me. We hugged long, a reunion after an interminable gap of space and time. He told me to get a new headlamp, and then suggested we forget the haul bag until morning. It was his way of neatly removing any burden of responsibility and laying it at my feet, to take or leave as I liked. Whether it was because I was still elated after completing the lead, or from some cloak of martyrdom that I pulled around myself, I offered to fetch the bag.

"How?" he asked, but he was too tired and the question mark in the word got lost somewhere. He didn't really want to know. I needed to recapture the focus that had enveloped me while I was leading, but I was wired on emotion and the concentration was gone. I tried to center as best I could while Simon worked himself along the ledge. Finally I decided to rig a rappel with an end of rope. Some measure of despair did get hold of me as I descended the route, a sense of going the wrong way on a one-way street. A din of voices from inside competed for my attention.

"Forget about the haul bag for tonight, just get some sleep," my tired muscles screamed. "You don't need food; the bagels are moldy anyway. Why are you doing this?"

"Get the water. All I want is water." from my dry throat and cracked lips.

"Hardwoman saves young climbers from sleepless night..." my ego laughed at me.

Finally, I could make out the haul bag lurking maliciously under an overlap, and I yanked it free. Simon brought it up as I climbed back to join him.

I couldn't believe it was almost midnight when I looked at my watch. There would be no long sleep tonight—tomorrow we had to summit through the most difficult part of the route. As I crawled into my sleeping bag, the climb's tension crept out of my body and curled itself up neatly in a corner of the ledge to wait for me until morning.

REFLECTIONS ON MY FIRST
EXPEDITION

Deb Piranian

▲ ▲ ▲

ONE NIGHT IN January 1986, I was aroused from a deep sleep in my Leadville, Colorado home by the phone's ringing.

"Hello, Deb? This is Nancey Goforth in Alaska. Do you remember me? Did I wake you up?"

"Ya," I answered, still mostly asleep. "I have to get up really early tomorrow for work." I had two part-time jobs, one as an instructor for Colorado Outward Bound and the other as a lift operator at a ski area. I had to be up by 5 a.m.

"Well, I won't keep you. Let's set another time to talk."

"How about Friday morning; I'll be home."

"OK. But just so you know what I'm calling about, I was wondering whether you'd be interested in an all-women expedition to China this summer. Anyway, we can talk on Friday. Bye."

By the time I had crawled back into bed, I was wide awake. China! A women's expedition! It was only Tuesday.

For the next few days, thoughts of China and the expedition permeated all my waking hours. I was on a continual adrenaline rush. Sitting still was impossible. My mind raced: "What gear would I need? What kind of training program should I start?" I was motivated to go to the gym, even after long days of work outside. I stayed up later than usual and did not mind early mornings.

I wanted to go, but had fears and hesitations. My partner, Jeff, and I had made major climbing plans for the summer. I did not like backing out on those. He pointed out that our plans could happen any time, but the expedition was a rare opportunity. Then came the internal doubts. I had been climbing for eight years, but the last three had been devoted mostly to rock. Although I had spent extended periods of time in the mountains, I had never been on a major expedition. Did I have sufficient skills? I needed to share these doubts with Nancey to see whether she still thought me a worthwhile member. She did.

That short, late-night conversation led to my involvement in the 1986 Women's Expedition to Mt. Kongur (25,325 feet) in China. The highest peak in the Pamir Mountains, a northwest range of the Himalayas, Mt. Kongur had only been climbed once, in 1981 by four British climbers.

In March, the whole team gathered for the first time in Colorado. The goals of the meeting included teambuilding, logistics and having fun outdoors together. I was nervous and excited as I drove to the gathering. I had met only two of the women in person. One was Nancey Goforth. We had met in Seattle several years before to talk about Outward Bound and we had numerous acquaintances in common. Because of her non-sporty dress, people seldom guessed that she had been on many expeditions, including a first ascent. At our gathering she told us that colleagues in her nursing program in Anchorage found out about her mountaineering life only after she started selling T-shirts for our expedition. The other woman I had met was Pat Dillingham. I felt comfortable with her. She worked in corporate training and was focused and organized. She turned out to be the primary one to keep us on task in the many meetings throughout the expedition.

I had talked with Kath Giel, the expedition leader, on the phone, but had never met her. At the meeting she struck me as friendly, enthusiastic and organized. At the time she worked for a utility company in California.

By the end of the gathering, I had some sense of the other women. Joan Provencher, a house painter from California, was quiet and looked strong. Nancy Fitzsimmons, from Idaho and an instructor for both the National Outdoor Leadership School and Outward Bound, was practical and down to earth. Our base camp manager, Suzanne Hopkins from Massachusetts, was a political activist. It was she who questioned seeking donations from companies that had political dark sides.

The other two women were from Colorado. Carole Petiet, a psychologist, was in charge of the psychological research we planned to undertake. Her tall, slender build belied the strength she would show on the mountain. The March gathering was at her home. Kathy Nilsen was a nurse in Aspen. She was an infinite source of humor, something I came to value dearly. When events seemed bleak in China, she could make us laugh, putting everything back in perspective.

The first night together, we each filled out a questionnaire as part of the psychological study. To become more cohesive as a team, we shared parts of the questionnaire: "What are your strengths and weaknesses? What is something that even a close friend may not know about you?" We worked through some logistical questions and put on a fundraising show at a Women's Week at the University of Colorado, Boulder. We even went backcountry skiing for a day. Driving home from the gathering, I was excited. It felt like a good group of women, and I was pleased with the process and sense of team so far. I dreamed of our becoming nine inseparable friends.

The next time we were all together was at Kath's home in Albany, California, the week before leaving. We could have used two weeks. There were endless lists of last-minute details, plus food and gear to pack. Numerous relatives and friends dropped what they were doing to help us for that week. We did more psychological and neurological testing for the studies. We sampled donated food and checked donated gear. At one point, Kath's small front yard had five tents set up; in between sat Suzanne and Pat, reading the instructions for the video camera with which we were going to film the expedition.

All that would have been more than enough, but there was still fundraising. We had a budget of $65,000. Being the first all-women expedition in China, we had a unique slant to offer the media. At first the media coverage was exciting. "Look! Our picture is in the paper! We're on the ten o'clock news!" But pressure came with the media coverage; we were presented as experts, as wonder women. I came to understand, especially after the expedition, the media's love of extremes. One article, based on their selective excerpts from our group journal, created the impression that we had been constantly fighting for our lives. It hardly seemed like the same expedition I had been on.

Finally we left. We flew into Beijing and had a day of sightseeing. I was struck by the similarity to the Soviet Union—the gray atmosphere and dilapidated buildings, roads and vehicles. We were whisked to the Ming Tombs and the Great Wall by our interpreter, a young woman with minimal English. The Wall, truly one of the great wonders of the world, stretched for thousands of miles along ridgetops, with subsidiary walls going off on adjoining ridges.

We also had our first face-to-face encounter with the Chinese Mountaineering Association (CMA). The Chinese had never dealt with an all-women expedition. Previous "women's" groups always included men, usually in leadership roles. Our first obstacle was a CMA official named Mr. Ying, whom we quickly renamed Mr. Ying-Yang because of his obvious efforts to create obstacles for us. He told us it was "surely impossible" to take all our baggage and specially crated oxygen on the plane with us to Urumchi (Urümqi), our next destination, and it would have to be shipped separately, which would take several weeks. "You have many problems. Why don't you just go trekking," he advised us. We decided to ignore his negativity and to counteract with the assumption that everything would fly with us. The next morning at the airport, we piled our seventy-five pieces of baggage in front of the check-in counter, blocking the area. All our baggage, including the oxygen, came with us on the plane.

In Urumchi, we met our two liaison officers, Su and Muhameti. Su spoke reasonable English, liked to be the center of attention and was an avid and talented photographer. Muhameti was Uighur, the predominant "minority" in northwestern China. Because of his Uighur language, he was invaluable in dealing with the local people, especially our camel drivers. Several years before, he had worked as a liason officer for the Japanese expedition attempting the north side of Mt. Kongur, on which several climbers had been killed in an avalanche. A gracious and humble man, Muhameti consistently tried to make our experience both positive and meaningful.

After numerous delays due to dust storms, we flew on to Kashgar (Kashi), an ancient oasis town on the Silk Road. The people in and around Kashgar are mostly Uighur, Kazakh and Tadzhik, thus they are Turkic and Iranian, not Asian. They are also Muslim. For me, this was the most fascinating part of China. It was like stepping into a different world, even a different era. There were few multi-story buildings in Kashgar; most buildings were hundreds of years old. People got around mostly on foot, by bicycle, on donkeys or on horse-drawn carts, and we soon learned that the carts with a blue or red canopy were taxis.

While in Kashgar, we had our second run-in with Mr. Ying-Yang's efforts to thwart our mountaineering attempts. We had shipped Gaz cartridges for our Bleuet stoves, which were to be our only source of fuel high on the mountain, well ahead of time from the United States. In Beijing, Mr. Ying had told us they had not yet arrived but that it was "surely possible" to buy some from the CMA in Kashgar. Although we were able, with the help of Su and Muhameti, to buy high-altitude cartridges from the CMA that were left over from a Japanese expedition, Su told us that Mr. Ying had called from Beijing with instructions not to sell us any.

Leaving Kashgar, we drove by jeep and truck along the Kara-koram highway. Right outside of Kashgar and the green of its oasis, we found ourselves in the bleakest countryside I have ever encoun-tered. The whole area was a flat field of large gravel. Only the tire ruts distinguished the road from the surrounding area. Gradually, barren hills showed on the horizon. At one point we passed a "high-way crew": people removing rock cut from the cliff road with crow-bars and moving it to the river side in wheelbarrows. The road grader was a camel dragging a heavy piece of metal along the road. The rocky hills gave way to snow- and glacier-covered peaks. What were unnamed nominal peaks there would have been major moun-taineering attractions anywhere in United States. At last we reached our destination, Karakol Lakes at 12,000 feet, situated in a high des-ert plain surrounded by towering mountains.

We spent two nights there acclimatizing, visiting a local settle-ment and trying to figure out which of the distant peaks showing themselves among the clouds was our destination, since no topo-graphical maps of the area were available.

Ever since we had met Su and Muhameti, they had made com-ments implying that they wanted to go above our base camp and be involved in the climb. We were definitely against it; this was to be a women's expedition. We decided we needed to impress upon them our experience. The night before leaving Karakol Lakes, we had a meeting with all eleven of us. "In the interest of getting to know each other," we each shared our background and achievements. It felt strange to brag about ourselves, but by the end of the meeting Su and Muhameti said that they were impressed and that we obviously knew what we were doing. They dropped all talk of going above base camp. In some sense, I think, they were relieved. Neither of them had much mountaineering experience. I suspect they had felt responsible to "protect" us on the mountain.

The walk to our base camp at 14,800 feet (elevations are approximate, based on altimeters) could have been done in one day had the camel drivers with our gear not tried to undermine us. Muhameti told them that they would not get paid if they did not take us all the way. By then, the drivers had procrastinated and dramatized long enough that we had to spend a night on the way. In the morning, everything was covered with snow, but it melted as we hiked the last eight hundred feet to base camp.

We spent the first day setting up tents and organizing gear. We had agreed to take a rest day the next day for people to acclimatize; we had come up almost 10,000 feet in three days. On the "rest day" I felt tired, but could not resist hiking up higher. Under a gray overcast sky I hiked above the camp to where I could see the Koksal Glacier where it squeezes between two ridges. There were more crevasses than glacier surface. Awed by the sight, I couldn't help being glad that our route was elsewhere.

The next day, Nancey and Kathy came down with respiratory infections. Kathy said she had felt the beginnings of it in Urumchi and, perhaps, should not have gone running there. Nancey was pretty sure she had picked up hers in a small settlement near the Lakes where she had drunk tea from a local's cup. Within a day, everyone except Nancy, Pat, Suzanne and myself were sick and on antibiotics. Suzanne was base camp manager, and a back injury prevented her from carrying loads, but Nancy, Pat and I were anxious to get on the route and start carrying loads. So, with great excitement, the three of us set off up the Corridor Glacier.

Each new view around a corner was exploration: What will we see? What is the best way to go? How long will it take to get to that col? What looked like a forty-five-minute distance turned out to take three hours, so unaccustomed were we to the scale of these mountains. Being neophytes to big expeditions, we were not clear about the best way to organize movement up the mountain, where to put caches or establish camps. Nancey and Kathy had the most expedition experience but were extremely sick. It was all they could do to wake up and crawl out of their tents to pee; they were certainly in no state to help plan an efficient system. So for the first three or four days, until the others began to recover and help carry loads, the four of us who were not sick made many of the organizational decisions.

The system we established remained more out of inertia than pure merit. We had two caches between our base camp and the advanced base camp—one at 16,200 feet and the other at a col at 17,300 feet. The lower one proved of some value as people recovering from sickness started to carry loads. It gave them a short, "conditioning" goal. However, as it turned out, having two caches was inefficient. As we adjusted to altitude, we could make longer carries. We still needed an intermediate stop between the two base camps; it was too far to make the round-trip in a day without a rest day. However, with two caches, we tended to set our sights on shorter distances.

Gradually, the other women got better. Everyone was eager to be involved in moving up the mountain and started carrying loads as soon as they felt better. Unfortunately, I think for some it was too soon. Nancey, Kathy and Joan never fully recovered. After a few days of carrying, they would be back in their bags sick. I cannot help but think that if they had been able to resist the strong drive to be out and involved, had taken a few extra days to more fully recover, they might not have continually relapsed. Of course, hindsight is twenty-twenty. As it was, they all got to the advanced base camp, and Kathy and Nancey made a trip to Camp I.

We spent two weeks traveling back and forth between the base camp and advanced camps, carrying gear and food. It was exciting to finally move up to the advanced camp, at 17,000 feet in the middle of the upper basin of the Koksal Glacier before it squeezed down toward base camp. With hindsight, I can now see that we carried too much food and gear above base camp. Our plan was for everyone to be at least as high as the advanced camp, if not higher, so we carried up food and fuel for eight people. We did not take into account the liklihood that at least some of us would be sick. We realized later that we should have carried up enough for five or six people; if we had been lucky enough to get all of us that high on the mountain, we could have carried up more supplies as needed.

For the advanced camp we had VE-25 tents, the largest of The North Face dome tents, and MSR stoves (both donated). For higher camps we had brought modified Bleuet stoves and smaller tents. Essentially, we had carried double the gear we needed to Advanced.

As people adjusted to the altitude, they worked on setting up Camp I at 19,300 feet on the southwest rib. On the morning that Pat and Nancy planned to move to Camp I, Nancy said she was too tired to go. Kath asked whether I would go; Pat was anxious to move up. Ignoring my own tiredness, I agreed. It was special to be the first to sleep there. We melted water, forced ourselves to eat and drink, and marveled at the view. Off in the distance, 7,000 feet below, we could see Karakol Lakes and the brown of the surrounding high desert. We could see into Pakistan and the Soviet Union. The next day we were tired and had headaches. Between resting and melting water for drinks, we worked on a snow cave for Carole, Nancy and Kath, who joined us that day.

The next night was one of the worst in my life. My head felt like it was splitting into pieces. Ordinary medication did nothing. I cried from pain and constantly shifted positions, hoping to find a more tolerable one. In the morning, at the seven o'clock radio contact, I asked the nurses (Nancey, Kathy and Carole) what stronger medication we had that I could take for headaches. After a few questions, they said I needed to descend; it sounded like edema. I felt like crying from disappointment as Nancy and Pat accompanied me down. Within 1,500 feet I felt tolerable. By the time we reached the advanced camp, I felt okay. It was hard to watch Nancy and Pat turn around to go back up.

Nancey was glad for the company. The previous day, she had been knocked off her feet by a sudden shift of the glacier. We had probed the area carefully when we had originally set up the advanced camp, but things were changing. We spent the next week together reading, eating popcorn and freeze-dried cinnamon apples, organizing gear, sleeping and talking. We went up to Camp I once, but I started getting a headache again. As our time on the mountain drew to a close, we cleared out everything extra from the advanced camp and moved down the mountain. Back at the base camp, overwhelmingly disappointed, I swore I would never go on another expedition. I wanted to get away from the mountains, go sightseeing in Kashgar and Beijing, and go home. I missed Jeff more than I had anticipated.

Meanwhile, Nancy, Kath, Pat and Carole at Camp I pushed higher. Camp II was set at approximately 21,000 feet. But when the weather deteriorated and avalanche conditions developed, they decided the summit was not worth the risk. In addition, our time was running out; the date for the camels to pick us up at base camp was set and could not be changed. That was unfortunate because there was still plenty of food and fuel at the advanced camp to wait for conditions to improve. Our only shortage was time.

Extra time would have also given people a chance to rest. Carrying loads had taken a toll. Carrying too much gear to the advanced camp, not having had a terribly efficient system, and sickness had eaten up time. Above 19,000 feet there is so little oxygen that your body deteriorates even on "rest" days. To really recover and regain strength, you need to return to lower elevations. If we had had more time, people could have returned to base camp for a number of rest days after stocking Camp I and then gone back up for a summit push. If . . .

It was a great relief when we were all safely back at base camp. We had a meeting to discuss our successes and what we could have done better. Watching the video of this meeting back in the States was painful. We had been so down about not making the summit, yet we were not talking about that. As we each talked about "successes," our faces shouted out sadness. At that meeting we were unable to share our pain with each other. It is true that reaching the summit was only the goal and that the process of the whole expedition was significant, but at that moment all we seemed to see was the goal not reached.

As if in accordance with our mood, a heavy snow fell the last night in base camp. The next day we walked out of the camp, each in our own world under a gray sky that matched the gray snow, eliminating any distinct horizon.

After seven weeks in the mountains, we retraced our steps through China. With the stresses of the mountain behind us, we felt more patience to go sightseeing and enjoy the culture. We began to talk some in smaller groups about the disappointments, but we were no longer a cohesive group with a common goal. We each had separate plans ahead of us.

I came away from the expedition full of new experiences and understanding, although at the time I did not appreciate them all. What I had known intellectually about expeditions, I came to understand on a personal, experiential level. The familiarity with expeditions gained on Mt. Kongur proved invaluable when, several years later, I ventured onto Denali with two friends who had no previous expedition experience.

There was also the time shared with the eight other women. We did not all become the inseparable friends I had hoped. Some of the time together was joyful, some of the interactions were rough and painful, but I feel a bond with most of the women because of our time together.

As I originally went through my journal to write this article, I was struck by two things. One was my own concern with doing everything correctly. I wanted a perfect expedition with no mistakes (whatever that means). The second was the marvel of the process. Yes, it was extremely disappointing not to reach the summit, or even the technical parts of the climb. However, I now appreciate that those would have been only final steps in a long journey. Not making those steps cannot negate all the steps we did take. With each of those steps came new experiences and understanding, and I feel incredibly fortunate to have been part of the journey.

SAINT EXUPERY

Sue Harrington

▲ ▲ ▲

I WOKE UP with a start, my right hip and arm numb, my back pressed into a sharp rock, and my feet hanging off the edge. Shifting my position, I noticed that Alan, sound asleep, hoarded most of our tiny bivy ledge. I shoved him over, feeling not the least bit guilty. "Hey, what did ya do that for?" he moaned. I ignored him, and tried to fall back to sleep, content that I wasn't the only one awake. Misery loves company.

As I lay there, eight pitches up on the North Face of Saint Exupery, I thought about my husband's (Alan Kearney) and my decision to climb together in Patagonia, mulling over some friends' comments on climbing with their significant others. Debbie once told me, "Because of Andy's and my different experience levels, I get worried that we can't complete long difficult climbs. I want to retreat too soon." Peter admitted to Alan that he fretted when his wife Rachel was leading: "I'm afraid she'll get hurt." Rachel's comment was that if she didn't do her share of the leading she didn't feel as satisfied with the climb.

Alan and I have shared similar experiences while climbing together. On a few climbs I have had to remind Alan, a much more experienced climber than I, that he was not climbing with one of the boys. We have had to retreat because I wasn't willing to be pulled up a route. Nevertheless, climbing together has remained a high priority. The chance for us to do a route in an exotic place such as Patagonia didn't seem to require a second thought. However, I began to realize just how much work it took to make an expedition with one's spouse successful. Certainly, one did not go on a climb like this for romance!

Our trip had been inspired by a desire to do a new route on Saint Exupery, a lesser-known yet striking twin-summitted spire of clean granite in the Argentine Patagonia. It had only seen four ascents, all by the East Ridge. Alan had been to the area on two other trips, and was intrigued with Exupery's unclimbed west face. When I asked him to climb the west face of Exupery with me, he agreed without pause.

Upon arriving in Fitz Roy Park, however, our plans were uprooted—Exupery had recently been climbed twice by new routes, once via the west face. Alan immediately lost interest. I was disappointed by Alan's change of heart, but after a lengthy discussion we decided on an alternative, Exupery's neighboring peak Torre Innominata. It had been climbed only once by a British team in 1974.

After three false starts due to stormy weather, our climb of Innominata went smoothly except for a long offwidth that poor route finding forced us into. We made the summit on a beautiful, clear day. From there, our view of the steep north face of Exupery revealed a perfect-looking ramp, rekindling our desire to climb the mountain—providing the weather held.

We returned to base camp exhausted. It had been easy to agree to climb Exupery while feeling the high of success on top of Innominata. But now I didn't want to move. I liked the peaceful forest, and was ready to spend a week there, reading, baking bread, washing clothes and getting my head together for the next climb. Secretly, I hoped for a real whopper of a storm.

On our third morning at base camp, when we went out to gaze at the mountains, Alan cheerfully announced, "Looks like the day for our next trip up the glacier." I could have killed him! It was bad enough to have my dreams of numerous naps and lavish eating smashed, but his enthusiasm was too much. I tried to convince him that the thin layer of clouds overhead was an ominous sign—to no avail. He insisted that we had to take advantage of the good weather, something that comes in rare spells in Patagonia.

I was beginning to see that Alan's drive and mine were much different. He was energized by the unknown, whereas I liked the predictable. I was finding it difficult to match his rising level of enthusiasm for climbing a new route on Exupery when a week before Alan had no interest in the mountain. But I knew he was right about the weather. So with dread and suppressed anger, I repacked, and began plodding toward high camp with heavy feet. Intuition told me this would be another false start.

That night I couldn't sleep. I was dreading the next day and not entirely sure why. Fatigue? Stress? A partner whose undying enthusiasm for this place was beginning to wear me down? I came here enthused to climb so I couldn't understand this change. I let anxiety rob me of sleep.

The next morning dawned beautiful. The surrounding peaks glowed orange in the morning light, but my mind was still a dark cloud. I tried to tell Alan how I was feeling but he didn't want to listen. Our spouse/climbing partner relationship was weakening. We were experiencing a conflict in roles. I wanted Alan to be a consoling spouse, not a driven climber, and he wanted the reverse of me. We were having difficulty balancing these competing needs.

I had decided long ago that I wasn't about to stay home in the kitchen while my husband gamboled about the world climbing, so here I was. And like it or not, it was a perfect day to climb. I told myself I would feel better once I started moving.

Three hours of scrambling over talus, up a snow couloir, and up steep loose slabs delivered us to the base of the wall. Alan led the first pitch, leaving me with the pack, which wasn't light (we had planned at least one bivy on the peak). He climbed over a bulge and into a steep, shallow chimney dripping with snowmelt. I followed, free climbing as far as the protrusion, where the pack threw me off balance. I thought, "Don't worry, you can always jumar," a task easier said than done. I struggled, I swore, I struggled some more, and I still couldn't get over the bulge. Finally, the tension from the past two days was too much—I cried.

I pictured myself hanging dead on the rope because I couldn't move. I hated Alan for taking me to this place and "making me" climb. I swore I would never climb again, provided we made it down. I felt utterly alone.

"What the hell are you doing down there?" questioned Alan,

tearing me from my tension-induced fog and inspiring me with anger. I was determined to get up this pitch just so I could give him a piece of my mind. With profuse cursing and animal grunts I was over the swell, through the chimney and finally into a crack where the going was easier. But when I reached Alan I was too short of breath to chew him out!

By now it was late afternoon and clouds were boiling over Cerro Torre to the west. Alan asked if I wanted the next lead. "No way," I barked. "I am tired, scared, sick of climbing and I don't like the looks of the weather." In a disapproving tone Alan said, "Guess we better go down then." I was flooded with both relief and guilt as we began rappelling.

Snug in our sleeping bags once again at high camp, we exchanged few words. I think Alan was afraid to say anything to me. I fretted over his silence for awhile, but finally I realized that what was really bothering me was me. I had let both myself and Alan down. It had been so easy for me to blame Alan for my problems on the climb. I rarely lost my temper with other climbing partners, and I didn't expect them to instinctively know how I was feeling. That was a large burden to place on one's partner and Alan was taking it surprisingly well. But he was becoming short with me. Maybe all this was why some couples prefer not to climb together. It dawned on me that I had been relying on Alan to keep the momentum going. Somehow I was going to have to rekindle the spirit that first inspired me to climb in Patagonia.

That night it stormed. The wind picked up, and the rain came down in sheets. No longer was high camp snug. We awoke to water dripping from the rock onto our faces. However, the sound of the rain and wind was reassuring to me. In my half-awake state I imagined it was a sign that we were not supposed to be on the mountain that night; maybe my reluctance to climb was due to an intuitive sense rather than to being a failure. With that thought, I pulled my bivy sack over my head and fell back to sleep.

By morning, the weather had not improved and it was obviously time to return to base camp. We had a difficult decision to make. Did we pack everything, or did we leave our high camp intact for another attempt? Alan left it up to me, encouraging me to do whatever I felt was best for me, and saying he would accept that decision without question. He knew that to push me would only create resentment. I thought that I really could climb the mountain if I didn't have to struggle with such a big pack. I suggested to Alan that we reduce the load and with a smile he said, "I'm sure we can take care of that." Leaving our gear behind, we headed back to the peaceful forest.

The skies soon cleared. With machine-like monotony we repacked, and although I was more optimistic this time, I hoped this would be our last trip up the trail. My knees screamed with the thought of all the boulders and uneven terrain we would have to cross again. Even Alan, who normally chatters away, was silent. We made it to high camp in five hours and cooked a quick meal of instant potatoes before bed.

Beep-beep-beep-beep! I tried to pretend I didn't hear it, but Alan did. Up he popped, as chipper as ever, to start the stove.

Awfully optimistic, I thought; he hadn't even looked at the weather. Having drawn the cramped side of the boulder, I couldn't see out, so I rolled over and waited until the water was boiling. It was 4:30 a.m.

After a hot breakfast Alan looked outside, then swore at seeing a bank of storm clouds. As I saw it there was nothing to do but go back to sleep. Six hours later the clouds dissipated and after a brief discussion we decided to go for it, regardless of a late start. We reached the base of the wall at 2:00 p.m.

I wasn't sure how I'd feel climbing. As I looked up and saw the ice-filled chimney on the second pitch I quickly grabbed the first lead. Gritting my teeth I tackled the pitch, feeling like I'd never climbed before. My feet rattled, my hands wouldn't grip, and I couldn't get in the proper pro. Why did I want to do this? I made it to the belay, letting out a big sigh of relief. Alan arrived, oblivious to my chattering teeth. He stopped just long enough to hand off the pack—it figures! I could see that leading was where it was at.

After two hundred feet of chimney climbing we hit a series of clean, parallel finger and hand cracks that led to the ramp we had spotted from Innominata. Every time it was my turn to lead I felt nauseous, but to overcome my illness all I had to do was look at the pack. Slowly, I began to regain my courage, and the climbing became more enjoyable with every pitch.

By dusk we had climbed two pitches up the ramp. Failing to

find the perfect bivouac site, we ended up on a tiny ledge eight pitches up, where sleep was hard to come by. I pondered the wisdom of climbing with my husband. Our relationship had been strained, but it was far from severed. By feeling free to yell and express some fears I had been able to work through things that bothered me. I wasn't holding grudges against Alan for "making" me be here any more. I was pulling my weight as a climbing partner, and Alan was being supportive. We were working as a team.

Morning came after an eternity, but the clear skies of the day before were replaced by somber gray clouds. Trying to be enthusiastic, I pointed out that there was no wind. Alan pointed out that there also was no sun. We lingered in our cramped one-person bivy sack and hid beneath its thin layer of warmth. Finally, we wriggled out of the sack and stomped our aching feet back into stiff, cold rock shoes. Doubts began to resurface, but I quickly squelched them, focusing on moving instead.

I again drew the first lead of the day, starting off cold and shaky. But I warmed up quickly. As my confidence grew I became more talkative, and Alan responded with an improved mood. We climbed easily together and swapped leads with little fuss. The seven-pitch ramp yielded enjoyable 5.7 and 5.8 climbing—more my speed. At the end of the ramp a short wall with flaring shallow cracks led up to the East Ridge. We dropped our plans to continue up the north face with the onset of light rain. The top of the East Ridge route was circuitous, made more so by our stubborn desire to free climb the route.

After nineteen pitches, we arrived on top, elated. But clouds and rain already obscured the tops of Poincenot and Fitz Roy to the north, so we quickly began an endless succession of rappels. Finally, we dropped into the snow gully after seventeen rappels. It was 11 p.m. and I could barely see Alan in front of me. We were thankful that the threatening storm never fully developed. Unfortunately, we didn't make it back to high camp that night. Totally exhausted, we opted to spend the night out above the gully.

The next morning we awoke—if one really wakes up from not sleeping—to a brilliant sunrise. Sitting on our ledge and looking across at Cerro Torre glowing pink in the distance, my feelings gelled—this *was* romantic! What better person to be with than your spouse in such a magnificent place? We had worked hard to over-

come some unforeseen stresses which climbing placed on our relationship. We would share this experience forever. It was with a
stronger bond that we packed up our gear and headed off toward
camp.

RISKY BUSINESS

Alison Osius

▲ ▲ ▲

I HAVE KNOWN since sixth grade that the pyramids in Egypt were tall, when I saw in the encyclopedia that one named Cheops was "137 m." and earnestly read in my report to the class that it was 137 miles high. At first, none of the slumped listeners noticed, but then a few doubtful questions stalled me mid-oration.

Sixteen years later, my family and I rose at 4:15 a.m. from my brother's apartment in Garden City, Cairo, to climb Cheops, known as the Great Pyramid, forty stories tall. An hour later we reached the three pyramids at Giza, on the edge of the city, left the car half a mile away, and walked along the silent road.

Darkness and mist concealed the pyramids—5,000 years old, and among the seven ancient wonders of the world—until we were one-hundred yards from Cheops. Then, like an idea forming, its edge began to take shape.

Sudden and eerie, the drawn-out wail of the *muezzin* sounded, calling the faithful to prayer. We six thought of ghosts and grave robbers and guards—in fact, there was one following us now. "He's got a gun," I whispered to my younger sister, Lucy, 20. With us too were my mother, Nancy, 54, and cousin Deb, a year older than I at 27, and a friend, John Kerr, 23 like my brother Ted.

The guard trailed us. As we neared the base of the Cheops Pyramid (the largest, 146.5 meters when constructed in 2690 B.C., its base still covering over thirteen acres), another guard, in hood and long *galibea,* approached. "No climb today!" he exclaimed. Climbing on the pyramids is forbidden. Various tales exist about how many people have been killed doing so. The three most often mentioned were a Marine, an Englishwoman, and an American mountaineer: Rand Herron, in the early 1930s, had just finished an attempt to climb Nanga Parbat in India when he fell descending one of the pyramids. Jack Mansfield, a retired U.S. Air Force officer presently living in Cairo, told me he had heard of five deaths in just this decade.

Now, two more guards approached us. John Kerr spoke with them in Arabic. "Negotiating is half the fun," said he, veteran of twenty such excursions. Eventually he turned back. "Hm. Somebody fell off a few days ago."

"Died?" I asked.

"Well, yeah."

They resumed conversation. I reflected that I was the only experienced technical rock climber in our group.

My mother, trying not to sound too relieved, speculated that orders had come from above to clamp down on climbers. She does not like heights.

John reached into his pocket, and gave the guards their *baksheesh:* ten Egyptian pounds. More words. "He wants ten extra because somebody fell," John added, tossing "Nah!" over his shoulder.

"I don't think I want to do this," Deb had been venturing for some moments, but she followed as we began stepping up onto the lower stones. It was still pitch dark, and the wind was blowing above fifteen knots.

"After the first part, the rest is easier," John assured us. We climbed up several corners, each person pointing out footholds for the next. Lucy began protesting after twenty feet when we had to traverse a twelve-inch wide, down-sloping ledge. I dropped back to help. My hand on Lucy's back, I could feel her shaking.

The ridge was a series of big, uneven steps, like staggered rows of molars, each about two to four feet high. About 2.3 million blocks of stone make up the structure, weighing an average of two-and-a-half tons apiece, some as much as sixteen tons.

After forty feet, Lucy announced indignantly she was going no farther. With difficulty we coaxed her ten feet more to a wide platform where she could wait: Camp I.

At about one hundred feet, Deb tersely declared she'd sit tight. We left her at Camp II. The route now had two *in situ* cousins.

The pyramid loomed hugely above us, and it did seem that no one who didn't want to should continue. I was in front, squinting to find the way, watching my mother. We wound around the northeast ridge, me nervous about finding the easiest way possible, fearful of leading onto the wrong sections.

By 200 feet my heart was audibly thumping with apprehension. My mother, in uneven tones, mentioned that she was afraid to look down. She never did again on the ascent. The rock was sound, no blocks loose, but the exposure stark, and emphasized by the fact that we could not see the ground. I wished for a rope between us, and some Friends. Looking down that black drop, you couldn't help wondering, would you bounce? Or would those protruding rocks strain you like a sieve?

A rock climber and instructor, I got more scared on this easy climb than on any other I can think of. An admission: I have instructivitis. I can no longer hide the symptoms. Its prevalent characteristic is an eternal feeling of responsibility. If my mother slipped, the fault would be not my brother's, whose idea this had been, nor John's, who took his friends up regularly, but mine: as the experienced climber, I should have known better.

Firing my fears was the fact that both our father and John's had just died. Our dad, aged fifty-four, had died very suddenly of a heart attack six weeks before, in a marsh, wading offshore in his hip boots after a goose he'd shot. John's father, Malcolm Kerr, president of the American University in Beirut, had been assassinated ten months earlier, shot as he walked into his office. Two gunmen had run out. No one knows who was responsible for the murder; as always in the Middle East, various terrorist groups claimed it as theirs.

Just as a surgeon shouldn't operate on a relative, no climbing instructor should take her mother up anywhere unroped. Fear for another is worse than fear for oneself. And if Lucy and Deb had not dropped out, I would have been, silently, wild.

I kept telling my mother we were almost at the top, sometimes believing it myself, when darkness hid the ridge thirty feet ahead and I thought it ended there.

I had a flash of imagined conversation between my Mountain Rescue Service friends in New Hampshire:

"What *happened?*"

"She was crazy to take her mother there."

But my mother moved steadily along.

We reached the top before 6 a.m. Now it was time to worry about getting my "clients" through the descent. In a few hours, I thought, this heavy weight would be off me.

We looked at the sky; only a faint film of pink showed.

To get out of the wind, we huddled behind a desk-sized block on the top platform, making conversation. I wedged myself into a niche, and smelled urine. Now we began to worry about Deb and Lucy below. Cold, too antsy to wait for a slow dawn, I stood up abruptly, saying I'd start down to give them the car keys and maybe an escort.

It was veritable shades lighter now, and I skittered along fast, finding the two moving together only twenty-five feet from the ground. Deb had, half an hour before, first made her way back down to Lucy. The two had huddled together, speculating about how much money it would take to make them climb up.

"Would you do it for a thousand dollars?"

"No way."

"How about a million?"

"Um . . . I don't know. I would try very hard."

Lucy hadn't been able to shake the feeling that the whole pyramid was about to tip over and slide her off.

Below, a shadowy figure had crept up. Lucy's spine had straightened in fear as a guard climbed toward their ledge. What if he grabbed her foot and tried to fling her off?

He only ordered, "Go down!"

When I reached the two, Deb, steeped in responsibility, had forgotten her own fear and was coaching like a pro. "Just think of it like going down bleachers. OK, face in here . . ."

On the ground, several robed figures gathered around us, all in turbans or hoods. One opened the dirty blanket on his shoulders wide, trying to gather Lucy into it.

I had doubts about leaving Deb and Lucy, both excruciatingly blonde, with the guards, but more about leaving my mother up top.

I clambered back onto the worn rock. When I was at thirty feet a loud whistle shrilled. A fellow in a white turban sprinted across the sand toward Cheops, blowing his tin whistle. "Madam! No climb!"

"Hi," I waved airily, and continued.

The whistle shrieked in rage. I stopped.

I could hear Lucy's stern voice. "There's a *mother* up there."

"Mother. Mother. Mother," the men repeated among themselves. They grew reverent.

"She is *old*," Lucy continued. She looked up, forehead furrowed. "Don't tell her I said that, Alison."

The whistler nodded. I continued uninterrupted. By now a man was offering the girls "hubbly-bubbly"—hash. When I next looked the two were hurrying toward the car.

I leapt from one palm and high-step to the next, panting, rocking right foot to left in the most patterned climbing I've ever done. Two-thirds of the way up I met the other three descending, weary of waiting for sunrise. My mother was more afraid now because she had to look down. But it was light enough to see the way clearly. Seeing she was in good hands, with the gentle guide John, I made one more sprint to the top with Ted to look around.

We could see the other two of the big three pyramids, built by grandfather-father-son pharoahs; nearer was Cephren, second in size, which looks tallest, being on a higher section of the plateau. Some of its original limestone casing still sheathes the top. Below us were the smaller structures created for the pharoahs' wives and children, some rows of square adobe dwellings, and beyond them, the empty, dun-hued desert. Ted pointed out the Sphinx, from here preposterously small, actually eighty meters long and twenty-two tall, enclosed by a wall. Layers of mist separated us from the highway, and beyond that, from the lights of Cairo. A rooster, then several, crowed, and I noticed for the first time today the incessant cacophony of horns, which only tapers off in the hour or two before dawn, and in the nights made me stuff my ears with toilet paper.

As we hurried back down to join the others, I felt curiously liberated. I had been unprepared for death when it hit my father; my comfort was that he had lived his short life well and fully. I had since been excessively fearing death for my loved ones. That was no way to live well, and now was time to stop it. At some point, you *feel* what it means to "go on." Climbing and loving people are both risky businesses. Worth it.

Seven guards clustered at the pyramid's base, gesticulating. Two had rifles. One had a pistol.

When my mother's feet touched ground, they sprang forward to shake her hand in congratulation, then got on to business as usual and asked for more money.

One planted himself before John, asking in Arabic, "Hey, where you been lately, man?" He had once seen John there three times in a week.

"This is the *last* time!" another told John.

Freed, perhaps, of some self-absorption, I questioned, for the first time, whether it was right for us foreign tourists to pay to tread all over one of these Egyptian and world treasures. Only crassly entitled by the payment of *baksheesh,* to wear it down even further. As for the armed guards, well, they *were* only doing their job, which was to guard. I wouldn't have questioned possession of a gun by a guard at the Lincoln Memorial.

"I wonder if he was making that up about the guy just getting killed," John mused, walking away. "Maybe they change their strategy every time like I change mine. Usually they just tell me they'll take me to jail."

We went next door to see the Sphinx, and the sun came up.

THE AMERICAN TEAM

Denise Mitten

▲ ▲ ▲

AFTER TWO DAYS of flying, we arrived in Kathmandu, Nepal. We would be climbing in the dry rain shadow of the Annapurnas, I told our climbing group, meaning that the Annapurna Mountains create a weather block, making the area to the northwest of the massif dry relative to the surrounding area. I had been in this same area three years before on my first trip to Nepal and had fallen in love with the mountain scenery and the people. I feel good when I am in Nepal. I feel I fit in. I connect easily with the people and respect their Buddhist traditions and teachings. I love the views. When someone asks me why I climb, I typically reply "for the views." I seem to get in a better and better mood the higher I walk. I feel both invigorated and calm when I hike and climb in the Himalaya.

Our group—Georgia, Kris, Deb, Linda, Charlea, Valerie and myself—came from Minnesota, Illinois, New Mexico, Washington and Colorado. All seven of us came with our own hopes and expectations. Our goal was to walk around the Annapurna Circuit and to climb Pisang Peak en route.

The Annapurna Circuit is a popular trekking route that opened to outside visitors in 1977. The route, which circles around the Annapurna massif, includes trekking over a 17,000 foot pass, and takes about twenty-one days to hike. During this adventure a trekker covers about forty-five miles while going up and down over 30,000 feet.

Standard maps showing elevation in Nepal do so in 1,000-foot contours; the norm for the United States is between twenty- and one hundred-foot contours. Even so, Nepal maps are covered with lines; only seventeen percent of this tiny country is flat. The mountains rise sharply, and the people literally carve their villages into the hillsides. The trails we would hike had been local trade routes since the fourth century.

Halfway around the circuit stands Pisang Peak—a beautiful cone-shaped, snow-capped 19,900-foot mountain with permanent snow fields starting at 16,000 feet. Pisang Peak boasts a reputation as a trekking peak: that is, you need mountaineering skills to climb it, but it is not as hard to climb as Mt. Everest.

In Kathmandu, I did the trek and climb negotiating, hearing the typical "no problem, memsahib" answer to my requests and then having to follow up each request at least twice. We obtained the proper climbing permits and checked the first-aid kit and other gear. I knew from previous expeditions that thorough planning and checking in Kathmandu pay off many times during the expedition and set a good tone for the trek support crew.

In 1985, Kathmandu had a population of 350,000 people, yet it felt like a small town. I had met a number of Nepali people on previous visits, and I always seemed to run into some of them or people who knew them each time I returned. I met one man—Lakhpa Gurung—through an odd set of circumstances. A day after arriving in Kathmandu in 1982, a young Nepali man came up to my friend and me and offered his services as a guide. From our reading we knew to ask him for a reference, and he brought us a written one. But when we checked his reference in person, we found that the author of the reference did not know the young man. However, he did know a Sherpa who had a friend who knew another man . . . the trail took us to Lakhpa, and he became our traveling companion. He was interested in gaining guiding experience and, in addition, his family lived on our route and he had wanted to see them.

Lakhpa's presence had opened many doors then, and we had formed a strong relationship; he was like a brother to me. By the end of my first trip, we would even squabble over who had the heaviest load to carry, but I knew I could trust him with my life. I had been able to hire him for my 1984 trip. He had been, as usual, most helpful. Now in 1985 he was with me once more, and I looked forward to visiting his family once again.

The village where Lakhpa's family lived hadn't changed much since 1982. Toddlers abound and it's typical to see five-year-olds taking care of two-year-olds. The Nepali women work hard gathering firewood, cooking, cleaning, weaving and tending to sick babies. The men appear to spend most of their time socializing either sitting in front of the fire or, in warm weather, kneeling in front of the houses talking about politics or playing dice.

Lakhpa's sister is the matriarch of the house. On this visit she delighted in pointing out photographs on the wall of their family and myself that I had sent them after my first visit. During that visit I remember being struck by the familiar family dynamics. Lakhpa had wanted his sister to cook us a special yak meat treat "the way their mother used to." When his sister began preparing the meat, however, Lakhpa couldn't contain himself and got up and began to help, insisting that he knew better how "mother used to do it."

Although slight of stature, quiet and obviously poor, Lakhpa quickly won the hearts and confidence of our group members with his attentiveness and his almost uncanny instincts of knowing who needed what as well as how to get it.

Lakhpa had been especially pleased to be our guide in 1982 because as a Gurung, and not a Sherpa tribesman, he had been unable to get into the guiding business. The word "sherpa" is often confusing because it is both the name of a race of people—the Sherpas who migrated to Nepal from Tibet about 450 years ago—and a job position. Most people in the sherpa job position are Sherpas, and it is very difficult for a person of a different Nepali race—there are about thirty different ethnic groups in Nepal—to be hired as a sherpa.

Trekking in Nepal typically proceeds in the British style. Porters (Nepali people of any race) carry the food (most of it fresh), tents and personal gear in baskets held by a tumpline around their foreheads. The baskets are weighed each morning and distributed. The government regulates that the porter's load can be no more than sixty pounds or they must be paid double. Sherpas carry a more moderate load, typically in a Western-style backpack. They help set up camp and do the cooking. The trekkers carry day packs with their rain gear, water, snacks and incidentals. Once at the mountain the porters stay below the snow level, and only sherpas accompany the mountain climbers. The sherpas help climbers stay on the correct route, but climbers carry their personal gear as well as group gear starting at snow level.

When I began organizing my first group trek, I was appalled by the amount of gear and support people used to travel in this style. I remember telling the trekking company, "No, don't bother bringing the table (two sheets of plywood) and chairs (bamboo stools)." Then I thought about the situation and learned more about the Nepali people. The British style of travel gives tourists who are trekkers more time and energy to interact with the Nepali people. Relationships form that continue by letter for years afterward. These relationships help bridge cultural gaps and promote understanding. This kind of "luxury" travel also makes it possible for trekkers to see and experience Nepal, in contrast to many independent trekkers who, because of the strenuous conditions, spend their time in a survival mode and as a result accidently offend the Nepali locals and miss meaningful experiences with the people.

I have found that except for a few environmentally conscious ones, independent trekkers contribute to the deforestation and pollution of Nepal by relying on local teahouse service and by not having an awareness of minimum-impact travel standards. Teahouses have been used for centuries by local Nepalis as they travel for trade. Teahouses are heated, and meals are prepared with wood fires. As trekkers also use teahouse services, more of the limited forests are harvested, and often in the more remote areas the local food supply is seriously diminished, contributing to malnutrition. In the Nepali culture no one is turned away from the hearth—even trekkers who simply choose not to bring their own food or didn't know to. Trekking groups, on the other hand, are now required by the Nepali government to carry their own kerosene fuel and food and provide a cook. Although this adds to the expense of a trek, it greatly reduces the wood requirements and other impacts of the tourists.

Because we were a women's expedition, I wanted to be sure our members had opportunities to get to know Nepali women. Therefore one of the requirements of our expedition was to have several sherpanis—women sherpas—join us. These opportunities for women are another benefit of our trekking style. The sherpanis help do sherpa work, help us over cultural bridges and physically give us a hand while on the trail. In addition to their pay, we teach them English, which significantly helps their future employment prospects. The sherpanis are spontaneous, playful and fun to travel with. For them the trek is an adventure and a way to travel as well as employment. A sherpani who had been on our first trek has now opened her own trekking company.

When the early European explorers and mountaineers wanted to hire people to carry loads in the mountains of Nepal, the village elders usually provided them with older women because these woman were not needed as much for village work—men did not work much and also did not think it was within their role to carry loads. However, somewhere along the line this practice changed, probably when tobacco was introduced as the payment for work. Then men started to want the jobs. In 1984 it was hard to convince trekking company administrators to hire Nepali women. On the first trek I organized we were promised women; however, when we arrived there were none. After I resorted to "no women, no trek" and did not pay until all negotiations had been completed, the company did come up with four women. They were runaways—women who came to Kathmandu from the hills to seek their fortune much the same way that some young women in the United States run away from farms to big cities. These women formed special relationships with our American trekkers and were hard workers. Even though our trek had been only sixty miles from where they had grown up, they, too, were seeing the area for the first time. The Western women on that trek had admired the sherpanis, who were quick and eager to help when footing was difficult, always seemed to know the correct path even though they had not been there before, and laughed easily and often. And the sherpanis had to work hard to communicate with the other Nepali women in that area because they spoke different languages.

This year was similar. Mingma, the wife of our trekking company administrator, finally decided she would fill one of the slots. She said she had lived in Kathmandu for the last ten years and had not been able to get as much exercise as she used to. Before that she had been one of the very few Nepali women who had worked on a trek. In fact, she had started the trekking company we were using in

Nepal, which was unheard of because the trekking business is considered men's business. She was supporting herself and her young son and had the determination and skill to become very successful; however, when she remarried she had given the business to her husband to run and took the role of homemaker and mother. As might be expected though, she helped direct the business from the sidelines, and the desire for adventure was still in her soul. Given the opportunity she eagerly accompanied us.

Mingma is my age, and we talked a great deal about our lives, women in Nepal and women in the United States. She thrived on the contact with us because she could share her own feminist views—not popular with Nepali men or many Nepali women. Mingma is an unusual Sherpa woman and one of only a handful of Nepali women who have divorced their husbands. She divorced her first husband for having extramarital affairs, something Nepali women generally tolerate. I was delighted with my contact with Mingma and felt privileged to learn so much about the country from her perspective. I was impressed with her presence, how much she tried to learn from us and how much she gave to us in the process. Group members slowly began to rely on her for her Buddhist prayers for us all and for her funny stories, which kept us going when we sometimes wanted to call it a day.

Mingma started our trek in city shoes and a skirt and walked at the end of the line. By the third day she had shed the skirt and shoes for pants and tennis shoes. We never found out exactly where these had came from. Nepali people never carry many personal belongings, but they often appear with new clothes or other belongings. Before European influence, Nepal was quite egalitarian. For example, if it started to rain, a person could walk into the nearest house, pick up the umbrella, use it and expect it to be picked up by someone else, if it was available at her house during the next rain. Although that attitude is changing, there still is an expectation that everyone will share what food and material goods they have. That is one reason early foreign travelers in Nepal had such wonderful trips. As they traveled the country Nepali people would literally take care of all their food needs. As more people began to visit Nepal, the meeting of values between Western travelers and Nepalis caused friction. The Nepalis can't understand why the Western travelers in their country don't share what goods they bring, and usually the

Westerners bring a great deal more clothes and gear than the Nepali people have.

I was not happy with our sirdar, or head Nepali person, Dowa. He drank heavily and tried to get out of working whenever possible. His favorite T-shirt, given to him by a Western man, had printed on it, "How can I tell you I love you when you're sitting on my face?" Needless to say, women in our group insisted he either not wear it or turn it inside out. He did, but he still was cause for concern, and I knew I would have to work hard to keep our expedition on track to meet our goals.

We started by taking a five-hour bus ride on winding, dirt roads—the highways of Nepal. Our group was nervous and still in the process of sorting out all the new sights and smells. At the trail-head we milled around, as climbing groups typically do, working side by side with our porters and sherpas sorting our expedition gear into manageable loads.

The mountaineering experience of our group members varied. Kris had climbed Kilimanjaro, a 19,340-foot trekking peak in Africa, as well as all fifty-two peaks above 14,000 feet in Colorado. Charlea had climbed a peak in the Three Sister Range in Oregon as part of a wilderness experience course. But their group had been instructed to climb a certain peak one afternoon and it had turned out to be impossible to make the climb and return to base camp in one day. They'd had to spend the night out, unprepared. It did not surprise me then that Charlea questioned each of our decisions a couple times to be sure she was getting all the information she needed.

Deb and Linda had been no higher than 2,000 feet, being from Illinois and Minnesota respectively, and had no mountaineering experience, but both were strong women with an openness to learn and experience. Linda came with plastic see-through rain gear purchased from a discount store, not appropriate for a mountaineering expedition, a common type of mistake for those with little or no climbing experience. Valerie's experience included climbing and hiking in the Sierra Nevadas and participating in a previous Woodswomen trek. She was our medical specialist and my co-guide. Georgia had been on an earlier Woodswomen trek in Nepal and had begun to learn mountaineering skills in the Pacific Northwest. Georgia's humor was dry and funny, so she always had a hiking partner.

Motley as we were, we were prepared for our adventure. The group members had an amazing amount of trust in me as their leader and in our pre-trip preparations. Yet before the expedition, I hadn't really thought about my role as expedition leader. I had been to Nepal twice and led trips for fifteen years, often in remote places, but this was my first time leading an international climbing trip, and I don't think the enormity of the job hit me until two years after the trip. I also placed a great deal of trust and confidence in the women on the expedition. In guiding women's trips it is crucial not to underestimate what women can do—this only creates unnecessary obstacles.

So why did I decide to lead a woman's climbing trip in Nepal? I really liked the concept of giving women an opportunity to gain more mountaineering skills and experience being at altitude, something usually reserved for "serious male" climbers. Kris in particular wanted to use this experience to "break into" international and high-peak climbing. I had no idea of the complexities and risks that would be involved on this particular expedition. Fortunately, I was prepared for them. At the same time, the burden of responsibility for the safety of the group members was heavy. At times I was scared too; it was then I'd find my temper short and I'd have to bite my tongue. In all, leading the expedition was exciting and challenging for me, and I did have fun.

The first few days we got our routines down: wake up and be served coffee, tea or hot water as we dressed and packed our belongings; eat breakfast; walk, eat lunch and rest; walk some more; arrive at camp and have tea and biscuits; wash up; eat dinner; chat, and go to bed. Our meals were ample and delicious. Expedition cooks are excellent at their trade. They are trained to prepare British-style meals, beginning at tea time with English tea and biscuits and moving on to a continental meal of soup followed by a main course, dessert and finally tea. I specifically requested that our cook prepare traditional Nepali and Tibetan dishes for our main course. I had learned through experience that although the Western dishes were good, the traditional dishes were even better. Our expedition members also had the opportunity to learn more about

Nepali and Tibetan culture through eating this delicious food. Our cook creatively used the fresh food our porters carried—potatoes, kale-like greens, rice, beans, apples and flour.

On our trek to the mountain, we learned more about each other and got in better shape. I noticed how much land development had taken place in the three years since I'd traveled in this area. I was appalled. So much had changed, even the people. Many Nepali people have a low opinion of Americans, considering us mentally slow, because we do not bargain, and physically weak, because it usually takes an American woman or man twice as long to travel the same path as a Nepali person. The Nepali people in this area had become more commercial, less kind and colder toward tourists. I couldn't help but notice the sharp contrast to the people in the part of Nepal where I had trekked the previous year, a part seldom visited by foreigners.

Now we walked through the rapidly disappearing forest, which was being cut to build tourist hotels and to sell to boost the economy. It was sad to think how influential money and power are in any culture. The customs of sharing and group support were rapidly disappearing in Nepal.

After a week of trekking we saw Pisang Peak. It was beautiful and inspiring. We hiked to the village of Lower Pisang to begin our final preparations for the climb. The locals referred to us as "the American team." It took us a while to understand that we were the American team—it sounded so official, I felt like we had entered the Olympics. There were also Japanese, Australian, Italian and Nepalese teams climbing Pisang. We were the only women's team, although the Italian team included several women.

I'd picked the beginning of October to climb because typically that time offers the best chance for clear weather. However, the day after we arrived in Lower Pisang, the weather started to change to cloudy and drizzly. As the clouds hung on, the group members reminded me, more than once, that I had said we would be climbing in the dry rain shadow of the Annapurnas.

As we left the village to start our climb, it started to snow. Soon we were walking in a whiteout. But after several hours the snow stopped, and we again hoped for a window of clear weather. We arrived at 10,000 feet and decided to set up camp; the weather had made the climbing harder than we had anticipated, and we needed a break.

The views were incredible. Annapurna II had been directly behind us as we walked; I had never seen such beautiful mountains. And I was very excited by our group's successes. Several women had used ice axes for the first time, and Deb and Linda had climbed higher than ever before. We camped in the snow—another first for some. I couldn't resist the clear skies and ran around snapping pictures.

The sherpas were to accompany us to base camp at 14,000 feet. Then we were to climb to 18,000 feet, sleep and climb the last 2,000 feet the next morning. This is alpine-style climbing, meaning we would travel light to the last camp in order to minimize the amount of time we spent above 14,000 feet. We had planned to start using our ice axes at 16,000 feet and then put on crampons and rope up at 18,500 feet. However, the lower snowline (8,000 feet) meant that we had started using our ice axes, to help with stability, sooner then planned, making our progress slower than I had anticipated.

By morning it was snowing again. I wanted to stay put and resume our climb the following day. Unfortunately, Dowa had brought up only enough food for one day, even though I had specifically told him to bring enough for three. He had actually wanted this to be a short trip; besides being lazy, he had no confidence that women could climb. We had to go down.

Our crew was creative and negotiated to pitch our camp in a local villager's house under construction. The framing and roof were up, which gave us shelter from the snow, but no particular comfort. We cooked and kept a fire for drying clothes in the basement, or stable, of the house. It was warmer and drier than being outside but much smokier. In fact, Valerie got a migraine from the smoke and was uncomfortable most of the time. We celebrated her thirty-fourth birthday with a huge cake baked by our Sherpa cook, Nima, while she lay motionless in her tent willing her headache away. We shared the stable quarters with the Italian team—four men and three women— all friendly, enthusiastic and quite noisy and rowdy. The team had unsuccessfully attempted to summit the day we arrived in Lower Pisang and hoped for another opportunity. However, when it hadn't quit snowing after two more days, they bid us farewell and began the trip back to Kathmandu.

As it turned out, it snowed for five more days. We watched the snow keep falling and falling. Some of us hiked to the village of Minang for exercise and recreation. With Lakhpa's help, we gained access to the famous local traders of Minang and enjoyed some pleasant cultural exchange as well as shopping. We also spent time in the smoky guest house a short walk from our camp where the climbing teams and Nepali travelers congregated hunched down on the dirt floor in front of the hearth swapping stories.

The days of snow wore on. It snowed twelve feet that week in an area typically dry. In fact, snow in that area at 8,000 feet is unheard of at the beginning of October. After three days we knew we would have to choose between making another attempt to climb Pisang Peak, then returning the way we came, or completing the trek over Throng La Pass and around the Annapurna Massif. There was a bit of tension in the air as we prepared to decide our course.

I called a group meeting and asked the question everyone had been thinking. What are we going to do? The response was interesting. Some women were reluctant to say what they wanted; they seemed to want to hear what others wanted. Kris immediately said that she wanted to climb again. Charlea noted that the schedule said we were going to complete the circuit, so we should—a convoluted way of saying what she wanted.

We talked. I encouraged them to voice their personal wants. After all, most people only get to Nepal once in a lifetime. It turned out that Linda and Charlea wanted to do the circuit. Georgia, Valerie and Kris wanted to attempt the climb again, and Deb would do anything as long as the group stayed together. When we knew who wanted what, I saw the emotions of "Oh, the majority want to climb, so I guess we will all climb," from Deb; "only two of us want to do the circuit so how can we argue our case to win over the others," from Charlea and Linda; and "I'm glad I get to climb, but now we probably won't make it, because two of the women really don't want to be there" from the rest. For mountaineering to be successful, let alone safe, it requires commitment.

I suggested we split into two groups, one to go over the pass and one to climb. It took twenty-four hours of negotiating both within our group and with our Nepali support crews to finally work out the details of our respective adventures and our conflicting emotions so that we all felt safe and comfortable about our endeavors. Thank goodness I have stamina. At first Dowa was surprised and resistant to the idea of dividing the group. Oh great, I thought, I finally get the women to say what they want and I think we can make it happen, and now I have to convince our support crew it can happen. I was impressed, though, when he came through and acted with maturity. I knew splitting up trekking groups was not typical and was happy that he decided to cooperate. Mingma was a big help in these negotiations. She was as intent as I was on each woman achieving her goal. She strongly encouraged Dowa to give us whatever support we needed from him. She is a soft-spoken but very persistent women who expects to get what she wants.

We later discovered that these unusual snowfalls were all over the tiny country and that the recent earthquake in Mexico had touched off a tidal wave in Southeast Asia that had touched off a mini-monsoon in Nepal. There were also torrential floods in Bangladesh. We saw rescue helicopters several times, which added to our nervousness; we found out later that several people, including two sherpas, had died of exposure on Throng La, the high pass on the Annapurna Circuit, during the snows.

But as I said, we didn't learn the severity of the situation until later, and on the morning of October 13, we were up and ready to go. Linda and Charlea were off with Dowa, our sirdar, to complete the circuit, and the rest of us were off to climb. Our parting was upbeat but nervous. Both groups would be taking risks inherent to their respective agendas. Completing the circuit meant that Charlea and Linda would climb a 17,000 foot pass that was covered with ten feet of snow. Several of us walked with them for about an hour, waved good-bye and then turned our focus to our climb. The others rested and packed. Dowa was brotherly toward me when we split the group, he to lead the trek over the pass, and I as his counterpart to lead the climb. It felt nice for us to share kind words of encouragement with each other. Although there were hard parts to splitting, the potential rewards were evident to me.

I remember posing for a group picture before we departed for our second summit attempt and Georgia commenting, "Our group is shrinking." It felt good that we could acknowledge it. Mingma snapped our picture and asked us all to be careful. She waited there for our return. Off we went. I had checked and double-checked our food and equipment. The trekking company had neglected to send enough fuel, assuming we would burn wood some of the time. This made our situation difficult as the snow precluded wood gathering and made building fires impossible. I was personally uncomfortable with the ecological impact of using wood for the expedition anyway.

As we started our climb for the second time, we hiked up the same trail we had traveled a week earlier. We got to our first base camp, which we called pre-base camp, and hiked by it to the traditional base camp at 14,000 feet. There we were met by our cook, Nima, Lakhpa and an apprentice cook. They were our support crew for the climb. None of them had had mountaineering experience.

Another evening of gorgeous views captivated us as I prepared the group for the morning. We were going to rise early and climb while the snow was still hard. By midday the snow would be soft and those of us with short inseams would suffer.

The women rested fitfully, but I was pleased that everyone was coping well with the altitude. Valerie, our medical specialist, had been invaluable in getting the women to drink enough, dress properly and feel comfortable with their exertion. Deb, for instance, had said at one point that she could not go on because her heart was pounding so much. Valerie took her pulse and found it to be sixty beats per minute. Deb was in such good shape that a fast heart beat to her was a normal one for most of us. On the other hand, Valerie had had to work to keep her pace steady and slow enough to hold her rate at less then 180 beats per minute.

In the morning we started out later than I wanted, but our spirits were high. We were climbing again, the weather was good and our pace was fine. After about one hour of walking, the terrain became quite steep. Because of the snow it was impossible to follow the trail. I broke trail for part of the time as did our sherpa support crew. I gave a lesson on ice axe use and decided, because the snow was new and still soft enough to kick steps into, that I would not have the women put on their crampons. I also thought it would be safer not to rope up. I told them that this climb was going to be hard and that we had to pay close attention in order to be safe, but I did so in a way that did not scare them with the magnitude of our task. Unnecessary fear could contribute to accidents. What started out to be a physically challenging trek and short climb had turned into a long and difficult mountaineering experience. Still everyone's spirits stayed high all day. We made good time and used our ice axes like accomplished mountaineers. I was nervous, but confident that each woman could do the mountaineering necessary for the climb as long as yet another twist to our expedition did not occur.

At one point a piece of plastic fell off my pack and slid down 500 feet. Lakhpa was below me and picked it up as it came his way. The feeling in my stomach reminded me of being on amusement park rides. I said a silent prayer that none of us would go for such a ride.

By early afternoon we were starting to post-hole, sinking into snow up to our hips on each step. Progress was slowing. We stopped for a snack and decided to go only a little further to camp. We arrived at 18,200 feet at about 2:30 p.m. The women rested. I hoped they were proud of their accomplishment. I helped Lakhpa and Nima dig out a platform to set up our tents. In deference to weight, we had brought a four-person tent for five women and another for the three Nepali men. We figured that we would not sleep much as we wanted to begin our summit attempt at about 3:00 a.m. We tried to eat a dinner of Ramen noodles. It hadn't been stirred very well and Valerie reacted to a pile of salt in her bowl and tossed hers up. Each woman coped with being at altitude in her own way and had her own problems. Valerie could not eat after the salt episode. Kris was constipated and found it unbearable to spend the time exposed she needed to relieve herself. Deb was still worried about her heart rate, and Georgia continued enjoying her after-dinner cigarette with the sherpas. I took pictures.

There isn't a lot to do at 18,200 feet on the side of a snowy mountain, so shortly after dinner and another look at the view, we went into the tent. It was a tight squeeze. I was on the outside, furthest from the entrance. We chatted some and tried to sleep, but if one woman turned, we literally all had to, so none of us slept much. I woke up several times feeling I wasn't getting enough air and breathing very shallowly and rapidly. At the altitude we were at, this frightening phenomenon—called Cheyne-Stokes respiration—is common. About midnight it started to snow. The wind picked up, and by 3:00 a.m.—our wake-up time for our summit attempt—the wind was blowing ferociously at about sixty miles an hour, and it was still snowing. I went out of the tent for a moment to get a better feel for the weather. Although it was spectacular, I realized our summit attempt was probably doomed. I decided to sleep until 6:00 a.m. and check again then.

The storm continued, and it looked like it was settling in for yet another dumping of snow. It was truly incredible weather. If it had looked even a little as though it would change, we would have endured an uncomfortable day in the tents waiting to see. Instead we decided to retreat to the village. We could only dress one at a time. After the first two women got out, they asked if they could start with the cook-turned-mountain guide. I answered with a very strong no. The weather was too severe to risk separating. They complained as they waited, but fortunately they trusted me enough to wait.

We left camp at 7:00 a.m. in a ferocious whiteout. After a short way, we were able to glissade, that is, slide down the mountain using our ice axes as steering devices. The descent was quick. We slid about 4,000 feet, a slide any amusement park would envy. When we stopped, at about 14,000 feet, I told the group that we were just then equivalent to the top of Mt. Rainier in the United States. That gave a useful perspective to the elevation we had achieved.

The rest of the way down was tricky. At one point it was obvious that the sherpas were lost. Fortunately, when I stopped them to discuss our route, Lakhpa was able to convince the other sherpa to come my way. He was confident in my ability and agreed with me.

We got back to the village discouraged, tired, cold and wet. We knew that because of time this had been our last attempt, that tomorrow we would begin our trek out. We were all disappointed. The cook, Nima, who had left earlier than the group, showed up several hours later, having gotten lost.

While we rested and dried out a bit that night, I had time to reflect on our group's successes. The women on the climb did well. Every woman in our group, with the exception of Kris, ended up climbing higher then she ever had. Everyone slept higher then she ever had. No one got sick from the altitude—a large risk and an unknown for every expedition. I think our good health was due to Valerie's dedication as a medical person. She had a strong preventive approach.

The next day, we started our trek out only to find that our expedition was not over yet. The heavy snows in the highlands meant torrential rains in the lowlands. As we lost altitude we saw the effects. There were many mud and rock slides. Mingma showed her strength at keeping the porters together and calm enough to continue doing their job. Our fears returned. We wondered how Charlea and Linda were doing, and hoped they were safe. We were starting to get reports of accidents and deaths; the grapevine works very quickly in Nepal. I was glad I had access to it, though in this case no news was good news.

At one point we crossed the river to avoid walking on a fresh rock slide. The Italian team had been on that trail when the slide happened, and two women were buried alive. It was an eerie feeling to know that people we had camped with were lying there under the debris. With so many trails and bridges washed out, we were using any route that worked. We crossed rivers on rope bridges with no planks, hiked slippery hillsides, sunk knee-deep into mud, and finally reached the road-head. There we caught a bus, and to our amazement on that bus were Charlea, Linda and Dowa.

Their timing was as precise as ours. We had arranged to return to Kathmandu that evening at the latest. We traded stories. They confirmed that as a small group they had had an advantage that helped them navigate the pass safely. Most groups had turned back, but they were able to cross the 17,000-foot pass and had a great time doing it. Our reunion was joyful, and everyone was delighted that her adjusted goal had been met or at least that she had had the opportunity to try. All of us felt fortunate that we had completed our journey safely in the midst of such danger and disaster. The climbers had a strong sense of unfinished business, and I suspected some of them would return. Deb, who had not liked splitting up the group, was very glad we were back together.

Even though it had been hard to split the group, by doing so we each were able to get what we wanted. If in fact Charlea had talked the whole group into wanting to complete the circuit, it would have been in vain, because the snows made it possible for only light, small groups that did not need porter support to navigate the pass. Our larger group would have been forced to turn back at Throng La Pass, making it impossible for any of us to meet our goals. And, when attempting a peak climb, it is important for all team members to want to be there. If two members had only agreed to climb begrudgingly, the expedition's safety would have been compromised.

. . .

In Kathmandu we reflected on our trip. The climbers were extremely disappointed not to have reached the summit of Pisang Peak. For many this overshadowed their achievements. Only upon reflection after a number of years could we accept how extraordinary a trip it had been. After all, "the American team" had climbed as high or higher than any other expedition team on Pisang Peak that season and returned safely. In an international setting, dominated by male teams of greater experience, we had been the most successful. I was reminded of how true it is that especially as women we tend to dismiss our accomplishments. Some group members said they had had no idea they had done anything hard. If they could do it, anyone could. We were a group of ordinary women, but we had completed an extraordinary task.

Kris has continued her mountaineering career and has successfully climbed Mt. Fuji, Aconcagua and Mt. McKinley. Georgia continues to climb in the Cascades and has returned to Nepal to lead treks for Woodswomen. The following year Valerie was mountaineering in the Alps of Switzerland and Austria. Deb, Linda and Charlea have also continued their outdoor pursuits. I continue to lead mountaineering expeditions, including a successful ascent of Mt. McKinley. After our trek, Mingma said she would never again stay away from trekking that long, and in fact she was out trekking again three days after we returned—a changed woman.

A Women's Winter Walk
Across the Presidentials

Laura Waterman

▲ ▲ ▲

New Hampshire's Presidential range was first traversed in winter in 1896. Since that time, making this trip has become the test piece for the New England winter mountaineer, the Grand Prix of winter climbing, the one big trip to which most practitioners of this mad art dedicate their ambitions.

The typical itinerary is to ascend the Valley Way to the col between Mounts Madison and Adams, go up Madison and back, and then to slog across the entire Presidential range over Mounts Adams, Jefferson, Clay, Washington, Monroe, Franklin, Eisenhower, and Clinton; Mounts Jackson and Webster are sometimes tacked on at the end. For New England winter climbers this is a pinnacle of achievement, as it involves prolonged above-treeline exposure.

Most parties make the trip in three or four days, though some crawl along more slowly or get pinned down by bad weather. Others whisk over in less time, even in one day or—supreme madness—in a moonlit night. The success rate is low, however, because the notorious Mount Washington weather frustrates the majority of attempts. Although victorious parties feel like tigers, success or failure on a winter Presidential traverse is often more a measure of the weather conditions than of a party's strength. In good conditions, the trip can be almost easier than in summer; in bad even to attempt the Presidential traverse is the mark of an accomplished winter mountaineer.

In the winter of 1980, several of us women climbers decided to try a Presidential traverse. As far as we knew, a group of women had never successfully made the traverse. In fact, we had never heard of an all-women's team even trying it.

I myself had wondered just why this winter walk was considered the big test piece. As I mentioned, if the weather is foul (which it is most of the time) the trip is impossible, and if the weather is fair it's a waltz—like walking along a slightly bumpy sidewalk. There might be a fair day once or twice a month in winter, according to Mount Washington Observatory statistics. I'd read that the fastest observed land surface wind speed ever recorded swept over the Observatory building on Mount Washington's summit at a devestating 231 mph. But more to the point, for me anyway, I knew that winter climbers above treeline can normally expect to be staggered by winds of thirty to sixty mph. Gales of seventy-five to one hundred mph or more—elsewhere regarded as a hurricane—occur regularly in winter. So didn't it boil down to luck in hitting those rare good days more than skill?

Then again, there were those "marginal" days. Maybe, I thought, that's what the winter traverse is all about: using skill and judgment on the marginal days. That raised the next questions: just how marginal is marginal? What is my limit? I'd heard the stories: climbers carrying horrendous loads staggering across the peaks and being repeatedly knocked down by those infamous Presidential winds; rime ice building up on their windsuits, wolf-ruff hoods drawn down so tightly as to obscure vision, though with a blanketing whiteout the climbers probably couldn't see much beyond the breath in front of their faces anyway. To me it sounded like what polar explorer Admiral Richard Byrd, caught in an Antarctic blizzard, described in *Alone* as "extravagantly insensate":

Its vindictiveness cannot be measured on the anemometer sheet. It is more than just wind: it is a solid wall of snow moving at gale force, pounding like surf. The whole malevolent rush is concentrated upon you as upon a personal enemy. In the senseless explosion of sound you are reduced to a crawling thing on the margin of a disintegrating world; you can't see, you can't hear, you can hardly move.

I think some people don't consider they've really done a winter traverse if it doesn't approach Admiral Byrd's description. We didn't see it that way. We decided that if we had to cross the range wearing a wolf-ruff hood, in conditions approaching "insensate," we wouldn't cross. Besides, none of us owned a wolf-ruff hood.

I believe it was Natalie Davis who first came up with the idea, putting it something like this: "Why don't we women forgo the luxury and ease of winter trips with our male friends and husbands and try something on our own—like a Presidential traverse?" Natalie had thrown out that last part airily and I hadn't taken it seriously. But a few weeks later, while I was kneading bread (an occupation which leaves the mind calm and free), Natalie's idea surfaced, and immediately I thought, why not? What a wonderful goal! Whether we were successful or not, we'd gain tremendous experience trying. What a great thing, being up there in that alpine world by ourselves, making our own decisions. We wouldn't have our male companions to fall back on. A scary thought, but also exhilarating.

I next saw Natalie on a March backpack into the White Mountains. We talked and made plans, deciding to do our traverse the following winter with a party of four. To complete the foursome, we invited Peggy O'Toole, who was strong and enthusiastic, and Ellen Sturgis, whom we knew to be dependable and comfortable in winter conditions. We then asked Debbie O'Neill, who was a very strong hiker with tremendous spirit, if she wouldn't mind putting up with the really difficult position of being an alternate. The team was set.

We had all met through hiking, in particular winter hiking, and all of us were instructors with the Appalachian Mountain Club's Winter Mountaineering School, which has been teaching winter mountaineering in New England's mountains for more than thirty years. In everyday life, Peggy, Ellen and Natalie were school teachers, Debbie was a physical therapist in her town's school system, and I was a homesteader and writer.

Although we had all hiked together in a group situation, we had never shared the same tent or cooking chores. When we had camped in winter we had always shared these cooking and camp jobs with our men friends or husbands, so we thought it would be a good idea to try a summer backpack together—a dress rehearsal in which we would have the experience of setting up tents, getting meals, making group decisions and taking care of ourselves on our own. On the appointed day I showed up at the trailhead. And waited. No one arrived. After an hour and a half, I left to go hiking with my hushand, Guy, instead. "So much for a women's Presidential traverse," I grumbled to Guy, "We can't even organize a summer hike!" Of course, there was a good explanation, and when all came to light, I decided it was certainly worth another try.

Besides, wouldn't it be marvelous if we really pulled the thing off! We were very aware that we might be the first all-women team to cross the Presidentials in winter. But we didn't want this thought to dominate our trip. For us, being on our own in winter seemed most important. We all wanted the experience of functioning as a group of women together, without male support. But we had picked a challenging trip—the most challenging above-treeline traverse the White Mountains had to offer. And that was important too.

Debbie was satisfied with being the alternate until sometime in the fall, when she decided she really wanted to *go,* not sit on a fence. About that time Peggy got married and her life became so complicated that she had to drop out. We were all very sorry about losing Peggy, but there couldn't have been a better replacement waiting in the wings.

In November Debbie, Natalie, Ellen and I (with male friends) convened at our house in Vermont for the weekend. While the men chopped down trees for our winter firewood we got down to serious planning. We decided to allow five days for our traverse. That would give us several days of leeway if we had bad weather, since ideally one can cross the range in three days and two nights. We would take two MSR-type stoves, two sets of cookware, one four-person tent, four dinners, four breakfasts and five lunches.

Most important, we agreed on our objective. We'd heard about too many expeditions that had failed because climbers came with diverse objectives, agendas and expectations. Determined to avoid this impasse, we laid out all our cards and reached the understanding that for us a traverse meant crossing over the summits, not just taking the loop trails around them. We wanted to do the real thing. Going over the summits would make it harder, but it's also what the traverse is all about. We also talked about going over Mounts Webster and Jackson, two optional peaks, just to finish with a flourish.

Our plan all along was to think big and cut back later if forced to. As our planning concluded, I could tell we all felt a strong sense of commitment as well as great anticipation. We found the trip planning—this detailed thinking-through of each move from gear to route—exciting, and it moved us into functioning as a team right from the beginning.

A week before the trip, I began to have the usual pre-trip anxieties. I was worried about how our camping arrangements would work out. As alpinist Miriam O'Brien Underhill said many years ago, "I don't mind hardship as long as I'm perfectly comfortable." I subscribe to that philosophy of winter camping: like a hibernating animal, all I want is a dry, warm spot. Would that be possible on this trip?

Guy and I have such a fine system worked out for winter camping and understand each other so well that many tasks are done without comment or direction. Also, Guy does the cooking when we're camping. He calls it "taking me out for dinner." So although cooking on the tiny stove, balancing the pot and melting snow were familiar routines, I hadn't had that much experience on my own.

I wondered what would it be like camping with people I'd never shared a winter tent—or, for that matter, any tent—with before? I envisioned chaotic piles of frozen gaiters in the tent's corners, gear strewn haphazardly around the camp, dinner up-turned into my sleeping bag—and me feeling miserable in the midst of sordid disorder. How could I have so underestimated my teammates!

A few days before departure the worst of Ellen's fears came true: she had the flu and, sadly, couldn't join us. In her place, she sent a dinner, which we planned to eat on the second night.

It was down to Debbie, Natalie and me. We'd talked earlier about the possibility of having to go with three and had all agreed we'd still be willing to do it, so we were able to gear down to the lesser number at the last minute. We rationalized convincingly that a group of three would have its advantages: there would be more room in the tent, three people could move faster than four, and with the possibility of a two-two split eliminated, decision-making would be simpler.

The night before we left we became utterly ruthless about pack weight because we couldn't carry everything we had planned to take with four. The second stove and cook pots went, as did one of the dinners and one lunch each. We were now down to three dinners and four lunches, plus emergency hot drinks we could bolster into a meal if we needed to. We dumped the second first aid kit, pared down extra clothing, and left our snowshoes. Jettisoning the snowshoes meant we might have to sacrifice Jackson and Webster. It was also risky if we were forced to drop down into one of the snowier ravines, or if it snowed heavily during the time we were out. But it had been an unusually snowless winter, so it was a risk we felt we could gamble on—we knew the lighter the packs, the faster we could move; after all, doesn't Yvon Chouinard say, "Speed is safety"? We set the alarm for 5:00 a.m. and Debbie and I went to bed, lulled to sleep by the sound of Natalie sharpening her crampons . . .

Early the next morning, with a great sense of expectation, we walked up the Valley Way headed for Madison Col. The day was windy, but not too cold. Clouds moved about at a fast but not threatening clip. As we gained elevation we talked about where we should camp. We decided that we didn't want to set up our tent in Madison Col—it was too windy for that. Around 11:00 a.m. we stopped at what we judged to be the last feasible place in the trees and set up our tent just off the trail. It was a tight spot and not quite level. With our ice axes we hammered in the large nails we'd brought to secure the tent. The foot of snow cover on the ground was frozen to the hardness of concrete. It was quite windy even though we were in the trees, and we took our time making sure the tent was well-anchored. We rolled out pads and unstuffed sleeping bags in the tent, all the time eating and drinking water. We then put on our wind gear, as we wanted to climb Madison that day. We even had dreams of knocking off Adams.

As we were preparing our camp, three women came down the trail. I guess they were as surprised to see us as we were to see them, for one of them commented that it was nice to see other women on their own in the winter woods. We agreed! They had camped in Madison Col the previous night and had just climbed Adams and Madison, but because it had gotten windier, they didn't think those peaks were climbable now. I remembered Ellen's parting words about the tent: if it gets real windy, just drop the center pole. When you hear a remark like that inside a heated room, it all sounds very adventurous. But the romance of playing arctic explorer fades fast when you are faced with the actual possibility. By camping in the trees we had, we hoped, avoided these heroics.

Despite the other women's lack of optimism, we left our camp intent on climbing Mount Madison. The thermometer we'd hung on a spruce limb near our tent read sixteen degrees Fahrenheit when we left. The footprints of the women's party were completely blown away as we walked through the drifted sections of the trail, sinking in a foot or more, but our climb up Madison was relatively easy. The wind was at our backs, coming out of the southwest; we guessed that was why it wasn't too cold. We were glad we had made it to the top, but we knew it wasn't going to be easy going down. We sat on the summit in the lee, finishing off the food and drink we had stuffed in our shirts for the climb. The wind whipped up and blew the snow about as we helped each other put on our face masks so that we could better face into the wind during the descent.

I started down first and found the best way to travel off the summit ridge was on all fours—crawling. I thought about Admiral Byrd and his "being reduced to a crawling thing." I was amazed, though, by how much less resistance there was at that lower level, and by how impossible it was for me to stand upright. Once off the summit ridge, we could walk at a crouch. The wind was blowing right at us, and twice, wondering why my chest felt cold, I discovered that the wind had completely unzipped my wind parka. The climb was tremendously exhilarating, but my legs felt tired by the time we reached our campsite, probably from the strain of fighting the wind.

Debbie elected to cook dinner that first night, and a difficult time she had of it. Something was wrong with the stove, and it took hours and hours to melt enough snow for the water we needed for drinking and cooking. Finally, we had snow melted for our water bottles, and water for the cook pot for the morning. Debbie had done a great job under trying conditions: we were warm and well fed.

As we snuggled down into our bags for the night we could hear the wind still roaring. If it didn't lessen by morning, we knew we couldn't cross the range. It was one thing to crawl off Madison with no pack and quite another to crawl across the Presidentials fully loaded. We went to sleep with slim hopes of crossing the next day.

. . .

The alarm inside Debbie's sleeping bag went off at 5:00 a.m. No matter how much one *wants* to get about the business of the day, it is always hard to get up out of that delicious downy warmth. But we all made a stalwart effort, and soon I was attempting to cook breakfast. The stove again wasn't holding pressure properly: it had to be pumped every few minutes, and the action was very stiff. We looked at each other. Finally one of us said, "I don't think we should let a faulty stove stand in the way of crossing the range." We talked about this and agreed that the stove *did* heat, although slowly, and if it failed we would eat cold food, which we had enough of. Getting water was a bit shaky, but we hoped we could chop into the small pond near Lakes of the Clouds hut, our destination that day.

As soon as we got out of the tent, our spirits rose. We hardly dared hope, but this looked like *the* day to cross the Presidentials; sunny, warm, and most important, calm. Our weather prediction was confirmed by the time we got to Madison Col. With windbreakers stowed in packs and hats and gloves off, we ambled uphill. We visited the summit of Adams. Then on to Jefferson. Noon. We'd been walking four hours. Then down to Sphinx Col, one of our favorite spots in the mountains, and up Mount Clay. The weather was holding beautifully. We couldn't imagine a nicer day. To the west the Franconia Ridge stood out to perfection. We waved to Guy, who we knew was over there and cheering us on.

We had been seeing what we judged to be fox tracks since Madison Col. The fox had bypassed Adams, but had gone up Jefferson and Clay, nearly to the very summits, often on the path. Natalie speculated as to whether it might be a female fox. We couldn't tell, of course, but we were aware of gender that day. The delicate imprint was beautifully preserved on this all but windless day. It was fun to be walking along with the fox, all of us enjoying a rare day above treeline. It was 4:00 p.m. as we left Washington's summit and coasted down to Lakes of the Clouds hut, arriving at 4:45. The hut is boarded up in winter but a dungeonlike room in the basement is left open for backpackers. This ten-foot-by-ten-foot refuge with stone walls coated with frost on the *inside* is not a very cuddly place, but it keeps the winds on the other side. We dumped our packs and walked out to the lake. All was solidly frozen, probably to the bottom, and we chopped in vain around the fracture lines. We had less than a pint of water left between us and we knew we would be in very bad shape if the stove didn't work that night.

But we couldn't stop to worry about water then. Climbing Mount Monroe was the first order of business. Who knew what tomorrow's weather would bring? Besides how pleasant it would be to run up Monroe without our packs! And run up it we did. The next day's route, the southern Presidential peaks of Franklin, Eisenhower and Clinton stretched out along the ridge before us. We almost considered going on then and there, they looked so close, but knew we'd be caught by darkness within an hour. The moon was coming up as we descended. It was dead calm at the hut.

In our basement quarters, I spread out sleeping bags and pads, and Natalie began to organize dinner. Debbie lit the stove but very quickly noticed that the valve where the fuel can connected to the burner was leaking gas. For a moment we stared transfixed as the oozing white gas burst into flame. In a split second Debbie plunged her arms up to the elbows in the snowbag next to the stove. Repeatedly she reached for snow and doused the flames which were shooting wildly up toward the ceiling. Then she calmly picked up the stove and set it outside. We breathed again. A little fiddling with the stove revealed that a connection had been loose. In fact that had been our trouble all along. Now it held pressure, and no gas leaked out. Nonetheless, we kept the door open, ready to heave the thing out if it should misbehave.

We were elated as we ate Ellen's out-of-this-world dinner—a rice-chicken curry. We'd crossed the northern peaks—and on such a day! How could we be so lucky? But in the back of our minds lurked the thought that we didn't want it too easy. We wanted to find out how we would manage in bad weather, too. That was one reason why we were out here. Our climb of Madison was a taste. But we needed more. Not that we were hoping for bad weather— one's never foolish enough to do that in the Presidentials. We just didn't want it to be too easy, because then we wouldn't really know what we were capable of.

We need not have worried. At nine that evening, as we were falling asleep, we heard the familiar sound of—wind. It roared like an angry lion all night. And I, for one, had nightmares of bailing out down the nearest ravine . . . in a whiteout . . . without snowshoes. Or being stuck in this dungeon for days . . . and days . . .

We allowed ourselves an extra hour of sleep the next morning and got up at 6:00 a.m. It was just getting light. Debbie turned on the stove, and its mellow roar drowned out the noise of the wind. As we ate breakfast, we formed a plan. We'd go a little way down the trail to see how strong the wind was. We wouldn't pack up until we decided whether we could move in it. I recounted a particularly harrowing crossing of Mount Lafayette I'd done in freezing rain and strong wind that seemed to blow me over with no trouble at all. I had been wearing a frame pack, which, acting like a sail, caught every gust. With a big pack on, the amount of wind I could take and still walk was disturbingly little.

We put on our wind gear. It was quite a whiteout, but we could deal with that. The wind was coming from the northeast, which was good; we'd be sheltered from the worst of it as we went around Mount Monroe. How glad we were that we'd climbed Monroe the previous day! We couldn't imagine going over it with our big packs in the wind. After our short scouting trip we judged it a go and returned to Lakes hut to pack.

At 9:00 a.m. we started out. Now we were on the path that rounds Monroe. But what had happened to the wind? It was blowing directly at us and it was hard to put one foot in front of the other against it. Suddenly a gust toppled me. Then Natalie was down. We really didn't want to return to that stone room. We wanted to cross the southern peaks—that day. We all felt very strongly about that. But we didn't think we'd be able to walk upright all the way over Eisenhower. With reluctant steps we turned toward Lakes hut. Our footsteps slowed as we felt the wind lessen. A glimmer of hope. Debbie turned to Natalie: "Do you want to go on?" she asked. Natalie got a very decided look on her face: "Yes!" We all about-faced and started walking quickly—fighting the wind, but still standing. As we got around Monroe, the wind slackened and switched back to the northwest again. What had happened back there? Why was the wind from the southwest? Had it been funneled through in an odd way? We couldn't figure it out. But we were feeling jubilant again. Soon we were over Mount Franklin. The next hurdle was Mount Eisenhower—and soon we were over it. The wind was particularly strong as we walked on to Mount Clinton. But by now we were down in the scrub, with just a few exposed places, so the going was easier. Dumping our packs at the base of Clinton's cone, we walked unencumbered to the summit. Our last mountain. We'd done the traverse! We shook hands, jumping up and down, hugging and thumping each other on the back. It was a good last day; we'd had to work for it. It was a great feeling knowing that the decisions we'd made all along the way had come out right. "Doing this makes me feel so strong!' Debbie exclaimed.

That evening, back in civilization, we had the third dinner we'd carried over the range. I was cook, and Natalie and Debbie offered to open the doors and windows so as to create a proper atmosphere . . .

That was how it was for some of us Northeastern winter hikers in 1980.

Today, I wonder if the feel on all-women's trips is quite the same. Somehow, I don't think so. Women, in the last decade especially, have proved themselves in sport, in the marketplace, and have thrown over the confines of diapers and dishes. That early flush of finding ourselves together doing something we'd only done before with men has, I believe, long worn off. That self-consciousness of being a group of women has slid away. Instead, now we go into the mountains with a friend, a friend we choose to do that particular trip with, aware, naturally, whether that friend is a man or woman but less preoccupied with the fact of gender. That, it seems to me, is how it should be.

In 1980 we women climbers felt like pioneers. We felt we were learning something new, something important about ourselves, about working together as a group of women in the tough mountain world. We were each other's teachers and role models, and we were learning in a way that we could never have learned with men. We were excited by this feeling of being on our own, of finding out on a deeper level who we were as climbers and what we were capable of achieving in the mountains.

A wonderful side effect or spin off, you might say, was that when we hiked with our men friends we had much more to contribute, from doing camp chores to route finding to making crucial decisions along the way. We had gained confidence and inner strength from our all-women trips, and our men friends were quick to respond to this. Our mountain trips with them became even more rewarding and enjoyable—for *all* of us.

Since that Presidential crossing, I've gone on many winter trips in the mountains of the Northeast with various women friends. I've tried large groups of eight or ten, but I much prefer the smallest unit possible—the company of just one other woman.

My good friend Sue and I do a nearly week-long trip every winter. We both like to work hard, get dirty and feel tired at day's end. We like just being in the woods together. We find our winter trips to be a good time to talk. We like setting up our base camp in a way that makes us comfortable in spite of the elements, yet keeps us close to the wildness we've come to experience. We each try to be quick to anticipate the next camp chore. We like the problem-solving aspects of finding the best bushwhack route up some snow-drenched ridge. Sometimes Sue goes first, sometimes I do. We like cramponing our way up some off-the-beaten-track slide, assessing the avalanche danger, being alert, keeping an eye on each other.

Some of the pioneer edge of climbing with women has worn off now. That was inevitable. It's an important point—that we're women together out there—but not dominant. Now I go into the winter mountains to share the joyous fun of climbing with a good friend, who, by the way, happens to be another woman. But it still gives me the "out on your own" feeling that I learned to value so deeply on that 1980 Presidential traverse.

The Rope Between Us

Beyond the Climb

QUEEN OF ALL SHE SURVEYS

Maureen O'Neill

▲ ▲ ▲

I

MY MOTHER calls, and in her voice I can hear her wonder if she is the first to reach me: "Have you heard? One of your climbing friends, Eve, died on Mt. Index this weekend. They think it was an avalanche. Her partner died, too; they fell roped together. Your sister just heard it on the six o'clock report and said to call. She said you climbed with her." I tell her I know already, and she is relieved, then asks quietly, "Do you think she suffered much?" My mother is from the East, and these Northwest mountains are foreign to her. I doubt she can even imagine the landscape against which a woman's body fell and shattered.

I can imagine it only too well. How many times have I scrutinized an ice-lined corridor such as the one Eve died in to see if it might *go*—lead magically, without dead ends, to the summit. I can feel the angle of snow so steep it seems to push her outward, her calves straining to support her body on only the front points of her crampons, forearms trembling as the urgency to move quickly is telegraphed from mind to muscle: hurry, this gully feels unsafe, the warmth unseasonable. Why this stillness in the air? This heaviness?

Did she sense the avalanche? The pulse of kinetic energy about to snap? I cannot stop myself from imagining the moment she fell, delivered into the wide hands of that warm, blue air. I know she screamed in terrible frustration—she always screamed, at even the most minor defeat. This day it was not simply a move she could not make and a fall of a few feet, but her life wrenched from her hands as quickly as she was torn from the ice. Two days later, her body, broken in many places, was discovered half-buried in avalanche debris.

Other climbers have said that she pushed beyond the limits of even her brilliance, that she was somewhere she shouldn't have been, but few climbers can claim never to have found themselves in the wrong place at the wrong time. "Pushing" is only the natural impulse to grow, to improve. I answer with less than complete assurance: "I don't think she suffered. She was probably unconscious or dead when she hit the ground." Maybe it helps my mother to know that some die quickly, although it seems little comfort, given the fact that both her daughters climb and that climbing is a sport in which risks, however carefully considered, are an essential element.

When the mountains claim another life, a single aspect of climbing—the possibility of death—invades and eclipses all other meanings. For we survivors, the significance of her death pales against the fullness of a life anchored in the mountains.

The Olympics, Rainier, the Cascades: whether you climb them or not, the mountains of the Pacific Northwest are impossible to ignore. From the beginning of my life, I heard them praised. Whenever we plowed down a certain hill in the old Rambler, my Dad would say, "Look at those Cascades!"

Inevitably, on even a vaguely clear day, people will ask, "Have you seen the mountains?" If the reference is singular—the mountain—they are referring to Rainier, who so dominates her territory that on a sunny day thousands of city workers step outside on their lunchbreaks and turn their heads to the southeast, to the star-white glaciated peak transcending, or is it levitating, above the clouds.

Such a climate of appreciation for the environment produces people who seek immersion in the wilderness. I began climbing my last year in college for the most common reason in the world—because my best friend climbed. She took a course through our college, and it sounded like fun. Because she had shown the potential to become passionately involved in the sport, I knew I'd never see her unless I signed up, too.

It seemed easy then. Beg or borrow the gear, grab someone, set your sights on a place very far or very high—say that humpback peak or the one with a shark-fin ridge or the glacier-frosted cupcake that was Mt. St. Helens—and then do it, by placing one foot in front of the other, over and over and over.

My friend and I and another friend completed that college mountaineering course and did our first climb together. In our desire to make the summit, we made a typical beginner's mistake and neglected to turn back early enough. Benighted, we were forced to descend an entire glacier, honeycombed with crevasses, without headlamps. At eleven p.m., after what seemed an eternity of tenuous footwork, we reached the moraine. With a heavy sigh, Vaughn sat all six long feet of himself down on a rock, looked up at the moon, and cried, "I want my mother."

Those early climbs were endurance tests, and we always found ourselves equal to them. What a feeling! We ran up trails just to see how fast we could go, wondering if our legs would accordion under us, if we would ever reach the limit—but we didn't. We discovered we did what we had to do. The climbs were simple, often long snow slogs with a bit of scrambling on rock and more than a bit of tortuous bushwhacking if you lost your way. Climbing The Brothers, a peak in the Olympic range, we got lost on the descent and spent the night first lowering ourselves down a series of small cliffs by swinging on slide alder and, when that was done, swimming through a sea of neck-high foliage, wild spring growth coated with sap that shellacked the hair and tasted sweet when licked off a bare forearm. My companion navigated by the stars, aiming to bisect a foot-wide path, and to my great surprise, the plan worked. On the trail out, I learned to sleep while walking, since we had taken twenty-three hours instead of the usual eight to complete the climb.

I progressed to more technical climbing with a group of women as ignorant as myself. We banded together from a lack of money for instruction, a determination to climb and a desire to learn with other women. Our motivations were as varied as the individuals involved, but we all wanted to take complete responsibility in all aspects of climbing, including leading, and felt that being in a group of women best served that purpose. One spring weekend we packed up and drove across the Cascades to a cluster of sandstone formations set like prehistoric monoliths behind an apple orchard. The area resembled an outdoor jungle gym with a wide range of climbs to choose from. After consulting the guidebook, we chose peacefully named climbs located on gently angling slabs and avoided routes such as Vertigo, Bomb Shelter, Testicle Fortitude, Slender Thread, and Cro-Magnon.

Eventually we felt brave enough to try an imposing hunk called Orchard Rock, scary because of its verticality. I went second on the rope and had an easy time of the first thirty feet, which led to a secure resting place—a ledge with enough room for two feet at once. The crux move lay just beyond this ledge and involved climbing around a corner out onto an exposed face. I made one brave attempt, slipped, and retreated to the ledge. Clearly, it was impossible. How had I gotten into this fix? Because I was being belayed from above, any fall would have been minimal, but that seemed irrelevant. My tongue sealed to the roof of my mouth, and although I was perfectly still, I began to sweat. In short, I was gripped. Ten fingertips made pathetic forays across the rock searching for a decent hold (that is, a big one) but my body would not follow. I was rapidly becoming living sculpture.

Below me, third on the rope, Laura waited patiently. Dusk shadowed her face as her brown eyes gazed with maddening serenity over the orchards and dusty-green fields stitched together with roads and fences. Above me, birds chimed on a sunlit ridge and the air had the feeling of an embrace. "This really is for the birds," I muttered. "That's OK. Take as long as you want," she responded. I took forty-five minutes. How the hell could she be so calm while I agonized before the fact that this rock wasn't going to move for me. *I* had to move. With the bloodless precision of a slowly developing photograph, those forty-five minutes of deliberation revealed nearly everything I know about fear. Since then there have only been exquisite refinements.

To the climber, fear serves several purposes. It can make you attentive to possible danger, can warn you, infuse you with energy, serve as a gauge of your mental condition, and prevent you from taking risks beyond your ability. Fear deserves recognition but not one iota more of your attention, though it is usually eager to consume all of it. The natural flow of fear must be channeled or paralysis can result, and paralysis is serious. For me, fear manifests through resistance and hesitation, both of which cause unnecessary energy loss.

Those first few years taught me the simple things: eat before you're hungry and drink even if you don't want water because often the body reacts to stress and cold by erasing the desire for food and water at exactly those times when it is most needed. If you wait until your hands are cold before putting on gloves, they take an immense amount of heat to rewarm, creating an unnecessary energy drain. If you forget even the smallest thing—a spare mitten, an extra bulb for a headlamp—the consequences can be disastrous. If your upper body is so strong that you can haul yourself up a rock with just your arms, instead of using your legs, which are much better suited to hold your weight, you are a wastrel. In the words of Yvon Chouinard, climbing depends on conservation of energy, which translates into economy of movement coupled with reasonable speed.

Those years also taught me the range of movement involved in climbing—from the clumsy ferrying of loads to the base of the "climb" to the delicate moves or sequences of moves that were the cream and usually took only a fraction of the total time spent out. Yet what I grew to love above all was the pure luxury of spending two uninterrupted days with someone. As a teenager I spent a summer at a hiking camp; I remember being startled and disturbed at how naked people appeared outside the city: no makeup, no fancy clothes or houses, no supporting actors (parents). All the girls were tiny figures, cut and pasted against a background of sea and trees. As an adult I began to appreciate this nakedness. I was no longer disturbed by it and grew less afraid of the emotional exposure climbing creates.

This intimacy, this insight into the wilderness that is another person, is a gift. Not to mention a true test of friendship. Let me count the ways: withstanding the smell of your partner at night, stripped down to her fragrant long underwear and equally fragrant wet socks; the shove she gives you in her sleep, pushing you toward the wall of the tent dripping with condensation; the rude way she steps on you in the middle of the night as she heads out for relief; the hours spent reading to you by candlelight; the bites of chocolate fed to you at each bend of the trail to inspire you onward.

Seven years later I still climb with the woman who couldn't stop laughing at the sight of me splashing in a creek in midwinter like some huge woolly beetle trying to right herself with a pack on her back. From the other side, she offered only these words of consolation: "I told you not to cross with your snowshoes on."

Certain climbs are described as "committed." Put simply, a committed climb means there is no easy escape: once begun, both ascending and descending are difficult. These climbs require a firm intention to finish, simply because the alternatives are unappealing. Ptarmigan Ridge on Mt. Rainier falls into this category. My partner Kathy, her friend Karl, and I planned to do Ptarmigan Ridge one Memorial Day weekend. It was to be an apprentice climb for me; Kathy and Karl were to share the leading, and I was to go along as a third, knowing it would technically approach my limits. I read the route description with growing apprehension: "... steep snow/ice slope... snow/ice apron... rock buttress... steep ice chute... crevasse/serac pattern... sustained rockfall... gentle slope above...." Fortunately, preparation left little time for worry.

The day of the climb finally arrived, and we left the parking lot at 7:00 a.m. After a lengthy approach we at last reached our high camp, a breezy rock perch with just enough space, if we squeezed, for our three bivy sacks. Sleep came easily, and the next morning we were wakened at 3:00 a.m. by the steady pulse of an electronic alarm. The day promised to be windless and clear—ideal conditions. Karl, propped up on one elbow and still enjoying the warmth of his bag, was kind enough to boil water for coffee. After eating, we packed quickly and set off, arriving at the base of the climb before light. We had agreed to rope up at the start, and happy to shear weight off my load, I took out the Mammut and laid its brilliant, diamond-back coils loosely on the snow. Kathy glanced at our faces, barely defined in the twilight. "Ready?" she asked. I nodded, palm resting on my ice axe, and waited for the rope to stretch out between us. Cold seconds passed as the steel of the adze bit clear through my woolen mittens to the skin. With agonizing slowness, energy dammed up in my legs and lungs. I wanted desperately to move, to step out of that moment of extreme tension that marks a beginning, and start climbing the mountain.

We all commented on the perfect snow conditions; cramponing

was effortless. My primary responsibility was to follow and keep myself on my feet at all times, always a challenge. It seemed my two partners must have tremendous faith in me: if I fell, and I was the most likely candidate, we would all fall. I thought about that a good deal and paid the closest attention to each step, no small task when ascending a thousand feet of snow.

After perhaps an hour, Kathy stopped to rest on a bit of rock. As I drew near her, I detected a difference in texture in the ground ahead, a smooth pond of light in the wind-scored snow. I stood still for a moment, "testing the water" with a delicately placed front point. ICE. "Oh, that bit's easy," said Kathy, between hearty bites of her sandwich, "and it's just a taste of what's up ahead." As I was afraid, she was completely right.

We continued to inch upward, in a race between three snails and the sun, which upon reaching its zenith, would begin to warm and dangerously soften our route. At the apex of the slope, we began our traverse of the "apron." Each footstep punched in the rotten, icy snow seemed likely to give way with the weight of the next person, but somehow never did.

Just under the rock buttress we stopped for lunch. Removing my gloves, I laid three fingers against the pulse in my throat. "Hey, it's 120 per minute," I said. Kathy and Karl were unimpressed, already surveying the next fifty feet—a sheet of ice rounding a hump of rock with a nice, clear view several thousand feet down. Lunch was rather short and strained since we were all anxious to move.

Karl took the lead and danced over the ice with typical, angular ease. Kathy went next. Then he and Kathy waited quietly for me to cross. Too quietly. They seemed to be holding their breath, as though afraid any small draft might prove fatal. Using two tools, I began my crablike traverse and suddenly understood why Gwen Moffat, the famous British climber, titled her book *Space Below My Feet*. Midway through, I panicked and briefly hesitated, but standing still was much more terrifying than moving. I kept on, if only to evade the nasty fall line, making small explosive noises as I tried to place all four points with decision. The hip belt of my pack came unbuckled, and my hat (tied on the belt) began a direct descent. From the corner of my eye, I noticed Kathy wishing it a silent bon voyage.

Breathing deeply, I reached the other side, but there was no time to reflect, as Karl was nearly up the next lead, a narrow icy chute that was actually easier climbing but complicated by a cascade of spindrift, dreamily blowing down. From the top I heard Karl shouting at me to hurry, afraid heavier snow would follow and knock me off. His voice sounded remote, and his directions impossible to follow. I was overcome by the altitude and the odd sensation of moving against the flow. Under a misty white veil, I climbed steadily upward, groping for contact with ice and fighting to maintain my balance, constantly threatened by the swaying of my pack.

The chute led to the crevasse/serac pattern, a section of slopes tiered like a giant, white layer-cake and riddled with crevasses. Probing carefully, Kathy led out and immediately fell into one up to her hips. She climbed out and promptly fell into another. Turning back, she grinned and said, "Think light." Somehow we managed to weave our way out to what appeared to be the final tier leading to the fabled "gentle slope" and to the ridge for which the climb was named. As Kathy made a few tricky moves over the chest-high ice shoulder and onto the slope, Karl and I felt the entire crust shift and drop below our feet. Fired by wildly beating hearts we nearly jumped over the shoulder in our eagerness to reach solid ground.

At last Ptarmigan Ridge resembled a ridge, with that exhilarating combination of firm ground underfoot and airiness on all sides. The worst was over, and I began to relax, although we were at least two hours from the summit with the descent yet to come. As we ascended, clouds blew in and we were forced to use compass bearings for direction. Soon we all needed a rest from the effects of fog and altitude, especially Karl who, exhausted from the lower part of the climb, stumbled and lurched like a drunken man. In the shelter of an overhanging crevasse, we nestled together sharing an ensolite pad and gingersnaps. "Look at where we are," I said, "this is heaven." "Now if we could only be sure of that," Kathy joked.

Suddenly the air cleared and *voilà,* the sun. Kathy and Karl leapt up and scurried off in different directions to see if they could sight any landmarks. Serious business, obviously. Their quick, neat movements temporarily distracted me, but finding myself out of cookies, I began rooting in Kathy's private stash. She'll never know, I reasoned, absorbed in the luxurious ebb and flow of the clouds, teased by views through windows with drifting and torn edges. My reverie was cut short by a shout from Kathy. She had recognized Sunset

Amphitheater, an unmistakable western slope of Rainier, scooped out as though to form a gargantuan rock echo chamber.

Greatly encouraged, we slogged forward until the clouds descended again. This time, however, we were certain of our direction and felt our way with the Braille of steps kicked by Kathy, seventy-five feet ahead. By early evening we came upon the false summit, Liberty Cap, and were able to inform several other climbers, who had converged through the whiteout from different routes, of their location. Since we had neither time nor energy to build a snow cave, we scraped out a hollow in a small bank, which protected the lower half of our bodies. Kathy and I shared a bivy sack for warmth. She crawled in right away, uncharacteristically leaving her gear strewn about. As I was relatively refreshed, I put everything away in her pack, then lay awake most of the night, amazed at how warm we were at 14,000 feet with only three thin layers between us and the snow. Kathy slept the twitching, jerking sleep of the exhausted. Since it was impossible to keep the top of the bivy sack closed, downy flakes of snow caught in her red hair and melted slowly. She seemed infinitely vulnerable, protected only by skin that tears so easily. I gently pulled her hat over her head, marveling again at my warmth and the brightness of a night that never seemed to fall.

Climbing, like any exacting activity, draws one deeper and deeper into its own territory, a territory often as narrow as the ice-blue thread of a couloir. In return for this extraordinary sacrifice of energy, the climber receives visions of earth. In the moment before a difficult move, she may turn her head away from what is directly before her and the beauty—or is it the fear—lays her open. Her eyes are the eyes of God, the land flows in and through and from her like a river. As night falls she may gaze across an oceanic glacier rinsed with aqua to yet another sea of black peaks, wreathed by coral clouds. She has a view of earth where everything seems unmasked, naked. Forces corresponding to her own emotions are at work, visible in the sudden rapid devastation of avalanche, in the moraine foaming up and around the tip of a glacier as that tongue of ice furrows through earth, century after century. Something inside says yes, yes, I recognize this. I want to see the earth above all with nothing hidden. The same laws that govern this world govern the life of my body and soul and it is a relief, finally, to see violence and beauty erupt, both parts of the whole.

Venturing into the wilderness the climber inhabits two worlds. Place them side by side, and the contrast makes each distinct. What does it mean to survive in the mountains? What does survival in the city mean? What defines courage in the mountains; when is one courageous in the city? What is the nature of commitment in the mountains? In the city? None of these questions are easily answered. I am a slow learner and understand best through my body. The lessons I learn in the wilderness work into my urban life. When I have moved through fear and taken a risk, such as crossing a stretch of ice unroped at 12,000 feet, other risks, especially emotional ones, become easier.

My survival in the city has not meant physical survival (although there is always the threat of violence against women). I have not gone hungry or been without shelter. Usually I must contend with less tangible forces, such as the volatile energy created by many lives denied expression and many voices silenced. The physical stress of climbing can actually be a reprieve after, for example, the mental stress of searching for work. Both are difficult. One simply gives me the strength to face the other. I need to see success measured in physical terms: climbing a mountain, or weathering storms and changing conditions.

We all know intuitively that our survival depends on each other, but in the city, recognition of our interdependence is often reduced to providing and paying for services. In the mountains, climbers are bound by absolute necessity. We depend on our partners and routinely, through the use of a rope, trust them with our lives.

The climber is vulnerable to her companions the way she is rarely vulnerable in the city. Observing the way in which a woman climbs can be an intimate experience without the exchange of a single word or touch. You may learn more than her mother knows about how she approaches problems and whether she can persevere. You are allowed to witness your friend struggle and eventually reach the top, or fail and learn to accept that failure. You will perfect the art of encouragement: when to speak and when not to, what to say when your partner is frightened, and how to praise her when she succeeds. On occasion, you will be graced by the sight of a woman when everything in her being says yes: when intelligence and skill are transformed into strong, sure movement upon any medium—snow, rock or ice.

I have been asked how I can justify taking risks with my life. I often respond that driving to work scares me more than climbing a pitch of ice. Some days, when asked that question, I remember a thunderous crack that split open a sunny August morning as three women, strung together like pearls, scanned the rocky cliffs for the source of the sound. I remember how I stood perfectly still, keeping mute vigil as, seconds after the crack, a gully directly above my sister and my friend came alive, showering them first with a pressurized spray of snow and rocks and then, after a pause the length of three breaths, with car-sized blocks of ice. During that pause I remember the sense of terror radiating from Nancy's body as she realized she was trapped, and how she moved as though the ice itself burned her. And my sister's face, tilting upward, with an expression I cannot describe. Later she told me, "I thought I was going to die."

Why are the three of us alive today? The only answer is grace. We were roped, parallel a yawning crevasse twenty feet below us. If not crushed by rocks and ice, we could easily have been swept into the crevasse. Why did we do it to begin with? For me, that question alone is easy to answer: I climb from a deep love for the wilderness, for my partners, and for my own body and its amazing strength. I don't climb *because* of the risk, although that element must be reckoned with.

Eve Dearborn took a risk, and she lost. But I remember her alive: she climbed hard, she pushed, she had not yet accepted any limits. Many women in the climbing community were influenced and inspired by her. Eve was one strong woman. Clearly, her spirit was a gift to us, and her spirit lives.

Even now, the promise of future climbs and expeditions shapes my days. I try to soak up the Arizona sun and store it like bear fat against the coming sub-zero temperatures. During my daily run I compare road grades to the slopes I will ascend on unknown mountains. I want to sweat out all the poison and worries clinging to my skin. I want to be so tired that my only desire is to put my back against the earth. A ritual of purification? Yes. And I wouldn't trade anything for a bird's wing embossed on the snow or the morning I woke above the clouds to find the spiraling tracks of mountain goats beside my tent. I long to visit again that land between earth and sky, the middle kingdom, to see the red hair of my partner flame in the sun, casting a jeweled light on the white hand of the mountain.

II

Nine years have passed since I wrote the first part of this essay. Last year, on January 28, 1991, Kathy Phibbs and her partner Hope Barnes died in a climbing accident in the Cascades. Six months later, another member of our community, Nancy Czech, also died in a climbing accident. Hope and Kathy had been friends and climbing partners; Nancy and Kathy had been friends, climbing partners, and lovers. The deaths of these three well-loved women sent waves of shock and grief through Women Climbers Northwest; many of us will feel the reverberations for years to come.

As Eve's death was the occasion for writing the first half of this essay; Kathy's is the occasion for the second. I remember that one of my initial responses to Eve's death was to worry about how my mother would feel if anything should ever happen to me. Recently, I found an eerie echo of that feeling in a letter written by Kathy, days after Eve's death. After describing the accident and the viewing of Eve's body at a funeral home, she gives an account of the memorial service, where she met Mrs. Dearborn for the first time. Talking with Eve's mother, she said, gave her faith for her own mother's strength in a similar situation.

I remember writing the first half of this essay with a kind of desperation, hoping to shift my mother's gaze away from the accident; climbing was about living to me, not death, and I wanted her to understand that. For some, risk is the primary element in climbing's alchemy; for me, it's friendship. Women, adventure, a whole shining world: that's what I wanted to talk about. Then, as now, climbing was surrounded by concentric rings of questions. On the outside, I heard the world asking, "Why climb?" or "How can you justify risking your life?" Inside that, I heard myself asking, What does it mean to climb with women? And last, the inner circle, the cauldron: What is the nature of my friendship with this woman? With Kathy? Still, I am most interested in the last questions.

When the first half of this essay was published, I was ready to move in a brand new direction, satisfied that I'd put risk in its place, or at least explained myself to my mother.

It took years, but late last January, I had slogged forward to what I hoped was the end of another essay on climbing. I knew it needed more work, but I was excited because I'd made a start in the direction I'd long since mapped out. I couldn't wait to hear what Kathy thought. The day I finished it, Hope and Kathy fell from Dragontail. Three days later, when the search party went into the mountains, I heard about the accident, and I put the essay away.

Now, shortly after the first anniversary of her death, I find myself completing this, a good-bye to Kathy, and discover that something has changed in the nine intervening years.

In the face of her death, the old questions are raised, and though I still love climbing, I find I don't want to talk about it at all: not to defend it, or explain it, or glorify it. I feel tired when the subject is brought up, because I am more absorbed with her loss than the vehicle of her loss. And this perspective, finally, feels right: climbing was both the means of her death and a wonderful expression of our friendship when she was alive.

When a climber dies, you hear a lot of people say, "At least she died doing what she loved." That was never much comfort to me, but I was happy that Kathy spent so much of her life climbing—as Eve did, as Hope did, as Nancy did, as many of us still do.

Now, instead of dreams winging into the future, I have only memories of our friendship and a deepening, pervasive sense of mystery. My last image of Kathy belongs to a cold, wet day in January when I went to Leavenworth, Washington, with several of Kathy's friends, to view her body in a funeral home. I had been away on a writing break in Arizona when Kathy died and had flown home immediately when I received the news. A public viewing had not been scheduled, but Mr. Phibbs was kind enough to arrange a private one at my request.

I drove to Leavenworth with Saskia, a woman with whom Kathy had recently begun a relationship. Both Saskia and Hope's companion had joined the rescue party that carried the bodies out of the mountains. Through Monroe, Sultan, Startup, Goldbar, Index, the drive we could have done blind, I listened to Saskia describe the accident and how Kathy looked when she found her frozen in the snow beside Colchuck Lake. Seconds ticked by; I scanned the passing sky, the pastures heavy with standing water, the road—all were colored a dull gray-green that worried my eyes with its sameness. Again and again, I came up against the familiar fringe of dark firs corralling the dumb land. On the east side of Stevens Pass, I looked out at the winter forest and wanted something from it—we were so close now to where they had died—but I was met again with silence.

When we arrived at the funeral home, the owner tried to discourage us from seeing Kathy, saying she hadn't been prepared. Nancy spoke to him, politely, but made it clear she would brook no interference. He gave in reluctantly, adding that he was sorry but because of the short notice, he didn't have a room for her—the hallway was the best he could offer.

We filed in one by one, Nancy and Saskia first. They gasped as they walked through the door, then reached out to each other and stepped back, leaning against the wall. Kathy was lying on a hospital gurney in a maroon corduroy body bag zipped up to the neck, a white silk scarf covering her throat. Her head was tilted back slightly, and an agonized expression drew all her features tight. Her face was cut and bruised, and her mouth was open, as if she were still breathing hard and in pain.

Looking down at my friend, I knew I had found what I came for—the story of Kathy's death was written on her face. I could see the anger, the loneliness, and the fear of her last moments. She had fought hard before leaving this world.

The long habit of touching her moved my hands hesitantly toward her, to the cold that had overcome her body, hardening her skin and draining the light from her hair. I was filled with an immense desire to continue loving her even through death.

Yes, she was gone. But this home of flesh and bones was where we had known her, and the only place we could come to say good-bye. Our hands laid gently on her beautiful, strong body, our tears, the words whispered alone to her, were our good-byes, and the first step toward loosening the knot of grief that bound us to her.

We stood in a circle around her, and then each of us spent a few minutes alone with her. While we were all in the room together, Mr. Phibbs called and asked Nancy to say good-bye for him and to tell Kathy he was proud of her.

On the drive home, Nancy said it looked as if her death had been as hard as her life, the past year; Donna said she would have liked to stay beside her longer, she would go again to see her if she could; Bill said he'd kept looking up to the corners of the room, thinking he might catch a glimpse of her—he wondered if she was with us.

. . .

We'd planned to climb in Alaska in the spring. Instead, I returned to the Southwest, this time to the high desert of northern New Mexico. I think of her constantly, during days so hot that thousands of creamy pods from the elms near my house fall to the ground, fluttering and swooning in dizzy descending circles.

Her death feels like a retort that left me silent. The jokes I had saved to tell her, the new essay I'd written that needed her point of view. Always in these months, I look up to the night sky for signs of her, as if a galaxy might suddenly reshape itself in her image, or a string of stars form the profile I loved—even an ice axe would be welcome. Couldn't you at least do that, I ask.

The cottonwoods, so tall the tips of their branches brush the sky, are closer to her than I am. She is at once everywhere and nowhere, and the words I want to say to her work themselves inside, becoming hard seeds in the muscle of my heart.

Then she finds me, through the memory of a climb. It's almost as if she re-enters the day so that she can leave this life and our friendship on her own terms, as if in death, time has softened between her hands.

The memory is of the day we climbed Sahale. We didn't set out to climb it, we'd planned to do the North Face of Forbidden. It was summer and we slept out on the moraine in just our bags. A small wandering pack of deer woke us before daybreak, happy to find salt in patches of bare dirt near camp, our boots, and our pack straps. Shapely hooves and big, casual licks. Only half-awake, Kathy muttered something about the deer lacking manners, and how it was entirely possibly we'd be trampled in our sleep.

It was time to get up anyway, so we rose, ate, and packed. I realized my sore throat had developed into something more serious, but I couldn't bring myself to say anything. We started off and she immediately gained fifty yards on me. Realizing I was too weak to do the climb, I sat down on a rock and cried with shame and disappointment. Her back slowly disappeared into the twilight, then she turned and came back into focus. We decided to go back to bed and get up at a decent hour to climb Sahale. Kathy dispensed a few Sudafeds, her cure-all, and we slept soundly until the sun warmed our bags.

We woke the second time to a blue sky, which grew brighter by leaps. Sahale looked friendly, and Kathy was the best of company with her gift of taking great pleasure in the smallest things—in this case, a bit of tiptoeing between two crevasses, a chance to use an axe like an ice tool, a single move causing a few quick beats of the heart. All ease she was and so pleased with herself she treated me to a running commentary on my style and the "route." The fact that we had full packs was not to be forgotten or discounted, indeed, and neither was the proximity of the only two crevasses on the glacier, just inches away, nor the flexibility I demonstrated with my cramponing technique, nor the presence of the ferocious North Cascades, kept at bay for at least one glorious day.

Then we gained the summit, and Kathy, with her ready box of gingersnaps and red crown of hair, seemed queen of all she surveyed. She talked about routes, first stabbing the air with her finger, then rubbing her hands together in excitement and wiping the sweat off against her legs. So northern, she said, of the rich greens, browns, and grays, and I remembered that unlike me, she knew and loved other ranges.

But the best was yet to come—the walk down Sahale Arm. The day grew bigger and bigger and finally burst into night, shedding the light softly, for a quiet dusk. We descended the sandy, winding path, arm of the giant, through heather where tiny white blooms shone like footlights. All around us rose the night mountains, sisters of the day mountains, but black and splendid and jagged and twice as fierce, baring gleaming slopes of snow and ice.

But we were happy and safe, enjoying the evening's warmth. I will never forget how she walked, the discipline of years showing in her steady stride, always a sense of purpose about her. I didn't ever want the trail to end. I would have followed it with her forever, watching the falling light melt into the snow, happy to carry one more succesful climb home.

Once she paused, and when I reached her, she took my hand without words. We continued walking, and everything fell into place—our bodies on the path through meadows among mountains on an earth spinning in an ocean of stars.

Finally we reached Cascade Pass, and this is where the memories diverge. Instead of descending the endless switchbacks as we did on that summer evening, she pauses at the pass, and I notice how the darkness clusters around her, dense and purple. Then she waves, a single wave that doesn't ask for a response, and I understand she is leaving now—this is the moment she's chosen.

She gives me the smile I know so well, the one she saved for summits and hard leads, and I can't help but smile back. Not so much leaving me, she seems to say, but going home, home from this last evening walk in the mountains.

She turns and begins moving away from me, back into her Beloveds, whose sleeping profiles are now barely visible. Her body vanishes, sinking like a torn leaf into the smooth vast darkness.

IT'S THE DANCE THAT COUNTS

Susan Edwards

▲ ▲ ▲

IF YOU HAVE been climbing for a while, you've probably noticed yourself progressing through different stages of development. Broadly speaking, these are at first more predominantly physical, followed by mental and spiritual. None of these stages are clear-cut, but they characteristically follow a pattern of forward movement followed by a period of plateauing or non-movement. To move beyond a plateau requires making changes in ourselves, and if these changes are significant they generally have a profound effect on us.

Physical movement is so elemental, so obvious, that we often overlook the ramifications it has on us mentally and spiritually. I had reached a plateau in my climbing, and making changes in my range of motion had such a major effect on my psyche that the topic of movement itself became a fascination for me.

I had essentially been unaware of the way I moved and did not regard it as an aspect of climbing I needed to work on. It was the same with any activity I was involved in; movement was something I did automatically; somehow it just took care of itself.

I realized this level of awareness was not unusual when I picked up a book, *The Arts and Psychotherapy,* and read the following: "Most of us go through life unaware of our most essential mode of expression and survival, kinesis." Kinesis can be described as the feeling of movement within our bodies, through being aware of the way muscles, joints, tendons and bones work together. The author of the book, Shaun McNiff, points out that all of us are in constant relation to, and interaction with, ourselves, others and the physical environment through movement, but that we are generally blind to this because we have little opportunity to train our kinesthetic sense. I myself had only considered movement intellectually until I began practicing Wu-chu, a discipline of movements similar to the Chinese exercises called Tai Chi.

From the moment I first watched my Wu-chu teacher, I was struck by the beauty of the movements, and knew I wanted to reach the same level of fluidity. As I practiced I began to experience some loosening and flexibility in my body that I had never before thought possible.

Most of the sports I had previously followed, like swimming or running, required a predominantly forward type of movement which was not very demanding for me. When I tried skiing or dancing, however, where more flexibility was required, I noticed a rigidity in my body. As much as I wanted to improve my performance, I thought the mental and physical tension I was experiencing were just part of the way I was, and I saw little hope for change.

The practice of Wu-chu required so much precision, relaxation, concentration and balance that in learning the complex movements, I was forced to turn inward. This approach transferred over into my climbing. Until then, climbing had been pleasurable, but was sometimes a struggle. I also felt uncomfortable with the aggressive, conquering quality I had been assigning to the sport. I had managed to get by with my form but then had reached a plateau; and paying attention to the movement seemed to be the next step forward.

Small differences appeared in my ability to stretch sideways, to be more delicate and deliberate in my movements. As my awareness for what was required increased I began feeling smoother, and more in control. I started to enjoy watching others, and tried to visualize and feel their movements in my body. I was not sure how to do this, but just experimented and used my intuition. The shift was from an experience that had been mainly external, to one that was more internal.

Accompanying the physical changes were some mental ones, that is, changes in the way I perceived myself. As described by the movements themselves, I felt more gentle, deliberate, delicate, re-laxed, flexible and, at the same time, more powerful. These mental and physical changes held out the possibility for more consistent en-joyment in climbing and gave the whole experience of the sport more depth and meaning.

The effects were so positive that I wanted to know more. Just what was going on in this whole process? What were the stages be-yond this? And what were other people's experiences of movement? My excuse for further study was a thesis that I needed to complete in the field of Consulting Sports Psychology.

I decided to devote a section of my thesis to movement motiva-tion and awareness. I wanted to see if people regarded the forms of movement in their sport as part of their motivation toward the sport. I was also interested in whether different sports, and the level of involvement in them, were related to the degree of awareness a person had for movement. I also hoped that elite athletes might re-veal some aspects of experience beyond movement.

I had my own speculations about a number of these topics. I thought, for example, that even though we may be doing it uncon-sciously, we are always seeking ways to alleviate stress, freeing our minds and bodies for a more productive life. We may therefore choose a certain sport, in part, for the particular movements it re-quires. Research has shown that people hold tension in their bodies differently, and that this tension can be relieved to some extent using techniques such as acupuncture and massage. It seemed to me that making a particular combination of movements in a sport could provide similar effects, shifting and releasing the held tension. The more perfect the movement, the more relief one would feel.

It is not only the body musculature, however, that holds tension. Research has indicated that we may hold tension both somatically (in the body) and cognitively (in the mind). People who hold more somatic tension find relief in the pursuit of athletics or dance, whereas those with more cognitive tension take up activities like meditation. Because rock climbing exercises both mind and body, it may appeal to people holding both somatic and cognitive tension.

As for the connection between movement and awareness, it seemed to me that there were elements in both the sport and the athlete that would dictate the degree of awareness possible. Those sports requiring a broader range of movements, and greater precision, possibly in the face of danger, would require higher levels of attention to the inner aspects of the sport. At the same time the athletes would have to be willing to continually make greater demands on themselves in order to gain this awareness.

In rock climbing the ultimate goal would be to perfect the movements so that mind and body were no longer fighting the rock but flowing with it.

I started my investigations by sending out questionnaires to a number of women rock climbers. I was interested mainly in the responses of those currently pushing the limits in the field. I then compared their responses with those from climbers of average experience. I was interested to find out if the movement was a conscious motivation for climbing, or if an awareness of it was something that developed with experience. I requested a description of movements experienced, not only to see how people would interpret the attention given to this aspect of the sport, but also to see what their response told me about their level of awareness.

I then turned to the literature on movement awareness, and the mind-body connection. Most of the literature on movement was in the fields of dance, running and martial arts. I did, however, come across several articles by climbers in which movement was covered fairly extensively, not in terms of technicalities, but of inner experiences.

John Gill, who climbed in the 1950s and 1960s and introduced gymnastics, bouldering and chalk(!) into rock climbing, seems to be the guru for movement awareness in climbing. He has written a number of articles about movement, and as if touched by his influence, others who knew him, like Yvon Chouinard, also expressed thoughts about a deeper aspect of climbing.

In "Bouldering: A Mystical Art Form," Gill writes about the boulderer as an artist seeking self-realization through kinesthetic awareness. He says the aim is to turn inward and attain this awareness during the demanding technical moves. In his words, "when intellectual analysis is past, and pain and fallibility have receded, there remains this intoxicating and fundamental quality of inner climbing." He explains that this path is nevertheless a choice and that it requires removal from the external pressures and distractions of the climbing scene. But why would one want this awareness? Because, as Gill explains, this is where meaning lies:

In those moments when your mind becomes saturated with kinesthetic awareness, cosmic chaos assembles in a sharp and meaningful design, inseparably combining climber and rock in an interlude of destiny.

In an article written in 1986 about John Bachar, one of the top free-solo rock climbers of our day, Bachar describes his experiences as follows:

To me free climbing is a form of Tai Chi. You learn how to deal with your energy and what you can be mentally, physically, and spiritually, using climbing as the medium. I'm trying to perfect my movement to learn about myself. Every day I go out and climb, like a dancer works on his dance . . . this is how he expresses himself. Both he and I are interested in the same thing. It's the dance that counts.

One can imagine that removing any of the "props" in rock climbing can only increase the intensity of the experience. John Gill was doing short, intense climbs without a rope; now John Bachar is doing climbs of at least the same degree of difficulty, but of much greater length. He describes a very internal process that would seem to be the only way one could survive. At this level the sport clearly demands a looking inward, but the athletes also demand it of themselves.

Several aspects of awareness I found mentioned in the literature were substantiated by the women rock climbers. All of them felt that movement was one of their motivations for climbing. This was not the case for athletes from at least two other sports I investigated—ultrarunning and mountaineering—neither was it the case for the less experienced athletes. This suggested that the focus on movement, and the enjoyment of it, developed with increasing experience and was dependent on the type of sport practiced.

Climbers variously described the movement as a slow form of vertical gymnastics or a free-form yoga. And the diversity of movements—stretching, crouching, squeezing, pulling and controlled lunging—seemed to be part of the appeal. The physical and mental requirements to perform these movements—and which thus were an integral part of them—were described as control, fluidity, grace, flexibility, coordination, timing, balance, power, spontaneity, good judgment, commitment, relaxation, strength and self-confidence. Obviously perfection could be a lifetime pursuit!

One woman described how her movement seemed to be in response to a relationship with the rock; that is, in many respects the rock dictated the movements, but at the same time allowed room for creativity. The climbers felt that through their endeavors they gained a sense of being involved in a mental and physical challenge. The rewards were a sense of achievement, strength, a sense of balance, health, personal growth and close friendships.

It seems that although the experiences in climbing may be very different for each person, becoming aware of movement from a physical and mental perspective is essential for experiencing what might be called the essence of climbing.

Many people have probably had experiences along the spectrum of mind-body awareness, but development and open expression of them are rare in our linear and rational thinking Western culture. It has been said by some that, through lack of training, we have forgotten our right-brain capacities for other levels of knowing. Eastern paths of knowledge lay more emphasis on development of the right brain capacities for intuition, sensuality and creativity, all of which are closely linked to our movements in climbing. The West is showing an increasing interest in this approach and, as these aspects are integrated and spread among the climbing community, I am convinced we will witness the emergence of a totally different approach to the sport.

I don't believe one has to excel in climbing to develop this awareness, but it may be arrived at only after a good deal of dedication and a willingness to change.

If we choose to, integration of mind and body awareness can then progress to levels where we are able to transcend both. At that point, it may be that movement will be all there is.

Bibliography

Ament, P. *Master of Rock. The Biography of John Gill* (Boulder, Colorado: Alpine House Publishing, 1977)

Gill, J. "Bouldering: A Mystical Art Form" in Tobias, M.C. & Drasdo, H. (Eds.), *The Mountain Spirit* (London: Victor Gollancz Ltd., 1980)

Gill, J. "Bouldering at Fifty—A Wayward Commitment." *The Climbing Art,* #7, 5–8 (January, 1988)

Gill, J. "Option—Soloing" *The Climbing Art,* #20, 32 (Fall, 1991)

Mc Niff, S. *The Arts and Psychotherapy* (Springfield, Illinois: Charles C. Thomas, 1981)

Steiger, J. "Johnny Rock" *Climbing,* 31–39 (October, 1986)

FEAR OF FALLING

Lorna Millard

▲ ▲ ▲

I WAS ATTACKED three weeks before I went rock climbing in Squamish.

It had been my last day as a counselor for the federal employment office in Nanaimo, a mill town halfway up the east coast of Vancouver Island. I had left my job to take some time for rock climbing, hiking, writing, traveling and starting a new phase of life outside the civil service.

After a day of cards, gifts and packing up my office life, I should have gone directly home to finish stuffing my personal possessions into boxes destined for storage in numerous attics of friends and family. Instead, I indulged in a farewell stroll along my favorite trail in Morrell Sanctuary, a quiet park near my home.

My usual walk wove through mossy fir and cedar trees, skirted a small beaver pond, then circled larger Morrell Lake. Dividing the lake was a string of logs chained end to end. I hiked as I had every day to this spot, kicked off my sandals and walked out on the first log, which abutted the shore. Reaching the point where it submerged, I sat down on the sun-silvered wood. Watching dragonflies and newts, I swatted the odd, annoying mosquito and let the summer sun toast the air-conditioned office out of my bones. Reluctantly, I finally got up and started to retrace my steps. Fifty feet into my return hike along the lake, I was jumped by a naked man.

In the second before he sprang from behind a stump, I saw him. My mind did a strange thing, spinning that eye-blink of time into a ponderous eternity. "My god, it's the weirdo I saw the last time I was here."

That day he had intruded on my dragonfly watching by skinny-dipping less than fifty feet from my log, and I had made a nonchalant but speedy departure to a more populated end of the lake. When he didn't appear to be following, I had struck out on the remote trail that led to my mountain bike and the park entranceway. But the skinny-dipper put on shorts and shoes and caught up to me. He asked for directions, which I gave him, and then he ran ahead, only to reappear from one trail after another, intersecting my route. Finally, I arrived at my bike and the safety of other people.

The incident had spooked me enough to disrupt my daily hikes, but today, a week and a half later, I had convinced myself that there could be no repeat of that bizarre, chance encounter. Not on my last day of work, a day that deserved to end with my cherished ritual walk.

Now, here he was. "He looks ridiculous—squatting there like a naked gnome!" My voice was whizzing through my head. "Damn him! This isn't real. I have a whole new life to start at the end of this walk. Don't look like a victim! This can't be happening!"

"Hi," I said aloud, looking him square in the eye.

"Hi." He said it automatically, as if he couldn't stop the word coming out so inappropriately.

My endless second of eternity ran out. He leaped.

Screaming, I lunged sideways as he grabbed for my legs. He knocked me into a tree, then slammed me down onto the fir needles. I landed on my shins and hands, legs folded beneath me, arms braced against his crushing weight. Screams tore from my throat. I heard them echo through the empty woods and stopped, knowing with a sick certainty that no one was there to hear.

His right hand moved from its hard grip on my shoulder to my mouth. I wrenched my head down and to the left. His palm crushed my teeth into my lips, but I broke his hold. I knew I had to keep my mouth free. There was only the sound of the two of us panting.

Feeling the weight of fat and muscle pressing down on my back, I knew I was pinned helplessly until he moved. The edges of terror and fury pulsed through my body, but I didn't have time to deal with them. "What if . . . ?" danced on those razor edges. I refused to consider the question.

Then that unreal feeling of timelessness descended again. In the space of two pounding heartbeats, I found the very center of myself, and from there, a place I had never felt before, a deep calmness settled over me, pushing the fear and panic out the bottoms of my feet. Within that quietness there was strength.

Around my throat, I felt the necklace my co-workers had given me the night before. I thought, "I'm loved! And I am strong! You will not hurt me, I won't let you! You don't know who you're dealing with."

I found the words to talk him out of raping me. I reminded him that when we had met before, I had helped orient him on the maze of trails—I deserved far better than this in return for my kindness. He said it was too late for second thoughts—I said no, that so far he had only scared me.

Through swollen, bloody lips, I said he had done nothing to hurt me, we could both walk away and forget this had ever happened. I added that I was leaving town, I had no reason to tell anyone, and I wouldn't be around to pursue the matter. He could trust me.

After five endless minutes of desperate salesmanship, he stood me up and brushed the bark from my shoulders. "Don't turn around and don't come back, or I'll kill you," he said, and gave me a push down the trail. Walking quickly, but with control, I kept my head up and hoped my back radiated calm and confidence. And I listened hard, in case his footsteps pursued me.

Once I was well away, I glanced back. There was no one following. I ran as far as I was able, then slowed to a fast walk. For half an hour I fled through the woods, until finally I reached Westwood Lake. The beach was crowded with people. Knowing I was safe, I felt my control ebbing away. I didn't have much longer. I had to find someone fast, before I broke down.

Scanning the beach, I zeroed in on a middle-aged woman. She looked like someone's mom, steady and unflappable. Walking up to her, I said, "Excuse me, I need some help." My voice caught and stumbled over the rest of my sentence, "Someone just attacked me."

I don't remember her name. She drove me home, where I

picked up my van, and then followed me to a friend's office. My friend heard me come in the door and was halfway across the lobby by the time I reached him. "Someone just tried to rape me." That was all I could say before, overwhelmed by safety, I began to shake and cry. I couldn't talk anymore. If he hadn't been holding me then, I couldn't have stayed on my feet.

He took over, sat me down with a glass of water and heard the whole story. When I was calm enough, he phoned the RCMP. The rest of the evening seemed an endless numb dream. A police constable came and took a statement. Then the three of us went to the park, where I had to lead them to the site of the attack. I looked hopefully for an earring I had lost, a tiny silver dragonfly. We never found it.

From there, to the police station. Another taped statement. Pictures of me: my scraped and bruised legs, swollen lips, bruises and cuts on my back and shoulders. A cup of coffee and pages and pages of mug shots. He wasn't in any of them.

Later, my friend congratulated me: "The way you handled all the police questioning was great; it seems like you've already dealt with the attack and moved on."

"I don't know," I said. "Right now I feel, 'Wow, I did that!' But I know I haven't begun to get in touch with the uglies. They're still down there, waiting for me."

Unfortunately, I was right.

For the first two weeks, I did little but sleep. I was bruised, stiff and had no energy. My sleep was shattered by nightmares, and from those I catapulted into another frightening after effect—panic attacks.

One struck me while I was walking in the woods with a friend in a perfectly safe place—a wave of icy terror spun up from my feet and engulfed me. My throat closed, and I could hardly breathe; my body shook, my teeth chattered uncontrollably. Legs buckling, I groped for support. When the panic subsided, I was exhausted and frustrated. Even the woods had been taken from me and I didn't know if I would ever get them back.

Healing had to take place. The first important step was to talk about the assault. The second was completing a composite drawing of my attacker with a police artist. Once I had accomplished that, I had done as much as I could to protect myself and others from my attacker and no longer had to hold the image of his face in my mind. The last thing I did in Nanaimo was to go for my old walk—with a friend—and sit on my log in Morrell Lake. It was scary, but every time images of the attack came over me, I stopped, took a deep breath, let the memories flow, and then concentrated on the peacefulness I still found there.

By this time, I was overdue in Squamish, the rock climber's mecca just north of Vancouver. I wanted to do some climbing there with my friend Al.

On our first day, getting to the start of the first climb almost did me in. We clambered up to a ledge from which a series of cracks reached up to the top of a sixty-foot cliff. Just hoisting a pack over my head and onto the ledge left my legs trembling with fatigue and my chest heaving. "What are you doing here," I asked myself.

But Al scaled Cat Crack and then belayed me up behind him. As I began the climb, finger jams and hand jams sidled back into my brain. Twisting the toe of my sticky climbing shoe sideways into the fissure, I rotated onto the ball of my foot and felt the reassuring snugness of the grip. It held. I reached higher, relaxing and concentrating on the climb instead of my fear of fatigue—my fear of being afraid.

We did a few more climbs, then broke for lunch. I was tired but exultant. Climbing had been strenuous but fun. Best of all, it had taken my mind off everything else.

Halfway up the next crack, I was in trouble. Stretching for a hold, my left foot slipped, and I slammed both knees into the unyielding granite to stop my fall. Swearing loudly, I searched for the one contortion that might allow a comfortable rest stance. My legs were shaking. I realized the wisdom of retreat, but I just couldn't make myself stop.

I went at it again, struggling upward on precarious holds. Suddenly, the dam on my fear burst. Panic crashed over my pinched toes and coursed to my trembling knees. I hung desperately onto the rock edges as my body sank into an inky whirlpool of fear. It drew me into the hungry maw of the rock.

"Get me the hell out of here!" Al hauled, and I lunged upward against a sunless, sucking vortex of fear. I couldn't see the holds. I didn't feel the rock smash against my flailing legs. I knew I was drowning sixty feet up a dry cliff.

On hands and knees, I dragged myself onto the clifftop. Struggling to my feet, legs splayed and shaking, I braced my hands on my thighs to keep me upright and sucked air between my violently chattering teeth. Slowly, slowly the swirling waves of panic receded.

Why was I so afraid of falling? At worst, I would drop only a foot or two before the rope caught me. Falling is part of climbing. You don't get better if you don't push yourself enough to risk the odd fall. And since the most enjoyable climbs are mostly above the beginner level, if you don't push yourself, you miss the climbs that are most fun.

Then I realized, I had always hated falling. Up until the assault, I had just been able to hide it better. I had talked a good line, accepting falling as part of climbing—as part of life—but now I knew I had never believed it. Falling was failing. And I was afraid to fail.

I realized that since the assault, I had been constantly drilling for another attack. Instead of feeling empowered by how I had handled that situation, I felt it must have been a fluke. I was terrified that any experience that tested me would see me come up short next time. Here on this climb I had recreated the sensation of the drowning panic that was my first, uncontrolled reaction to the assault. Giving up on anything was allowing myself to be raped. Only now the victim and the attacker were one and the same.

That was a gut-shaking admission, but one I had to make. That fear and its denial had undermined my climbing. Now I began to see how they had sabotaged the rest of my life: I was always striving to be the perfect counselor, climber, hiker, traveler, writer. Anything less than perfect was a failure. I felt for the first time the burden of being onstage, madly changing from one costume and character to another, always trying to play my part perfectly in everything I did. Falling on a climb or falling flat on my face in any endeavor, it was all the same. Falling was failing. At every level, in everything I did, it seemed I had desperately covered up the imperfect, unacceptable, vulnerable me.

It had taken an attack from a stranger and the panic of dangling sixty feet up a cliff to make me see how viciously I had been attacking myself for as long as I could remember.

Swaying unsteadily on that Squamish clifftop, I made a decision: fear of falling had messed up my climbing and my life. I couldn't climb like that, and I certainly couldn't live like that!

And so I began the painful process of learning to trust my true thoughts and feelings and to let them out. After all, when I was assaulted there was no time for acting—it was all me. If being myself got me through the attack, what couldn't it get me through?

I started by climbing only as long and as hard as I really wanted to. The minute I said I "should" keep going, I quit. I even let myself fall a few times, on purpose, to get used to the feeling. On the first fall, my stomach dropped out through my feet. After that, it wasn't so bad. As a result, climbing became more relaxed and a lot more fun. I began to trust myself, and I didn't have a panic attack on any further climbs, even when I really pushed.

Buoyed by further climbs at Squamish, we headed back to Vancouver and up Crown Mountain. Crown is a peak accessible from the top of the Grouse Mountain gondola ride. After a gentle hike along a ridge, then down into and back up the other side of a steep valley, we reached the peak.

We camped on a ledge barely big enough for our two-person tent, just five meters below the summit and hundreds of meters above the moraine-strewn valleys that dropped away on all sides. To the south, the view took in the city fifteen hundred meters below us and on the clearest day our southern horizon stretched past the Olympic range to the massive white dome of Mount Rainier, over three hundred kilometers distant. West of us lay Georgia Strait and Vancouver Island. North and east, jagged blue and green peaks, capped with white, marched away in serried ranks.

We spent our days climbing on the secondary peak of Crown. It's called the Camel because it looks like a kneeling stone dromedary. There, I worked some more on my fear of falling. I climbed, and then backed off when I sensed I was continuing only because I was afraid to stop.

On our last day, Al coiled the rope over his shoulder and we scrambled up the Camel's back by the fourth-class route over its rump. The airiness was scary. Clinging to the arête, I looked down sheer rock walls to the furry green rug that was really a forest of tall evergreens and breathed deeply. After a bit, I relaxed enough to stop splaying like a starfish and sat up normally. Al continued toward the Camel's head, and I followed him over the hump.

The hump is actually a knife-edged spine with steep flanks that drop off on either side. We traversed by clinging to its sharp edge with both hands and walking our feet sideways along the steep rock face. It was easy as long as I didn't look down. Unroped as we were, a misstep would have been a deathfall.

Our destination was a flat block on the Camel's backbone that served as a station from which to rappel from the hump down into the bow of its neck. From there, one more rappel would have us at the base, where the Camel knelt on its granite pedestal. Separating us from the rappel block was a gaping hole in the spine. I watched as Al negotiated the empty air—one hand grasping the near rock, the other on the far side of the gap, feet straddling—then he was across.

Pausing a few meters short of the great hole, I hugged the warm, rough granite and dispersed my rising fear with deep breaths. A Grouse Mountain resort helicopter buzzed us, affording its load of camera-toting tourists close-up shots of the two crazy climbers. The angry sound of the blades seemed somehow malevolent and distracted me. Finally, the pilot veered back to the launch pad at the top of the tram, several kilometers distant. I had only a few minutes before his next pass.

Standing up, I grasped the last block before the yawning space and shuffled along it to the edge. As I craned my head around the corner, my gaze fell into the gaping hole, hurtled through empty air and crashed at the foot of the mountain. Then it swooped back up the sheer cliff, across the void and touched solid rock on the other side. The gap was bigger than I'd thought. I hesitated and felt the chill of fear begin to well up from my feet. Yanking my head around the corner, I carefully shifted back to a safer perch to regroup. I reminded myself that I didn't have to do this. I could retreat. But this time, I really wanted to push on.

The helicopter's warning buzz came faintly to my ears. I pulled myself erect and crab-walked to the edge again, this time barely slowing my momentum enough for one deep breath. "You can do it. You won't fall," I exhaled. Then I was stretching, reaching my left hand across the gap until my fingers curled over the edge of the far block. My left foot followed and touched down tentatively on the slanted face. I tightened my grip on the warm strong stone on either side and pushed off. My body swung across the void. My right hand gripped tightly beside the left. My right foot planted solidly on the far block. I did it. After that, the rappel down onto the neck and then to the base was like going down a playground slide.

At the end of September, it was time to move on. My ego said, take an exotic trip. But my heart said, go home, work, write, get outdoors. Settle for a while. I followed my heart and serendipitously found a great job, a nice place to live, and the time to write and to get outdoors.

I have begun to take the woods back, too. I miss the peaceful solitude I once enjoyed on my solo hikes, but because I can't feel safe hiking alone anymore, my compromise is to go with a friend. One of my best hiking partners is a massive mutt named Bear. He outweighs most people I meet on the trail and he doesn't interrupt my thoughts.

I have also found a new depth and satisfaction in my friendships and made a relieved, if rueful, discovery my friends have been able to see through my costumes all along. They have always liked me for who I am. I have fooled no one but myself.

Besides discovering a new honesty and closeness with old friends, I have made important new friends, too, and I manage to be myself around them, most of the time, even though they might not know me well enough yet to know the difference. And so, life is full, but there is time every day to write, to get outside for a run, a hike or a climb and to practice and refine the simple and unbelievably pleasurable task of just being me, to the utmost of my ability.

It comes in fits and starts, but it is coming: coming to terms with my successes and failures, with the fact that I don't have to be as ardent or adept a climber as Al to enjoy climbing; finding my peace in finding my own level in everything I do; feeling good enough just being me.

Being myself isn't always easy. I get scared, or I forget, and the old habits kick in. Suddenly, I'm up there in the footlights, playing the consummate character of the moment in full face paint, chanting "Falling is failing," over and over to myself. But it doesn't last very long. I suddenly remember that, as in climbing, most of the fun things in life are there for the doing, as long as I'm prepared to fall once in a while. Through my climbing, I have also learned that I can trust myself not to fall, not to fail, when I face a challenge for my own sake and not as a means of impressing others. I think about how awful it used to feel when I feared tackling anything because I feared failure. Then, I give voice to my new chant: "I can't climb like that, and I won't live like that!"

LATIN AMERICAN WOMEN
CLIMBERS TODAY

Rachel da Silva

▲ ▲ ▲

IN CONTRAST to the rapid development of women's climbing in Europe and North America, in Latin America progress has been, until recently, isolated and discontinuous. Few women practiced the sport and fewer still climbed at the highest levels, and when they did, they climbed as the lone woman in groups of ten or twenty men. As one might expect, they rarely were able to participate fully in expedition planning and decision-making.

Starting in the mid-1970s women climbers throughout Latin America began to discuss the the need for communication with one another, for an opportunity to learn from and with one another and to make decisions and take risks on their own. Many women experimented with a new concept: undertaking exclusively women's trips, in the process developing faith in themselves and each other as skilled and capable climbers. Many of these women dreamed of forming a women's climbing organization, a radical step they knew would change the climbing status quo forever.

By the mid-1980s this women's movement in mountaineering had reached critical mass. In 1986 twelve representatives from seven countries held the first convention of Latin American Women's Mountaineering in the Cordillera Reál of Bolivia and climbed Huayna Potosí (6,096 meters.)

In 1987 Argentine women organized the second convention.

Fourteen enthusiastic participants from six countries climbed the highest mountain on the continent, Aconcagua (6,959 meters). In July of the same year, Ecuador held the third convention, during which participants climbed three of that country's highest peaks, Iliniza Sur (5,305 meters), Iliniza Norte (5,116 meters) and Chimborazo (6,310 meters). Participation had grown to twenty-five women from six countries.

By 1988 word had spread and more women than ever wanted to participate. Peruvian women hosted the fourth convention. Thirty-three women from seven countries climbed two of the highest peaks on the continent, Vallunarraju (5,800 meters) and Huascarán Sur (6,768 meters.) They also put in motion concrete plans for the Congress that would inaugurate a Latin American women's climbing organization the following year.

With the help of the Association of Mountaineering and Exploration at the National Autonomous University in Mexico City, the First Congress of Latin American Women's Mountaineering was held there from September 11–23, 1989. Participating countries included Chile, Venezuela, El Salvador and Mexico, with the support and approval of Peru, Colombia, Brazil, Argentina and Ecuador.

By the end of the Congress the Union of Latin American Women Climbers (ULAMM) had been formed, and bylaws and regulations finalized. The Union was to function as a non-profit Civil Association, be apolitical, nonsectarian and racially non-discriminatory. Its objectives are to:

- create a Union of Latin American women climbers
- support Latin American women in their climbing activities as athletes at the national level
- encourage and develop women's participation in mountaineering
- raise the technical and cultural level of Latin American women climbers
- promote communication between women climbers around the world

To achieve these goals, ULAMM supports diverse sports activities, including related academic endeavors, outreach and administrative work.

ULAMM guidelines for conventions promote the goals of devel-

oping climbing at a high level, encouraging fun and mutual enjoyment of climbing rather than a competitive spirit, and placing the
safety of each individual ahead of the execution of any particular
objective.

ULAMM

The organization's logo is a profile of a woman's face with hair
radiating out in the shape of Latin America, and she wears a carabiner as an earring. The Union's motto "Unidas conquistando
ideales" is roughly translated as "Achieving ideals together," with
an undertone acknowledging the struggle involved.

In December 1991 the Second Congress of ULAMM was held
in Mérida, Venezuela. Topics discussed included mountaineering
medicine, high-altitude cooking and nutrition, and Venezuela's Himalayan expedition of 1991. A new area of focus was added to the
group's objectives: promoting care for the mountain environment
and governmental awareness of the scientific and natural resources
of these fragile areas. Participants then headed out for ten days of
climbing, including ascents of Pico Bolívar (5,007 meters) and the
"Five White Eagles," peaks just under 5,000 meters.

Since the formation of ULAMM each member country has held
annual national meetings. Many women in ULAMM feel that geo-
graphical barriers and self-limiting attitudes, rather than social pressures, contribute to the low numbers of women in Latin American
mountaineering. However, little by little there is a noticeable lessen-
ing of dependence on men as more women take initiative, guiding,
teaching and organizing expeditions.

In early 1990 Professor Evilio Echeverria of Colorado State University, an active climber, wrote me with names and addresses of over a
dozen women climbers in various Latin American countries whom
he knew personally or knew of from his climbing contacts. I wrote
them requesting their stories and many responded with enthusiasm,
some sending additional material—thick sheaves of newspaper clip-
pings, detailed write-ups of the various ULAMM conventions and

Newspaper spread of Rosa Pabón's climb of Pico Bolívar, 1986.

climbs, even a cassette tape of a radio broadcast about the 1987 Aconcagua climb. And a few sent photos of themselves. Since then I've received updates on the progress of ULAMM.

The three short biographies that follow are based on these letters and stories. Sandra Schwarz generously helped with the translations. I wrote the biographies of Luisa Gallardo and Rosa Pabón using their letters and descriptions of their climbs, which they kindly included. Julia Meza Ramirez's story is told in her own words. I translated it, adding explanatory details where necessary.

JULIA MEZA RAMIREZ
Chile

My life had a marvelous infancy. My parents were hard-working people of few economic resources, but they gave to my brothers and myself a home filled with love and understanding. They taught us from an early age to fight for what we wanted. I always loved active sports and did a lot of athletics in high school. This was perhaps because I had my father for a role model: he was a nationally-known competitor in cycling. After high school I entered the university to study law, but eventually switched to education. At the end of this five-year program, I received my certificate to be a teacher of emotionally disturbed children. Simultaneously I was studying for another degree, a four-year course in advertising. I also studied some theater. During this time sports had to go on the back burner.

I fell in love and got married, but sadly my husband left me after three years. We had one daughter, Valentina. She is enchanting. She's sixteen now and wants to study medicine. She's very intelligent and has always been a great support, like my parents, of my pursuit of sports. Many times she has given up being with her mom so that I could go on expeditions. I love her very much.

After graduation I dedicated most of my time to working with disturbed children. Almost all of them have been abandoned by their parents. Others are children of alcoholics. Around this time I began to climb again in a serious and coordinated way. I found it gave me great peace, and I discovered important friendships in the mountains.

I went with my daughter to live with my parents and every weekend I would go to the Cordillera to train or climb some peak. I belonged to the National School of Mountaineering and received the title of Instructor in the Federation of Andean Climbing. I worked with groups of twenty and taught rescue techniques, cooking, mountain travel, first aid, snow techniques, and so on.

In Chile the number of women who climb has been increasing. But at that time, 1983, there were only three women in the National School of Mountaineering. Nevertheless, we decided to achieve the great objective—to the men this was unbelievable—of being the first women's expedition to climb Aconcagua, the highest peak in the Americas. We planned the climb for 1983, the one-hundredth anniversary of the first ascent of the mountain. We worked for two years getting the money together, recruiting the final group of ten and training hard. In 1983 we succeeded in putting five women on the summit. As the leader, I had to accompany two members of our team who had become ill high up on the mountain back to base camp. I returned to summit alone, three days after the first group of four women.

On our return we were received with great admiration by our compatriots. They talked about what they called the "feat" and gave us the Medal of Honor in Sports. Our career as a serious climbers' group had begun. We had worked through many disagreements and in the end were very united. We knew that it was much more difficult for us to go to the mountains than for men, since all of us work and have children, but all the sacrifices were well worth it.

To stay in shape and improve our skills, we made many trips to volcanoes in the north of Chile; there are many over 6,000 meters. That year I worked a lot with children, teaching skiing and mountaineering courses. I participated in the Third Olympic Academy and participated in a seminar on Infant and Youth Recreation organized by the World Council on Education.

Together with some friends, all instructors with the National School of Mountaineering, we continued training to prepare for the First Women's Exploration of Antarctica in 1984. As before on Aconcagua, I agreed to be the leader. We all had to make a lot of sacrifices to gather the necessary economic and material resources. Obtaining the permits was another major job. Once in Antarctica, the five of us traveled 180 kilometers southeast from Base Bernardo O'Higgins and climbed and named various peaks in the region. On our return we were heralded in the media and given a second Medal of Honor and many other distinctions. A postage stamp illustrating our trip was issued.

In 1985 I became a ski instructor. That same year we went on the first women's expedition to the Austral Zone of Southern Argentina which was a great success with the first ascent—not a women's first but a true first ascent—of the volcano Macá.

On the emotional front my life took a big turn. After being single for eight years, dedicated only to my daughter, my work and my sport, I married a doctor—a specialist who had operated on my nose after it was fractured. We went to live in the city of Viña del Mar, about two hours from Santiago, far from my women's climbing group. Thanks to the understanding and love of my husband, I traveled every weekend to Santiago to continue training. I've lived in Viña del Mar now for three years. To continue with my sport requires an enormous sacrifice for me, but it's something that I will do until the day I die. I love the mountains, and I love climbing.

An idea occurred to me that I put before the Chilean Federation of Mountaineering, and the members accepted. It was to carry out the first Latin American Women's Expedition to Mt. McKinley in Alaska in 1989. It was a big challenge because it required a lot of money, a lot of training on ice and a lot of strength. But the idea was there, and we began to fight for it.

Again as leader of the group, I began to ask for support from more than one hundred businesses. Quickly I realized that this work was extracting a huge sacrifice from me. Every day, I would get up at six o'clock in the morning to go running for an hour on the shore alone, since my companions trained in Santiago. After running I would return home, have breakfast and leave to be at my job, working with emotionally disturbed kids, at 8:00 a.m. I'd leave work at 2:00 p.m., arrive, running, at my apartment for lunch and then go off to the university, where I was getting a Master's degree in Special Education. I would leave at 8:00 p.m. and hurry home to make supper and see my family, wash and iron and so forth. Fridays, I took the bus to Santiago to meet with my group and review equipment, food, transportation, and the other details for the Alaska expedition. Saturdays we'd go climbing, and I would return on Sunday. This life was a great sacrifice.

Without realizing just how quickly, we soon had our tickets to Alaska! For us, a place of dreams, like Antarctica had been. We climbed the north summit of McKinley; only two women had done so before us. Truly, it was an extremely difficult climb. The entire twenty-three days we were on the mountain, the fierce wind never stopped and the temperature never got above ten degrees below zero centigrade, and was usually closer to minus forty. We discovered we had less clothing than we needed, especially with the nightmarish conditions, and all of us suffered some degree of frostbite. But we returned to Chile triumphant and received praise from all sides.

Happily, I graduated from the university in December 1989 and took the postdoctoral exams, earning the highest distinction with a Grade Seven. Now I am a psychologist with a specialty in learning disabilities.

I was very pleased to be invited to the Fourth Assembly of the Pan American Union of Mountaineering Associations (UPAM) that took place in the spring of 1990 in Chile. All the heads of the mountain federations of Colombia, Peru, Bolivia, Ecuador, Argentina, Mexico and Chile were there. Very exciting for me was the formation of the "Andean Sisterhood" group, in addition to the establishment of a permanent UPAM commission in each member country through which women will be encouraged to get involved in mountaineering. In January of 1991 I will participate in the first Ecological Expedition to Mt. Aconcagua, following which UPAM will hold the first International Conference for the Protection of the Andean Environment.

Right now I find myself working with my problem kids, attending to my daughter, Valentina, and to my husband, training every morning on the beach and weekends in the mountains, doing housewifely things, and organizing some new expedition. Our next goal is to climb Chimborazo in Ecuador, if God's willing and we can come up with the money.

LUISA GALLARDO
Ecuador

"I have always been a climber; I was born into a family that loved going on trips," says Luisa Gallardo about her childhood. "Almost every weekend I went with my parents and seven siblings to some mountain near Quito, and when I was eight I began climbing on the snows of the Ilinizas." As a teenager she and her friends organized climbing and hiking trips to the mountains, "where we took our brothers, friends and lovers."

Luisa, who has a degree in economics, was working in the Ministry of Finance when she received an invitation to climb Cotopaxi, (5,970 meters) the highest active volcano in the world, with the climbing club Inti-Nan. This was the beginning of her "life in the mountains." She began to climb more seriously, staying away from home for several days at a time. Her mother and brothers disapproved, but since she had a job and was economically independent, there wasn't a lot they could do to stop her. They became used to her being gone every weekend. Soon she had climbed all the Ecuadoran peaks several times. She wanted more.

In 1986, Luisa decided to attend the first convention of Latin American Women's Mountaineering, held in Bolivia. Led by experienced climbers like Lucía Rojas, Magalí Campos and Narda Wuth, Luisa and the other women on the team overcame incredible obstacles on their attempt on Chearoco, a 6,000-meter peak, including last-minute logistical problems and an icefall that injured two climbers in their tents. In a driving white-out 180 meters from the summit they were forced to abandon the climb, heavy snowfall making the descent extremely treacherous. It was a real triumph of will that they continued and climbed their second objective, Huayna Potosí.

Inspired to help with the organization of the second convention hosted by Carina Vaca Seller of Argentina, Luisa became her country's representative. The successful all-women ascent of Aconcagua in 1987 was something of a watershed for Latin American women's climbing. It became a huge media event in every country that had a representative on the climb, and was a first for many of the women (even though it wasn't the first women's ascent). And it seems to have validated both the climbers and their dreams.

By now Luisa was an experienced organizer, and she took on the job of spearheading preparations for the third convention, held in Quito. From March through June she solicited support from businesses, clubs, agencies and individuals, gathering funds and in-kind donations that ranged from powdered milk to airplane tickets, from help with media contacts to the loan of a bus. Twenty-five climbers from six countries showed up for the gathering, and headed off to their first climbing objective, Cayambe. But the weather wouldn't cooperate, and neither this peak nor Cotopaxi could be climbed safely.

Although the wind and cold continued and clouds hovered low, the group was determined to push on to the Ilinizas. But well into the climb they were faced with another dilemma, as Luisa explains:

> Here we had to prove, one more time, our quality as human beings and the comradeship that reigned in the group. We realized that one group wanted to climb Iliniza North and the other Iliniza South, according to their respective abilities on technical rock and steep ice. We had two goals and one peak! We also had to minimize the risk of putting so many people on the South summit at one time. It was amazing to see how everyone rose to the occasion. Their discipline and desire to collaborate on a solution were clear.
>
> The following day a group of twelve left at 5:30 a.m. for the South summit, and at 8:00 five women headed for Iliniza North. Each group spent time on their respective summits and gathered together later at the refuge. There was a unanimous happiness among the group. Some of us had finally achieved the most technical of our objectives, and others had done another magnificent climb.

The last of the group's goals, the great peak Chimborazo, did not look inviting as they approached. But the weather finally did cooperate. Summit day was windless, and the sky clear. They left as early as they could, and at 8:45 a.m. seventeen women stood on the summit. They hoisted the flags of Argentina, Colombia, Chile, Ecuador, Peru and Venezuela in a brief ceremony, paying tribute to the dream of Latin American unity and freedom from oppression.

Luisa had been to Peru as a tourist and had become fascinated by the Cordillera Blanca. She wanted to climb there and eagerly participated in the fourth convention, climbing Vallunarraju and Huascarán.

> How happy I was when I joined the expedition to Peru. I was climbing again with women who were in situations similar to my own. We had all confronted fellow climbers who thought us incapable of climbing without masculine support. It was very emotional to realize that the idea [of the need for a women's climbing organization] had spread so wide, that there were so many women involved now, all working very hard so that these climbing conventions could take place. And more

than that, that the sisterhood was so strong and we had so much pride in ourselves that we were now going to be an institution at the Latin American level.

In addition to helping with the formation of the Union of Latin American Women Climbers, Luisa adopted a related project, the establishment of a chain of hostels, in all the major cities of Latin America, that would offer support, information and guide services to climbers, as well as traditional hostel services like inexpensive rooms and friendly people. The first of these was opened in Quito, Ecuador, by a group of women climbers, Luisa Gallardo prominent among them. It is affiliated with the climbing club Inti-Nan. She writes:

> It is with great satisfaction that we are helping the mountains, within our respective countries, to become better known . . . each of us is a medium of promotion and information for our women climbing friends throughout Latin America, and we are delighted to be able to offer them our support and friendship.

ROSA PABÓN
Venezuela

"In a conservative country like Venezuela, there are all kinds of obstacles—family, society, the media—to a young woman who would like to be free enough to go off to the mountains whenever she wishes. But I must admit that this isn't always the greatest problem. She herself, conditioned by fears and prejudices imposed by society, is often her own worst enemy. Many times I've heard women say, with a definite tone of frustration, 'Mountaineering is only for men!' How can we get rid of all these prejudices that don't get us anywhere? By working and demonstrating to ourselves that we *can,* that even though the first steps are shaky, with consistency, effort, and a good dose of will, we'll get where we want to go."

Rosa Pabón has followed her own advice and has, almost to her own amazement, found herself achieving her goals. As a result of a serendipitous meeting with a member of a mountaineering club while she was studying at the University of the Andes in Mérida, Venezuela, she became enamored of mountaineering and the marvelous intellectual and emotional escape offered by the mountains themselves. While earning her degree in economics, she also studied hard under the tutelage of members of the Jorge Eduardo Burguera Hiking and Climbing Club and participated in the Club's many outings. Early climbing expeditions to Mexico and Peru in the midseventies provided comradeship and nourished her love for the mountains. It also gave her the experience, skills and confidence essential in climbing major peaks.

In 1982 she had the chance to go to Europe, to travel and climb in the Alps. Of Chamonix she notes, "One can observe a tradition of family climbing. I saw children and adolescents happily climbing. We rarely see this in our country. Parents are very fearful to let their children climb, and reluctant with their teenagers." She herself has introduced her nephew and his friends to the joys of climbing in Venezuela and feels that it's very important "to give them a conscience about nature and its conservation, its joys . . . [this] doesn't exist in an organized fashion now [in Venezuela.] There isn't an effective 'politic' that teaches this to young people."

On her return from Europe, she dove into the work of promoting environmental awareness and knowledge of the mountains within her country through talks and slide shows organized by the Club. The ease of international travel Rosa had enjoyed in Europe, thanks to the sophisticated rail systems, now stood out in sharp contrast to the difficulties inherent in Latin American travel. Air travel is not always available and is even less affordable to the average South American than for the average European. Even communication is fraught with technical problems and poses obstacles to the spread of information within countries; for example, Venezuela has had regional television only since 1977.

On top of this, the devaluation of the national currency in February 1983, on a day referred to as "Black Friday," severely curtailed the Club's ability to accomplish its fundraising goals and carry out major climbs, like an ascent of Aconcagua planned for that year which had to be abandoned because of lack of support. These obstacles to major and expensive expeditions seem to have spurred Rosa on to climb and explore on a smaller but no less serious level. In 1983 she participated in a first ascent of a rock route on the north face of Pico Heriberto Márquez Molina (4,000 meters), did a rock climb of La Vieja (4,445 meters) and the Bourgoin route of Pico Bolívar (5,007 meters). During the next two years, Rosa continued to do talks and slide shows about climbing around the country and taught climbing courses for new members of the Burguera Club. She did a winter ascent of Pico El Carmen (4,850 meters) and many other major climbs. She led climbs and hikes for children, taught ice technique and climbed Pico Bolívar twice more, once to celebrate the fiftieth anniversary of the first ascent by the south route, and again to commemorate the bicentenary of the founding of the University of the Andes.

This latter ascent, Rosa's first all-women climb, was done with six other women from various climbing clubs. Among them was Nelly Chávez, a pioneer climber from Chile who now lives in Caracas and is still climbing strong at more than sixty years of age. "She has always been my inspiration," says Rosa. "I have received a lot of encouragement from her. She has followed my successes and has been like a second mother to me, a dear friend and companion. I've enjoyed the many opportunities I've had to learn from her experience; hers is a great example to follow."

On this climb of Pico Bolívar, the women encountered terrible weather on the route and had to turn back very near the summit. They returned a few days later and completed the climb under blue skies. Rosa recounts how this first experience climbing with women inspired her to try more:

> I felt that I was now prepared to attempt a climb of the north flank of Pico Bolívar, a route reserved for experts. It is the most difficult mixed ice and rock climb in the Sierra Nevada de Mérida. Two friends were interested but one backed out, saying she didn't have faith in us, which I understood to mean that up until then there had always been a guy on the rope, representing security and control to her. But Ana María Díaz was game for the climb. I knew this was going to be something of an experiment, but we couldn't turn our backs on this opportunity. At least we had to try.
>
> We planned our climb for March 7 and 8, 1986. Our friends were happy for us having made such a decision and giving free rein to our dreams. We started out early. On Pico Espejo—a lesser peak on the way—we ate a bit and continued on, crossing the west face, until we arrived at the Eagle's Nest, the point of departure for the north face route. We were full of confidence. A sixty to seventy degree section of the glacier led to the short sections of vertical rock . . . The details are unimportant. What matters is the experience. I couldn't believe my

eyes when we soon found ourselves on the summit, the sun burning, the air still. This time the mountains received us with open arms. It was a splendidly beautiful day. There were no words to express how perfect it had been. Night fell as the figure of Simón Bolívar received us, mute testimony to our boldness. [A bronze bust of Bolívar stands atop the summit.] We slept on the summit, under a sky crowded with thousands of stars. We were tired but happy to have attempted it, let alone succeeded.

Later that year Rosa and Ana María completed another women's first ascent, climbing the two-hundred-meter face of Pared del Abanico on the southwest side of Pico Bolívar.

Since these pioneering climbs, Rosa has been centrally involved in the promotion of women's climbing through her participation in the annual convention of the Union of Latin American Women Climbers. In 1986 she attended the first convention of Latin American Women's Mountaineering and participated in the ascent of Huayna Potosí. She was the first Venezuelan woman to climb Aconcagua in the very successful and much-lauded ascent during the second convention of Latin American Women's Mountaineering in 1987.

She continues to devote much of her energies to the promotion of women's climbing through her speeches and slide shows, and the example she provides to other women climbers. As she says, "Hay que permanecer"—you've got to stick with it.

MEET MISS DISH

Kathy Phibbs

▲ ▲ ▲

The persona of Miss Dish made her first appearance in 1983 at a ladies' tea party in Seattle, Washington. In a cocktail party dress for perhaps the first time in her life, Kathy Phibbs discovered that by dressing up she had found a new voice for many of the things she wanted to express about women and climbing. This alter ego eventually acquired a past, an Alice B. Toklas-esque partner, a small but fabulous wardrobe, and over the next few years wrote a series of essays about climbing. They were originally published in the Women Climbers Northwest *newsletter, and collected in* Women Climbing, *the 1992 Engagement Calendar published by WCN. Four of them are reprinted here.*

I
MEETING MISS DISH

I'll never forget the day I met Miss Dish.

I was in a bad mood. Above me, yet another "young protégé" worked casually up a climb I had just backed off of. The "young protégé" syndrome was a discouraging development in my recent climbing. All around me, brash young things swaggered up to climbs of a standard I had worked up to over many years, a standard I clung to tenuously, and flashed them without a second thought.

Where was the proper respect for "working through the grades"? As far as I could make out, these young tiger-girls kept me around for my skill in reading the guide-book.

It was all very discouraging. Mentally, I perused a list of my non-accomplishments to date: I was twenty-five years old and I hadn't yet been on a Himalayan expedition. I hadn't climbed a big wall. I wasn't famous. I was mildly notorious, in Seattle at least, as a founder of Women Climbers Northwest. In those days, women climbing together was a controversial concept. I had started climbing with women for all the normal reasons: purity of style, greater challenge, and of course, the relentless fun of it. It was a different game. We were on our own, learning from each other and from what we could glean from books and overheard conversations at climber hangouts. Not surprisingly, once out of the mainstream, our path tended to meander about.

As one who wanted the regular satisfaction of success and its resulting fame, I was going nuts with the pace. Various male companions had taught me so much in the early years of my climbing career. Now I yearned for a woman to continue the process, to teach and challenge me. So far, hardcore women climbers ignored me when I approached them.

Success as a climber wouldn't have been so important if my career in window washing was, well, more fulfilling. If anything was my "career," it was climbing, but it was increasingly clear that I was not going to be a Star. From what I read in the annals of climbing history, I could find precious few role models of devoted, passionate, yet mediocre climbers.

The young protégé danced past the crux and wondered aloud if the climb was not overrated. I sighed. Tired of watching the effortless acrobatics of my partner, I looked around.

That's when I saw her—the most astonishing little old lady . . . in tennis shoes. Her outfit wavered, reeled perhaps, along a razor-thin edge between elegance and tackiness: a white pillbox hat with fishnet veil, a red chiffon shift and cape with gold lamé, a combination ice axe/umbrella that she held lightly in one hand, rhinestone butterfly-wing glacier goggles, the mink stole arranged around her neck, and of course, the spotless white tennis shoes that simply confused the picture beyond resolution.

I gaped.

"My dear," she said adjusting the minks, "I'm not as young as I used to be, but I know a Thing or Two. I've been climbing for ages and ages. Why, my dear friend and constant companion, Freida Beckworth, and I have explored these parts since I can't remember when. You probably haven't heard about us or read about us in those mountain pornography magazines you young people are always drooling over. Heavens, no! Ladies, my dear, Ladies don't feel the need to Toot Their Own Horns. You'll find that we just tend to go about our own business and have a lovely time whilst doing so. But I know a Thing or Two, my dear, yes indeed. I'm not as limber as I used to be. I can't lead you up desperate climbs but you'll find I've got Stamina. My dear, I'm going to Take You Under My Wing, and I don't think you'll regret it."

I'd never met anyone who spoke in capital letters before. She wasn't quite the bronzed climbing goddess I'd had in mind for a mentor, a woman with a face lined by the sun, with big gnarly hands and a crooked, confident smile but this was the best offer I'd had. I became her protégé.

When I introduced Miss Dish to Women Climbers Northwest, she was quite delighted and immediately organized an expedition for all of us. Well, sort of an expedition . . .

This was the expedition brochure:

The Lady Climbers Northwest Expedition to Castle Rock
The major objective will be the swarming of Castle Rock by large numbers of ladies. On April 22, 1947, the first route was climbed on Castle Rock. On April 22, 1984, we will add another chapter to the history of this mighty lump. We need parties (tea, birthday, Tupperware) on every possible route . . .

Miss Dish Talks About Art and the Expedition
You see, don't you, that this is more than a climbing party. This is ART, an installation of climbing and women, the transformation of Castle Rock into a Hag Crag. Though it is important that we reach the top (because that's where lunch will be), this expedition's goals are not assault and conquest. Our goals are Spinning and Weaving, spinning with joy, weaving a web of multi-colored strands of shiny nylon braided material up and down and around Castle Rock. Just picture it, Ladies!

Except for the lawn chair that got permanently wedged into Midway Chimney, the expedition was a stunning success. Actually Midway Chimney has always been difficult to protect and the fixed lawn chair is now considered a blessing by some. There was some concern about the ethics of adding (albeit accidentally) protection to an established route, but Freida Beckworth, who did the first ascent, said it was a lovely addition and she wished she'd thought of it herself.

II
MANNERS IN THE MOUNTAINS

Miss Dish has noticed that the mountains and crags are becoming more and more crowded. As climbing becomes a media-glamorous sport in America, we need Standards of Behavior. Not ethics, new rules, or more complex rating systems, but something far more challenging. Climbers Need Manners.

Miss Dish realizes that she has a Duty to the climbing community to provide guidance in this matter. She has prepared a treatise on the subject for the women climbers because she knows they are Ladies and that in this matter will Lead The Way.

How to Be a Well-Mannered Climber
You (the climber) are a guest in Mother Nature's Home. The considerate guest remembers that above all—more important than the summit or even fun—she is a GUEST. The considerate guest does not leave a mess. She leaves things exactly as she found them. The considerate guest does not smear chalk on the walls.

Climbers, by definition, do not come over to Mother Nature's Home simply for the company. They come to work out in her Home Gymnasium. Sad to say, many climbers get involved in their workout and forget their Manners. They often excuse this lapse by saying, "I don't have time." "There was no other way." "The workout was dangerous." They commit a great sin—they Pit themselves against the challenge of Mother Nature's Home Gymnasium. The considerate guest does not Attack, Assault, Siege, or Gamble Against her hostess.

The Well-Mannered Climber does not Rush. She may climb in record time (and often it is important to be quick), but she never

Rushes. Rushing causes delicate terrain to be trampled, excrement to be left unburied, trash to be forgotten or ignored, and a snotty abruptness with other climbers. It causes unforgiveable Self-Importance on the part of climbers, grunting through mountains with no thought or sight of anything other than the summit. Rushing connotes a Contest, a Battle, a Test of Climber versus Mother Nature.

Miss Dish must say a severe thing: If you don't have time to do it right (with good manners), don't do it. Come back another day. Go fast, go efficient, go safe, but do not Rush.

The Well-Mannered Climber is Creative. She sees the vast physical, intellectual, and spiritual potential of climbing and is inspired. She brings her best to climbing. She is fascinated by the complexities of resolving Manners and Climbing.

III
ALL-MALE CLIMBS: FAD OR FOLLY?

Miss Dish has observed the growing trend of men climbing with other men. At first, she was shocked. Was it safe? Men together, alone, without a woman along? Then, she was concerned. Were these men trying to make some kind of political statement? Were they woman-haters? Later, she was curious. Were these men . . . gay?

After pondering these questions, Miss Dish considered that perhaps the poor dears needed to climb together for a while in order to gain confidence before they returned to REAL CLIMBING (with women).

Her protégé, that Kathy-girl, has tried to explain to Miss Dish about camaraderie, and the energy that men enjoy together. She has pointed out that even though men don't always approach climbing the Normal Way, they seem to gain a lot from each other's company. She has taken Miss Dish to task for implying that men who enjoy each other's company might be gay. She told Miss Dish this was a nasty scare tactic used to divide men, and besides, how delightful if some of them ARE gay.

Miss Dish was startled to hear such strong opinions from her protégé. She had never heard that Kathy-girl Speak Out. Perhaps the Younger Generation has some Backbone after all.

IV
WOMEN ARE THE HOPE OF CLIMBING

My protégé, that spineless Kathy-girl, had what her generation calls a "freak out" when she read this essay. "You're going to ruin me in the climbing community," she wailed. Tsk. Young people are so conservative these days, don't you think?

Miss Dish is ready to expound on the future of climbing and on the wonderfully positive things that women bring to climbing, a role that is growing each year. Why, the single most prevalent influence in climbing over the next years will be the greater and greater numbers of women. This is more than exciting. This is Big News. This is a Trend. This is the latest chapter in climbing history, like when climbing became more than an upper-class leisure sport and climbers from other classes brought new energy to climbing, changing it forever.

Women climbing have always had this effect to a certain degree. Today it is noticeable to all but the most recalcitrant. Women are the catalyst, the new energy, that will expand and inspire climbing. And, dare Miss Dish say it, women will SAVE climbing. Our influence is desperately needed, ladies. For while speed ascents, death routes, first firsts, solos and 5.16s are all fascinating trends, they are cut from the same fabric. They all spiral . . nowhere. They are interesting, even amazing, but it's really the squirrel in the treadwheel, going faster and faster to nowhere at all.

The prevailing definition of success in climbing—to be the best or do it first—is, in the final analysis, so limited, don't you think? Yet, Miss Dish must point out that it is a definition pursued with greater and greater frenzy. Yes, you boys are Rushing.

Ladies, climbing needs us. Many of us already find different joys and challenges in climbing. If we really think about it, we can create new ways to climb. Performance Art Climbing. Climbing with only the Best Manners. The slowest ascent of El Capitan, a peaceful pilgrimage from your home to the top.

As that Kathy-girl has learned while guiding, going slow can be a lot tougher than going fast. The possibilities are fantastic.

My dears, that Kathy-girl is moaning again about "radical feminist stigmas" and "renegade little old ladies." Poor dear thinks she will be tainted forever by our association. Hmph!

Miss Dish does not particularly welcome rebuttal to her statements. Miss Dish knows of what she speaks. A toast is always welcome, of course.

CLIMBING WITH KIDS

Diane Bedell

▲ ▲ ▲

IT'S EARLY morning, and the sky is a bright blue. Wind rustles softly through old pines in Taylor's Falls State Park, Minnesota. We are
at Taylor's Falls for a women and kids rock climbing clinic, sponsored by Woodswomen, Inc. Our group consists of six moms, nine
kids, and four instructors. I am the head instructor for the day.
Through the introductions I learn whose decision it was to participate in this clinic, the mother's or the kid's. I also ask them what
their expectations of rock climbing are, because it's important for
me to know what the participants want from the day.

During introductions I learn that some of the boys have previous
climbing experience from camp settings. One of the girls, Jessica,
has come to our clinic each year since its inception. Her mother,
Sarah, does not want to climb, but loves the opportunity her daughter has through our program. Sarah and Jessica have also participated in our other women and kids programs, formally called
Women and Children Bonding in the Outdoors.

Only one of the mothers, Sandy, has climbed before today, but
most are eager to try. Sandy's previous experience was as a partic-
ipant in another service project Woodswomen developed, Wilderness Experiences, for women felons. I have the pleasure to be
involved with both of these service programs.

• • •

Woodswomen is a non-profit organization dedicated to teaching healthy living skills to women, and women and children together. Founded in 1977 in Minneapolis, Minnesota as a women's adventure travel company, Woodswomen has developed into an organization with a strong service mission. Our mission statement reads:

> Woodswomen offers supportive and challenging learning opportunities for women and for women and children for the purpose of fostering individual growth and responsibility and relationship skills.

> This is done in the context of safe, enjoyable outdoor and wilderness travel experiences and leadership development courses that provide healthy living options, community-building activities, skills development opportunities and new perspectives on the natural world, history and society.

> Woodswomen is open to all women.

Woodswomen's Women and Children Bonding in the Outdoors programs were developed in 1989 as a way for low-income women and children to share the experience of being outdoors and learn outdoor skills. Initially the programs were funded by Woodswomen and a grant through the Emma B. Howe Foundation. Now they are completely funded by Woodswomen, and potential clients are contacted through several organizations serving low-income families.

Being involved with the outreach for these programs has been a tremendous learning experience for me. In speaking to women at various YWCA's, residential treatment programs and drop-in shelters, I realize that I'm not much different from the women I am contacting. Having grown up in a low-income family myself, the line seems very narrow between their situation and mine.

When I talk to these women about Woodswomen's programs, I meet a variety of responses. The majority of women look at me as if I were crazy: "You mean you actually sleep outside, with all the BUGS?!" or "But aren't there BEARS out there?!" are common reactions. But for some my talks strike a spark. When I ask these women if they have had any previous outdoor experiences, they smile and talk about fishing with their family, or camping when they were children, and they get excited about the prospect of sharing some type of outdoor experience with their own children.

After the introductions, I talk briefly about different types of climbing and the history of women in the sport, mentioning some of my favorite women climbers like Annie Smith Peck and Fanny Bullock. The kids cut me short though, as they want to get on with the business at hand. I pass around equipment we will be using—webbing, carabiners, ropes, and helmets—and I explain the uses of each piece. I then begin to teach the basic knots we use. I start with the overhand knot, then the water knot, which leads into making harnesses for everyone. My co-instructors and I check all the harnesses and knots and stress tying off the ends with an overhand safety knot. Next I show them the figure-eight and figure-eight follow-through. I have everyone practice this several times.

We then walk over to our bouldering area, where I teach them about spotting for each other and show them how to balance over their feet by not hugging the rock. We spend about twenty minutes practicing friction moves, smearing and opposition moves.

After our bouldering session we head down to the "bone yards," another climbing area in the park (climbers have an odd habit of giving climbing areas obscure names, but I never have figured out this particular one.) I have set up top ropes on four climbs of various degrees of difficulty, and one rapelling station. We teach the mothers, one on one, to belay (we don't let the kids belay), and the kids start climbing. I watch the kids move through their initial fear of being on the rock: they usually start out clinging to the rope, but after a bit of coaching—"Hang onto the rock, not the rope!"—they start balancing over their feet and reaching up to the next hold.

I also listen to the interaction between the mothers and their children. At first the moms are fairly quiet; they are not sure what to do or say, but their comments are supportive, helping the kids problem-solve through the climb. But after watching and listening to me, they begin to point out possibilities, offer suggestions and encouragement. I really enjoy the sharing that happens between the participants. The mothers even offer support to each other's kids.

I watch Sandy with her children, Mike (six), and Bethany (eleven). Sandy is quietly urging Bethany to reach up for that next hold, slightly overhung, and praising her success when she grabs it. Bethany is working on a tough climb, challenging, but short enough for her eleven-year-old frame. I think back to the day spent rock climbing with Sandy through Woodswomen's Wilderness Experiences program.

Wilderness Experiences, partially funded through the Minnesota Department of Corrections, introduces women felons to outdoor activities. Outreach for the program involves talking to parole officers, meeting with women in treatment programs and asking counselors to make referrals for their clients. Our program has met with a great deal of support in the corrections/social services community. The participants learn camping and rock climbing skills during three days at Wilder Forest, a wilderness retreat center near Taylor's Falls. After the initial three-day program, these women are invited to join our other programs. They can canoe with us, climb with us or join us for our women and kids programs. Some women participate in the outdoor leadership courses we teach, later assisting with other Woodswomen programs.

During Sandy's Wilderness Experiences climbing day, she told us that she had climbed with her father and brothers once as a child. Frightened by bees, she couldn't complete the climb, and her father ridiculed her as a failure. She hadn't climbed since and had serious doubts about her ability to do so.

We gave her the space and opportunity to climb for herself. We let her know that if she didn't complete the climb it would be fine with us. She not only completed all the climbs we had set up, but was extremely supportive to the other women who were climbing for the first time. Sandy knew she wanted to share this experience with her children.

To me, the high point of the Wilderness Experiences program is when the participants realize that the program is for them, freely given and without strings. So often these women hear that they don't count, that they are in the way, that they are bad people. They have difficulty understanding that the goal of the program is to have fun and, in the process, learn how to work together. It is not about success or failure, climbing or not climbing. What is important is that they take the day and the experience as their own.

I see this understanding develop during the climbing day of the program. As each woman rappels down the wall, something clicks, and she looks up to the top, grins and waves at the rest of the group. The group, in turn, cheers for the woman on the rope. They are having fun, and it is okay. They come away with a feeling of accomplishment. There are a lot of good-natured jokes about finding a new way to "get high" or learning a new meaning to "being at the end of my rope." Not everyone chooses to climb again, but that choice is part of the freedom offered in this program.

The women and kids day is progressing, and almost everyone has done two climbs. We break for lunch, and I offer a tour though the park. Taylor's Falls State Park is an area of great geological interest. During the last glacial period, potholes were ground into the basalt and remain today as reminders of the awesome power of nature. The park also offers beautiful views of the St. Croix river valley. We find a lunch site overlooking the river, and some of the participants talk about how their morning has been. The mothers are typically more articulate about their experiences than the kids are. They talk about moving on the rock or the feel of the rock or of not feeling strong enough to climb. I hear the word "wimp," and I tell them my definition of the word: "Women Improving Muscular Prowess." I get quite a few laughs from that one. One woman asks me about a climbing accident that has happened earlier that week at Taylor's Falls. I explain the difference between lead climbing and top roping and tell the group that the climber was lead climbing and taking a different type of risk than we are taking today.

The kids start asking questions about the rappel we have set up. It is off a thirty-foot-high rock bridge with about twenty feet as a free rappel. All the kids are eager to try this; the moms are a little more hesitant. Sandy shares her rappelling experience with the group: "You have to sit back in the harness, put all your weight in it, then you start taking small steps down the wall. The hardest part is that first step, but it feels great once you've done it."

After lunch we start a rappel rotation, some kids climbing and some rapelling. Jessica is the first on rappel. Sarah is there to talk Jessica through the toughest parts. Jessica wants to hold onto the fence at the top and is afraid of letting go. She starts to lean back into the harness and just at the point of balance where you commit yourself to the rappel, Jessica grabs the fence again. Jen, one of my co-instructors, is talking to Jessica: "Breathe deep, Jessica. Put all your weight in the harness, and lean back. Keep your feet in one place until you are sitting in the harness, then take little steps down the wall." Jessica finally commits to the rappel and starts down. At the point where the free rappel starts, Jen offers some more advice: "Jessica, keep your feet on the wall, and lower your rear below your feet. When you lower your rear far enough, your feet will follow.

This will help keep you from swinging into the wall." Jessica takes Jen's advice and swings free of the wall. She stops midway for a photo opportunity. At the bottom of the rappel, Jessica unties her belay rope and hustles back to the top to get in line again. I enjoy listening to all the support and caring that goes into the process. I encourage the women to try rapelling as well, and many of them do.

As we wrap things up, I ask the moms and kids to share a bit about how the day went for them. Mike pipes up, "It was great, but I wish I could have rappelled again. I think that part was the most fun." I laugh and say, "So three times wasn't enough? Well, maybe next time." One of the mothers confesses, "I didn't really know what I was getting into; David wanted to do this, not me. But I enjoyed it. I don't think I would want to do too much more, but I finally understand what David is talking about when he talks about biners or belaying. I feel like I learned a lot today." I know that Sarah and Jessica will be back next year for more. Jessica, at nine years old, is already quite fearless on the rock. Perhaps Sarah will want to climb next time.

Sandy, Mike and Bethany are excited about their next climbing day. They will be joining us for our next women and kids climbing day in a few weeks. Sandy is in a treatment program, and these outings provide a chance for her to have some fun with her kids. The three of them are also scheduled to go canoeing with Woodswomen, but that is a different story.

While working on these women and kids programs, I have heard women say that it is usually dads who get to have most of the outdoor fun with the kids. I'm delighted to work for an organization that provides some fun for moms, too.

Carol Snetsinger just below Camp II on Pumori in the Nepal Himalaya. Led by Shari Kearney, the 1989 American Women's Pumori Expedition was extremely successful, with five of its seven members summiting and all returning healthy. Besides Carol, expedition members included Sue Giller, Shari Kearney, Lucy Smith, Kathy Phibbs, Diane Taliferro and Lynne Wolfe.
Photo: Carol Snetsinger collection

Top: Julia Meza Ramirez instructing
climbing students in rappel technique,
Santiago, Chile.
Photo: Julia Meza Ramirez collection

Right: Rosa Pabón on the summit of Pico
Bolívar, 1986.
Photo: Rosa Pabón collection

Opposite page: Top: Joan Firey on the east
side of Mt. Triumph in Washington's
North Cascades.
Photo: Carla Firey collection

Bottom left: Maureen O'Neill in the
Washington Cascades.
Photo: Maureen O'Neill collection

Bottom right: Laura Waterman on Cannon
Cliff in New Hampshire.
Photo: John Dunn

Top: Temporary collection site for garbage built and filled by the 1990 Everest Environmental Expedition.
Photo: Lorraine Bonney collection

Right: Lorraine Bonney shows off a hand made sheet of paper produced from recycled junk paper during the Everest Environmental Expedition, 1990.
Photo: Lorraine Bonney collection

Opposite page: Kathy Phibbs dressed in the spirit of Fay Fuller during the 1990 Fay Fuller Centennial Climb of Mt. Rainier. Phibbs led thirty-three women on a climb of the 14,410 foot peak to commemorate its first ascent by a woman, August 10, 1890.
Photo: Rachel da Silva

Top: Denise Mitten at Joshua Tree, California.
Photo: Kathy Phibbs collection

Left: Diane Bedell and student at a Woodswomen women and kids rock climbing course, Taylor's Falls State Park, Minnesota.
Photo: Nina Roberts

ONE OF THE BOYS

Susan Fox Rogers

▲ ▲ ▲

"TY, YOU CAN'T go unless there's another girl along."

I sighed. We'd been through this before, my mother and I. In the past, I'd won, but it always took so much talking, persuading, convincing.

"Fine. Fine, there'll be another girl."

My mother turned to me, her eyebrows raised, her dark eyes set, staring into mine. Truth, she seemed to demand silently. She knew there weren't any other girls around who climbed. I looked away, but not with any guilt. After all, why should I be deprived of climbing just because there weren't other girls to join me? My mother, however, didn't seem to think she was depriving me of anything. She was protecting me. "Sixteen-year-old girls simply do not sleep alone in the woods with boys."

Tonight I didn't feel like doing battle, so I walked to the phone and dialed John.

"I can go," I said.

"Psych."

"You have to bring your little sister," I said.

"My little sister? I don't have a little sister."

"That's great. I can lend her some shoes. She has a sleeping bag, right?"

"Is your mom enforcing the 'another girl' rule?"

"You got it. Pick me up at seven. I want to climb all day."

"Seven-thirty." And John hung up.

I walked past my mom who was standing in the kitchen near enough to listen.

"I didn't know John had a sister."

"She's only seven."

"Isn't that awfully young?"

I shrugged. "She's a girl."

I was ready and standing in front of my house at six-forty-five the next morning. The air was cool and moist, early spring when everything smells green and brown and my body aches to move, to pull, to lunge. To climb.

I pushed against the large oak tree in our front yard and felt the muscles in the back of my legs slowly loosen. Then I propped one foot against the tree and leaned over it, stretching further. I hoped John would arrive before my mother woke up. She would appear in her blue bathrobe at the door to ask me if I'd had breakfast, or she'd peer out the window and see there really was no girl along. I thought it was such a silly rule. What would another girl do: ask me to stop making out or to stop having sex? How far did my mother imagine I went? I wasn't interested in any of that, so I really didn't feel bad about lying. I just didn't want to get caught.

John and I had been climbing partners for two years and were best friends. We met at lunch in the cafeteria and again after school to builder, that is climb on the walls of buildings. We spent our weekends together climbing at the local crags. I never thought of us as a couple, though I bet most of our twelfth-grade class did. I knew I trusted and loved John but in that push-and-pull way you love a brother. There was nothing close to romantic about our hugs after a climb, or even when we huddled up next to each other in our sleeping bags. We were family, part of the climbing family that came and went and had random reunions at the Gunks in the fall or Joshua Tree in the winter. We shared meals and stories and tents, and sometimes the climbing blood seemed richer and thicker than family blood. So I wasn't interested in sleeping with John. Or any guy for that matter. I liked being one of the boys. I just wanted to climb.

I heard the purr of John's truck, and as it approached I could see someone sitting in the passenger seat. I threw my pack and sleeping bag into the back and then squeezed into the cab. I made the stranger sit in the middle. I would have offered to be the sardine, but as the smallest, or maybe because I was the only girl, I was always chosen (and sometimes I offered) to sit in the middle. This morning I decided I'd sat there too many times, my butt going numb and John knocking my knees every time he shifted.

"Tim this is Ty, Ty, Tim. I met Tim down at the wall yesterday. He's at Penn State."

"Where from?"

"New Hampshire."

I nodded.

"We're going to take a road trip to New Hampshire this spring."

"I've never been there," I said.

"Best climbing on the East Coast," Tim said.

"No, the Gunks is."

"Depends on what you're looking for."

"The Gunks has everything."

"Wait till you see New Hampshire. Routes ten pitches long." He turned to me and smiled. "You'll love it," he said. "I promise."

John slipped in an Emmylou Harris tape. We always listened to country to get us ready for our future lives out West. We were both saving our money to go the minute we graduated, and we'd spent the winter dreaming and planning: Eldorado Canyon, the Wind Rivers, Vedauwoo, Tuolumne, Yosemite—we were going to go everywhere.

"I'm going to stop for coffee," John said.

John was a caffeine fiend. He always drank too much then ended up shaking on the rock.

"Get me a donut," I said.

"Did you guys eat breakfast?" Tim asked. "I'm starving. Let's stop for breakfast."

I was hungry, too, but I didn't have the patience to stop and eat. "I want to get to the rock. Let's get something to go."

"Fine with me," John said. Everything was usually fine with John.

We stopped at Jim's Deli on the west side of town and each got an egg on a roll and a large coffee to go. The truck smelled of eggs and coffee. John was juggling, trying to eat, shift, steer and drink at the same time. Usually when we drove and ate, I shifted for him while he clutched. We had it pretty well coordinated, and I'd only once thrown us back into first instead of third.

"These things aren't bad," Tim said holding up his egg sandwich.

He was right, but I didn't want to agree with him.

We went to Hunter Rocks, a bouldering paradise on a piece of private hunting land. John and I were the only ones who climbed there a lot, and so we had put up most of the routes. We'd work through the boulders in a set order each time: first the warm-up rocks and then the test pieces we threw ourselves at. We'd push each other, fall off, and try again all afternoon. Today, John started with one of our warm-up climbs that used to be a test piece until we figured out the secret hold.

I was going to suggest we let Tim try it first, but John was already on the gritty sandstone, his feet smeared onto the first holds.

"There's nothing when you start, except this." John grabbed a large hold with his right hand. He moved his feet up, smearing and crouching low. "Watch," he said. His body extended completely off of the big hold as he reached, half lunging for our secret hold out left. We'd worked for months to find that hold and when we did we laughed and laughed. And then we'd done the problem a dozen times as a victory dance. When John walked around to the front of the boulder, Tim was already on it, moving his feet up to crouch and reach.

"That's it," John said.

In one motion Tim had the hold and was moving up the rest of the boulder. He made it look casual, easy.

"Great," John said. He turned to me. He looked happy, his eyes shining, his mouth curved into a soft smile.

I smiled back. "I'm going to head up to the slabs. I'll meet you guys there later."

"Wait for me to try the Super," John said.

I jogged up the hill to a set of rocks that formed a perfect circle. The sides of the rocks are smooth, dotted with sharp, thin holds. This was my favorite section of the rock. "If you like this, you'll like Tuolumne," John had promised. "It's like this for days." I already liked Tuolumne—the name rolled out of my mouth, and it felt magic and strong.

I sat down to put on my shoes. The ground was still damp and cool. It felt good to breath deeply, to be quiet and alone.

Once I touched the rock and started to move, I felt great. My muscles tightened and relaxed, and I stepped high for holds that felt sharp and cut into my fingers with a secure bite. I did the five problems I knew, and they all felt good and solid. Then I turned to the Super Slab. It was the highest boulder, and the hardest moves were at the top. John and I always jumped off, half trying the last moves. At one point we decided the last move wouldn't go; it was a problem we just couldn't do. But we both still tried it each time we were at Hunter. We didn't want to give up.

I had the first moves wired and did them quickly and smoothly. I hadn't felt this secure in a long time, and when I got to the top I suddenly saw how it should go. It meant standing up on a nothing of a hold, using a pebble to move up left and then smearing on a slight indent to reach for the top. Maybe I'd seen all of this before, but it had never seemed possible.

I didn't hesitate, because I knew I could psych myself out of any move. Everything hit right, and my hand slapped, then stuck to the top. As I pulled myself up, I heard John and Tim whistle and clap.

I stood up, turned around and smiled.

They were sitting in the sun, perched on a nearby boulder.

"Thanks for the spot," I said. Though I knew if anyone had been there, standing behind me, I wouldn't have made it.

"I tried," John said. "Tim wouldn't let me."

"I didn't need it," I said.

"That was obvious," Tim said. He turned to John. "She's good."

"Don't tell me," John said.

Tim sat down and then stretched out on the rock. His body was laced by the sun that filtered through the new green leaves. "This place is great," he said.

John and I smiled at each other.

John sat down beside Tim, taking in the warmth of the sun.

I walked over to join them, and as I approached I almost expected to see them holding hands, their bodies connecting in some way. They looked happy together, resting, exposed in the woods. The both had their eyes closed, and Tim's face was smooth and relaxed as if he were asleep. But I could tell his eyes were moving under his lids. He had deep brown eyes, the color of rich Pennsylvania soil, and they were always moving, searching. The slow afternoon sun reflected off the gold in his dirty blond hair.

John opened one eye and looked at me. "Show me how you did it?"

"I'll tell you," I said. I'd done this in the past: tried to repeat a difficult move I'd just done only to fail. Then the success becomes a fluke, and the happiness of that moment of inspiration vanishes. I'd try it another day, but I knew I couldn't do it again today.

John stood up and walked down to the slab.

"You looked good," he said.

"I feel good."

"Tim's all right," John said. "He likes you."

"What's that supposed to mean?"

John shrugged and winked, then turned to the slab. He moved up the first section quickly and then hesitated.

"See that sliver of nothing? You have to stand on it. Reach left, there's a pebble you can use to balance."

John stood, shifting his weight on the small holds; then little by little he moved his weight onto the wrinkle. Each time his foot began to slip, he returned to his more solid holds.

"You can't do it slowly," I said. "Move through it. Move upward. Do you see how it goes?"

"Yeah, but you made it look so easy."

I laughed.

John concentrated, breathing steadily, preparing himself. I stood with my arms in the air, spotting him if he fell, and shielding my eyes from the sun. I watched his calf muscles flexing and tensing, as if they were thinking, breathing, contemplating what they had to do. Everything was still, and I was almost holding my breath waiting for John to move when, in the silence, I felt something near me. I turned to see Tim leaning against the rock directly behind me. I hadn't heard him approach, and it surprised me to see him there, so still and calm, standing as if he'd been there for a while. He smiled, his face wrinkling into a grin. I turned back to John.

Soon John came sliding down the rock and landed heavily on the ground. I caught him under the arms as his body tilted backward.

"I can't do it," John said. He stood up and shook himself out. "You really stood on that?" he asked.

I nodded. "You have to believe."

"No, you have to invent."

"You did it because you're a girl," John teased. He imitated our friend Ron's voice: "Girls have amazing footwork." Ron categorically believed women had better footwork and so should be better climbers. It was only our own personal failings that held us back from being genius climbers.

I punched John on the shoulder. "And you can't do it because you're a boy."

"No, it's because I'm out of shape."

"When will you be in shape?"

"1997. Or thereabouts."

John and I were playing in our usual way, ignoring Tim. I turned to him. "Want to try it?"

Tim looked at the wall and shook his head. "Maybe in 1997."

We spent the afternoon climbing, alone and together. I got used to Tim, but he treated me differently than John did. He'd go back and get my shoes for me, or chalk up a hold to show me where to put my foot.

This is too easy, I thought. This is easy to accept. And then easy to expect.

When Tim caught me when I fell, he helped me up, holding me under the arms. He'd squeeze me quickly. Small tight hugs.

At 3:30 we were all burnt. We lay in the sun for a while, each on our own rock, resting and warming.

"Let's go for a swim," John said.

"Where?" Tim asked.

"There's a swimming hole off 45. It means driving back toward town a few miles."

"The water will be cold," I said.

We stopped at Edson's country store for a root beer and vanilla ice cream. An older lady served us our sodas in glass bottles, and we finished drinking before she managed to scoop out the cold, hard ice cream.

Back in the truck, Tim turned up Emmylou real loud. I sat in the middle, and we all rocked against each other, our shoulders touching as we licked our ice cream cones.

John was the first to jump out of the truck. He took off for the pond, running in long strides. Tim and I walked side by side, carrying towels over our shoulders.

"This place is beautiful," Tim said.

I nodded, but I didn't feel like talking.

We walked past the no trespassing signs onto the narrow path. I walked in front of Tim. He walked close behind me; I could feel his eyes peering into my back, into the nape of my neck. I felt as if he was trying to look through me.

I spotted John flying through the air on the rope swing. He let out an ape-man yell as he let go of the rope and arced into the water, his naked limbs flapping in the air. Tim and I laughed.

I stepped back from the edge of the pond and watched as Tim pulled his T-shirt over his head. His back was smooth and glowed with a layer of sweat. He dropped his shorts and stood naked. The blond hair that ran down his legs started off as soft wisps on his buttocks. I stared at his long legs and firm, round bottom. I knew he knew I was staring at him, and that was fine.

John popped out of the water and climbed up next to Tim. John was breathing heavily from his swim.

"Try it," he said. "The water's freezing." He turned to me and smiled. "What's the matter with you?"

I shrugged. "Nothing." I never wore a bathing suit when it was just me and John, but suddenly I wished I'd brought one.

John grabbed the rope and swung out letting out his tremendous call one more time. He dropped into the water and for a brief moment it was silent as he swam underwater.

Tim turned back to look at me. Just his upper torso turned. He had half a smile on his face. For a moment I thought he was going to step completely around and walk toward me. But he turned, reached for the rope and arced into the air before dropping into the water. I watched him disappear for a few moments then surface, gasping, not for air, but from cold. I laughed as I quickly pulled off my shirt and slipped out of my shorts. Then I ran for the rope and swung out high over the water.

AIRBORNE ON HOMEMADE
WINGS

Kristen Laine

▲ ▲ ▲

THE STORY I remember best is this one: A group of climbers from
Minnesota, in Yosemite to climb their first big wall, started up the
Nose route on El Capitan but realized it was beyond their abilities
and decided to turn back. In their rappel retreat down the face, the
first climber down the rope clipped his carabiner around the chain
between two bolts instead of through the bolts themselves. That was
the first mistake. The second mistake came when the last guy cut
loose the haul bag from the pitch the others had just rappelled:
when the bag hit the end of its long free fall, the force on the bolt
pulled the metal from its mooring to the rock. One by one, the men
(I remember there were three) hanging at the belay station slid off
the now free-hanging chain to their deaths. The climber who told
me this story, then my housemate, had been doing another route
higher up on the face. He heard noise and looked below him, but
saw only a sleeping bag, escaped from the exploded haul bag, floating to the ground.

   I heard this story the first winter after I started climbing, in
1981, when I shared a house with a couple who also climbed. He
was a veteran of hard ice climbs in Alaska and Canada; she had
climbed Mt. McKinley as a teenager. Both had worked many years
as wilderness instructors. I spent much of that winter sewing gear
slings and double-layered climbing pants on their foot-pedal ma-

chine and learning the grammar of the climbing culture from their stories.

When my housemate told me about that accident, he didn't stop with his memory of the floating sleeping bag, but moved right into the cautionary moral of his story: at a belay, never clip in to a sling or chain; always clip directly to bolts. This advice, which I have never forgotten, is not why I remember the story almost verbatim more than ten years later. I remember it now because it was my first awareness that you can die climbing. No single, blatant mistake cost those three young men their lives; they made a couple of small, but fatally multiplicative, errors.

The young and inexperienced climbers from Minnesota were like youthful Icarus in the Greek myth. Thrilled at being airborne, Icarus forgot to heed his father's advice to fly the middle path between the waves and the sun. He plummeted into the sea when the wax that held his homemade wings together melted. In its most archetypal reading, the story of Icarus and Daedalus is about the delicate balance of risk, knowledge and desire in any challenge. There is always the sucking pull of the waves and the deadly heat of the sun—the dangers that exist beyond your intentions. Knowledge says there is a way and then tries to find it. Daedalus tried different techniques for layering the feathers and tested out the apparatus before teaching his son. But it is Icarus, in his ecstatic flight, that we tend to remember. He is the embodiment of desire, the part of us that thrills to the thought of something not yet done.

By the time I heard that winter tale, I knew I wanted the challenge that lay in climbing. I had already felt the thrill of standing on a thin ledge of rock a hundred feet above ground. The story my friend told me was a warning, yes, but it also held out an incredibly seductive answer: If you do this and this, you will succeed. If you don't, you can die. What was seductive was that few things in life are ever so clear. I vowed to find the middle way and waited for my second climbing season to begin.

The Adventure

People often ask climbers why we climb. There are famous non-reasons—because it's there; it was either that or life insurance[1]—but

---

[1] Thanks to David Roberts for this phrase. It can be found in Patey Agonistes: A Look at

these are designed more to put the non-climber in his or her place than to answer the question. In fact, much ink has been spilled over the question of why people climb. Generally, we agree that the climber seeks adventure. We disagree when we try to dig below or beyond that desire.

I can't remember when I didn't want to have adventures. When I was a child, books gave me an outlet for dreaming about what an adventurous life could be. Through them I could live the voyages of Marco Polo or the Kon-Tiki; I could be a trapper in the Far North; I could ride a spotted pony across the Great Plains. I didn't know what was possible for me, but the books fed my desire for a life out of the ordinary.

The drive for adventure is captured by the great myths of all cultures—by the twelve labors of Hercules, the trials of Odysseus and Buddha's search for enlightenment. Adventure follows naturally from a quest for riches, knowledge or truth. Joseph Campbell, scholar of mythology, called it the hero adventure.

> The usual hero adventure begins with someone from whom something has been taken, or who feels there's something lacking in the normal experiences available or permitted to the members of his society. This person then takes off on a series of adventures beyond the ordinary, either to recover what has been lost or to discover some life-giving elixir. It's usually a cycle, a going and a returning.[2]

Climbing is a modern version of the adventure quest. Like other quests—explorations are an easy example—spending one's time getting to the tops of mountains is a difficult challenge, often ambiguous even as it's being undertaken, yet the final outcome is seldom ambiguous: either you find the far-off land or you don't; you get to the top or you don't. All these quests ask the potential hero for skills he isn't sure, that he has. The result? When the quest is complete and the outcome known, the hero returns home, where he accepts the duties of a leader.

The hero adventure is a ready metaphor for the transition from childhood to adulthood. The hero acquires new knowledge, under-

---

Climbing Autobiographies, collected in *Moments of Doubt* (Seattle: The Mountaineers, 1986), 187.
[2] Joseph Campbell with Bill Moyers, *The Power of Myth* (New York: Doubleday, 1988), 123.

goes tests of character and skill, and earns a place in the world. John Long, writing in a climbing magazine, described the rite of passage into manhood through climbing:

> Sometimes when I'd return to Camp 4 after a long climb, boys who I'd left but for a couple days had suddenly become men. A single big wall—slugging their way up ancient Half Dome, battling through thunderstorms and sleeping in slings, soaking wet and hating life—had hurled them straight into manhood. Their youth lay behind them like snakes' skins, and their faces had set overnight.[3]

Climbing has also been—or was, before it began to receive media attention in the 1980s—the refuge of the outsider. Climbing essayist David Roberts jests about the Standard Life of the climbing autobiography, which he says would start with the Anemic Childhood: "The boy who, inept at sports, weaker than all his playground chums, accused of being a sissy, finds in adolescence in the solitude of the mountains an overcompensator's paradise."[4] The mountains and the cliffs become the refuge—the "adventure beyond the ordinary"—of the emotionally inarticulate and the control freak. In this twist on the hero's adventure, the unlikely candidate succeeds through extraordinary effort or intelligence.

What happens when the outsider in question is a woman? In Campbell's masterwork on the hero adventure, *The Hero With a Thousand Faces,* women are either reward or temptation for the hero: "woman represents the totality of what can be known. The hero is the one who comes to know."[5] In the index of Campbell's book under *woman,* we find "symbolism [of] in hero's adventure," "as temptress," "as hero's prize," and "*see also* mother." There is no mention of a heroic role for a woman separate from her relation to man or child. If the classic hero's story, the *Odyssey,* is the story of the versatile, brave man (Odysseus) and the faithful woman

---

[3] Back Then, *Rock and Ice* (Nov/Dec 1991), 17.

[4] Roberts, *Moments of Doubt,* 184.

[5] Joseph Campbell, *Hero With a Thousand Faces* (Princeton, N.J.: Princeton University Press, 2d ed., 1968), 116. Even Campbell's last work, *The Power of Myth,* while giving women a hero role, portrayed them as heroes of two specific hero adventures: finding a mate and bearing children. See p. 125.

(Penelope),[6] then what does a young woman do when she wants to take that archetypal journey of self-discovery?

This is no intellectual question for me. I still remember a sort of stifled anguish in my youth, when I began to notice that all my heroes—the world explorers that I read about in for-young-reader books—were men. When I saw this difference between my heroes and myself, I began to seek out models like me, female, but the best I came up with—Jo March of *Little Women;* the two Indian women Pocahontas and Sacajawea; Pippi Longstocking; Clara Barton, the nurse—were not, though I couldn't admit it to myself at the time, nearly as exciting as the others. When I reach back to that stage in my life, I have a vague memory of confusion, and, I think, fear.

My muddy sense of something I wasn't happy with corresponds to some well-defined patterns in female development. Carolyn Heilbrun's book *Reinventing Womanhood* is an extended essay on undoing the paradox of being fully functioning and fully female. In the book, Heilbrun describes a study conducted by Dora Ullian on young girls' attitudes toward themselves and toward men:

> From six to ten in the stage Ullian calls Assertion, she found that girls resent boys. From ten to fourteen, they begin to swerve toward support of them, the stage Ullian calls Ambivalence. By fourteen, girls have accepted the need of underpinning males and have entered the stage she calls Accommodation.[7]

At age eight, I was discovering that there weren't many strong, active women in history (much less in my neighborhood) for me to model myself after. However, everywhere I looked, I could find models of supportiveness, attractiveness and dependence. Because I wanted to have an exciting, challenging life *and* be a woman, I took the same path as many other young women with ambition: I split my search for what was possible in life into two parts. On the one hand, I tried very hard to put myself in the shoes of the people, predomi-

---

[6] Carolyn G. Heilbrun, quoting Robert Fitzgerald, translator of the *Odyssey,* in *Reinventing Womanhood* (New York: W. W. Norton, 1979), 41.

[7] Heilbrun, *Reinventing Womanhood,* 188. The results of Ullian's study were presented in 1976 at the National Council of Family Relations. More recently, Carol Gilligan's work with young girls, published in *Making Connections* (Cambridge, Mass.: Harvard University Press, 1990), has supported Ullian's findings.

nantly male, whom I wanted to emulate—those Thor Heyerdahls and Marco Polos of my adventure reading. On the other hand, I modeled myself after the most interesting women I could find, trying to understand the glory and the power of their more supportive roles, as portrayed by the books I read (Pocahontas to John Smith, Sacajawea to Lewis and Clark). By the time I entered high school, I already practiced accommodation. It was like stepping on my own feet to keep from moving. I worried about becoming too excited about things, because I'd been told that when I did, I was loud, and that this was unattractive. I tried to remember what being attractive meant, because I seemed unable to make sense of the definition. I was also storing anger, but I did this without being aware of it.

I was twenty-three years old when I first said, "I want to learn to climb." This simple statement of interest in an obscure sport would reverberate for years through my psychic landscape of accommodation and anger. I was introduced to climbing gear by a man I was dating. This followed the pattern I'd learned to find out about new things: find a person (man) who knew something about it, ally myself with him (date him) and ply him for information about what I wanted to know. I scorned women who used "feminine" ways to pursue the promised security of marriage; I pursued knowledge, not marriage or financial security, yet I used methods similar to the women I disdained to reach my goals.

This man told me he climbed. He impressed me with descriptions of the several climbs he'd done in Yosemite. One evening, he showed me his many-hued climbing rope coiled and hanging on a hook inside his closet. I said I would like to try climbing, too, someday. He took the rope off the hook and draped it over my neck, added a gear sling with many clinking pieces, stepped back and said, "Now, would you really want to carry all this weight around?" I felt vaguely chastised; looking down at all the gear, I felt that I had to keep to myself the thrill the weight of it gave me.

A few months later, I was in Southern California interviewing students for the University of Puget Sound in Washington state. I drove into the foothills near Santa Barbara to be near my appointment the next day. Not far from my hotel, I noticed a tall white rock a short distance from the road. The late-afternoon sun had dipped it in pink and orange. A desire formed in me, obscure and somewhat puzzling, to go out to that rock and touch it. Early the next morning

I hiked through the low brush a quarter mile until I stood below it. I wanted nothing more than to move onto the rock and to its top. I circled the base until I found a low-angled wide crack. I began to walk my tennis shoes up the gritty face, just as I had heard my friend describe. About fifteen feet up, the crack steepened and narrowed. I didn't know how to keep going, and for the first time I looked below me. I tried to back down, but found out that great truth in all climbing—going down is much harder than going up. So I held on and experienced for the first time the dithering panic before a fall, that Saint Vitus's dance of fear. I don't know how long I clutched the rock after the shakes overtook me, but eventually I fell from my stance into a prickly bush at the base of the rock. Luckily, I was unhurt, though shaken and scratched. I'd been stupid, perhaps, to try to climb something without training, and I vowed to get some. But I had felt stronger emotions than fear—desire, focus and energy—and I wanted to feel them more, soon.

This simple experience set in motion the next years of my life. In a simple acting out of desire and interest, I had begun to unlearn the lessons in accommodation I had absorbed as a young girl. I was embarking upon my own hero journey.

When I returned to Washington, I signed up for a class in basic climbing. As I learned the names of equipment and practiced compass bearings in the rain, I had the odd sense that I was picking up with the self who had been me at eight years of age. The soggy, overgrown forests of the Northwest were nothing like the rolling, lake-dotted farmlands of my childhood, and yet I was continually reminded of summers spent at a family cabin in Wisconsin. Going into the mountains brought up sweet memories of a lost self who had built forts on islands and spent full days learning the lakeshore and its woods. Although I didn't have this language for it then, I was reconnecting with the girl who had yearned for great adventures and had started giving them up (or at least questioning whether she could ever have them) when she was eight years old.

Partway through the climbing course, I attended a slide show on women and climbing at the University of Puget Sound. I invited another woman from my class to join me. We were the only people who showed up. I was embarrassed for the presenter, but she seemed not to notice. Once the slides and music began, I forgot my discomfort and watched with amazement a woman leading up a steep snow slope, two women laughing together in a tent, a woman turning around from desert sandstone to smile into the camera.

I finished the climbing course, then quit my job and, in the absence of any strong career goals, decided to climb full-time. I entered into that blissful state familiar to other climbers, where climbing more beautiful and more difficult climbs was all that I asked of life. (That, and that I not be forced to work more than the barest minimum to fund my obsession.) It shocked me, and it definitely shocked my parents, to note the satisfaction with which I threw over the traces of what was supposed to be adulthood and hitchhiked around the country to the major rock-climbing areas.

The adult responsibilities I turned my back on differed from those of my male compatriots. The men I climbed with were resisting the idea that they were supposed to support a wife and family and not take "unnecessary" risks. I was rebelling against being the stay-at-home wife, or the wife with the jobette, whose primary role was to support her man. I wanted the same adventurous life that the young men did; I was their comrade in flight. For a time, I identified happily with the men around me and took their stories for my own. Then in my second season of climbing, on an extended stay in Yosemite Valley, a female mentor entered my life.

I first saw Katy Cassidy washing her hair. The bathroom in Camp 4, the climbers' campground, was just across the dirt path from my campsite. The morning after I'd set up my secondhand A-frame tent on the scuffed dirt, I crawled out into the frigid seven o'clock air and headed for the bathroom. As I walked inside, I saw a slight woman with long, dark hair dunking her hair into the basin. I knew that no hot water came out of those spigots; at this early hour and this elevation, frost still coated ripstop, cars and picnic tables. But she had her head under the freezing water and was humming. I remember thinking, that's a good definition of a mountain woman.

I met Katy later that morning in the grocery store, when she startled me with a warning about too conspicuously eating the grapes from the fruit bins—the store management had been known to bar climbers from the premises for such infractions. Her hair was still damp, and she wore faded cotton running shorts with the name of some college barely visible across one leg. She looked grungy and well traveled; she looked like she belonged there. We exchanged climbing pleasantries in much the same way that dogs sniff each other. It didn't take me long to figure out that she climbed at a level I'd hardly dreamed of. She said she'd just finished climbing a wall on El Cap; possibly it was Tangerine Trip, but I didn't know enough at that point to distinguish between walls. I would have been equally impressed if she'd climbed Half Dome, a much easier climb. She asked if I was looking for a climbing partner. Or possibly I was bold enough to ask her. I'd just led my very first 5.8 (a one-move crux) at Smith Rocks a few days earlier, and I'd followed a few 5.9s. In keeping with my personal style (a step or two ahead of reality), I told her that I led 5.8 and was ready to try 5.9s. Translation: I had led that one-move 5.8. In keeping with her personal style, Katy told me she was also leading 5.8s and 5.9s. I didn't get the translation until later. We agreed to climb together the next day.

We hitchhiked down the valley to the Chicken Delight area, which has a plethora of 5.8 and 5.9 routes of one to three short pitches. Katy gallantly asked me if I wanted the first lead of our chosen two-pitch climb. It was averred a solid, if unexciting, 5.8 by the guidebook. I peered up at a nearly vertical and awkward-looking crack that seemed to go on much too long. I would be pleased to follow her this first time, I said. I struggled up behind her swift lead and arrived at the belay stance already sheepish and deflated. As she quickly started the second pitch, I watched with admiration—and new clarity—as she moved across the chicken heads on the face. For the first time since I had started climbing, I was in the company of a woman who was a very good climber.

I fell several times following Katy to the top of our climb. She must have seen me struggling on the first pitch, because she hadn't offered the second lead. I arrived at the top sorry I had puffed up my meager talents and aware of a new dynamic, though I wouldn't have talked about it this way then. Everyone I had climbed with before was either as much a novice as I was or a man much better than I. With the men, I had ("instinctively" is the word that comes to mind here, but I can no longer use such an easy out) fallen into a passive role. I tried to be assertive. But I always knew they were in charge and would bail me out if necessary. Never while climbing with them did I feel as if I were looking at someone I might become. I was climbing their sport until I climbed with Katy.

I apologized while I made fumbling attempts to help Katy set up our rappel. She didn't respond, and when we returned to the base of the climb, she asked me if I wanted to lead a nearby 5.8 climb. But I had done far more that day than I had bargained for. Grasping the bedraggled feathers of my borrowed plumage, I said, no, I did not want to lead that pitch, though perhaps I might another time. I was torn by equal desires: wanting to confess my exaggeration, harmless though it may have been, and wanting to beg Katy to climb with me again. She took matters out of my hands by asking me if I wanted to climb together the following day.

For a full week, Katy was my climbing partner. I discovered that yes, she led 5.8s and 5.9s. Also a variety of 5.10s, most of them, it seemed to me, off-widths. After my first attempt at an off-width, I invested in a pair of kneepads just like the ones Katy wore. When she wasn't using hers, they rested on top of her shoes at her ankles. I slavishly imitated her in this, just as I tried to imitate her actions on the rocks. Katy, small-boned and birdlike, with knobby knees sticking out from the one pair of shorts she owned, had enormous tenacity in her small body. I knew (and if I'm honest, I knew it with a sense of loss) that Katy's very presence denied me the easy excuses I'd been using without even thinking of them as excuses. Katy was just about my height; her musculature was slight; she was a woman just like me, and yet she saw herself, and me, too, as capable of so much more than I'd expected. I could never again say, even if only to myself, I can't do it because I'm a woman.

I don't remember much of what we talked about together, though certain moments stand out in my mind. I have a distinct memory of walking proudly through the parking lot with Katy, our climbing rope strapped to my back and my hands leprous with gashes and missing skin. I remember drinking lemonade with Katy in the meager shade of a manzanita scrub one hundred feet up Arch Rock on a very hot day. The heat radiated from the speckled granite and swept past me in warm blasts on its way up the wall. While we rested between pitches, Katy and I swung our legs from the smooth branches and appreciated our bird's-eye view of the lower Valley floor. Our climb was considered a hard grunt, so it was both a surprise and a pleasure when we realized that the leader of the party coming up behind us was another woman. She joined us in our shrub stance to belay up the man who was her second. From the grunts and gasps that drifted up with the hot air, we could tell that the climb was a stretch for him. Katy and I talked to the other woman for almost an hour before he arrived at the belay. At some point the conversation touched on abortions. One by one, around our small circle, each of us admitted to having had an abortion. We were unduly pleased that three out of the four climbers on this over-hanging jam crack on this particular day shared such a woman's history. We gloried in this brief overturn of the climbing norm, a norm in which hard climbs weren't done by people who had abortions or menstruated—weren't women.

Katy taught me how to wrap my hands with tape so the tender skin between my thumb and fingers didn't get torn, and how to save the tape gloves for a second and even third day. She showed me how to wedge my body into squeeze chimneys, pushing my hands palm out against the opposite wall and rocking first my knees and then my ankles against either side while I wormed up the passage to her belay. "You're doing great," she'd sing down as I flailed through a move or hung against the comfort of the rope from above. I knew not to believe her, but believe her I did.

In Katy Cassidy, I found a mirror of what I might do and be. Katy and I traveled together that summer. When I returned to Seattle after seven months on the road, I had surpassed my earliest dreams and embarked on new ones.

The Community

If my first two years as a climber initiated me into adventure, the next several gave me a community that supported my new self. In January 1983, two months after my triumphant return (in my own eyes) to Seattle, I became a charter member of a new climbing group called Women Climbers Northwest. Katy Cassidy had shown me a mirror of what was possible for me as a climber; Women Climbers Northwest was that mirror refracted into multiple possibilities. The dervish force behind this new group was one Kathy Phibbs. WCN was her most recent attempt to bring together the two overriding passions in her life: mountains and women. This time, the concept took.

Between twenty and thirty women met one rainy January evening to talk about organizing a climbing group made up of women, for women. Almost no one in the room that night would have been recognized as important in the larger climbing community. Other than Kathy, who had done first ascents in South America, and Carla

Firey, who had been putting up new routes in the North Cascades since she was a teenager, no one had any first ascents to her credit, and no one was climbing the highest numbers in rock climbing. Several of us had aspirations in that direction, however. Collectively, we wanted to climb big walls in Yosemite, go on Himalayan expeditions, be mountain guides and climb ever harder.

As organizations go, Women Climbers Northwest was pretty free-form. We didn't follow the highly structured committee system of the Mountaineers, the oldest and biggest climbing organization in the area, or the clubby hierarchy of the American Alpine Club. Our affinities were more to the Gunks' prankster Vulgarians (the rowdy band of climbers and ne'er-do-wells who rattled the Victorian sensibilities of the East Coast climbing establishment), or, closer to home, to groups who gave themselves names like the Dead Boys Climbing Club to apply for expedition grants. We did have some structure: we elected a board of directors, asked for dues, mailed out a monthly newsletter and organized meets and group trips. But mostly the organization was a mailing list loosely connecting women who wanted to climb with other women. We mimicked the back-fence network of women everywhere: "So-and-so seems gung-ho. You might try asking her to go on your next trip."

One of my goals in joining Women Climbers Northwest had been to find a climbing partner with whom I could continue to push myself, as I had with Katy. I zeroed in on two climbers in the group who seemed as ambitious as I was—Eve Dearborn and Kathy Phibbs. Like me, Eve had been climbing only a year, but she approached climbing with a discipline and an intensity that she'd acquired in an earlier career as a dancer. Kathy was one of the most experienced mountaineers in the new organization and wanted to improve as a rock climber.

After a while I realized that I'd met Kathy before. She had given the slide show on women and climbing when I was taking my basic climbing course. Kathy knew of me as well. A few months earlier, we had both been in Yosemite, Kathy with several other Northwest women climbers. I was alone after my travels with Katy, on month six of my climbing circuit tour. Only one hundred dollars stood between me and having to get a job, so I had started collecting cans and bottles for refunds at the recycling station. This bit of entrepreneurship paid my fifty-cent fee each night in the climbers' camp-

neurship paid my fifty-cent fee each night in the climbers' campground and allowed me to stash occasional dollars in the local bank. By day, I climbed with a group of Ohio boys who'd moved to the Valley after high school. By night, we drank rotgut vodka and orange pop before raiding the garbage bins for cans. When I began climbing, I had rediscovered myself at eight years old; one year later, I was having a blast acting a lot like a teenage boy. Not everyone considered this progress. Someone had pointed me out to Kathy and her friends as another Northwest climber, but they had not been thrilled with what they saw of my lifestyle and had kept their distance.

When we met again in Seattle, however, we recognized in each other a passion for climbing and an affinity for hamming it up. Kathy pursued her dreams with a wild energy that I found appealing. It seemed to me to be the same energy I'd tried to suppress in myself back in high school. Soon the word "wildness" appeared regularly in my journals.

We had considered calling the climbing group Crag Hags, after Mary Daly's revisionist definition of "haggard hags"—wild, untractable women, untamed by men.[8] Women Climbers Northwest was my first experience with the pleasure of running in a pack. We were loud, we were silly, we acquired a reputation for flamboyance.

Kathy had an ever-expanding collection of climbing literature, through which I learned that we were not the first women to have banded together for this purpose. In the 1920s, Miriam O'Brien Underhill and several other women did "manless climbs" in the Alps. They were initially met by scepticism, as Underhill recounts in her climbing autobiography, *Give Me the Hills:*

> Henry de Segogne went to some pains to explain to me why a woman could never lead a climb. There is a lot more to leading, said Henry, than first meets the eye, a lot that must be learned, and that is best learned by watching competent leaders attentively and coming to understand their decisions. Women, however, never bother to do this. Since they know that they will never be allowed to lead anyway, they just come walking along behind, looking at the scenery. Therefore,

---

[8] Mary Daly, *Gyn/Ecology: The Metaethics of Radical Feminism* (Boston: Beacon Press, 1978), 14-16.

even if they were given an opportunity to lead, they would be completely unprepared.[9]

Fortunately, Underhill ignored this advice and went on to do the first "manless" ascents of the most important Alpine climbs of her day. When she and Micheline Morin accomplished the first all-woman unguided ascent of The Grépon, a well-known climber bemoaned, "The Grépon has disappeared—there are still some rocks standing there, but as a climb it no longer exists. Now that it has been done by two women alone, no self-respecting man can undertake it. A pity, too, because it used to be a very good climb."[10]

Beyond improving as a climber, and even beyond the new leadership skills I acquired, I tried to fill holes in my upbringing and acculturation. I called it self-sculpting. I had been molded in attitudes, behaviors and expectations by the culture I had grown up in. I now wanted to break that constricting mold and devise a better one. I wanted what Carolyn Heilbrun defined as androgyny, which "seeks to liberate the individual from the confines of the appropriate."[11] Why should it be inappropriate for me to climb hard, for me to climb with other women, for me to be powerful?

The more time I spent with these strong women, the more I learned to love myself as a strong woman. I didn't worry so much about being loud when I was excited, or wonder if I was too muscular, or get anxious about how I smelled.

I had congratulated myself on my open-mindedness in becoming friends with Eve and Kathy, since they were both lesbians. In fact, I was hyperaware that they were interested in women, not men. My own anxieties initially blinded me to the truth: I was desperately attracted to Kathy. When it finally dawned on me, and when she responded to my clumsy overtures, it was as if I'd never felt love before. All my growth seemed to culminate in this relationship.

Kathy and I were together a short time, a matter of months, before our respective immaturities got the better of us. But during those months, climbing was a metaphor for all the ways I was learn-

[9] Miriam Underhill, *Give Me the Hills* (Riverside, Connecticut: The Chatham Press, 1956), 149.

[10] Underhill, *Give Me the Hills,* 158.

[11] Carolyn G. Heilbrun, *Toward a Recognition of Androgyny* (New York: W. W. Norton, 1964), x.

ing to be a strong woman. It made perfect sense to me to have discovered the love of women through this activity that had given me such joy and strength. At our best, Kathy and I were young lion cubs, wrestling together in the sun. We had great plans and the energy to match. We read in a climbing magazine about two climbers who trained by doing "Half Dome days," in which they climbed as many pitches as on Half Dome (24) in a day. We took it as a challenge to match the feat. We raced from one climb to another, counting up the pitches and exhorting each other to try this one or that one. After we broke up, I moved away, went to graduate school and became involved with men again. We corresponded. When Eve died in an avalanche on Mt. Index, I was immensely grateful that it was Kathy who called me with the news, so that I knew instantly the call was not about her.

After I received my graduate degree, I returned to Seattle and began working full-time. For a while, my life followed the trajectory I'd envisioned when I first started climbing: increasing prowess as a climber translated into increasing strength and skill in all areas of my life. I was in good shape physically and well practiced as a climber. On rock, I sometimes attained a pure match of purpose and ability, when I could focus completely on a series of moves. In my first years of climbing, fear and desire had occupied nearly equal roles. But now, it seemed, my fears merely fed this focused energy. The only other experience I could relate these feelings to was a religious one, my separate self completely emptying into an absolute present.

But then, gradually, something changed. One season I wanted nothing more than to keep getting better. I spent most of the winter plotting new routes and new challenges. But when summer arrived, even though I didn't want to believe it, my desire began to ebb. I became afraid. Was I losing my touch? Was I not, perhaps, the incredible mountain woman I'd led everyone, myself included, to believe? Was this it?

I stopped climbing. It wasn't a conscious choice at first. Initially I attributed the change to a new job, which was very stressful and fast-paced: The weekend would arrive, and I'd only want to recover from the week before. The idea of going out and taking on even more stress began to seem very strange indeed. I told people that climbing had been an early way for me to harness my energies and ambitions, but now I harnessed them to my career. Fair enough, perhaps, except that I also felt dead, numb inside. This sense of dying deep inside seemed related to my job and to giving up climbing, but the connection wasn't one I understood. I was scared that I'd lived my glory days and that I was a fake.

I began to feel unsafe at any speed: in the mountains, at the office. When my depression was at its worst—when it was a struggle to get up, get dressed and go to work—Hope Barnes, a good friend, called and asked if I would attend a lecture series with her. One evening every month during that long winter, I shook myself from my stupor and met her for dinner and a lecture. After the lectures ended, Hope and I met once a week for breakfast. Kathy forced me out of the house on training runs. We didn't talk much of climbing; it was as if my friends were nursing me back to health.

It is always painful to realize that an approach to life that has taken you great places no longer works. My approach had been to push myself and to ignore my fears. It had brought me certain achievements, but it had also kept me from being connected to myself. I was like a tire—all hard shell on the outside, nothing on the inside.

I'd used climbing as a drug, much the same way others use alcohol or cocaine. I'd used it to act with strength and with assurance, but behind that learned competence had lurked other, more vulnerable emotions. I had climbed in part both to avoid those scarier emotions and to disperse them without having to admit to their presence.

During this time of reassessment, I had dinner with a man I'd known since I first learned to climb. He was now a world-class mountaineer; when we met for dinner, however, he was unhappy with his life. He was beginning to believe, he told me, that his emphasis on climbing had made it easy for him not to think about a painful past. As he remembered that past, he found his urge to climb diminished. For both of us, climbing had served an important purpose, but we had used it to stay in behavior patterns that were ultimately harmful. The choice to climb, as David Roberts eloquently says, can have its darker side:

> How much of the appeal of mountaineering lies in its simplification of interpersonal relationships, its reduction of friendship to smooth interaction (like war), its substitution of an Other (the mountain, the challenge) for the relationship itself? Behind a mystique of adventure,

toughness, footloose vagabondage—all much-needed antidotes to our culture's built-in comfort and convenience—may lie a kind of adolescent refusal to take seriously aging, the frailty of others, interpersonal responsibility, weakness of all kinds, the slow and unspectacular course of life itself.[12]

I knew I didn't want to climb any longer to avoid dealing with the painful or even boring aspects of life. I wanted to enjoy climbing without needing it to fill empty spaces within. Was there still a place for climbing in my life?

Climbing had been a powerful metaphor for me from the beginning. When I first started climbing, it was an image of self-growth and an expression of rebellion. In the early years of Women Climbers Northwest, climbing was a metaphor for my love of myself and others as strong women. Most recently it had been a metaphor for risk-taking and success.

As I considered a new approach to climbing, I promised myself that I would no longer outreach myself in what I wanted. I would heed the dozens of lessons I had accumulated over ten years; though I would continue to think of climbing as primarily a metaphor for self-discovery, I would not harness my drive for achievement to it. Going to a rock-climbing area or into the mountains would now be more of a mind-clearing release, I decided.

With this revision firmly in mind, in the winter of 1990 I once again talked of climbing.

The Risk

"A dangerous path is this, like the edge of a razor," according to the Hindu saying. The new year came—1991, a palindrome. I spent the last days of January skiing with my sweetheart in Utah. We skied all day in the weightless powder and fell asleep early every night. Our schedule shared a simplicity with my early climbing trips: get up, ski hard, eat and sleep. While I was in Utah, I wrote in my journal that I wanted to go climbing with Kathy again. Our old wounds seemed far enough away, and I missed her powerful energy.

We returned from our trip on Sunday night. A note was pinned to our front door. It said, "Dear Kristen—We have some terrible

---

[12] Roberts, *Moments of Doubt*, 189.

news to tell you. Both Hope and Kathy were killed climbing Dragontail this week. . . . " and it was signed by two friends. Those two sentences formed a red-hot coal that dropped down my throat. I could feel it burning through me, and no matter what I did, it kept burning.

In the first days after their deaths, I was driven to act. I edited the accident report. I restlessly sought out others who had known Hope or Kathy and talked about them, refusing to use the past tense. I dreamed that I found a book of instructions for putting Hope back together. It had pictures and diagrams, like a repair manual for a dishwasher. I read it carefully, memorizing all the procedures, happy that something so concrete was all I needed to bring her back.

Their deaths brought home to me the three fallacies I'd been climbing under: that I could avoid death by careful study; that only the stupid or reckless die climbing; and that climbing is a metaphor.

Every climbing death I'd known about until Hope and Kathy died could have been avoided. The three young men on El Cap hadn't clipped properly into their belay; Eve had been climbing on an unseasonably warm day, when the avalanche risk was too high; a teenager at Devil's Tower had died soloing—a completely avoidable death, I thought. But I couldn't find what Hope and Kathy should have done differently, unless it had been not to go at all. They had climbed in good conditions, they were careful, and still something had happened so that they fell more than 1,500 feet to the base of the climb.

Before Hope and Kathy died, I firmly believed that if I listened to my mentors and learned from the mistakes of others, I would not die climbing. The non-climbing world seemed to me to have a gruesome fascination with deaths in the mountains and on rock cliffs. I tried to avoid talking about climbing deaths to anyone who didn't also climb. I don't climb to seek or taunt death, I thought, so why even mention the risks?

But the truth is, if I flirted with death as a climber in my early years, it was in believing on some emotional level that I would not die. It's hard to admit that you may die doing something you love, so I metamorphosed that terrible risk. I was wrong: The risk in climbing is not metaphoric. The self may believe it is going to die when you give a speech or reveal your most vulnerable emotions, but it does not actually risk physical death. Risks in climbing are actual. Objective, the guidebooks say.

Katy Cassidy was in Yosemite by herself during the spring of 1982 because her boyfriend, who was also her climbing partner, had died in a climbing accident some months earlier. She came to the Valley to see how it felt to be among climbers again and to see if she wanted to climb. She slummed with me, possibly, because I was safe. I was challenged by climbs that kept her well within her abilities. And maybe she derived some vicarious pleasure from watching my progress from novice to skilled climber. I don't know, because callous and unaware as I was, I didn't fully grasp the tragedy of her situation. I only tried to knot lessons gleaned from her partner's death into my string of things to avoid, placing another admonitory bead on my rosary. Tie enough knots, my reasoning went, and I would be spared.

I wanted to cheat death by proving myself worthy of being passed over. Where others might have gathered good-luck charms, I gathered information and knowledge. Without being fully aware of it, I was trying to deny that by climbing I accepted certain basic and unavoidable risks. Even with the best of intentions and the highest level of skill, I could be seriously injured climbing, and I could die.

Should Hope and Kathy not have climbed? Should I no longer climb? For several months after they died, I imagined death around every bend in the highway and beyond every curb I stepped from. I tried to find reasons that would explain why they had died when they did. I was surprised when my search released me into a paradox: I saw that the end of every life on earth is death. It wasn't as if Kathy or Hope could have avoided death for all time; at best, they could have avoided this particular death. I started to see that if I focused on avoiding death, I would also avoid living. I had been doing that unwittingly in my climbing, by scrutinizing every accident for how it might have been avoided—as if death itself could be avoided. It was useless to fear death, and a waste to court it; beyond that, the best I could do was to live as fully as possible.

Hope and Kathy died, as we all will, because they had lived. In the year since they died, I haven't stopped missing them or regretting all that I never said to them, but I have remembered to appreciate how they lived. And I still take the old wings out for a spin, now and again.

KEEP THE PIGS OFF
THE PEAKS?

Lorraine G. Bonney

▲ ▲ ▲

MOUNT EVEREST. Words that magnetize! They tingle the spine...capture the imagination...evoke emotions of fear, awe, wonder. Yet, on July 15, 1989, the mystique of Everest was shattered. According to *The New York Times,* six explorers were heading across Antarctica by dog team and skis. Why Antarctica, the expedition's publicist was asked. "Oh, Antarctica is the hot spot now. Mount Everest is out. It's been done every which way. It's been trashed!"

Mount Everest, the great mysterious silent center of the Himalaya, the third Pole, the climbing challenge of the twentieth century, trashed? Was it true? How could this tragedy happen? Because it's the tallest object on the planet? Because climbers are pigs? Or is it really all that simple?

Though the British "discovered" this vaguely located but extraordinary object and named it for Sir George Everest, they didn't find it easy to pursue the conquest of this, the highest peak in the world because of its position on the border between the closed kingdoms of Nepal and Tibet. However, in 1921 the Dalai Lama, the incarnate deity of Tibetan Buddhism, finally permitted the first British reconnaissance-climbing expedition to approach Chomolungma, Mother Goddess of the Earth, the Tibetan name for Mt. Everest. Citing scientific inquiry to justify their intrusion, this team of explorers and surveyors was fortified by four experienced mountaineers including the already well-known George Leigh Mallory. The cavalcade with its hundred mules carrying provisions and equipment barged into the Rongbuk Valley and camped near the highest monastery in the world, the first white men ever seen there.

Base camp was established at the snout of the Rongbuk Glacier and from there small "advance" camps were pushed upward. Despite disorganization and bad weather this group discovered the feasibility of the North Col route. More important to this story, they brought into the near-virgin Rongbuk Valley the first massive loads of boxes, food tins, ropes, oxygen bottles and other paraphernalia needed to sustain their five-month probe of Everest. Thus did this large and costly expedition shape the future of Everest.

Even larger expeditions under General C. G. Bruce approached Everest in 1922 and 1924, again via the Rongbuk Valley and again heavily laden with supplies and equipment. This time the lama of the Rongbuk monastery gave permission to proceed but included a few ethical guidelines: they had to behave like pilgrims, preserve the holiness of the region, kill no animals in the valley and remove no rocks.

We all know the results of the 1924 expedition: On the first summit attempt, Major E. F. Norton pushed himself up to 28,125 feet with no "gas," turning back a scant 903 feet below the summit. On the now famous second attempt, Mallory and Andrew Irvine disappeared into the clouds close enough to the summit to create a controversy that lingers to this day: did they reach the top of Mt. Everest?

A magnificent memorial to the twelve men who had died in the three expeditions was built on the prominent moraine overlooking base camp. Tibetans later pulled down the monument, angered by the disruption the expeditions had caused to the countryside.

Five similar British expeditions followed, three of them large and costly, two of them inexpensive and lightweight. Calling the earlier expeditions "extravaganzas that failed," Eric Shipton was determined to place a small, well-equipped party on the North Col for one-tenth the cost and only minor impact on the countryside. However, he dallied, the monsoon struck, and he too failed. The British conquest of Everest was then interrupted by the war. Volatile politics then slammed shut Tibet's door to Mount Everest in

1949, not to be reopened until 1980.

When Nepal's south approach opened up to climbers, the lucky Brits got first crack at the unclimbed south side, and in 1953 Mount Everest became a household word around the world as a New Zealand beekeeper, Edmund Hillary, and the Nepalese Sherpa Tenzing Norgay made the first ascent of Mount Everest. Eric Shipton had been first choice to lead this significant 1953 climb. He wanted it lightweight but was overruled, this would be Britain's last chance at Everest for several years, and the Brits threw everything into the assault led by militarist Colonel John Hunt, who built up and supplied the high camps like they were beachheads. His military strategy paid off.

Later Hunt wrote that the Everest story was "finished." In fact it had scarcely begun, and its ramifications on Everest's future were significant: Heavyweights became the formula for Himalayan climbing for the next twenty years. Everest was "booked" years in advance. The small armies came, climbed, filmed, dumped, retreated and, in doing so, made the South Col infamous as "the highest trash pit in the world."

The deflating blow to extravaganzas came in 1978 when Reinhold Messner and Peter Haebler accomplished what Major Norton had just missed doing in 1924—they climbed Everest without canned oxygen. Standards were shaken; Shipton was vindicated!

And what of the north side? After the Chinese poured through Tibet in 1959 like a dose of salts, destroying monasteries, one-fifth of the population and a significant part of the Tibetan culture, they locked off Tibet from the outer world and had Qomolangma, as they called Everest, all to themselves. They made the most of it. They pushed a quasi-road up the Rongbuk Valley to base camp; they summitted Everest via the North Col route in 1960; and in 1975 one Chinese and eight Tibetans including the second woman to climb Everest, a thirty-seven-year-old Tibetan mother of three children, summitted again.

Then—oh joy!—in 1980 word flashed like wildfire around the world that Tibet had opened its doors again to foreign climbers. Requests for permits flooded in, but this time the Japanese snatched the plum—the first foreign permit to open Everest's almost virgin north side. Their successful massive assault is best remembered for the gross disasters called campsites that they left behind.

Superstar Messner further revolutionized mountaineering in 1980 by paying $50,000 for the privilege of adding "super" to the word lightweight. In a spectacular display of skill and self-confidence, he climbed Everest solo with a twenty-kilo backpack from a camp below the North Col. Lightweight was in style!

In 1981, Galen Rowell led the first American trekkers since the Chinese revolution into the Rongbuk monastery. In his *Mountains of the Middle Kingdom,* Rowell described the monastery as a shambles, "without a single ceiling; just broken walls stretching a hundred yards up a hillside devoid of life, where hundreds of lamas and pilgrims once worshiped... (Here) expeditions have performed a sacrilege that turns my stomach...Tears came to my eyes...Cans. Thousands of cans. None of them very rusted. All from expeditions since 1975. Chinese labels. Japanese labels. German labels. Boxes, paper, decaying food, metal and just plain junk. And Rongbuk is accessible by truck!"

Everest, "special mountain," like a battered Atlas trying to shrug off his load, like a Gulliver trussed up in ropes with Lilliputians crawling all over him, took the assault from every side as the litter piled up. How long would climbers stand for this assault on their senses, their dignity and on the mountain, the only "resource" they really influenced?

When Ellen Lapham came back from the American West Ridge expedition in 1986, she reported "debris scattered all over everywhere...It looked like an American landfill...Climbers don't pack things out. If somebody wanted to do a cleaning expedition, there's plenty to clean. The question is, does anyone give a damn?"

Well, somebody did give a damn. It all began in 1987 when Scott Fischer's American Everest North Face Expedition tried to put the first American woman on the summit and failed by only a thousand feet. Although it failed in its main goal, this expedition gave birth to an idea that would have far-reaching impact on Mount Everest.

Why was Fischer's expedition any different? Because it made a precedent-setting commitment *before* it left the States, according to Liz Nichol, "to our sponsors and ourselves to leave Everest a better place than we found it." Beaten out by wild storms and high winds, nevertheless they pulled out all their camps and cleaned up the messes of others.

Two of its members, Liz Nichol and Bob McConnell, sensitive, dynamic and eloquent people totally committed to the environment, were deeply revolted by what they found at Advance base camp, a perfect camp, according to Nichol, "except for the piles of human waste in and by the stream and toilet paper littering the pond. It took two of us most of three days to dig a hole big enough to bury the cans and broken glass we collected from an area the size of a football field." Their group shared base camp that year with some four hundred other climbers. While Nichol's team members dug latrines, not easy in the stony ground and at the oxygen-starved atmosphere of 18,000 feet, others just defecated on the ground.

"Trash is a Western phenomenon," Nichol said. "People in the Third World don't know what to do with trash because they don't generate it. Everything is reused or biodegradable." Enter Westerners from the twentieth century who bring with them a culture wrapped in plastic and cardboard. Their calling card is trash, and they leave it around the world!

Liz Nichol and Bob McConnell, now married, conceived the idea of the 1990 Everest Environmental Expedition, E-3, in January 1988. They would return with a garbage collection team in an international effort to clean up Mt. Everest. They would concentrate on the Tibetan side where the trash pileup was only ten years old.

Well, as the pundits always say, undertaking a big project is like eating an elephant—you do it one bite at a time. The first bite was to tell the world of their project. They did that so well that even I, way out in the Tetons and Jackson Hole, Wyoming, heard the call. By the end of the next two hectic years, they had a money-raising slide show, nonprofit status, a bank account, a budget of $165,000 for research, planning and execution, and a staff.

E-3 set three goals for itself. The initial goal of cleaning up the ten-year pileup of trash at base camp and Camp I was at best a "quick fix," not a solution. Long-term goals had two approaches: first, to work with the Tibetan officials in establishing some systems to help climbers and trekkers clean up after themselves; the second, and toughest, to educate expeditions back home in ways to minimize their potential trash. That meant attacking the curse of Everest—packaging!

As word spread about the Everest clean-up, two groups of fifteen volunteers each signed up for this first expedition targeted solely to pick up other people's garbage in the harsh, high-altitude environment on the Tibetan side of Everest and, what's more, paying for the privilege. One support group consisted entirely of Ohio Explorer Scouts and their adult leaders who enthusiastically plunged themselves $74,000 in the hole to join this venture. The other was a miscellaneous bunch ranging from high schooler John Barlow to Wyoming's famous "old man of the wilderness," founder of the National Outdoor Leadership School (NOLS), Paul Petzoldt. The trip wasn't cheap at $5,865 per person, plus a tax-deductible $650 contribution to E-3. Seattle's Mountain Madness, a mountaineering and adventure travel company, was behind the exciting, smoothly coordinated, trek-style itinerary.

A staff team of seven left in mid-July for Lhasa, Tibet, and the Everest base camp at the foot of the Rongbuk Glacier, where they set up two camps, evaluated the situation, set priorities and prepared for the arrival of the first support team.

That was us—the least likely bunch of trash pickers Craig Seasholes, our group's leader, had ever seen. Or so he declared when he met us at the San Francisco airport to shepherd us on our Great Experience all the way through our itinerary to Kathmandu and Bangkok.

Once at Lhasa, acclimatization began immediately because we had flown from sea level to 12,500 feet. To avoid the dastardly "Lhasa-tude" (a Seasholes gem), we drank at least three liters of water a day. We were further conditioned by walking and climbing thousands of steps following tireless Johnny Wang through cities, villages, palaces, monasteries, shrines, market places, private homes, gardens—everything between Lhasa and Shegar, 1,000 kilometers to the west.

At Shegar (alias Dogtown, infamous for its many dogs and the outrageous "gone-to-the-dogs" plumbing in the three-month-old "new" hotel) we left Tibet's No. One highway, the Friendship (read Hardship) Road and headed south on the ultimate four-wheel-drive challenge, a primitive, often washed-out track obviously not built to last in 1959. We checked into Chomolungma Nature Preserve and jolted the 110 kilometers south up the Rongbuk Valley, the "valley of precipices and steep ravines," an apt phrase. We reacted to our first unclouded view of Qomolangma in 1990 much as Mallory did on his first trip in 1921: "We paused here in sheer astonishment . . . We asked no questions and made no comment, but simply looked. . . ."

Like many expeditions and trekkers in the seven decades before us, we camped at the Rongbuk monastery at 16,500 feet, rebuilt since Galen Rowell's poignant description in 1981. Roofs had been replaced, the trash removed or hidden. It was now a quiet and near-empty shell echoing, not with the soft tread of hundreds of monks, but of eight monks and three nuns trying mightily to carry on the old traditions such as ceremonial blessings for the success of expeditions like ours.

Two days later our bone-cracking truck ride ended as we jolted into the famous Everest base camp at 17,000 feet, a huge, barren mosaic of boulders, pebbles and powdered rock of a river floodplain, moraines, scree slopes, crags and snow-capped peaks. We passed the campsite first used by the early Brits and, a half mile beyond, jerked to a halt at our cook tent about noon, at the same site used three months earlier by the well-publicized International Peace Climb. At last!

Bob McConnell welcomed us with joy, bear hugs and apologies because Liz wasn't there too (the birth of their son, Christopher, interrupted her co-leading plans, so she instead coordinated our expedition with the outer world from the headquarters in Colorado Springs). Then McConnell turned us over to Louisa Willcox. Back home in Yellowstone, Louisa is an environmental wildcat as program director of the Greater Yellowstone Coalition, and here she was no different, attacking Everest problems with the same fireball energy and enthusiasm. Talking up a storm, she whisked us off to inspect the facilities, the memorials to dead Everesters on the moraine above camp, and the immensity of our garbage-collecting project. The staff had surveyed the situation the previous week and had already built eleven stone temporary holding areas for the trash.

We caught up with Tom Leech, graphic artist from Colorado Springs, who taught us how to turn junk paper into sparkling note paper with his simple outfit set up on the cement satellite pad built in 1988 for the 252-person Tri-National Expedition of China, Japan and Nepal.

E-3's first goal, the physical cleanup of Everest's north side was *not* a piece of cake. To scour the place required 709 person-days of back-breaking, heavy breathing work, collecting and bagging almost a ton and a half of trash (2,863 pounds exactly). We each dragged around one of the huge donated "Tough Bags" emblazoned with Leech's great E-3 logo, packing them with smelly, rotten, broken collectibles—mostly glass, cans and human waste.

Headaches and hacking coughs became a routine part of our daily life, and instant breathlessness attacked us, not because of the scenery or excitement, but from the lack of good old O_2. Had any of us become really knocked out by the altitude, the staff would have stuffed the sufferer in a Gamow bag, and in effect taken him or her down as much as 6,000 feet just by increasing the air pressure in the bag.

The most trashed-out site was at the north end of base camp, just below the semi-reconstructed Mallory memorial. We spent a lot of back-breaking hours at this international "Camp of Horrors." It was easy to see why the early British climbers chose that particular campsite—it was the one green spot softening the rocky landscape, with a little pond next to the stream. We could easily imagine gentlemen in Harris tweeds sitting around a camp table, dining on quail in foie de gras (tinned, of course) and sipping Montebello 1915 as they did in 1924. The same spot when we arrived boasted water bilious with slime and crap, a miserable thing to clean up. Incidentally, we identified trash from every nation that had sent an expedition into Tibet.

Earlier, in April, the thirty-strong American-Chinese-Russian International Peace Climb team had scaled the heights of Everest and come back down leading a string of yaks carrying two tons of garbage left by earlier climbers on the North Col route. It was a pity they tried to bury the trash in the base camp floodplain because our outfit arrived to find high waters had flooded it all out again. Re-collected, it filled a couple of holding bins.

Our dedicated team spent several days prying into filthy rock outcrops long used as toilets and garbage hideouts. From all the broken glass we had to pick up, including Rainier beer bottles, there must have been one helluva party that ended by tossing, with joyous abandon, hundreds of bottles onto the rocks, while beyond loomed the majestic mountain itself.

Six decades after the Brits had left base camp to establish their Camp I, a group of us left base camp to follow in their footsteps, along what had become a well-established, well-littered trail. We moved quickly through a hazardous, narrow trough between high moraines that we called the "tube," heads up and eyes on the rocks constantly rolling down toward us, mostly dislodged by blue sheep. Where the river was pinched in by its gorge, we each roped across via a Tyrolean traverse, the torrent's raging frothy boil grabbing at our feet. We then moved due south up the main Rongbuk valley, climbed "Heart Attack Hill," crossed through an 18,500-foot pass and finally straggled around a last corner of the seemingly endless moraine that until then had blocked our view.

Suddenly there she was, the vision of a lifetime, a breathtaking mountain of ice, the legendary Chomolungma, so close she filled the southern sky, dwarfing her peers, tantalizing the dreamers. Tucked within the moraine was a little Shangri-la, a jewel-like cirque shel-tered from avalanches and wind, our advance camp, at 18,000 feet. Rejuvenated, we spurred ourselves on, feasting our eyes on the Mother Goddess of the Earth in her vestal snow robe, her north face seamed with sun, shadows and cliff bands, her west ridge flung out like a protecting wing, denying the hazards of the avalanche tracks thereon. The cirque overlooked the massive Rongbuk Gla-cier, spectacular with seracs, a jagged sea of ice pinnacles, like face-less pilgrims, "los penitentes," in stark white robes paying homage to the Mother Goddess herself. At the edge of the cirque a stream trickled out of the rocks to form a shallow pond. Moss formed a lush emerald-green carpet nearby that was a sheer delight to our green-starved eyes.

Fluttering on the ridge above the stream were colorful strings of tattered prayer flags of hope, the Tibetan's way of gaining merit and showing reverence. Festooning the rock outcrops below the ridge were more tattered prayer fla . . . no, not prayer flags but toilet paper scraps dotting the rock outcrops, unmistakable mementos of white men passing through this holy valley. Its mere presence there screamed irreverence! The spell of Shangri-la was shattered.

Instinctively my shocked eyes sought the ground near my feet and saw the litter there. How incredibly embarrassed I was as I looked at the cans, candy wrappers, cigarette butts, broken glass, but mostly the obscene toilet paper decorating piles of human waste. Climbers did this, my type of people who love mountains and all they represent. Closer inspection of the little stream and pond revealed a vile green slime. I was revolted. Then the significance of it all jolted me into reality. After all, I was here not to climb Everest but to clean it up. In other words, get used to this Lorraine, quit your wild dreaming and start hauling trash!

How could climbers do this? How could a scene change so fast—from Shangri-la to a place that would later, when I personally dealt with the human waste problem, make me puke.

So what did we accomplish on the mighty Mount Everest? Did we, with the Tibetans, establish a system to help climbers and trekkers clean up after themselves? Can recycling be seriously considered? Yes! Yes! to both! The trash we collected from the glacier and Camp I all the way down the mountain to base camp was carried by backpack and yaks. At base camp it was faithfully weighed and tallied, then the mountain of trashbags was hauled out the 110 kilometers to Shegar (now Xegar) by tractor and truck. Because recycling in Tibet is limited at present, the trash ended up in a landfill—that is, a big hole—near the "new" hotel. Ten fifty-five-gallon barrels were brought in and left at different locations in base camp for trash. A shiny new truck, donated by E-3 and the Woodlands Mountain Institute of West Virginia, was promptly put into service by Preserve officials for regular removal of trash.

Recycling, a partial solution to Everest's problems, must involve Tibetans. The Rongbuk monastery and nearby villages already collect unused food and useful equipment left at lower altitudes. They enthusiastically absorbed Leech's paper-making ideas. Aluminum cans and unbroken bottles can be recycled in Zhangmu, west of Shegar, with the added economic incentive of ten *fen* (less than one cent) per bottle.

My room/tent/yoga mate, geologist Anne Schwab, described the scene at Shegar's "landfill" when the new truck arrived loaded with garbage: "It was really weird to stand there and recognize trash that you had picked up! Tibetan children retrieved any interesting items that fell out of the bags—it was great! Incidentally, the trash bags will be reused by Preserve officials. We've also donated a year's salary for a ranger."

What about incineration? I say no way! Give up the filthy habit. We learned the hard way how expeditions, just before pulling out, heaped up their trash, poured kerosene over it and set it afire. What didn't burn (most of it) was left there, an obscene glob of broken gear, bottles, cans, plastic and foil packaging. Ask first-year university student Cathy Brown about it. At Camp I she discovered a half-burned, half-buried snake pit of medicinal trash close enough to the water source to poison it for the next few years.

Burying? No way! Burying trash at base camp means someone else re-does your dirty job. The water table is only about two feet below the surface so buried trash will wash up in the next big run-off. The Peace Climb's groundwater test proved that.

Crevassing? Don't you dare! Your grandkids will stumble over the junk in a hundred years.

And what about the human waste? In 1989, 10,000 visitors in the Khumbu Region in Nepal and 3,000 in the Rongbuk Valley deposited tons of human waste. Mount Rainier climbers deposit six tons in an average year. The difference, however, is that it's collected and not left all over the landscape! In the Rongbuk the rocky ground and altitude do nothing to assist biodegrading bacteria. Despite the vastness of the Rongbuk Valley, there are very few good camping sites along approach, base camp and climbing routes, and they all get heavy use. The E-3 summary report recommends establishing a series of permanent campsites with well-built outhouses over removable fifty-five-gallon barrels at all the heavy-use sites; the human waste could be used as "night soil."

At base camp we discussed garbage a lot. Paul Petzoldt recounted the method he had used on his annual New Year trips up the Grand Teton: "Everyone urinated and crapped in plastic bags, and we threw some quick lime in to destroy all the germs." He added that the person who comes up with a simple way to neutralize or reduce human waste into harmless powder that could be dumped anywhere including in the local water would be an instant million-aire and he wished he were smart enough to figure out how to do it!

One day we got into a big garbage and ethics discussion about E-3's most important goal—how to educate expeditions back home about minimizing their potential trash. Louisa Willcox suddenly popped a question to Petzoldt, her old mentor, "Where do *you* think wilderness ethics needs to go, and how do you think the mountain community should handle this?"

Petzoldt was ready. He's been on a clean-up-the-wilderness kick ever since he started NOLS back in Lander, Wyoming, in 1965 and turned loose hundreds of kids into Wyoming wilderness. Now, as the president of his more recently founded Wilderness Education Association, he has been trotting around campuses and into auditoriums with his wife, Virginia, preaching good wilderness habits to professors and students alike.

Petzoldt raised his great bushy eyebrows at Willcox, a spectacular gesture in itself. "Well," he rumbled, "first you have to tell people what they should do. Most of our research has been on what people have done; we need research on what the expedition should be. You've got to develop the moral standard and get it accepted by the leaders of the fraternity, not easy because mountain climbers are the most intelligent and most obnoxious group in the world. But you've got to have it so that when Joe Blow, the leader of an expedition that trashed up a mountain, comes back, the whole fraternity knows about the trashing and he's in the doghouse."

McConnell asked, "Do you think he ought to be denied a permit to climb?" Louisa added, "Yeah, or maybe probationary action . . . ?"

Paul said, "You mean keep the pigs off the peaks! Nope, you can't condemn a person for a law that hasn't been enacted until you've set the standards."

"In other words," Louisa said, "it has to be put down in writing and accepted as standard operating behavior and moral conduct."

"Right," Petzoldt said, "and I think the mountain community is ready for it. Set the standards—carry it in, carry it out, whatever! If it doesn't work," he said, emphasizing the words with his eyebrows, "*then* you take the drastic action."

He's right, of course. But what's so new about that! Grand Canyon river runners, for instance, have been running the Colorado for years—haul it in, haul it out, famous shit cans and all. The alternatives are fines and forfeited privileges.

Mr. Shrestha, mountaineering officer in the Nepal Ministry of Tourism, said as much at the December 1988 American Alpine Club meeting in Atlanta, "We want clean expeditions more than we want cleanup expeditions." In 1988 Sir Edmund Hillary wrote Nichol and McConnell that he too had "been deeply disappointed in the casual discarding of rubbish by expeditions." For a long time he wanted Everest closed off to all climbing for five years to let it recuperate.

Does that sound unlikely? The king of Nepal has already decided to close some areas to all climbing and trekking. Such "solutions" imply that climbers are irresponsible and put the climbing community on notice that, unless it adopts a more responsible approach, it will either be denied access, or will have to respond to rules created by the nonclimbing bureaucracy.

Big changes are coming! Pakistan, for example, now requires climbing expeditions to pay a two-hundred-dollar environmental clean-up fee AND hire extra porters specifically for carrying out garbage and human waste. Meanwhile prices to climb Himalayan peaks are skyrocketing! We'll pay through the nose for all our bad habits.

The E-3 summary report which was submitted to the Chomolungma Nature Preserve, to the expedition's sponsors and to international climbing and trekking organizations, called for host nations around the world to establish codes of environmental ethics for visitors to their fragile mountain environments; called to adventure travelers around the world to voluntarily comply with these codes; called to the sponsors of future expeditions to ask expeditions seeking their sponsorship how they plan to deal with environmental issues *before* sponsorship is granted; and finally—the biggie—called to international climbing organizations to support enforcement of environmental codes by fines, expulsion and denial of future visas or climbing permits when voluntary compliance is not forthcoming.

Would enforcement of rigid policies such as the "carry in—carry out" policy work? Count on it! On their way out, at the request of the abbot, the E-3 team left a list of rules for visitors at the Rongbuk monastery to follow. One of the rules: clean up or pay up. Call their bluff if you want to. Be a pig!

The fact is climbers must become a part of the solution instead of part of the problem. Imaginative planning is vital. Biodegradable packing, burlap, or recyclable containers are in. Minimize packaging! Buy local food and stimulate the local economy. We did it and wolfed down what our Tibetan cooks served up. Plan and budget for packing gear in *and* garbage out.

Maybe the glory-hungry adventurers are all heading for Antarctica, but I doubt it. Every climber has dreams of climbing Everest. It's traditional, a habit. There are those of us who still dream of challenging the roof of the world—not to get our names in the books, or to set any records, or to get on TV, but for the traditional reason of dreamers everywhere challenging the quintessence of challenges—Mt. Everest. But by God, we've got to do it clean!

ON MOTHERHOOD

Nancy Kerrebrock

▲ ▲ ▲

I AM A full time "hausfrau" and mom by choice, so please understand that I'm not bemoaning my lot in life when I say that domes-
ticity lacks something. I have a two-year-old daughter who is in
many ways still just a baby, and babies need security, comfort and
routines. Providing all that is immensely satisfying to me, but leaves
me feeling rather anesthetized. So what's a housewife to do for
thrills? With the help of my cooperative husband and generous
friends, I've discovered that having a kid doesn't mean Mom has to
give up climbing. Nor does it have to mean a fortune spent on
babysitters.

I climbed until I was about seven months pregnant, when I
could no longer see my feet. The good fit of my one-size-fits-all harness was what allowed me to keep climbing as long as I did. When I
fell, which I did with increasing frequency as the months went by,
my harness took the load around my back and the back of my legs
so there was no pressure on my belly. I didn't lead so my falls were
short. Perhaps Renata's delight in being tossed in the air was
learned in utero!

Born on Groundhog Day, by Easter Renata was sleeping
through the night, and my energy level had recovered. I got back in
shape by bouldering at a local university; climbing on walls at this
university is technically forbidden, so Renata provided good cover

when the security guards came around. She slept nearby in her baby carriage or watched from blankets on the grass. My husband and our climbing partners helped; whoever was resting took a turn playing with her.

I nursed Renata for almost eight months, and during that time I never left her for more than an hour or so. When I went climbing, she came along. Infants sleep as much as sixteen hours a day, but they wake frequently, and Renata usually woke hungry, which meant I could never get very far away from her. So instead of climbing long routes, we spent our time on first pitches that were too hard for us, taking turns on the rope, working out the moves, falling frequently—hang-doggin' is what climbers call this activity. Although doggin' is considered ethically impure by some traditional climbers, it does have its advantages: I now lead several grades harder than I ever did before Renata was conceived.

We have taken her on day trips to the Pinnacles, weekends at Lake Tahoe and in Yosemite, and longer trips to climbing areas in Southern California and Oregon. We learned early on that we needed to have at least three adults on these trips, so that someone would always be free to tend to the baby. One day my husband, Clint, and I took Renata to the Pinnacles and tried to do it all ourselves. That is to say, Clint led out and left me to do all the rest. Renata was mobile by then and fascinated by precipices—she'd see one and head for it full speed, damn the torpedos. That day she saw one and off she went, just as Clint was working his way through the run-out rotten upper half of "Cosmos." What could I do? It was my baby or my husband...I tied Clint off to a dubious sapling, the only anchor readily at hand, and ran to catch Renata, just as she, face lit with delight, threw herself off the edge. Since then Clint has periodically suggested that we leash her, to which I reply, "Our daughter is not a dog."

Since I've stopped nursing Renata we've had more flexibility. Sometimes I go climbing for the weekend while Clint stays home with Renata. More often Clint goes without us. Occasionally my mom stays with Renata so Clint and I can get away together. And sometimes we take her with us.

Renata enjoys these outings. One typical trip was a day in the Pinnacles with friends Alice, Sean and Roger. In the car she napped. As we sweated up the switchbacks of the Juniper Canyon trail, she bobbed along on my back, guzzling juice from her bottle, cooing at the orange lichen and wildflowers. We spread out her blanket in a meadow between two short spires that offer a selection of topropes and leads from 5.2 to 5.10c. Sean set up top ropes on a 5.7 and a 5.9, and while we all took turns on them Renata ate lunch, chased butterflies in the meadow, and, yes, bouldered (with continuous contact spotting by mom.) I had my eye on the 5.10c, "Aliens Ate My Buick." I started up it and was feeling solid, had clipped the fourth bolt and was moving into the crux, when Renata began to wail. She was about fifteen months old then, and often cried when she saw me moving away from her, whether it was up the rock or just across the playground. Having read the child development books, I knew it was a normal phase and tried to remind myself of that, but my concentration faded as her howling escalated. My fingers suddenly felt greasy and my boots sandy. Alice rescued us by popping something sweet in Renata's mouth; my cruise control returned with the ensuing quiet. I rapped down to a big chocolatey kiss.

Any parent knows that outings with a small child are not easy, and climbing trips are no exception. Baby needs diapers, food, naps and vigilant attention. I remember vividly one cold morning at Smith Rocks—it was too cold to climb—when everyone else was snuggled in the car with the heater on, while I stood outside with my hands in a bucket of icy water, washing baby bottles. Renata has definitely made climbing trips harder on me, but I wouldn't have it any other way. I can't imagine life without her anymore, and I don't want to give up climbing.

I think of the state of my hands as a symbol of the compromises I've had to make. I would like to let my fingers get calloused so that tiny edges wouldn't be so painful. I could wear gloves when I do dishes and bathe Renata, and skip the hand lotion. But how could I touch Renata with climber's hands? How could I rub her soft little back when she's having trouble falling asleep on a hot night? The memory of my own mother's hands—soft, plump and infinitely comforting—came to me with startling force when I was in the excruciating last stages of labor in Renata's birth. Neither my husband's presence nor all the Lamaze techniques I'd learned did as much to help me with the pain as did Martha, the labor nurse. Martha gave me her hand to squeeze, and it felt exactly like my mother's. So I keep my hands soft for Renata, and shred my fingertips every time I climb. But as I said, I wouldn't have it any other way.

Some women climbers stop climbing when they become mothers. One reason is simply logistics: add the demands of a baby to two full-time adult schedules, and something has to give. I'm sure that mixing climbing with babies is easier when one parent doesn't work outside the home. Were I employed and Renata in day care, Friday evenings would probably find me just wanting to spend the next two days playing with Renata and getting the laundry done. As it is, on Friday evenings I want to get out of the house and away from the laundry baskets. I want to let someone else play with Renata for a little while. The monkey in me wants to romp.

A more compelling reason women stop climbing when baby arrives is that risk takes on a whole new meaning when you become a parent. Suddenly a helpless little person is depending on you, and you realize that you won't be the only one who will suffer, should you, for example, crater. You ask yourself, perhaps for the first time, whether climbing is worth it. For me this transition was probably easier than for most women because I had experienced a climbing loss—the kind that leaves you questioning your reasons for climbing—long before Renata came along.

I lost my older brother, who died in a tragic mountaineering accident on the north side of Denali in May 1981. Chris and I grew up climbing mountains together, and at the time of his death it was mountaineering, not rock climbing, that I loved best. In May 1982, still haunted by his death, I went to climb Denali with a guided group. Standing high on the West Buttress I looked down at the Peters glacier, where Chris spent his last days. I had his journal and knew how deeply impressed he had been by the beauty of this remote side of the mountain, how satisfied he was with the grueling days behind him, and how thrilled he was with the prospect of the climb to come. Somehow from my perch I shared his feelings, and from that moment his death haunted me less and the happiness of his last days remained with me. I decided that I would continue to climb, as long as it felt right.

As it turns out I did very little climbing for the next five years because it didn't feel right. I had no confidence in myself or my partners; I was scared and it wasn't worth it. Then Clint invited me to Yosemite for a weekend, and I felt totally secure on the warm granite with him at the other end of the rope. I learned to love rock climbing, and I hope to be a honed grandma someday, but I doubt I will ever climb another big mountain.

While there are some very good reasons to quit climbing when baby arrives, I think we will be seeing more and more climbing moms in the future. Recently in the City of Rocks four women gathered, purely by chance, at the base of a rock one afternoon. Two were hugely pregnant: one was climbing 5.10, while the other found climbing too painful at eight months, and was belaying her husband. The third (myself) had one child, and the fourth woman was about to get married and start a family. She seemed fascinated and encouraged by the other three. Scenes such as this are rare, but I think the elements of change exist. I think of all the young women who have discovered and become hooked on climbing in the last ten years, women who are only just now reaching their late twenties or early thirties and beginning to think about having children. This is a generation of women who are used to the idea that they can continue, after they become mothers, to do many of the things they enjoyed before. I predict it is only a matter of time before one of the high-profile female competition climbers takes a year off to have a baby and then returns as formidable as ever. She will spark a trend, and before long we will be seeing lots of baby backpacks, bottles and happy, grubby pink-cheeked cherubs at the crags.

I feel an especially keen sense of satisfaction when I see pregnant women and young families in the mountains, because it means that more and more little girls will grow up blessed by an early introduction to the power of their own bodies. I think girls who clamber up mountains when they are young learn two all-important things: that they are just as strong and able as boys, and that climbing is FUN! What's more, they learn these things before society gets a chance to teach them otherwise. I am forever grateful to my father (who loves the mountains) and my mother (who doesn't so much, but cheerfully goes along with my father's passion for the sake of family unity) for taking me climbing as a child. We scrambled up innumerable peaks when I was in grade school, and my father taught us to use ropes and ice axes and crampons when I was eleven. I climbed Mt. Rainier at fourteen and Mt. Robson at sixteen. I learned to climb steep New England water ice when I was in high school. It never occurred to me that I shouldn't be good at or shouldn't enjoy climbing, and my parents never doubted my abilities. They encouraged me just at they did my brothers. True, I grew up in the sixties, when few people had heard of "women's lib," and I know there were moments when my parents wondered what sort of daughter they were raising. But I honestly think it was only my image they worried about.

When I was fourteen my family spent a vacation mountaineering in the Washington Cascades. We all carried identical Kelty frame packs, with the exception that mine and my mother's lacked extension bars on top for lashing on extra gear, for example, a tent. To lash my share of our gear on my pack, I had to use yards of cord, and even then the gear often shifted and slipped off to one side or flopped forward onto my neck. I complained to my father that he and the boys had extension bars, and that I should get one, too. In his most provocative teasing manner, he answered, "But you're just a girly, and you're supposed to carry delicate little loads." Enraged, I socked him in the gut with all the strength my scrawny adolescent arm could muster. Fortunately my father knows how to take a punch, and is blessed with a great deal of wisdom in dealing with his children. Although nothing more was said about the extension bar, it was not long before one appeared on my pack. Later, when I was in college, my father, while helping me sharpen my crampons in preparation for a trip, and listening to me chatter on about all the spectacular ice climbs I planned to lead my (male) partner up, said to me, in all seriousness, "You know, you have to be very careful with men's fragile egos." I didn't have to worry about his warning very often because most of my partners were better climbers than I, but when I did think about what my father said, I honestly didn't see why men couldn't take care of their own egos. I still don't.

These days parents can raise their daughters to be strong and sure without worrying about whether their girls will appear unfeminine or unattractive. In the last few years, the glossy climbing magazines have shown us Lynn Hill climbing 5.14, Lynn Hill in an evening gown, and Lynn Hill in a wedding veil. The message is clear: we are ready to accept as a standard of attractiveness and femininity a woman who can outcrank most of the men on the planet.

Mixing climbing and motherhood will, I'm sure, raise a whole new crop of issues, most of which I can't even begin to imagine. But I've had glimpses: already I wonder how I will respond if Renata doesn't want to climb. Based on the short time we've had together, I know I have a strong tendency to favor her wishes over my own, so I doubt I would deeply resent giving up Saturdays on the rock in order to drive her to ballet lessons, for instance. Actually the alternative worries me more: what if she does want to climb? How will I respond when I see her taking risks, even the same risks that I take regularly? I suspect it will be very difficult not to overprotect her. I am only just beginning to appreciate what it must have cost my mother to see me continue to climb after my brother died. I can only hope to handle myself as gracefully as she does.

For now I am simply enjoying my days at the crags with Renata. While climbing trips with her are still about twice as exhausting as trips without her, they have become more interesting and more fun as she's grown. Now a sturdy toddler, she prefers walking to being carried and puts in several miles on her own little legs in a typical day. Her curiosity about the natural world has reawakened me to small wonders—soft moss, spider webs, mouseholes. Best of all, as I watch her doing what comes naturally (toddlers know no other way), I can see that much of the behavior we think of as peculiar to climbers as a breed—endlessly fondling gear and rearranging the rack, scamming free food whenever possible, climbing itself—is really just a grown-up version of child's play. Renata loves to sort the rack by color and size, and then do it again, and again. She's also an accomplished scam artist, cruising the other groups of climbers at lunch time and watching them eat with such devoted attention that they never fail to offer her a handout. And like any child her age, she loves to climb. Furniture, fences, trees, rocks—it all delights her. She no longer cries when I start up the rock, instead she clamors for a turn. It probably won't be long before we're resoling her sneakers with sticky rubber and tying her in. And then, as one friend teasingly points out, it probably won't be long before she outclimbs me. I hope so. Maybe she'll lead me up "Astroman" some day.

Glossary

abseil British term for rappel

adze the wide section of the head of the ice axe, used for chopping, digging, etc.

aid climbing using the rope and anchors for pulling yourself up the rock; used instead of natural holds

anchor to attach a climber to the rock, ice or snow by means of one or more appropriate devices: chocks, ice screws, pickets, etc. Also, the device itself plus the necessary webbing or rope and carabiner required to attach it to the climbing rope

apron a wide, relatively featureless expanse of a rock face, usually at the base of a mountain or cliff

arête a large corner formation on a mountain

bannock a type of flat bread; a staple of various North American native peoples

barndoor to lose one's balance or hold on a rock or ice face so that the body swings out and away to one side

belay a procedure of securing a climber by means of the rope

bergschrund a large crevasse formed where the glacier pulls away from rock headwall or summit block

biner see *carabiner*

bivouac; bivy to make camp or spend a night out with an absolute minimum of equipment

bolt an artificial anchor placed in a hole in the rock drilled for that purpose

boulder to climb on small cliffs or actual boulders without the protection of a rope; often in order to work out complex or difficult moves with the relative safety of proximity to the ground

builder a variation on *boulder*, but refers to climbing on buildings or artificial surfaces instead of natural rock

buttress a major cornering or projecting formation on a mountain, larger than an *arête*

cagoule upper body rain gear, usually extending to or below the knees, often with a hood

cam a metal anchoring device in roughly the shape of a round-cornered half-circle, used as a chock for protection in rock climbing.

Camalot a particular make of mechanical camming device used for protection which adjusts automatically to any size and shape of crack within a certain range

carabiner an aluminum alloy link with a spring-loaded gate to allow insertion of the climbing rope or a runner, used to connect things, e.g., the rope and protection, rope and climber; also *biner*

chicken heads protuberances of rock, usually numerous within a local area, found on slabs and faces

chock generic term for any of several types of rock climbing anchoring devices designed to wedge into cracks. Ususally a small piece of extruded metal (aluminum alloy) with a short length of rope or wide cable attached allowing for placement in cracks and connection to the climbing rope by a carabiner. Rarely, chocks may also be a small stone or a knot of rope or webbing used similarly.

chute a topographic depression steeper than a gully or couloir

col a steep, high pass, narrower than a saddle

cornice an overhanging lip of snow on a ridge or mountain top caused by prevailing winds

couloir a deep chute

crampon a steel device with multiple sharp teeth attached to the sole of a climbing boot to aid in travel on steep snow and ice

crevasse a crack or fissure in the surface of a glacier, extending downward from a few inches to 150 feet or more

crux the most difficult section or move of a climb or pitch

down climbing climbing back down the route of an ascent, rather than rapelling or walking down a trail, both easier methods of descent (though not necessarily safer). Down climbing is harder than climbing up since holds for hands and feet are farther away from climber's eyes and movement with the pull of gravity is usually more uncomfortable.

edema swelling of body tissue as a result of water retention, as in pulmonary or cerebral edema, both severe reactions to being at high altitude

edging rock climbing technique that uses the rigid angled edges of the shoe's sole to enable the climber to stand on tiny, horizontal projections of rock. Compare to smearing.

étrier a short ladder made from webbing, usually attached to a piece of protection or ascending device and used to stand on during aid climbing

face a relatively unbroken expanse of rock

free climbing climbing using only holds provided by the rock, as opposed to aid climbing; rope and anchors can be used for protection but the climber doesn't pull or stand on them.

Friend a type of mechanical camming device; see *Camalot*

friction move see *smear*

glissade to descend a snow slope quickly by either balancing on one's feet and 'skiing' straight down the slope, or sitting on the snow and sliding down using the spike of the ice axe to steer and control speed

go, goes a route is said to "go" when it is proved to be actually climbable, versus being hypothesized

gripped to become immobilized by fear

hanging bivy camping style in multi-day ascents, usually of big wall rock climbs; a type of hammock or sling (Porta-ledge) is anchored to the rock and a climber makes camp and rests in place.

haul bag a duffel-type bag containing climber's extra gear and food which is hauled up the rock after each pitch

haul line a rope separate from the climbing rope(s) used only to haul the haul bag

headwall where the slope of a mountain, rock face or glacier steepens markedly

hone to work out, practice, refine one's skills and physique

horn a protuberance of rock useful as an anchor for belaying or rapelling

ice axe standard equipment for anyone traveling on snow or ice; has a spike at one end of an arm-length shaft and a double-ended head at the other consisting of a pick for self-arrest and an adze for digging snow or cutting ice. Axes for ice climbing are shorter and of various specialized designs

icefall a steep part of a glacier, where the faster flow causes greater and more random crevassing and serac build-up

jam crack a crack climbed by means of jamming the hands and/or feet into the crack and expanding or twisting them so that they exert pressure against the rock

jug a large hold in the rock; also, to ascend using jumars

jumar to ascend a rope by means of mechanical ascenders that slide up the rope but not down; also, *Jumar,* a particular brand of ascending device

lead   to climb first, placing anchors and threading the rope through them so that one is protected by the belayer; also, a *pitch*

lunge   a quick, dynamic move up or sideways while climbing

mantel shelved, mantel   a climbing move used to gain a ledge, similar to getting out of a swimming pool. Climber places her hands palms down on a ledge and jumps up to transfer her weight to them over her straightened arms. One leg is then raised to stand on ledge and ascend

massif   a bulky, expansive mountain mass culminating in one outstanding summit

moraine   area of rock, scree, gravel and/or sand, usually at the sides or toe of a glacier, exposed by glacial action

notch   a small col or a sharp depression in a ridge

offwidth   a crack too wide for a foot jam and too narrow to admit the climber's body; awkward to climb, often requiring two-footed or two-handed techniques

opposition moves   techniques requiring that the climber push or pull against two opposed surfaces simultaneously

overhang   rock or ice that slopes more than ninety degrees away from the horizontal; as it approaches 180 degrees, it is called a *roof*

piece, protection   a stopper, hex, nut, mechanical camming device, ice screw, picket or other anchor used in rock, ice or alpine climbing

pitch   a section of a climb between belays, up to the length of a climbing rope but usually between eighty and one hundred forty feet

piton   a metal spike driven into a crack in the rock with a hammer; has a hole for attaching a carabiner and the rope; also called *pin* or *peg*

post hole   to sink into soft or new snow when climbing or hiking without skis or snowshoes

problem   a challenging move or section of a climb

protection   an anchor in snow, ice or rock climbing; also pro or piece

prusik   to ascend a rope by means of stirrups and a seat attached to the rope with *prusik knots* which slide freely up the rope unloaded but tighten and remain in place when weighted; also, the stirrups or loops of rope themselves when used for the purpose

quick-draw a short loop of webbing with two carabiners clipped to it, carried on the rack and used when speed is important in attaching the rope to an anchor.

rack the selection of carabiners and assorted nuts, quick-draws and camming devices the leader carries, used to protect the climbing team; usually worn on a sling over the shoulder or on a specially made waist belt with loops stiffened for that purpose

ramp an ascending ledge, from a few inches to several yards wide

rappel to slide down a rope, usually doubled, anchored to the rock above; can be done using only the rope wrapped around the climber's body or with one of several types of mechanical devices rigged for the purpose

rime ice crystals built up on any solid object usually parallel with and facing into the wind

ripstop a kind of nylon fabric used in outdoor gear that incorporates a latice of stronger threads within the weave, slowing or preventing long rips or significant unravelling should the fabric be torn

rotten snow; rotten ice snow or ice that appears to be solid but which when weighted compresses unduly or dissolves

serac a standing ice tower, usually found where a glacier steepens, either at the intersection of crevasses or in an area of icefall

scree small, loose rock or gravel, as found on moraines and at the base of volcanic or other mountain formations

sling a short length (usually about five feet) of webbing or rope tied into a loop; used for many purposes but most commonly to attach a carabiner and rope to an anchor

sluff a shallow avalanche involving light or powder snow or just the top layer of the snowpack

smear to maximize contact between the sticky rubber sole of a climbing shoe and the surface of a rock face so that it adheres by friction, as distinguished from edging; same as *friction*

squeeze chimney an opening in the rock so narrow that the climber can only just get her or his body into it

test piece the hardest climb within a particular group, style or rating of climbs

top rope to climb while roped, belayed by means of a secure anchor above; also, the rope when rigged for this purpose

topo   a topographic map, showing details of elevation by means of contour lines

traverse   to travel across a slope rather than directly up or down it; also used to describe a climb involving more than one summit of a mountain or range and different routes of ascent and descent

trek   a long walking tour

whiteout   a condition of near-zero visibility due to blowing snow or fog

Sources

Beckey, Fred. *Cascade Alpine Guide, Columbia River to Stevens Pass* (Seattle, WA: The Mountaineers, 1973).

Graydon, Don, Ed. *Mountaineering: Freedom of the Hills,* Fifth Edition (Seattle, WA: The Mountaineers, 1992).

Loughman, Michael. *Learning to Rock Climb* (San Francisco, CA: Sierra Club Books, 1981).

Long, John. *How to Rock Climb* (Evergreen, CO: Chockstone Press, 1989).

Grading Systems for Rating Climbs

North America

Most of the early rating systems originated in Britain and Germany in the late nineteenth and early twentieth centuries. Since that time climbs have been classified in grades according to their degree of difficulty. In the 1920s Willo Welzenbach developed a rating system that used Roman numerals and the British adjectival system. A modified Welzenbach system was introduced to North America in the 1930s and became known as the Sierra Club system. At California's Tahquitz Rock in the 1950s the Sierra Club system was modified by adding decimal figures to class five climbs. This system, called the Yosemite Decimal System (YDS), is now widely used in North America and uses both a class system (which refers to degree of technical difficulty) and a grade system (which refers to the average time it takes to complete the route).

Yosemite Decimal System

Classes:

1–2	Walking and scrambling.
3–4	Easy climbing. Rope and belays may be needed.
5	Serious rock climbing/free climbing. Artificial protection needed.
6	Aid climbing. Tools/rope/anchors needed to move up a wall.

Class 5 climbing is divided into degrees ranging from 5.1 (five-one) to 5.14 (five-fourteen). 5.10 and above are further divided into letter grades: 5.10a,b,c or d, with "a" the easiest and "d" the most difficult.

Grades:

I	1–2 hours
II	4–6 hours
III	1 day
IV	1 day or longer
V	1½ – days
VI	2 days or longer

International

There are several other rating systems used internationally. Brief descriptions of a select few follow. Please refer to the books listed in the Sources for more information.

The *Australian* system uses open-ended numerals ranging from 1-33. The *UIAA* (Union Internationale des Associations d'Alpinisme) rating system describes climbs from I-X with levels V-X subdivided with a plus or minus: (-) easy, (nothing) moderate, and (+) hard. The *British* system also uses two kinds of grading: The adjectival grade and the technical, or numerical, grade. The adjectival grade describes overall difficulties (ranging from Easy (E) to Extremely Severe (ES)), including protection, quality of rock, etc.— and the technical/numerical grade rates the hardest pitch of the climb.

How Ratings are Assigned

When a climber establishes a new route, she or he gives it a rating. Ratings are communicated in guidebooks and through word of mouth. It should be noted that each climbing area has its own peculiarities, type of rock, conditions, and so on. There is no absolute correspondence between ratings in different areas because of regional differences as well as variables in the current equipment and average skill levels of climbers.

Sources:

Gerrard, Layne. *Everybody's Guide to Rock Climbing Equipment* (Berkeley: Ten Speed Press, 1990).

Graydon, Don, Ed. *Mountaineering: The Freedom of the Hills*, Fifth Edition (Seattle: The Mountaineers, 1992).

Loughman, Michael. *Learning to Rock Climb* (San Francisco: Sierra Club Books, 1981).

Resources

There are hundreds of outdoor organizations that offer mixed or women-only trips and courses. The following were selected for their focus on climbing or trekking and related services to women. Please check with the groups individually for current status and schedules, as these tend to change. For a more complete listing see *Women Outdoors: The Best 1900 Books, Programs and Periodicals* by Jennifer Abromowitz. (Self-published; order from Jennifer Abromowitz, RD 1, 345C, Williamsburg, MA 01096.)

Adventure Associates
P.O. Box 16304
Seattle, WA 98116
206-932-8352
Offers trips, management training and personal growth programs for women in the U.S. and abroad. Write for more information.

Alaska Women of the Wilderness
Box 775226,
Eagle River, AK 99577
907-688-2226
Year-round one- to ten-day trips and courses for women, including hiking, trekking and other sports.

Alpine Club of Canada
Box 1026
Banff, Alberta
T0L 0C0 Canada
403-762-4481
Canada's national mountaineering club, with trips, courses and facilities throughout Canada. Publishes newsletter and journal. Welcomes international membership.

Everest Environmental Expedition
3730 Wind Dance Lane
Colorado Springs, CO 80906
719-578-9061
Promotes environmental awareness and action through education and expeditions to the Himalaya.

Mariah Wilderness Expeditions
P.O. Box 248
Point Richmond, CA 94807
1-800-4 MARIAH
Offers women's trekking trips, as well as whitewater rafting, kayaking, SCUBA diving and ballooning.

The Mazamas
13734 N.E. Thompson
Portland, OR 97230
503-227-2345
Oregon's oldest and largest outdoor and climbing club. Offers courses, trips and facilities.

The Mountaineers
300 3rd W.
Seattle, WA 98109
206-284-6310
One of the oldest and largest outdoor and climbing organizations in the country, offering trips, courses and facilities for members.

National Outdoor Leadership School (NOLS)
P.O. Box AA
Lander, Wyoming 82520
Professional outdoor school offering a wide range of outdoor leadership courses from fourteen days to semester-length.

Outward Bound
384 Field Point Rd.
Greenwich, CT 06830
800-243-8520
International organization offering a variety of outdoor courses, many tailored to particular interest groups.

Personal Challenges, Inc.
1852 Ashland Ave.
St. Paul, MN 55104
612-646-2063
Climbing trips for women, focusing on connections between spirit and the land.

Stonewall Climbers
P.O. Box 445
Boston, MA 02124
Gay and lesbian climbing organization. Publishes a quarterly newsletter; members organize ice, rock and alpine climbs throughout North America and beyond.

Union of Latin American Women Climbers (ULAMM-Mexico)
Apartado Postal 97-059
Mexico, D.F., Mexico
Phone: 763-09-18 or 583-18-69
Sponsors annual conventions and climbs, and gatherings within each member country. ULAMM welcomes new members from all nations. Dues are $8 per year plus a $4 initiation fee. There is a National Coordinator in each of the capitols of Brazil, Chile, Columbia, Ecuador, El Salvador, and Venezuela. Contact them through local climbing clubs or guide services.

Washington Women Outdoors
P.O. Box 301
Garrett Park, MD 20896
301-474-4403
Non-profit women's educational organization offering one and two-day trips including rock climbing and leadership training.

Womantrek
1411 E. Olive Way
Seattle, WA 98112
206-325-4772
Offers trekking and other trips
for women in the Northwest and
around the world. Write for
catalog.

Women Climbers Northwest
P.O. Box 20573
Seattle, WA 98102
WCN welcomes new members.
Dues are $15 per year. Publishes a
monthly newsletter, hosts monthly
gatherings and members organize
climbing and other outings.

Women Outdoors
55 Talbot Ave.
Medford, MA 02155
National non-profit network with
chapters throughout the U.S.,
offering trips including leadership
training. Publishes quarterly
magazine.

Women Outdoors—New Zealand
P.O. Box 68-296
Newton, Aukland
New Zealand
Members lead co-op rock climb-
ing, hiking and sea kayaking trips,
and publish a newsletter.

Woodswomen
25 West Diamond Lake Road
Minneapolis, MN 55419
Phone: 612-822-3809 or
1-800-279-0555
Offers numerous and varied outdoor experiences and leadership
courses for women and women
and children. Contact them for
complete catalog.

CONTRIBUTORS

Diane Bedell is the Logistics Coordinator and a wilderness guide for Woodswomen, Inc. She teaches rock climbing, backpacking, canoeing, and dogsledding skills to women and children. She received her B.A. from Eastern Washington University in Recreation Management and has participated in a five-month Outdoor Leadership Training Seminars program based in Denver, Colorado. Diane lives in Minneapolis, Minnesota, and enjoys exploring the Boundary Waters Canoe Area in northern Minnesota.

Lorraine G. Bonney was born in Edmonton, Alberta, Canada, in 1922. She began climbing and skiing in Banff while working her way through college as a waitress. She has climbed on all the continents except South America, and is also a whitewater kayaker, skier, biker, and SCUBA diver. She and her husband, O. H. Bonney, co-authored numerous books including the *Guide to Wyoming Mountains and Wilderness Areas* and *The Grand Controversy: Beginnings of Teton Climbing to 1934.*

Susan Edwards is a microbiologist and sports psychology consultant. She has a practice with SPORTMIND in Orinda, California, where she teaches mental training methods to athletes. She is also a rock climber, mountaineer and trail runner.

Sue Harrington's climbing career started on the side of a dormitory building while attending the University of Rochester School of Nursing in New York State. From there she progressed to climbing rock on the Niagara escarpment and mountains across the United States. Her love for the outdoors inspired adventures in Alaska, Mexico, Canada, Argentina and Nepal. Sue received her master's degree from the University of Washington and now works as a family nurse practitioner in Bellingham, Washington. The neighboring Cascades are her favorite mountains to explore.

Louise Heinemann started climbing at the age of sixteen in the days of big boots, hauser laid ropes and nut runners made from actual nuts with the threads drilled out. Between 1967 and 1970 she and her climbing partner were known as "the hardest girl climbing team in the North East," leading V. Severe to H.V. Severe. She has been a teacher, editor and anthropologist, traveling or working in China, Japan, Australia, France, Spain, Peru, Pakistan, Canada and the United States. She has climbed Lotus Flower Tower in the Northwest Territories, as well as numerous routes in California and Colorado.

Nancy Kerrebrock lives in Palo Alto, California. Since writing this essay she has gone back to work part time as a research economist, and given birth to a son, Skyler. She still climbs whenever possible.

Ann E. Kruse has been climbing for twenty years. She has rock climbed from the Gunks to Joshua Tree to Squamish, and her mountain experiences range from the Sierras to the Rockies to Alaska. She is a member of Women Climbers Northwest and of the American Alpine Club. She practiced law in Seattle for twelve years and currently is an organization effectiveness consultant in Pasadena, California.

Kristen Laine has called Seattle home since 1980. She works in the computer software industry. She also writes fiction and raises money for organizations working to improve the lives of women and children. Kristen has degrees in English literature from Harvard and Radcliffe Colleges and the University of Wisconsin.

Jill Lawrenz grew up climbing mountains in New Hampshire. She climbed Mt. Rainier in August 1990 to celebrate the one-hundredth anniversary of the first female ascent. She works as an advocate for homeless women in Seattle, Washington.

Lorna Millard is a lapsed bureaucrat who writes, travels and enjoys the outdoors. She lives in Nanaimo, on Vancouver Island, but is usually found in a tiny village named Errington, home to a big dog named Bear.

Denise Mitten is the Executive Director of Woodswomen, an outdoor adventure travel organization for women based in Minneapolis, Minnesota. She has led climbs on McKinley and in the Himalayas, treks through Nepal and Switzerland, backpack trips in the Tetons, and sea kayak trips in Alaska. She also teaches skiing, rock climbing and whitewater canoeing. But her first love is leadership philosophy, which she has developed through Woodswomen's acclaimed Leadership Training Program and as a faculty member at Metropolitan State University in Minneapolis.

Gwen Moffat was born in Sussex, England and educated at Hove County Grammar (High) School. She was the first woman guide appointed by the British Mountaineering Council, and has climbed professionally in North Wales, the English Lake District, the Highlands, the Isle of Skye, the Swiss and French Alps and the Dolomites. Her autobiography *Space Below My Feet* (1961) describes the thrills and philosophy of climbing. She has written seventeen novels, fifteen of them mysteries, most of which feature Miss Pink, an elderly alpinist who can still manage a moderate route, a small peak or a spooky house if pushed. Since her first trip to the United States in 1979, many of her stories have been set in the wilds of the American West. Moffat has worked as a book reviewer, broadcaster and columnist, but now concentrates on crime writing.

Maureen O'Neill is thirty-seven and has lived in Seattle all but the first two years of her life. Maureen came out as a lesbian and started climbing at the same time, fourteen years ago. Currently, she divides her time between writing and climbing. She lives with her dog and climbing partner, Asa Mercer.

Alison Osius, senior editor of *Climbing* magazine, has climbed worldwide and is a member of the U.S. climbing team. She has consistently been a top performer at national climbing competitions, and has won two national titles. She also has placed in the top ten in numerous world climbing events. Her writings have appeared in more than twenty-five newspapers and magazines, six adventure anthologies and *The Encyclopedia of Climbing.* She lives in Carbondale, Colorado, where she maintains an active schedule of climbing.

Bachendri Pal was born in 1954 and grew up in the hills of northern India. As a very young child she developed a fearlessness and love of nature that propelled her to become a mountaineer. She became the first Indian woman to climb Mt. Everest and now directs a climbing program and promotes adventure programs for young people in India.

Jeanne Panek is a graduate student in Forest Science at Oregon State University in Corvallis. She returned to school because she is concerned about the health of forests in an environment of increasing human pollution. In her free time she climbs at Smith Rocks or escapes to the high glaciers of the Cascades to climb, ski, hike or just immerse herself in the outdoors.

Kathy Phibbs grew up and attended school in Washington and California, and climbed extensively in the Cascades and the Sierras. She also climbed in Mexico, in the Alaska Range, Peru, Bolivia, the Canadian Rockies and the Himalaya. Her most notable ascents include the West Ridge of Huayna Potosi in the Cordillera Real in Peru, and the Southwest Ridge of Pumori in the Himalaya, an all-women's expedition. An active member of Seattle's lesbian community, Kathy helped develop an outdoor program for gay and lesbian youth through the Seattle American Friends Service Committee. Kathy was the driving force behind Women Climbers Northwest for many years, and for five years the Northwest Director of Woodswomen, an outdoor adventure travel organization for women. Kathy died in 1991 at the age of thirty-three, climbing in the Washington Cascades.

Dorothy Pilley, born in 1893, first climbed in Wales and the English Lake District as a teenager. Introduced to the Alps in 1920, she went on to become one of the most active and best known climbers of the period. She participated in many first ascents, most notably that of the north ridge of the Dent Blanche in 1928. She was a founder of the Pinnacle Club, and eagerly participated in early "manless" ascents in the Alps. Additionally, she climbed in Europe, Asia and North America. A journalist, she became an expert on Chinese art, culture and religion, and was one of the first to travel professionally to the People's Republic of China. Dorothy Pilley died in 1986.

Deb Piranian's interest in climbing began when she received a copy of Maurice Herzog's book *Annapurna* for her tenth birthday. She moved to Washington State for graduate school and started whitewater kayaking, mountaineering and rock climbing in Washington, California and Canada. After receiving her Ph.D in Slavic Linguistics, she moved to Tucson, Arizona. In 1984 Deb began working for Outward Bound, concentrating on teaching women's courses, wilderness therapy, and international courses in the former Soviet

Union. Some of Deb's more significant climbs include Mt. Kongur, an attempt on Denali, and a successful ascent of The Nose on El Capitan with another woman. Deb is currently pursuing an M.A. in Art Therapy.

Colette Richard grew up in Versailles and in spite of having become blind at the age of two, learned to love and trust nature. She began climbing and caving in her early twenties, and went on to climb the Mont Tondu, Col du Géant, the Infranchissable and Mont Blanc du Tacul. Her speleological adventures included the Bedeilhac Cave with its prehistoric sculptures and the Caverne de Gargas where she spent a night alone in a remote part of the grotto, the first person to have done so.

Janet Roddan is a rock and ice climber. She is currently working on a degree in film, getting a guiding certification from the Association of Canadian Mountain Guides, and climbing whenever she can. Some of her favorite climbs include *Grand Wall* and *Angel's Crest* at Squamish, B.C., the latter being the location of a film she is producing. She is a member of the Sport Climbing Committee of the Alpine Club of Canada, and lives in Vancouver, B.C.

Wendy Roberts is pursuing her doctorate in Zoology at U.C. Berkeley. She divides her time between her research in the forests of Costa Rica and life in Northern California. Besides climbing, she enjoys skiing and bicycling, and has been a member of Women Climbers Northwest since 1983.

Susan Fox Rogers is a writer and editor who has been climbing for the past sixteen years. Her work on climbing has appeared in *The Village Voice, Climbing* and other outdoor publications. She is currently working on two books about women, sports and the outdoor experience.

Louise Shepherd has been a professional rock climbing instructor since 1982. She is co-director of The Climbing Company, based in Natimuk, Victoria, Australia, which offers professional climbing instruction at Mt. Arapiles. She is a founder of the Climbing Instructors Association, a lead guide for Wildwise, a women's adventure company, a member of the Victorian Climbing Club, and editor of their new Mt. Arapiles guidebook. She is an active environmentalist, having used her climbing skills in three Greenpeace protests, and serves on numerous organizing and advisory committees dealing with issues ranging from the ozone layer to fishing to parks management.

Cyndi Smith was born and raised on a cattle ranch along the shore of the Red Deer River in the heart of the Alberta badlands. She studied biological sciences at the Northern Alberta Institute of Technology in Edmonton. Since 1980 she has worked for the Canadian Parks Service, first as a naturalist, then as a patrolwoman, and now as a park warden. She has published several books and articles about the Canadian Rockies including *Off the Beaten Track: Women Adventurers and Mountaineers in Western Canada* (Coyote Books, 1989) An avid skier, backpacker, sea kayaker and mountaineer, she has explored many of Canada's wilderness areas.

Miriam O'Brien Underhill learned to love the outdoors from childhood trips to the White Mountains of New Hampshire. By her mid-twenties she had become an adventurous mountaineer. Between 1924 and 1932 she climbed throughout Europe, but especially notable were her first ascents and first "manless" ascents in the Dolomites and the French and Swiss Alps. With her husband, Robert, she later climbed in Idaho, Montana and New Hampshire. Miriam died in 1976.

Laura Waterman is a New England climber. She has co-authored with her husband, Guy, *Backwoods Ethics: Environmental Concerns for Hikers and Climbers* (1979) and *Forest and Crag: A History of Hiking, Trail Blazing and Adventure in the Northeast Mountains* (1989). She and Guy are currently working on three books, all to be published in 1993: *Yankee Rock and Ice: A History of Climbing in the Northeast* (Stackpole Books), *Wilderness Ethics: Preserving the Spirit of Wildness* and a revised edition of *Backwoods Ethics* (Countryman Press). Laura's first female ascents on ice include the Black Dike on Cannon Mountain and the first (known) female lead of Pinnacle Gully on Mount Washington.

ABOUT THE ARTISTS

Joan Firey (1928–1980) called herself a "mountain portrait" artist, although her artistic terrain covered a wide variety of subjects. She was largely self-taught, taking occasional instruction from local artists and institutions. She worked in oil, watercolor, sumi ink, acrylics and silkscreen (serigraph) printing. Joan's work has been seen in many shows and juried exhibits.

As a climber, she has thirty-three first ascents to her credit in the North Cascades of Washington, the Coast Range of British Columbia, Southeast Alaska and the Alaska Range, many of which she did with her husband, Joe. She also climbed in Peru and Mexico, and participated in the 1978 American Women's Himalayan Expedition to Annapurna. Joan worked for many years with The Mountaineers and served on the Board of Directors of the American Alpine Club. She worked professionally as a physical therapist, and, with her husband, Joe, raised three children.

Carla Firey began accompanying her family on trips to the mountains at the age of nine months. She started mountain climbing as a teenager and rock climbing during her last year of high school. She has climbed all over Western Canada and the United States, especially in the Washington Cascades and rock climbing areas such as Yosemite and Squamish, B.C.

In her twenties Carla formed her own business doing freelance and custom design and manufacture of tents, packs and outdoor wear. She majored in geology in college and completed her BFA in painting in 1989. These twin interests are joined in her mountain landscapes. She has worked in oils, acrylics and a variety of drawing media, often working from on-site sketches. Carla's paintings represented here were influenced by Joan's work and by memories of trips taken with her mother.

About the Editor

In 1972 Rachel da Silva bought a letterpress and some handset type; four years later she co-founded Seal Press and has worked in printing and publishing ever since. She climbs whenever she can and is a member of Stonewall Climbers, The Alpine Club of Canada and Women Climbers Northwest. Originally from New York City, she now lives on an island suburb of Seattle where she and her partner are building their home.

Selected Titles from Seal Press

Water's Edge: *Women Who Push the Limits in Rowing, Kayaking and Canoeing* by Linda Lewis. $14.95, 1-878067-18-4 An inspiring book that takes us inside the world of competitive rowing, kayaking and wilderness canoeing through ten profiles of women who have made their mark in these sports, from the first pioneers to today's Olympic champions.

Rivers Running Free: *Canoeing Stories by Adventurous Women* edited by Judith Niemi and Barbara Wieser. $14.95, 1-878067-22-2 This spirited collection of writings that spans a century of women's canoeing adventure is sure to please the avid paddler as well as anyone who has ever been attracted to the romance and excitement of outdoor adventure.

Uncommon Waters: *Women Write About Fishing* edited by Holly Morris. $14.95, 1-878067-10-9 A wonderful anthology that captures the bracing adventure and meditative moments of fishing in the words of thirty-four women anglers from—finessing trout and salmon in the Pacific Northwest to chasing bass and catfish in the Deep South.

She's A Rebel: *The History of Women in Rock & Roll* by Gillian G. Gaar. $16.95, 1-878067-08-7 This lively history of women in rock & pop features interviews with dozens of performers, great photos and a behind-the-scenes look at the music industry.

Hard-Hatted Women: *Stories of Struggle and Success in the Trades* edited by Molly Martin. $12.95, 0-931188-66-0 Women employed in non-traditional work—ironworkers, carpenters, firefighters and more—vividly describe their daily experiences on the job.

Closer to Home: *Bisexuality and Feminism* edited by Elizabeth Reba Weise. $14.95, 1-878067-17-6 A dynamic anthology of essays by and about women who are bisexual, *Closer to Home* breaks new ground in feminist and 'queer' discourse.

Getting Free: *You Can End Abuse and Take Back Your Life* by Ginny NiCarthy. $12.95, 0-931188-37-7 The most important self-help resource book in the movement to end domestic violence. Also available on audiocassette, $10.95, 0-931188-84-9.

Seal Press, founded in 1976 to provide a forum for women writers and feminist issues, has many other books of fiction, non-fiction and poetry. You may order directly from us at 3131 Western Avenue, Suite 410, Seattle, Washington 98121 (add 15% of total book order for shipping and handling). Write to us for a free catalog or if you would like to be on our mailing list.